BRITISH CERAMIC ART
1870-1940

John A. Bartlett

77 Lower Valley Road, Atglen, PA 19310

ACKNOWLEDGEMENTS

I am indebted to the many dealers, collectors, authors, museums, libraries and auction houses who have provided information and allowed their collections to be photographed.

I am also particularly indebted to the following collectors and specialists in decorative arts for their valuable input to this edition:—

Reg Adams, Patrick Beasley, Michael Buckland, Michael Bruce, Graham Davis, Katherine Dickson, John & Audrey Edgeler, Roger & Shirley Edmundson, Lady Elton, Peter Gooday, Joy Hallam, Malcolm Haslam, John & Heather Hockings, Michael John, Pat & Charles Lancaster, Alastair Lamont, Steve Loud, Harry Lyons, Carl Rosen, Barry Stock, Cynthia Weaver, Eva & Glyn White, Mary & Bernard Wright;

and to the following museums, art galleries and auction houses:-

Blake's Lock Museum, Reading (Sue Read)

Carisbrooke Castle Museum, Isle of Wight (Roy Brinton)

Chelmsford & Essex Museum, Chelmsford (Anne Lutyens-Humfrey)

Christie's South Kensington, London (Mark Wilkinson & Jane Hay)

City Museum & Art Gallery, Stoke-on-Trent (Kathy Niblett)

Hampshire County Museum Service, Chilcomb House, Winchester (Margaret MacFarlane)

Huntly House Museum, Edinburgh (Gordon McFarlan)

Ironbridge Gorge Museum (John Powell)

Leatherhead Museum (David Bruce)

Maidstone Museums & Art Gallery (Henry Middleton)

The Watts Gallery, Compton, Surrey (Richard Jefferies)

and to Denby Pottery (Linda Salt)

and to Julia Johnstone for transcription services,

and to Stephanie Bartlett for editorial services.

Photography by John Bartlett, with the exception of certain plates which are acknowledged as they appear. Photographs marked "HCMS" are of pieces owned by Hampshire County Museum Service. Photographs on the following pages were taken by Mr. M. Bruce: 69, 84 bottom, 161 top, 162 bottom, 163 top. Thank you.

Also by the author:

English Decorative Ceramics

Published by Schiffer Publishing, Ltd.
77 Lower Valley Road
Atglen, PA 19310
Please write for a free catalog.
This book may be purchased from the publisher.
Please include $2.95 postage.
Try your bookstore first.

We are interested in hearing from authors
with book ideas on related subjects.

Contents

Typical Arts & Crafts decor.

Preface

The purpose of this book is to provide collectors and dealers of British art and studio ceramics with a comprehensive guide to the artists, potteries and their products from 1870 to 1940.

The book aims to be a single source of reference, directing the reader to further detailed reading (where this exists) via a References section for each chapter and a practical Bibliography.

Our knowledge regarding the many artists, studios and potteries that existed during the period is rapidly increasing, and the interest that now abounds in their creations has prompted a surge of research. Much still needs to be done, however, and the obvious gaps in this current volume are evident of that continuing need.

I remember bringing a Linthorpe bowl designed by Christopher Dresser to a well known London auction house in the early 1970s, only to be met by a strong rebuff that it was not the sort of thing they were interested in! How the climate of opinion and taste has changed since then, with such pieces now regularly valued at three or even four figures! Who would have thought that Clarice Cliff wares selling for only six pence at Woolworth's during the 1930s would now be selling for several hundred pounds?

The popularity of pre-war British ceramics has clearly given us a thirst for knowledge, such that I hope this volume, which includes details of potteries hitherto unpublished, will provide not only a ready source of information to all those interested in the subject but also will act as a catalyst for encouraging further research.

Organisation of this Book

Each chapter is arranged in alphabetical order of the pottery, studio or artist most commonly associated with the wares produced. Readers not finding a particular name as a chapter heading should consult the comprehensive Index.

For ease of reference the chapters are divided into Historical Background; Products; Production, Quality and Availability of Wares; Marks; and References.

The References sections list additional information regarding each chapter heading, such as publications for further reading (also listed in the main Bibliography), specific museum collections, etc.

Examples of many of the wares described in this book may also be seen in the larger national collections, such as the City Museum and Art Gallery, Stoke-on-Trent, and the Victoria and Albert Museum, London. These collections, because of their general coverage of British ceramics, have only been referenced under certain chapters. Likewise, museums displaying small representative collections of British ceramics through the ages, such as the Holburne Museum, Bath or the Curtis-Allen Gallery, Alton.

With few exceptions, the photographs in this book are of pieces which were typical of an artist's or pottery's output. It is hoped that this gives a more representative view for the dealer and collector, than by showing rare or unusual pieces.

The marks shown in each chapter are those most commonly associated with a particular pottery, studio or artist. They are certainly not designed to be exhaustive and there will always be deficiences and exceptions. The reader is urged to consult the References sections for publications which may provide more detailed information on marks. Additionally, the author is always willing to hear from readers who may provide further information on marks, or indeed any other aspect of a particular pottery.

The plus minus signs (*) in the marks sections indicate that a particular mark, device or legend may or may not occur.

An attempt has been made at categorising pottery **Production** and overall **Quality**, based on quantities of output (known or estimated) and average ceramic quality (body and decoration). The categories can only be approximate, however, and, naturally, views vary considerably as to what is good and what is poor quality. Also, many potteries unfortunately destroyed vital records of their production and styles, not thinking of any future need for such information. The attempt at categorising has been thought worthwhile, however, as indicated from a usefulness point of view from many dealers and collectors.

An attempt has also been made at assessing the **Availability** of pieces for the buyer. This category is more difficult to assess because of changing fashions and demand. For example, a particular type of ware suddenly becoming favourable might result in a sudden flooding of the market.

The use of all three categories together should assist the reader to make an assessment of demand and worth. The categories are:-

Production	Quality	Availability
Very Low	Poor	Rare
Low	Fair	Scarce
Moderate	Good	Uncommon
High	Very Good	Common
Very High	Excellent	Abundant

Advertisement for the British Institute of Industrial Art Exhibition, 1920.

Cranston Vase, 237mm high, stamped "Cranston Pottery, PP & Co. Ltd., England" and pattern no. 73/619

Introduction

The period covered by this book, though representing only seventy years of elapsed time, witnessed a phenomenal development in ceramic art, not only through the influences and innovations of artistic movements and styles, but also through significant technological achievements in ceramic science.

It was a period which saw the birth of Art Pottery, the growth of Studio Ceramics, the influence of the Arts and Crafts Movement, the Modernists and Vorticists, and the impact of the Art Nouveau and Art Deco styles.

Many potteries existed only during this period, established on a wave of enthusiasm and enterprise, capitalising on a late nineteenth century renaissance of British pottery manufacture, only to be extinguished by the impacts of two World Wars or an inability to cope with changing markets and fashions.

There were those, however, that stood the test of time. Their sheer size, diversification of operation, or ability to react to the many changes of style over such a relatively short period, ensured their survival.

Today, that great centre of ceramic production and endeavour, Stoke-on-Trent, is a very different place from the nineteenth century town. Few bottle-kilns remain, and gone are the persistent black clouds of smoke from its furnaces. It still retains, however, its importance as a pottery producer, and though much of the old is gone, its links with past glories are maintained through the great names of Doulton, Minton, Moorcroft and Wedgwood, and such time-capsules as the Gladstone Pottery Museum; and the City Museum—that leviathan monument to ceramic art.

Renaissance

The late-Victorian period was without doubt a milestone in the history of British ceramics. Traditional shapes and decorations were giving way to new and revolutionary styles, opening up exciting possibilities for anyone with the imagination and creativity to undertake pottery design and production.

Ceramic pioneers and champions such as Henry Doulton, the Martin Brothers, Henry Tooth, Harold Rathbone and William De Morgan, together with designer pioneers such as Christopher Dresser and Walter Crane, launched such a tide of creativity, that, by the end of the nineteenth century, their work had resulted in the achievement of some of the finest creations in the history of ceramic art.

Various styles started to evolve from this late-Victorian renaissance, the most widespread of which was the *style art nouveau*, which flourished through to the end of the century and beyond, finally losing favour by the start of the First World War.

The style found expression in several art forms, not the least of which was pottery. For pottery, however, it meant the chance for designers to break away from the strictures of earlier styles and embark on a form which would shake the very foundations of traditionalism.

The new style, recognisable principally by its swirling leaf and flower patterns and sinuous feminine forms was well suited to the ceramic medium. The plasticity of the clay enabled art nouveau forms to be constructed easily, and the florid patterns could be made to fit almost any shape. With a choice of several means of decoration available, plus an increasing range of coloured glazes, the style found ready accord with the artistic expression of the period.

The wealth of output was amazing. It seems that every pottery made some attempt to embrace the new style, such that the term *art nouveau* came to be applied increasingly to anything that looked different.

There were other strong influences on pottery design, however, such as from the Arts and Crafts Movement—a body, which included the designer William Morris, the illustrator Walter Crane, and painters Dante Gabriel Rosetti, Ford Madox Brown and Edward Burne-Jones among its members. The Arts and Crafts Exhibition Society was formed in 1888 in order to display the work of artist craftsmen and encourage the establishment of workshops and studios.

A strong interest sprang up in reviving ancient styles and incorporating them into new designs. Revivals of Gothic, Grecian, Roman and Medieval shapes, Hispano-Moresque, Persian and Isnik styles, featured strongly in ceramics of this time. There was also a preoccupation with Oriental styles; and Japanese and Chinese designs, shapes and glazes were taken up by many potteries. Museums of the day attracted many artists and designers, who were inspired by the exhibits they housed. The Franks Collection at the British Museum, for example, was a source of inspiration for potteries such as Castle Hedingham, Farnham and Dicker; whilst Schliemann's excavations of Troy and the excavations of the Romano-British town of Silchester inspired the potteries of Rye and S.E. Collier, respectively. Published works on design, such as Dresser's *Principles of Decorative Design* (1873) and *Studies of Design* (1875), and Owen Jones' *Grammar of Ornament* (1856) and *Grammar of Chinese Ornament* (1866) were also a major influence on ceramic designs of this period.

A tendency towards medievalism was frequently shown through the work of Morris and Burne-Jones, and recurring themes, such as the medieval galleon or knights in armour were evident in ceramics through the work of William De Morgan, Harold Rathbone at Della Robbia and Mary Watts at Compton.

Country studios flourished and became important centres of experimentation. Even large potteries set aside small studios in order to encourage creativity and give free rein to artistic talent. They were as much commercial considerations as well as benevolent acts, since large potteries could capitalise on any chance discovery or winning design. The technological development of ceramics owes much to these small studios, whose craft output often complemented mass-produced wares for a lower-priced market.

Arts and Crafts doctrines were vigorously taken up, and country potters such as Elton and Watts readily encouraged the proliferation of local crafts as a reaction against the machine age. "The proper place for Arts and Crafts is in the country... away from the complex, artificial, and often destructive influence of machines and the great town" wrote Charles R. Ashbee, a prominent member of the Arts & Crafts Exhbition Society, in his book *Craftsmanship in Competitive Industry* (1908). Ironically, country craftsmanship was regularly used by architects in urban design, and potteries such as Della Robbia fulfilled ceramic commissions in several towns and cities.

Many local centres of art, societies and recreational organisations had sprung up throughout the country during the 1890s, and these organisations, according to John Phillips, director of the Aller Vale Pottery, fostered "a greater enjoyment of life, from a growing appreciation and the use of the good things around us." The President of one of these societies, the Recreative Evening Schools, was Princess Louise, a daughter of Queen Victoria, who included sculpture and other crafts amongst her own hobbies.

Amateur art was regularly promoted, and the ceramic retailers Howell & James promoted much amateur work at their shop in Regent Street, London, and at regular exhibitions from 1876. The South Kensington School of Art held frequent competitions for students, whose winning work often was featured in national publications such as *The Art Journal* and *Magazine of Art*.

Edwardian Growth & Georgian Decline

The beginning of the twentieth century was a boom period for art pottery and ceramics in general. A Board of Trade Production Census recorded that 68,168 persons were employed in the "china and earthenware trades" during 1907. Production was concentrated on the Staffordshire potteries, but other large centres, such as London, the area around Derby, Torquay in South Devon, Barnstaple in North Devon, Kirkaldy in Fife, and Ironbridge in Shropshire, were all important areas of production, where the clay was good and abundantly available.

Great strides had been made in ceramic chemistry. Pioneers, such as Joseph Burton, Bernard Moore, Cuthbert Bailey and Charles Noke, experimented widely in reduced atmosphere glazes, producing marvellous effects of colour and texture.

Art Schools, such as South Kensington, Glasgow, Burslem, Hanley, and smaller centres such as Barnstaple, and Farnham provided a continuous flow of resource to local potteries. Stoke-on-Trent, as the undisputed centre of pottery production, naturally had more than one Art School, and in 1905, whilst under the direction of the ceramic designer George Cartlidge, the Hanley School of Art stated its principal objective as being "to further art as applied to pottery." Burslem School of Art, at this time under the direction of Stanley Thorogood, held a similar specialist view, and these two Schools alone, because of their bias towards ceramics, performed an important supporting role to the industry.

The London store of Liberty & Company, founded in 1875 by Arthur Lasenby Liberty, was a major promoter and influencer of artistic fashion, giving special emphasis to craft work. Many pieces bore the mark "Made for Liberty," which has now become an emblem of distinction for collectors. Other stores and retailers, such as Lawley, Selfridge, Thomas Goode and Howell & James contributed to the promotion of ceramic art, and the London precinct of High Holborn became a recognised retail centre for the pottery trade.

The boom of the early Edwardian period, however, was soon to dissipate in the years leading to the First World War. Studio potters gradually found it more difficult to sell their new art wares, and the shops that had encouraged their creations, such as Liberty and Selfridge, were soon stocking more restrained, classical lines. The Pilkington Pottery was selling its brilliant lustreware at less than the cost of production, and a general slump in the industry at this time did not help matters.

Ironically, a short-lived boost was given to the Staffordshire potteries by a Royal Visit of King George and Queen Mary in 1913. This was reported as the first visit by a reigning monarch to the area since that of Edward II in 1323! Queen Mary was already known as a keen collector of contemporary ceramics, and regularly patronised Staffordshire potteries and studios, Moorcroft and Bernard Moore in particular.

The First World War was a significant breakpoint in the continuity of production. The loss of labour and the restrictions on the production of pottery using coloured glazes were prime causes for factory closure. Some potteries managed to keep going; others did not reopen, often merely because their product was no longer fashionable.

Between the Wars

The austerity of First World War ceramics quickly gave way to a demand for colour, though output at first was generally restrained and simple in form. A catalogue from the Poole Pottery for 1920 suggested, "the demand for simplicity, which is the keynote of present day furnishing, is combined with a more artistic perception of what is essential decoration. Profusion of ornamentation is now recognised as defeating its object, and in Pottery the beauty of form, which is its chief attraction, must not be marred by a diversion of the eye from the symmetrical outline. The ornamentation should be just sufficient to emphasize the shape without detracting from its purity of line."

After the war, the range of high temperature colours available (i.e. those that could withstand temperatures greater than 1000°) was augmented. This, together with increased developments in lustre glazes, enabled a greater variety of colour and surface decoration to be applied. S.Fielding & Co. of the Devon Pottery, Stoke-on-Trent, for example, set about producing colourful hand-painted, ornamental wares and tablewares, bearing distinctive lustre glazes.

Annual exhibitions, such as the British Industries Fair, held in London from 1915 to 1957 (except 1925 and 1941-46), and also in Birmingham from 1920, promoted high quality products through fierce competition. One-off exhibitions, such as the British Industrial Art Exhibition at Knightsbridge during the summer of 1920, the British Empire Exhibition at Wembley in

1924 and 1925, the Exhibition of Contemporary Art for the Table at Harrod's store in 1934, and various exhibitions abroad, such as at Paris in 1925, helped to place the pottery industry on an international footing.

Competition to build new markets for those lost during the war was rife, and rival showrooms vied to satisfy the public's taste through the latest ceramic lines. New types of ware were proudly displayed, such as the floating-flower bowls and toilet-sets which were popular at this time.

There was always a danger that the ornamental side of ceramics would become too commercialised, and, with the increase in moulded wares during the 1920s and 1930s, this almost became so. Wedgwood and other large concerns were mass-producing wares, even though much work was done by hand, and many potteries thought it necessary to write "hand-painted" or similar legends on their moulded or slip-cast shapes in an attempt to decry their mass-production.

The larger potteries, besides mass-producing wares for the lower market, kept alive their craft sections. Doulton's Sung and Chang wares and Wedgwood's Fairyland Lustre were successful attempts to strike a balance of production.

Many wares were given individuality by the addition of silver or pewter mounts, and some bore wicker handles, many of which were supplied by the Lichfield Basket & Cane Works, Hanley. True individuality, however, could only be achieved by the studio potter, a new breed of which emerged after the First World War. Roger Fry's Omega Workshop, founded in London in 1913, produced tin glaze earthenware for table and ornamental use. Fry, as a trained artist, represented a link between painting and ceramics, encouraging other artists to embrace the ceramic medium. He trained at the Camberwell School of Arts and Crafts, which was also a starting point for many of the inter-war studio potters (Charles Vyse, Reginald Wells and William Staite Murray, for example).

Ceramics at Camberwell owed much to the influence of its principal, W.B. Dalton, as did the Royal College and Central School of Arts and Crafts to Dora Billington. Suffice it to say that the style of inter-war studio ceramics was markedly different from that prior to the First World War. The Chinese and Japanese influence was still strong, but in a different sense. Whilst, prior to the war, a prime aim was to emulate oriental glazes, during the 1920's and 1930's particular attention was paid to emulating oriental bodies. An exhibition of early Chinese pottery and porcelain at the Burlington Fine Arts Club in London in 1910 was an initial influence on this trend.

Bernard Leach went to Japan specifically to understand the techniques of pottery production, and returned to take on pupils at his renowned studio in St. Ives, Cornwall. Oriental stonewares were recreated with vigour by studio potters such as Vyse and Wells, and many used the oriental techniques to create their own particular brand of pots, such as Murray and Katherine Pleydell-Bouverie.

Mintons Hollins Group of Astra Ware pieces.

Not all the successful studio potters came under the oriental influences, however. Michael Cardew, for example, was influenced by traditional English slipwares, and, later, African styles. Stonewares, though, seem to have been the most popular studio wares with the great collectors of the day, such as George Eumorfopoulos and the Reverend Milner-White. London Galleries, such as William Paterson's, Beaux Arts, Lefevre, Walker's and The Fine Art Society were important outlets for studio ceramics between the wars.

Tablewares became an increasingly important form of output for the larger potteries during the 1920s and 1930s, and their importance to the industry was brought home by C.E. Bullock's introductory address in 1935 to a lecture given by the artist Gordon Forsyth: "When you come to discuss questions of art and design in pottery, bear in mind that, of the many millions of pounds' value of china and earthenware produced, probably 90% represents tableware. Therefore, really the most important design is not that which is included for purely decorative articles, but for articles that are used in connection with the service of food and drink."

Forsyth's lecture concerned the Exhibition of Industrial Art at Burlington House, London, which was organised by the Royal Academy and the Royal Society of Arts. He stressed the "educational importance of the appreciation of beauty in mass-produced articles" and the need to break down "the barriers between the fine arts and industrial arts."

The art deco style, with its bold expressions of form and colour, was certainly suited to mass-production, and found favour with mainly utilitarian output. Designers such as Clarice Cliff, Charlotte Rhead and Susie Cooper left their own interpretations of this style, which prevailed during the latter half of the 1930s. The Denby Pottery was producing what it described as "industrially produced Studio wares" during this time, and The Pearl Pottery Company (PP & Co.) produced their Cranston range of ornamental jugs and vases to complement their production of Art Deco fireplaces.

Modernist designs were also a feature of the 1930s, and "good clean lines" was an advertising slogan for much domestic and functional pottery of the later 1930s. T.G. Green's Cornish Kitchen Ware, with its wide, concentric bands of blue, green or yellow on a white ground, exemplified the tenet for "cleanliness in the modern home." Its reproduction today demonstrates that simplicity and functionality can usually find a market in any age.

The outbreak of war in 1939 marked the end of another phase in British pottery. As with the First World War, restrictions in output and the shortage of labour took their toll on most potteries, many of which closed permanently. Studio potters were not exempt. Katherine Pleydell-Bouverie recorded that black-out restrictions prevented her firing her kiln at night, and shortages of essential materials affected most potters.

Today, economic recession is another enemy of the craftsman, whose ability to survive has much to do with a discerning public's desire for quality and uniqueness. An equivalent desire for hand-thrown and hand-decorated wares has ensured a future for studio potters, however, and there are pieces being produced today which will take their place alongside such historical landmarks as De Morgan's "Persian colours" and Elton's "Gold Crackle Ware."

Fielding's Devon Lustre Dish, 280mm wide, deep blue lustre.

Identifying British Ceramics

Marks

Not all pottery was marked, but although the absence of a mark can cause difficulty in identifying a piece, there are other ways in which identification may be made. Comparisons of style, shape and glaze can often be positive indications of identity, since many potteries were remarkably consistent in their output.

Dating a piece is more difficult, though even without a date mark good estimates can often be made. After 1891, for example, all wares made for export were required to be marked "England," and during the 1920s to the present time the mark "Made in England" was common-place. Also, many potteries utilised their own slogans, which can be helpful in dating their wares.

During the period covered by this book various methods of marking were in operation. In general, it is possible to recognise five basic types of mark: a *factory* mark, an *artist's* (or decorator's) mark, a *thrower's* (or designer's) mark, a *pattern* or *shape* number and a *date* mark. Each of the marks may occur independently or in various combinations. It is also possible that the factory mark, artist's mark and thrower's mark were one and the same, so common sense needs to be employed when using marks for identification.

Naturally, the collector desires the appearance of as many marks as possible, and several potteries in this book were particularly consistent in their marking. An example from a Pilkington's Lapis Ware vase exhibits the following marks:

1) *Royal Lancastrian* (impressed)—the Pilkington factory mark
2) *ETR* (incised)—initials of the thrower Edward Thomas Radford
3) *157* (incised)—the pattern number
4) *R* (painted monogram underglaze)—the mark of Gwladys Rodgers, the artist/designer.
5) *1928* (impressed)—the date
6) *Made in England* (impressed)

The **factory mark** is the most commonly found mark on pieces. It may contain the complete name of the pottery or the title of its ware (eg. "Carlton Ware"). It can sometimes be abbreviated (as the "P" for Pilkington) or occur as a picture or monogram (as the ship for the Della Robbia Pottery and the TTC monogram for the Torquay Terra-Cotta Co.).

The mark may be impressed or incised in the wet clay, painted or stamped underglaze, transfer-printed or painted overglaze. Sometimes the same mark may be executed in a variety of ways. Few potteries were totally consistent with their factory marks, and most changed their styles of marking to suit their output or ownership over the years. It is rare that one can date a piece precisely using the factory mark alone, but it is often possible to date a piece to within ten years.

The *artist's* or *decorator's* mark in addition to the factory mark is often taken as a sign that a piece was not mass-produced, but, again, common sense must be used to weigh a balance between the piece under scrutiny and the production habits of the factory. Artists were justly proud of their work, and it was common practice at large studios to encourage artists to be inventive with their designs. At Doulton, where a large number of artists was employed, we are fortunate to have detailed lists of many artist's marks as a means of identification.

The artist's mark is more often to be found painted underglaze. This really is a reflection of the process involved during the creation of a piece, since decoration would usually occur after the first (or "biscuit") firing. The artist would usually sign his or her initials in one of the colours used in the decoration, though for many years underglaze blue seems to have been a standard marking-colour in Britain and Europe.

The artist's mark need not necessarily occur on the base of an article. Arthur Eaton at Doulton regularly signed his name within the body of the decoration; and on the black and red landcsape flambés it is worth looking for the occurrence of his signature—so many people miss it!

The presence of a *thrower's* mark is greatly valued by the collector, since this generally guarantees the individuality of a piece, particularly if the mark is hand-written. On many studio wares the thrower was also the designer and decorator but on non-studio wares a thrower's mark is relatively rare.

At the Martin Brothers' studio, Walter Martin was the principal thrower, and signed his work accordingly. At Linthorpe, Henry Tooth undertook much of the throwing, but his mark frequently comprised his initials stamped in the clay, and was no guarantee that he personally threw a piece. The large number of pieces available without his stamp, however, together with the relatively short life of the pottery, tend to indicate that he had some involvement in all of the pieces so stamped. Such is the dilemma of positive identification regarding all pottery marks. They pretend to tell us much, but really tell us so little.

The addition of a separate *designer's* mark is not common. It is closely linked to the thrower's mark since the designer would indicate to the thrower the style of a piece. At Linthorpe, Christopher Dresser's signature was used on pieces made to his design, and often resides with the thrower's mark.

A mark which can give an indication of style, shape or colour is the *pattern number*. Researchers have spent long hours trying to interpret pattern and shape numbers of potteries, and we are often indebted to their labours. It is easy to be misled by the various codes and scratchings that appear with sometimes annoying regularity on certain wares, and not be able to identify their meaning because the pottery kept no records of their markings. Moorcroft collectors were, for years, puzzled by impressed O and X marks on many pieces. We now know that they related to the method of turning, and are actually useful in dating pieces.

In many cases, pattern or shape numbers related directly to a catalogue, and some potteries adopted quite intricate coding systems. At the Poole Pottery, for example, a painted code of **1OR** indicated a pattern of geometric lines, but a code of **OR** indicated the same style of pattern, but with the geometric lines further apart. This code was purely an indication of decoration, however, and gave no guide to shape. Generally, codes that indicated shape were incised underglaze, and would be marked by the thrower. Decoration codes were more often painted on, over, or under the glaze.

At some potteries number codes might refer to the quantity of pieces made, whilst at others they might merely be catalogue entries. At C.H. Brannam, pieces could be ordered by shape from the catalogue, and decorated to a customer's choice of colour.

In addition to the above marks there may or may not be a *date* mark. At the Pilkington Pottery, Roman numerals were used for many years to indicate the year of production (eg. XI for 1911), whilst the Martin Brothers incised both the year and the month on their wares (eg. **7-1889** as July, 1889). Moorcroft, however, rarely dated wares, and usually only during the first few years of production at their Cobridge works (1913 to 1915, approximately).

At Wedgwood, a complicated method of registration was used at one time to mark their pottery and glass products, but the codes can be readily interpreted using a guide[1], and reveal much about a particular piece. This "diamond registration" system was enacted by Parliament through the Designs Act of 1842, and allowed thirteen classes of ornamental designs to be registered via year, month, day, class and bundle codes.

Few of the potteries covered in this book made use of the diamond registration system, however, Wedgwood being one of the few. The system was replaced from 1884 by the Patents, Designs and Trade Marks Act of 1883, which allowed a single registered number to be used on ornamental designs; and many potteries made use of this simpler form of registration, marking some of their wares with the Registered Design Number.

Moorcroft, for example, registered several designs, and pieces of a particular pattern were usually marked with the same Registered Design Number. Interpretation of the registered numbers is difficult, however, since reference has to be made to Board of Trade records[2].

The collector will doubtless come across types of marks other than those described above. From an identification point of view, becoming familiar with the range of wares from a pottery is equally as important as knowing the main marks.

When examining marks the collector should beware of forgeries and restorations. A mark *incised* under the glaze would generally leave a burred edge where the displaced wet clay has been fired and then glazed. The displacement would be much less on pieces *stamped* underglaze. Collectors should therefore be wary of incised marks without any displacement, particularly on high value wares.

Reproductions can be a problem in authenticating wares. A good line is well worth repeating, and will often maintain a pottery business. The immensely popular Meissen figurines, for example, have been continually produced and reproduced all over Europe. Similarly, the boom in the houseplant business has created a market for reproductions of Victorian and Edwardian jardinières, particularly as originals are now commanding high prices.

Demand for Victorian and Edwardian tiles is also heavy currently, and reproductions using original moulds may cause authentication problems. If a new mark is not present, one can usually tell a reproduction from a certain freshness of style. The absence of wear or crazing may also be indicators of a reproduction.

The lack of a mark and a smooth unglazed base could indicate that grinding has taken place, something which is undertaken to eliminate basal chips. Grinding may have been performed at the factory or many years afterwards. At the factory, grinding was mainly undertaken using carborundum stone to smooth down sharp edges of glaze. The collector should be suspicious of any clean scratch-free base which might indicate that grinding has taken place since an article left the factory.

Kiln marks are often present on the base of pieces, and with some potteries they were almost a trademark. For example, most Elton pieces featured three equally placed, raised round marks, which were made by the kiln supports when firing the glaze.

General Characteristics of Wares

The form or feel of a piece is as much an aid to identification as the mark. Pieces may be heavy or light, thinly or thickly potted, thrown on a wheel, moulded, slip-cast, modelled or coiled. Ceramics can take many forms.

Pots which are hand-thrown will often not have completely smooth interiors, such that the collector should be able to feel the ribbing inside a piece where the thrower has "brought up" the pot on the wheel. Mass-produced pieces will invariably have smooth interiors, and moulded wares will often bear one or more straight lines revealing the egdes of contact of the mould. Moulded pieces are also generally much lighter in weight than hand-thrown pieces of similar size.

Pieces may exhibit a variety of glazes. Some glazes will be high (i.e. of high gloss), others matt, lustrous or crystalline. The chemical content of a glaze often dictated the finish, and the collector should be familiar with the different effects of ingredients such as wood-ash, feldspar, zircon, tin, lead, etc. Likewise, the manner of firing a glaze dictated the final effect. Many potteries experimented with flambés and other reducing glazes, created at very high temperatures in the kiln.

Apart from the glazes, a variety of clays may have been used to form the pottery body. Some wares were created from earthenware, others from terra-cotta, porcelain or stoneware, and within each type there could be many varieties. The pottery body is a useful additional aid to identification, and may frequently be revealed at the base of a piece. Some potters even marked the body used. Doulton, for example, marked some wares in this way (eg. *OB* for olive body).

---

[1] Ref. Diamond Registration System in Appendix II.
[2] Ref. Appendix III.

Ceramic Styles

Another aid to identification is the style of a piece.

Firstly there is the *shape*. Oriental influences were strong during the latter half of the nineteenth century, and vases with bulbous bases and tapered cylindrical necks were one exponent of this influence. The Ruskin Pottery in particular promoted Oriental shapes, and even went as far as producing Oriental style ceramic stands for some of their wares.

Bulbous shapes were a natural extension to the graceful curvilinear styles of the Victorian period, though the earlier styles did not fade. The Ault Pottery continued to produce Victorian classical pieces into the 1920s. Their jardinières were heavy in design, and exhibit the characteristic Victorian penchant for frills and scroll-work on boat-shaped or deep tulip-like bowls.

A Victorian zest for classical Greek scenes and shapes was well catered for by the art potteries. Mintons' pâte-sur-pâte wares were noble exponents of this art form, as were the impressive enamel wares of the Watcombe Pottery. The classical Grecian Urn was a favourite model for the Wedgwood factory, whilst the Ault Pottery used the outline of a Grecian vase as part of their factory mark for many years.

The ready extension of the artist's canvass to ceramics prompted many potteries to utilise flat-faced shapes such as plates, chargers, plaques and tiles for painting portraits and scenes. Mintons' South Kensington Studio, for example, using locally trained artists, produced painted wares of considerably quality.

By contrast there were also exponents of the *avant-garde* during this period. The designer Christopher Dresser put his ideas into practice at the Linthorpe and Ault Potteries where his use of angular shapes and modelling broke away from tradition. His curious South American designs appealed to a Victorian taste for the unusual, though his streaky glazes and patterns were less well received.

Dresser's designs did much to change the way people thought about pottery style, and in many cases he was original. Individualism was an increasing trend during the late nineteenth century, and potters such as Elton seemed to be able to embrace a variety of styles and absorb a variety of influences and yet retain individuality of output.

De Morgan produced vases in Persian styles, and the Aller Vale Pottery tried to emulate Moorish designs. At Linthorpe, Dresser produced some Japanese-style tea-wares, Bretby Art Pottery openly declared their Chinese and Japanese influences in named wares such as *Carved Bamboo Ware*, and Maw & Co. emulated Middle-Eastern designs in their large stoneware vases with ear-like handles. The Della Robbia Pottery existed solely to produce pieces in the style of the fifteenth century Italian Renaissance, and some unusual bottles and vases emerged from the Burmantofts Pottery strongly imitating North African wares.

Such was the range of international influences on British pottery—influences which surely had been spurred on by the international Great Exhibition of 1851. Europe, however, was not without its own particular style, and from the late 1870s, the Art Nouveau style made its mark on ceramics. New shapes emerged and asymmetrical forms appeared, accompanied by extensive modelling. Handles twisted over the necks of vases, often in the forms of reptiles, and many shapes took on floral forms.

Grotesques, whether derived on purpose or by accident through misshapen pieces, became popular. The Martin Brothers produced their stylised birds with human heads, and Brannam produced his devil jugs and other monsters.

Shape in ceramics, of course, is as much directed by functional use as by practical manufacture using the facilities available. The opportunity to deviate from this premise is often limited. Bernard Leach, however, once advocated that style was more important than functionality, and gave short shrift to a lady who wrote to him complaining that the teapot she had purchased did not pour adequately!

Studio potters between the wars were generally more concerned with the artistry of their shapes than their earlier counterparts, whose prime concern was for decoration. Harmony of shape and decoration was an Oriental tenet taken up by many inter-war potters, whose pieces exhibited Oriental foot rings, pulled handles and other characteristic trappings.

The work of the studio potters, particularly those producing stonewares, was visibly different from any output of the large potteries at this time, whereas prior to the First World War there was considerable emulation of studio wares by the larger concerns.

It was the larger potteries, though, that were quick to embrace the next dramatic change in shapes to come along—those which reflected the Art Deco style of the 1930s.

The Art Deco style gave rise to more exaggerated and angular shapes. Bowls were produced with square and hexagonal sides, and conical forms (such as cruet sets) appeared. An increase in moulded forms during the 1920s prompted more imaginative use of modelling, and contemporary subjects, such as automobiles and air planes were modelled, which doubled as teapots or salt-cellars. An interesting assortment of artistically influenced shapes was created, such as Louis Wain's model cats in the Cubist style.

Whilst it is possible to recognise style through *shape*, it is often easier to recognise wares by means of *decoration*. For some potteries, decoration was an individual hallmark and their decorative style never changed. Others changed their decorations to suit public taste and demand, or through the employment of new artists and designers, or to embrace new developments in technology.

At Moorcroft, for example, on wares produced between 1913 and 1945, one can see few differences in the overall decorative style, which was essentially slip-trailed floral patterns on stock shapes. At Wardle and Salopian, however, there was no overall decorative style, and identification of wares without a mark is often rendered difficult.

Although decorative style varied considerably throughout the period covered by this book, certain aspects are readily recognisable, whether they relate to slip-trailing in the traditional English manner, tube-lining, sgraffito, painting, enamelling, modelling or glaze effects, for example.

The use of glazes originally stemmed from practical considerations, such as ensuring a water-holding seal over the porous clay, but potters soon discovered the decorative importance of glazes, and the wares of many potteries can often be recognised by glaze alone.

Extensive use of salt-glaze by potteries such as Fulham, Doulton and the Martin Brothers during the early period of this book produced wares recognisable by their overall, translucent, silky effect, whilst the lead glazes used by many potteries, such as Farnham and Ewenny, until their effect on health was understood, produced a recognisable high gloss with an iridescence. Conversely, the wares of some potteries are recognisable by their limited use of glaze to achieve the full effect of the clay body, such as at Torquay Terra-Cotta.

Technical achievements in ceramics, which extended the range of colours available, were a significant influence on decoration. Experiments in glazes were a continuing occupation of potteries in the search for new and rival finishes. A large range of reducing glazes was produced during the first twenty years or so of the twentieth century, though not all potteries were able to make use of this complex and relatively costly technology.

Doulton's *flambé*, *sang-de-boeuf* and crystalline glazes were the result of laboured experiment, and much admired for their effects. Likewise the Ruskin Pottery's *rouge flambés, viridian flambés,* crystalline and *souffle* glazes. Bernard Moore's *rouge flambé* glazes were virtually a hallmark, and Moorcroft's use of *flambé* over slip-decorated wares won much acclaim.

Lustre glazes gave another particular type of decorative effect, and many potteries made use of different types of lustre decoration. The Pilkington Pottery produced a virtually unique form of lustre with mirror-like effects, whilst De Morgan's lustres rendered more matt or silky finishes. As a contrast, lustres on a porcelainous body, as utilised by Wedgwood and A.J. Wilkinson, often produced glassy finishes.

Use of colour can characterise a particular pottery or artist, often during a particular period. Designers such as Clarice Cliff and Charlotte Rhead were known for their bright decorative lines emphasising simple but often impressive shapes during the 1930s. The Art Deco style was noted for its dramatic colour combinations, such as yellow and black, orange and green, and bold, geometric patterns, such as zig-zags and concentric bands.

By contrast, the studio potters of the inter-war period adopted restraint in use of colour. Glaze effect and body were prime decorative considerations, and many potters of stoneware rarely allowed themselves the addition of surface decoration—a few well-placed brush-strokes perhaps for simple effect.

Sgraffito decoration was often a particular characteristic of certain artists. Hannah Barlow at Doulton was known for her sgraffito images of animals and children, and James Hartshorne for his images of ferns and flowers at Salopian.

When one thinks of modelling, names such as Robert Wallace Martin and George Tinworth (Doulton) come to mind, and when considering tube-lining as a decorative means, Charlotte Rhead must be thought of as a prime exponent.

Various types of decoration can, therefore, be associated with particular artists or potteries, and the same is true for decorative motifs. Gordon Forsyth's heraldic emblems for Pilkington and Daisy Mackeig-Jones' fairies for Wedgwood are two examples.

Recurring decorative themes were common, such as the medieval galleon (as utilised by William De Morgan, Walter Crane at Maw & Co. and William Mycock at Pilkington,) the "Liberty" cats (as utilised by Brannam, Baron and Aller Vale,) the "Liberty" owl (as utilised by Farnham, Brannam, Denby and Elton,) the John Dory fish (as utilised by Doulton and Pilkington,) and the leaping deer (as utilised by De Morgan and Honiton.)

Perhaps the most common of all decorative themes was the floral motif, whether depicted from nature or stylised. The more classical wares of the late-Victorian period regularly depicted flowers and foliage, and on Art Nouveau wares fruit, flowers and vegetable designs were typically employed, which often extended outwards from a piece as modelling in relief. The Devon potteries' beautiful painted renditions of flowers in the French barbotine style, and Doulton's similar impasto floral subjects showed the variety of expression which could be accomplished using the floral motif.

Doulton's method of impressing real leaves into wet clay and colouring the impressions to create their Natural Foliage Ware, was just one of many novel ideas thought up by potteries in the search for alternative means of decoration.

Many potteries merely copied decorative ideas. Artists did move around, and several potteries were clever at imitating other potteries' styles. Hancock & Sons' "Morris Ware" bore similar characteristics of motif to some of Moorcroft's wares, and attempts to emulate Pilkington's popular lustres were made by Maling and S. Fielding & Co.. Carlton's leaf-shaped dishes were also emulated by S.Fielding & Co. during the later 1920s, and the Devon potteries regularly copied each other's designs. More striking copies were made by Salopian, for whom few potteries' designs seemed sacrosanct.

The joy of looking at pottery, however, is in its infinite variety, and the collector will always come across similarities as well as surprises. It is all too easy to generalise, but it is hoped that by drawing comparisons between marks, style, shape and decorative means, the identification of wares will be that much easier for the reader.

Alphabetical list of Potteries

ALLER VALE ART POTTERY (1881—1924) —terracotta

Newton Abbot, Devon.

Historical Background

The Aller Vale Pottery was established as the Aller Pottery in 1865, producing initially brown bodied earthenware for domestic use.

In 1881, after the original pottery was damaged in a fire, John Phillips set up the Aller Vale Art Pottery, recruiting workers from the Newton Abbot School of Art which he had helped to found ten years previously. The Torquay Terra Cotta Company and Watcombe Pottery were already established and may have influenced him in his enterprise.

Phillips was particularly interested in the principles of the Arts and Crafts Movement, and encouraged the local community by running craft classes. He admired pottery hand-made in the traditional way, using locally obtained materials, and was careful to ensure that this was practised at Aller Vale. He also encouraged Edwin Beer Fishley of the Fremington Pottery (a pottery situated nearby which was run on mainly traditional lines) by introducing him to some of the national collections of ceramics in London.

In 1886, Phillips took on an apprentice by the name of Charles Collard, who later went on to found the Honiton Pottery and the Crown Dorset Pottery at Poole in Dorset. Collard executed some fine painted decorations whilst at Aller Vale, including some inspired by Persian and Isnik designs. He left Aller Vale in 1902.

In 1890, national attention was drawn to the pottery when Princess Louise, well known for encouraging local craft initiatives throughout the country, opened the fourth annual exhibition of the Kingskerswell Cottage Art Schools, Torquay.

More public attention was given through the London store, Liberty & Co., which is recorded as stocking Aller Vale wares between 1887 and 1901.

Phillps died in 1897 and the business was bought by Hexter Humpherson & Co., who also later purchased the Watcombe Pottery.

In 1901, the Aller Vale Pottery joined with the Watcombe Pottery at Torquay to form the Royal Aller Vale & Watcombe Pottery Company. The works at Aller Vale finally closed in 1924, much of the labour force having already moved to other local potteries.

Aller Vale Selection of wares.

Aller Vale Selection of 'barbotine' wares.

Aller Vale Examples of the 'Sandringham' pattern.

16

Aller Vale Advertisement, 1920.

Products

The early styles were crude and unglazed, pieces seldom being marked, but from 1887, there was a noticeable change of style and wares became heavily glazed and well marked. These often exhibited floral and insect designs in thickly coloured slips. These wares were in the manner of the French "barbotine" style, and comprised mainly vases with decoration in bright colours on a blue, yellow, green or red-brown ground.

A common characteristic of the Aller Vale barbotine pieces was the painting of a flower motif on only one side of a vase, the reverse usually depicting a simple complementary leaf pattern, such as a bullrush.

A pattern developed by Collard and known as "Persian" was introduced about 1885, being characterised by blue tulips and other flowers such as hyacinths and carnations on Persian shapes. Collard went on to develop this pattern further at the Honiton Pottery, reaching a peak in development in the late 1920s.

Another strong influence on design at Aller Vale was an Italian artist, Marcucci, who created Italianate scroll patterns from about 1890. His name is sometimes found on pieces of his design, incised or painted within the decoration.

Some of the wares were given specific titles, such as "Sandringham," "Abbotskerswell" (a simple daisy pattern named after a local village), and "Crocus." This latter ware consisted of an Art Nouveau crocus design, usually painted on tall-necked vases in green and white on a deep blue background, and included the stem, bulb and leaves of the crocus as well as the flower.

"Sandringham" featured a blue scroll pattern on a white ground, and was named by the Princess of Wales who purchased several pieces. Other patterns included "Scandy" and "Rhodian" (both reminiscent of Prince of Wales feathers) and various forms of cockerel design. The name "Scandy" appears to be a corruption of Scandinavian whilst "Rhodian" relates to Rhodes in Greece. The reference is misleading, however, since, as at the Salopian Art Pottery where the names were also used, it is sometimes difficult to see the connections between the designs and the places.

Floral motifs seem to have been a favourite means of decoration at Aller Vale, surface decoration being generally plentiful and colours bright. The deep red body of the wares was a suitable background for the designs and types of glaze employed.

Designs often emulated old Moorish and Mediterranean ceramic styles, and, although the majority of output was in terracotta, some pieces were created in white clay (particularly the Sandringham pattern) or a mixture of red and white clays.

Some fine grotesque wares were also produced, demonstrating that the pottery could produce interesting shapes as well as decorative ranges.

A great deal of ware was made for the souvenir trade, and many pieces contained popular mottoes, although it is believed that only one person was employed to etch the mottoes at any one period to ensure consistency of handwriting. Designs after 1901 included more and more souvenir wares, such as cottages and windmills, many of which were of low quality.

The collector should note that potteries in the Torquay area often produced similar designs, and recurring themes were common across the Devon potteries generally. The Longpark Pottery, for example, working from 1905 to 1957, produced a popular decoration of yellow daffodils on a bright green ground, the whole bearing a high gloss glaze. This design was reproduced at Aller Vale and elsewhere. Collectors will frequently find styles imitated at Aller Vale from a wide range of potteries—Linthorpe, Burmantofts and Brannam being just a few examples.

Suggestions for Further Study

Thomas, D & E Lloyd. *The Old Torquay Potteries.* Stockwell, 1978.

Cashmore, Carol and Chris. *Collard, the Honiton and Dorset Potter.* pub. privately, 1983. (includes details of Aller Vale pattern codes).

Torquay Pottery 1870-1940. catalogue of an exhibition at Bearne's and Bonham's, London, August 1986, Torquay Pottery Collectors' Society.

Cashmore, Carol. "Ceramics for Gentlemen of Taste: The Torquay Potteries and Their Products," *Antique Dealer & Collector*, August, 1986.

Monkhouse, Cosmo. "The Potteries of Aller Vale," *The Magazine of Art*, 1891.

Aller Vale Selection of grotesques.

ALLER VALE

Types of Ware	Production	Quality	Availability
Early wares	Low	Poor	Uncommon
Post-1887 art wares	Moderate to High	Fair to Very Good	Uncommon (grotesques: scarce)
Souvenir wares	High	Poor to Good	Common

Marks

Incised:	Phillips Aller	c. 1881-1887
Incised:	Phillips Newton Abbot	c. 1881-1887
Impressed	ALLER VALE	1887-1901

(early pieces often occur without a factory mark, but occasionally bear a small impressed "T," Maltese Cross or crescent shape; other marks have also been noted)

Impressed	ALLER VALE DEVON ENGLAND	c. 1891-1918

+/- H.H. & Co. *(after 1897)*

Painted:	Aller Vale England	c. 1891-1901

(N.B. 'Royal Aller Vale' refers to the post-1901 period)

+/- pattern numbers A to Z with numerals, indicating the variety (usually the colour of the background, eg. C2)
+/- decorator's mark
+/- impressed mark: Made for Liberty & Co. 1887-1901

There is no record of pieces bearing dates, except commemorative wares, where the date sometimes appears as part of the decoration, but never on the base of a piece. Early pieces tended to have an unglazed base.

THE ASHBY POTTERS' GUILD

(1909-1922)

—earthenware
—lustre glazes
—flambé glazes

Woodville, Derbyshire

Historical Background & Products

The Ashby Potters' Guild was a studio pottery established in 1909 by Pascoe Tunnicliffe, a ceramic chemist who was one of a family of potters. The pottery specialised in glaze effects, and often used multicoloured glazes over a red clay body.

Some fine blue and ruby lustres were produced, together with crystalline glazes (often in blue or green) and a rouge flambé. The Pottery Gazette records that a specimen of the pottery's crystalline glaze was sold to the Copenhagen Museum in 1913.

Some vases of varying sizes and good quality were produced during the early 1920s, together with floating-flower bowls, pot-pourri and ginger jars, plaques, covered vases, tobacco and bisuit jars, cake-stands and ink-stands. Many designs were orientally inspired. Some miniature pieces were also produced, and many of these were created using a white clay body.

Pieces were known to have been exhibited at the Ghent Exhibition of 1913 and the British Industrial Arts Exhibition of April, 1920. This latter exhibition included the Guild's "Vasco" art pottery, the manufacture of which had been temporarily suspended during the First World War. "Vasco" art pottery consisted of pieces decorated in variegated crystalline and lustre glazes and also enamel colours. At the exhibition an orange flambé glaze also attracted attention.

Besides the glaze effects, decorative styles included floreate designs, such as arrangements of oak leaves, many of which were quite individual in character.

In 1922, the pottery merged with William Ault's pottery to form the partnership "Ault and Tunnicliffe" (ref. Ault).

Unfortunately, little is known about the many ranges of ware produced by the Ashby Potters' Guild, and there are few speciliast collectors currently to promote extensive research. Individual pieces, however, are sought after, because of their high quality and attractive glaze effects.

Ashby Potters' Guild Small vase, 73mm high.

Ashby Potters' Guild vase, 135mm high, lustre glaze, marked "AB" in monogram.

THE ASHBY POTTERS' GUILD			
Type of Ware	**Production**	**Quality**	**Availability**
All wares	Low to Moderate	Good to Very Good	Scarce
Marks			
Printed or Impressed:	ASHBY (within oval) GUILD		1909-1922
+/- artist's initials			

Ashtead, Surrey.

Historical Background

The Ashtead Pottery was founded in 1923 by Sir Lawrence Weaver, who, as vice chairman of the Rural Industries Bureau, wanted to establish new careers for disabled ex-servicemen.

A fund was set up through a committee headed by Sir Lawrence Weaver's wife, Kathleen, which included Sir Bertram Clough Williams-Ellis, Stafford Cripps and the Reverend Edward Dorling among its members. Initial capital was provided by the British Red Cross Society and the Order of St. John and Jerusalem.

A small factory was obtained in Ashtead, and wares were marketed as Ashtead Potters Ltd. Lady Weaver became responsible for the welfare of the employees, whilst her husband actively marketed the pottery's products at every opportunity.

The first of these opportunities came in 1924 when Sir Lawrence Weaver was appointed Director of the UK section of the British Empire Exhibition, Wembley. He ensured that the Ashtead Potters were given ample press coverage; and King George V & Queen Mary visited the Ashtead stand at the exhibition. Ashtead pottery was included at the same exhibition the following year.

In 1928, the Duke and Duchess visited the pottery and were presented with a gift for their daughter, Elizabeth, of a "Christopher Robin" nursery set, which was subsequently issued as a numbered edition. The set was decorated from designs by E.H. Shepard, which were transfer-printed in black on to a white ground and then hand-painted.

Apparently Sir Lawrence Weaver was a great persuader, and many well-known artists gave their time to teach at the pottery or contributed their designs. Prominent among these was Phoebe Stabler, who designed extensively for the Poole Pottery, Doulton and Royal Worcester, and who designed some striking figure models for Ashtead.

Ashtead Group of wares, tallest 385mm high. (courtesy of Christie's Images)

Ashtead 'The Wembley Lion', souvenir of the British Empire Exhibition, Wembley, 1924, 102mm high, 129mm long. (courtesy HCMS, DA 1976.27).

Ashtead Selection of modelled pieces (courtesy of Leatherhead Museum). l to r:i) Eastern lady, 125mm high, by Phoebe Stabler, 1930, marked "M37". ii) Madonna and child, 210mm high, by Phoebe Stabler, marked "M34". (loaned by Mrs. Hardenburg). iii) Child with staff, 135mm high, by Phoebe Stabler, marked "M38". iv) "Corn Girl", 190mm high, by Allen G. Wyon, 1927, marked "M72" (loaned by S.E.D. Fortescue).

Another prominent modeller at Ashtead was Percy Metcalfe, a free-lance sculptor, who produced one of the designs for the well-known "Wembley Lion" model, which was sold as a souvenir of the 1924 Wembley Exhibition. A stylised version of the "Lion," designed by Frederick Herrick, appeared on souvenir beakers and circular boxes.

At the height of its operation, the pottery employed some forty workers who produced a variety of shapes and designs. Many designs were copied from pieces in museums (such as the Victoria & Albert Museum in London) or from other samples of pottery at home and abroad. Lady Weaver is known to have named the "Brittany" shape of jug, for example, following one of her holidays in France.

The bulk of the pottery's output was tableware, and several commissions were fulfilled for specialist products. A honey-pot was made for Australian honey and a ceramic chocolate box for Carson's chocolates.

Sir Lawrence Weaver's death in 1930, coupled with the general depression in trade, heralded the end of the enterprise, and in 1935 the factory closed.

Ashtead Four nine-inch soup bowls, 230mm diameter; marked P6V.

Products

Mostly tableware was produced, such as dinner, tea, coffee and breakfast sets. Several small items were produced, which were also of a domestic nature, such as egg-cups, cruet sets and ashtrays (most interesting of which were the "CHO-KR Patent Extinguishing Ashtrays.")

Several souvenir items, such as beakers and circular boxes, were produced for the British Empire Exhibition and featured the "Herrick Lion" as a decorative motif, and bore the legend "19.B.E.E.24."

Among the larger items produced were electric lamp bases and vases, though the largest pieces seem to have been no more than 490mm in height.

Most pieces were moulded, and were subsequently light in weight. Pieces heavier in weight were generally hand thrown. Some pieces were modelled, such as figurines or the "Wembley Lions," and were produced by such artists as Phoebe Stabler, Percy Metcalfe, Allan G. Wyon and Donald Gibson.

Surface decoration was noticeably minimal, but where it occurred it was usually accomplished by hand-painted scenes (cottages in landscapes, for example) or painted transfer-prints (such as the "Christopher Robin" nursery set or "Canterbury Tales" series.)

A series of face tankards modelled by Percy Metcalfe of famous politicians (such as Stanley Baldwin) was produced in white without any surface decoration save for the name of the face transfer-printed in black round the base of the tankard.

Shapes were generally simple and unadventurous, but their simplicity was effectively reinforced by striking use of bold monochrome colours.

On tablewares, in particular, the simple shapes and bold colours were given a feeling of lightness and delicacy through the use of a thin translucent high glaze (which was also used throughout the product range.)

Colours ranged from a bright yellow, turquoise green, cerise, etc., to a soft speckly beige and powder blue (similar to Moorcroft's but paler.)

Suggestions for Further Study

Leatherhead Museum, Church Street, Leatherhead, Surrey, has a good representative collection. (Museum closed during the winter).

Hallam, Edward. *"Ashtead Potters Ltd. in Surrey. 1923-35."* pub. privately, 1990; obtainable from PO Box 159, Epsom, Surrey, KT17 1NR, England.

Ashtead Selection of decorated wares (courtesy of Leatherhead Museum) l to r:i) small dish, 105mm diam., painted underglaze, marked "S5". ii) pepper pot, 85mm high, painted underglaze, not marked. iii) frog mustard pot (marked "Ml9") and owl pepper pot (marked "M20"), 95mm high, painted underglaze. iv) "Christopher Robin" plate, 235mm diam., transfer printed and painted underglaze, No.14 of a 24 piece set. v) "CHO-KR" ashtray, 80mm diam., impressed mark "CHO-KR PATENT" and marked "S25" , "Patent Extinguishing CHO-KR Ashtray" transfer-printed. vi) coffee mug, 80mm high, painted underglaze, marked "C10".

Ashtead Selection of wares (courtesy of Leatherhead Museum) l to r:i) plate, 235mm diam., decorated with concentric bands of colour, marked "Pl". ii) three-handled thrown vase, 130mm high, orange glaze, marked "V36". iii) moulded vase, 270mm high, yellow glaze, marked "V2". iv) moulded muffin dish/warmer, 230mm diam., marked "X75". v) moulded jug, ll0mm high, turquoise glaze, 'Liverpool' shape, marked "J35". vi) large moulded jug, 180mm high, powder blue glaze, 'Brittany' shape, marked "J16".

ASHTEAD POTTERS LTD.

Type of Ware	Production	Quality	Availability
All wares (excl. figures)	Moderate	Good	Uncommon
Figures	Low	Good to Very Good	Scarce

Marks

Transfer-printed:	Ashtead Potters (within outline of a tree on a hill)	1923-1935

+/- name of artist

+ pattern number (painted): Letter followed by number:-
e.g.   J2 (jug 145mm x 152mm); B8 (bowl 50mm x 152mm); M1 (Metcalfe lion); X7 (ink-well 56mm x 101mm). The number denotes the size.

+ colour code (painted):-
e.g.   a **dark green**; b **yellow**; c **Royal blue**; d **Celadon**; f **Powder blue**; g **ivory**; m **orange**; o **applegreen**; p **rose**; r **black**; s **mauve**; t **buff**.

+/- transfer-printed: (on later wares)	BCM / ASHTD MADE + ENG IN LAND	c.1926 - 1935

+/- date codes, as shown by the cross in the above example. Codes noted so far are: a cross, square, triangle, quarter-moon, swastika (believed to represent 1928), anchor and star.

Ashtead "Shy", figure by Phoebe Stabler, 385mm high. (courtesy of Christie's Images)

G.L.Ashworth & Brothers, (1862-1968)
Hanley, Staffs.

Historical Background & Products

About 1845, the rights to use the title "Masons Ironstone" were bought from the china works of Charles James Mason & Co. by Francis Morley & Co., following Masons' bankruptcy. When Morley & Co. also got into financial difficulties, the Rochdale woollen firm of George L. Ashworth & Bros. took them over in 1862 together with the right to manufacture Mason's "Patent Ironstone China."

With the collapse of the wool and cotton trade, G.L. Ashworth & Bros. was bought by the Goddard family, but continued to keep the company name as G.L. Ashworth & Bros.

J.V.Goddard started to experiment with flambé glazes, and from 1905 high-fired lustres were produced under the direction of the Austrian chemist Dr. Basch.

Dr. Basch was appointed to produce "interesting" glazes, and a range of wares was produced with a variety of special glaze effects, some of which were known as "Lustrosa" and "Esterella."

The quality of these wares was very good, and shapes were kept simple in order to show off the spectacular glaze effects. Mostly vases were decorated, in classical shapes, ranging from small squat vases to larger urns.

Colours were generally monochrome, but with a striking colour palette, such as apple green with a silky finish, for example, or royal blue with white flecks and a high glaze. A deep maroon was a particularly impressive lustre glaze, similar in effect to Pilkington's "Sunstone" glaze.

Dr. Basch's glazes were exhibited at the Louvre in 1914, but were never marketed as planned, and Dr. Basch returned to Austria with the approach of the First World War.

In 1968, G.L.Ashworth traded as "Masons Ironstone China Ltd.," and in 1973, Masons became part of Wedgwood, who currently maintain a colection of some 81 Ashworth art vases and 9 bowls.

Suggestions for Further Study

A collection at Masons Ironstone, Hanley, Staffordshire is open to view.

Ashworth Vase, 260mm high, marked "ASHWORTH".

Ashworth Vase, 80mm high, impressed mark "ASHWORTH" and pattern no. 78.

ASHWORTH			
Type of Ware	**Production**	**Quality**	**Availability**
High-fired lustres	Low	Very good to Excellent	Rare
Marks			
Impressed curve:		ASHWORTH	1905 - 1913

+/- name of ware: e.g. LUSTROSA
+/- artist's signature printed underglaze: e.g. W. Nash

Swadlincote, Burton-on-Trent, Staffs.

Historical Background

In 1887, the potter William Ault (b.1841) left the Bretby Art Pottery and his partnership with Henry Tooth in order to set up his own pottery at Swadlincote (ref. Bretby.)

He began to manufacture wares similar to those produced at Linthorpe, but which he termed "Ault faience" (though in the strictest sense of the word the wares were not faience.) He experimented continuously with coloured glazes, and with the help of his daughters, Clarissa and Gertrude, applied these to pressed and moulded wares.

In 1893, Ault won a gold medal at the Chicago "World's Exposition" where he exhibited his already renowned jardinières. Ault's wares at this time, however, were fairly classical in style and lacked inventiveness, so the designer Christopher Dresser was commissioned to design pieces for the Ault pottery similar to those he designed for Linthorpe.

Towards the beginning of the First World War, the demand for more decorative hand-painted pottery stemmed the production of Ault's coloured glazes, but these were revived somewhat during the 1920s and 1930s when many fine art pieces were produced.

In 1922, the firm amalgamated with the Ashby Potters' Guild and became known as "Ault and Tunnicliffe," but from 1937 traded as "Ault Potteries Ltd." until 1975.

Products

A popular piece produced at the Ault Pottery was a vase supported by a metal stand (a design which was used as a trademark,) but besides this and decorative vases of many shapes and sizes, plant-pots and large jardinières on ceramic pedestals were the speciality of the pottery. These were produced in quantity from about 1890. Pieces produced were of good quality and were offered for sale in the biscuit state with customised decoration.

Decoration was mostly in the form of coloured glazes (usually monochrome, or bichrome which tended to run into each other) applied over heavily moulded patterns in relief. Decorative subjects were at first mainly classical floreate designs with garlands, graduating to more art nouveau styles with bold swirls after about 1893.

Figure patterns on plaques and vases tended to be produced after 1893, together with animal models and figurines, moulded or slip-cast, or occasionally thrown.

Dresser's designs at Ault included double gourd-shaped vases and a vase with goat head buttresses. Both monochrome and streaked glazes were used, and the South American pre-Columbian influence is strongly apparent in many of his designs. Dresser also combined the use of metals with the ceramic medium and designed metal handles and rims for some of his creations. His designs continued in production well after his death in 1904.

Ault Two pieces designed by Christopher Dresser. l to r: flower holder, marked "236"; vase, 220mm high.

Ault Pair of vases, hand-painted decoration, 165mm high, impressed mark "AULT ENGLAND", "9".

Ault Jardinière, 212mm high, impressed early mark "E" with pattern no. 476 and raised Ault "tall vase" mark.

Ault Jardinière, 1200mm high, yellow and blue colouration.

About 1910, in consideration of workers' health, leadless glazes were introduced at the Ault pottery, and some items about this time are marked "Ault's lead-less glaze."

After 1900 certain named wares were produced, such as "Sgraffito Ware" (sgraffito designs of flowers and scrolls,) "Creke Pattern" (a scroll motif on a red ground,) "Mauresque Ware" (characterised by splashed and striated surfaces,) "Ebonite Pattern" (an ebony-like black surface with stars and figures of clowns in red, white and grey,) "Anemone," "Iris," "Honesty," "Bulrush," etc., (single flower patterns painted over transfer-printed outlines.)

During the 1920s, painted transfer-printed wares were produced in quantity as vases (often in pairs,) toilet sets, etc. Animals, birds and flower scenes were common, but though often decorative in appearance, the artistic quality of the work was not spectacular.

Suggestions for Further Study

Christopher Dresser. (see under Linthorpe for references).

Pinkham, Roger. "A Tale of Three Potteries." *The Antique Collectors' Fayre*, September, 1977.

Ault Pair of vases, 150mm high, hand painted pansies in purple and green on a cream ground.

AULT POTTERY

Type of Ware	Production	Quality	Availability
Art wares by Chr. Dresser	Low to Moderate	Good to Excellent	Uncommon
Art wares prior to 1922	Moderate to high	Good	Uncommon

Marks

(A great deal of Ault pottery was unmarked)

Impressed or moulded:	AULT	(on scroll, plus or minus a vase on stand design)	1887-1922
	APL	(in monogram)	1887-1922

+/- 'AULT's LEADLESS GLAZE' (*c. 1910*)
+/- 'Chr. Dresser' (in impressed signature, sometimes moulded; ref. Linthorpe)
+/- 'C.J.A.' (initials of Clarissa Ault on painted vases)
 +/- pattern number (three numbers and a letter; also occurs without a factory mark)

+/- 'ENGLAND' (*after 1891*)

Printed or impressed:	Aultcliff MADE IN ENGLAND	1923-1937
	APL (in monogram; similar to earlier mark)	1937-1975

27

—terracotta

The Pottery, Fulham, S.W. London

Historical Background & Products

C.J.C. Bailey was a civil engineer who, in 1864, acquired the Fulham Pottery which had been operated by the renowned potter John Dwight (1637-1703) over a hundred and fifty years previously.

The pottery had been producing mainly brown salt-glazed ornamental wares, and Bailey enlarged the works to accommodate the production of domestic, sanitary and architectural wares (mainly in terracotta.)

Bailey is primarily remembered for his ornamental salt-glazed stoneware which was often similar to Doulton's Lambeth wares. He was fortunate in recruiting good artists and designers, amongst whom was Robert Wallace Martin who was associated with the pottery from 1872.

Also in 1872, the French painter Jean-Charles Cazin, who had been Principal at Tours Art School, was made art director at the pottery. Cazin also undertook a teaching post at Lambeth School of Art before returning to France in 1874.

Stoneware jugs, vases, mugs, bowls, tobacco-jars and jardinières were the main ornamental output, and much use of sgraffito and applied bead work was made in their decoration. Cut-away decoration and lattice work were also employed, and many pieces were heavily ornamented. The colour palette was limited, but good use was made of browns, pink, blue, green and brown-red.

Floral patterns often featured on pieces, and a motif of acanthus leaves was regularly used around the base of wares. The architect J.P. Seddon designed some jardinières with foliate motifs, and the decorator Edgar Kettle is known to have executed foliate and floral patterns as well as birds, animals and medieval figure subjects.

After 1872, the sculptor E. Bennet is recorded as having been involved in the production of stonewares to Dwight's recipe, and producing some different shapes, together with unusual handles to jugs and vases. Certainly, pieces marked with Bennet's monogram exhibited an accomplished artistry and balance of decoration. Figured medallions often featured alongside beadwork, stippled backgrounds and colourful swirls of flowers and leaves, on elegant shapes. The entire surface area was often decorated.

In 1889 the business folded, and in 1891 the pottery was sold to George Cheavin who continued to use the name Fulham Pottery on industrial and sanitary wares.

CJC Bailey Vase by R.W. Martin, 110mm high, marked "R.W. Martin London SW 3-1875", and ".I.l."

C.J.C. BAILEY			
Types of Ware	**Production**	**Quality**	**Availability**
Salt-glaze stoneware	Low to Moderate	Good to Very Good	Scarce
Marks			
Incised:		Bailey Fulham	c.1864 - c.1889
		C.J.C. Bailey The Pottery Fulham	c.1864 - c.1889

+/- year
+/- artist's mark:-
    EK (incised) & outline of a kettle (*Edgar Kettle's mark*)
    EB (incised), (*E. Bennet's monogram*)
    R.W. Martin (incised), (*Robert Wallace Martin*)			

Impressed		CJCB (in monogram) FULHAM	c.1864 - c.1889
Variations exist.			

Mill Road, Rolle Quay, near Barnstaple, Devon

Historical Background

William Leonard Baron (1863-1937) formed his pottery at Rolle Quay in 1895, having previously worked for C.H. Brannam Ltd. from about 1885 to 1893.

Prior to joining Brannam, he had worked a short time at Doulton and some of his early designs clearly reflect a Doulton style. Whilst at Brannam he became an accomplished modeller and attended Barnstaple School of Art during his spare time. His interest in art prompted him to undertake several part-time teaching posts throughout his pottery career.

On leaving Brannam in 1893, he formed a brief arrangement with E.B. Fishley to produce his own wares at the Fremington Pottery.

At his own pottery at Rolle Quay, Baron had assistance from several staff as decorators, modellers or throwers. Output was remarkably similar to Brannam's "Barum Ware" both in range and style and consisted of art wares as well as wares for the Devon tourist market.

Considerable business rivalry thus existed between Baron and Brannam, particularly concerning Baron's enterprise in attracting tourists to his pottery by erecting a sign outside the town which gave directions to his pottery and by paying coach drivers a shilling for each coach load of passengers driven there.

The feud lasted for some years and was fuelled when Baron opened a shop about 1904 in a prime position in Barnstaple town. Baron continued to operate his pottery independently, however, until his death in 1937, when C.H. Brannam Ltd. absorbed the business, closing the Rolle Quay works at the outbreak of war.

Collectors tend to agree that, on the whole, Baron's wares were not as high a quality as Brannam's, and much of this may have been due to the quality of potting and firing rather than design. Notable pieces were produced, however, and some of Baron's better quality wares were exhibited at the British Industrial Arts Exhibition of 1920. Gold and silver medals were also won in earlier years at various exhibitions.

Products

Baron's wares were produced in a variety of shapes and sizes, though much of the output consisted of pieces small in stature. This was because many pieces were made for the Devon tourist market, and as such, often bore mottoes.

Apart from many pieces of simple form, some art vases were produced with more imaginative shapes. A typical vase style featured twisted handles on a pear shaped body, a form similar to that produced by Brannam. A more complex shape was a posy-holder produced by Baron originally at Brannam, which featured a small bulbous bowl supported by three dolphins on a lower, larger bowl. This was often highly ornamented with sgrafitto motifs and applied slip or cutaway decoration.

Baron Coffee set, inscribed "Baron Barnstaple".

Baron's wares were mainly produced using a red Devonshire clay, though a white clay was also used, particularly on later wares. Potting was generally poorer than Brannam's, but William Baron's own decorative style was well accomplished. A high lead glaze was characteristically used, which frequently produced a slight iridescence. Decoration was often solely monochrome glazes (typically blue, green, orange and deep pink,) such as found on the curiously quaint, but heavily potted, tea sets.

The finer art wares exhibited a more intricate decoration, with, typically, relief modelled bird, fish and floral motifs against a stippled ground. The result was particularly effective when dark colours (such as royal blue, sea-green and brown) were used for the decorative subject against a paler cream coloured ground.

Some interesting grotesques were modelled either as free-standing models or as face jugs, spoon warmers or candlesticks, etc. Other models included various styles of cats, dogs, rabbits, etc.; and the quality of modelling was often quite good. Some Toby jugs were also made during the First World War, and the collector will come across those depicting personalities of the day, such as Kitchener.

By 1930, the heavier intricate Victorian styles of the art wares had given way to art deco style motifs on simpler shapes. The boldness and brightness of the deco patterns was missing, however, as if Baron could not entirely bring himself to embrace the new style.

Suggestions for Further Study

The Museum of North Devon, Barnstaple, has some pieces by Baron on display.

Audrey Edgeler. *Art Potters of Barnstaple.* Nimrod Press Ltd. 1990

C.H. Brannam Barum Ware, a catalogue by Harry Lyons of a display of Barum Ware at the Liberty Arts & Crafts Exhibition, London, 1991.

Baron Vase, 165mm high, inscribed mark "Baron Barnstaple 101".

Baron Vase, 315mm high, marked "353".

BARON POTTERY

Types of Ware	Production	Quality	Availability
Earthenwares	Moderate to High	Poor to Good	Abundant

Marks

Incised:		W L Baron Barnstaple Fremington	1893 - 1895
+/- date			
Incised:		Baron, Barnstaple	1895 - 1939

(variations exist, such as "W L Baron, Barnstaple" and "Baron Ware, Barnstaple", though these are thought to be early marks, c.1895)

+/- incised number
+/- date (*to 1896 only*)

St. Ives, Cornwall (1925-1928)

Coleshill, Highworth, Berkshire (1928-1936)

Historical Background (see also Katharine Pleydell-Bouverie)

Norah Braden studied at the Central School of Arts & Crafts in London from 1919 to 1921, continuing her studies at the Royal College of Art until 1924.

She joined Bernard Leach at his pottery in St. Ives in 1925 and quickly gained his respect and praise as a "naturally gifted" potter.

She joined Katharine Pleydell-Bouverie at her pottery in Coleshill quite by chance, since she had only intended to visit there to make a stoneware floor for the kiln at her own pottery in West Sussex. Her technical skill with ash glazes and her expertise as a first-class thrower cemented a productive partnership that lasted until 1936, when she returned to Sussex to teach at Brighton School of Art.

It seems that she gave up potting after the war, having made only a few pots whilst teaching. She held other teaching posts until her retirement in 1967. Her stringent quality control and criticism of her own pieces prompted her to destroy much of her output, so that examples of her work now are rare.

Products

While having produced some pieces at St. Ives, the majority of her output was in stoneware made at Coleshill. Vases, bowls and dishes were predominant, often very similar to those produced by Katharine Pleydell-Bouverie, with typically ash glaze decoration.

Norah Braden was, however, competent at painting, and produced more decorative work than Pleydell-Bouverie. Decoration was characteristically simple, often consisting of brushed outlines (abstract, animal or floral) in an iron-red or black pigment against a grey-white slip ground. Many pieces were decorated with two or three concentric lines, with or without an accompanying motif.

Shapes were similar to Pleydell-Bouverie's, emulating Sung styles, and the quality of potting was good.

A commission in the early 1930s from Bendicks, the chocolate producers, for about a dozen ceramic containers, was fulfilled as a set of finely potted, circular, covered jars with brown brush-strokes decoration on a speckled, cream coloured ground. These are clearly marked "Made by N. Braden for Bendicks, Kensington."

Suggestions for Further Study

The Crafts Study Centre, Holburne of Menstrie Museum, Bath, has a collection of pieces, together with a list of glazes and clay bodies used.

Roscoe, Barley. *Katharine Pleydell-Bouverie: A Potter's Life 1895-1985.* Bath: Bath University Press, 1980.

Rice, Paul and Christopher Gowing. *British Studio Ceramics in the 20th Century.* Barrie & Jenkins, 1990.

Riddick, Sarah. *Pioneer Studio Pottery—The Milner White Collection.* Lund Humphries, 1990.

Watson, Oliver. *British Studio Pottery—The Victoria and Albert Collection.* Oxford: Phaidon-Christie's Ltd., 1990.

Norah Braden Group of stonewares. (courtesy of Christie's Images), l to r: dish, 282mm diameter, brushed brown strokes on mustard coloured ground, painted NB mark; jar, 260mm high, pitted blue glaze with black vertical bands; bowl, 268mm diameter, stylised fish decoration in brown on grey-black ground.

NORAH BRADEN

Types of Ware	Production	Quality	Availability
Stoneware	Very Low	Very Good to Excellent	Rare

Marks

Incised or painted:	NB (in monogram)	1925 - c.1928 ?
+/- "SI" impressed (*for St.Ives 1925-28*)		
Impressed	NB (in octagon)	c.1928 - c.1939 ?

BRANNAM POTTERY

(1847—present)

—earthenware (from 1879)
—terracotta

Litchdon Street, Barnstaple, Devon

Historical Background

In 1879, Charles Hubert Brannam (1855-1937) persuaded his father, Thomas Brannam, to allow him to use the family pottery in Litchdon Street, Barnstaple, for the production of experimental art pottery. He had become dissatisfied with the quality and type of ware his father was producing. Charles Brannam had acquired his pottery education both in his father's workshop and at the Barnstaple School of Art.

At the School he became acquainted with Alexander Lauder (1837-1921) who taught art and who later set up his own pottery business nearby. Brannam realised the potential of the local red clay deposits at Fremington and, being a skilled potter, set about producing a quality ware which would be acceptable to a discerning public.

He initially produced jugs, toilet sets and vases, to which he gave the name "Barum Ware" (after the Roman name for Barnstaple,) but he also produced more industrial items such as drain pipes.

Brannam himself undertook most of the throwing, but engaged assistants to help with the decoration. A brick-built kiln was utilised at the outset, which was fuelled by wood. Some crude machinery was employed, such as a horse-turned roller which was used for squeezing the air from the clay prior to working it.

In 1880, a contract was negotiated with Mr. James of the London retailers Howell and James to market Barum Ware to London dealers. This heralded the success of Brannam's art ware, which soon won many local prizes, and gave the firm its Royal patronage in 1885. The ware then became known as "Royal Barum Ware."

In 1881, Brannam took on a talented young decorator, James Dewdney, who was later to design and produce some fine art vases. It soon became necessary, however, to take on a second designer, and in 1884/5 William Leonard Baron was employed. Baron left in 1893 to set up his own pottery business in the neighbourhood (ref. Baron Pottery,) but during his time at Brannam he contributed much to the success of the company's wares. Other designers were employed, many on leaving school, such as Frederick Arthur Bowden, Arthur Bamkin, Thomas Liverton, Stanley Williams and Beauchamp Whimple. Another designer employed, Frederick Braddon, worked at the pottery on and off until 1930. The high complement of designers employed prior to 1900 gives some indication of the demand for Brannam's art ware at this time. Local art was encouraged, and a Barnstaple Guild of Metalworkers was formed in 1902. It is known that James Dewdney and Frederick Braddon both designed and executed work in metal as well as pottery.

Barum Ware was widely advertised and certainly became extremely popular. Pieces were shown at international exhibitions and sold at Liberty & Co. from 1882 through to the 1930s. Liberty acted as sole agents for Barum Ware between 1882 and 1914, and were also granted the use of Brannam's owl jug design for the production of a pewter version with sea-shell eyes about 1902.

The price of a large jardinière in 1881 was thirty shillings (£1.50p), a tall jar eighteen shillings (90p), whilst smaller items could be purchased for seven or eight shillings (35-40p). These relatively high prices reflected the quality market that Brannam sought.

Brannam Grotesques, all marked "C H Brannam Barum", l to r:-Pair of Griffin candlesticks, dated 1895, one marked "SW" (Stanley Williams), the other "AB" (Arthur Bamkin); Puffin jug, marked "SW", dated 1900; Devil jug, marked "BW" (Beauchamp Whimple), dated 1901; Grebe, marked "RP" (Richard Pearce), dated 1900; Boar, marked "AB", dated 1901.

Brannam Cachepot, 240mm diam., moulded, with fish decoration, monochrome green glaze, marked "C.H.Brannam England", c.1930.

Brannam Vase, 245mm high, by James Dewdney, signed "C.H.Brannam Barum", "JD", dated 1893.

Brannam Vase, 380mm high, by James Dewdney; pattern no. 1899.

Brannam Vase by James Dewdney, 590mm high, three twisted handles, peacock motif, incised mark "C H Brannam Barum JD 1896", shape no.38.

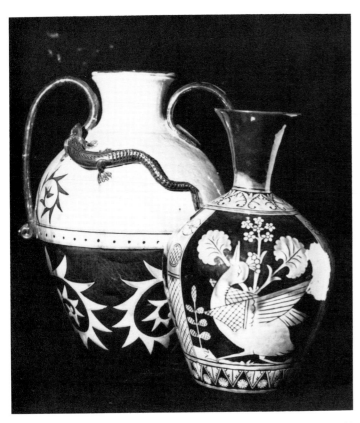

Brannam l to r: i) two-handled vase, 301 mm high, brown glaze with appliqué lizard, dated 1882. ii) Vase, 280 mm high, with stylised bird and geometric decoration in dark brown and grey-blue, dated 1881.

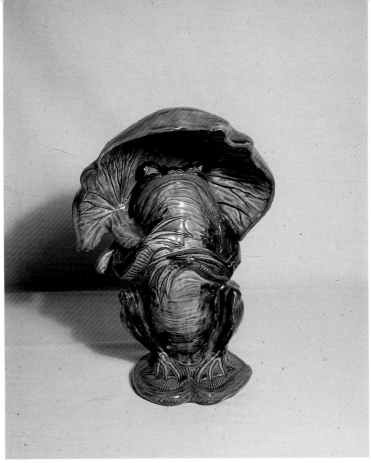

Brannam Model of a frog with lily leaf umbrella, 300mm high, marked "C.H.Brannam, Barum, 1901".

Brannam Large three-handled vase, 480mm high, with 3 panels of birds and anemones or chrysanthemums.

Brannam Two vases by William Baron in a Doulton style, marked "C H Brannam Barum", "WB", l to r:-large vase, 300mm high, dated 1886; small vase, dated 1885.

The art entrepreneur Horace Elliott is recorded as having collaborated with Brannam in 1889 to exhibit designs at the Arts & Crafts Exhibition Society, of which he was president. In 1892, Queen Victoria again patronized the pottery, as did many other members of the Royal Family and European royal families on other occasions.

In 1914, the pottery became a limited company, and wares from that date were stamped "C.H. Brannam Ltd." Control of the pottery then passed to Brannam's two sons.

At the 1920 British Industrial Arts Exhibition, Charles Brannam exhibited some fine examples of his work, among which was a range of toilet wares etched with scroll, bird and floral motifs and glazed in rich colours. Brannam claimed to be particularly successful in overcoming the difficulties of the soft red Devonshire clay when applied to such utilitarian wares. From 1920, the Fremington clay was purified by filter-pressing, and during the 1930s production included moulded, pressed and cast items (though moulded wares had been produced since the late 1890s at Brannam.)

Also during the 1930s, the firm earned the title "By Royal Appointment to Her Majesty Queen Mary." By then, the price of a large jardinière had risen to only fifty-two shillings and sixpence (£2.12p), whilst a tall 31-inch (790mm) decorated vase was sixty—six shillings (£3.30p).

Charles Brannam died in 1937, aged 82. The pottery continues today, however, making mostly terracotta wares.

Products

Initially, the pots were decorated with a thin layer of white slip. The red clay body was exposed by sgraffito work, and then the glaze was applied. The early glaze utilised was a plain beige colour, but, later on, lead glazes were developed in bolder colours. A two colour combination of brown and blue seemed almost to be a hallmark of the pottery during the 1880s.

The general style of art wares towards the turn of the century consisted of simple shapes decorated with coloured slips, with much carving and sgraffito work, depicting typically bird, fish, animal, seaweed and floral subjects.

Much domestic pottery was also manufactured, such as milk pans and bread pancheons, whilst a large amount of flower pots was produced well into the 1930s. Art wares were typically produced alongside domestic and light industrial wares.

A great variety of art wares was produced. Many bore characteristic twisted handles applied to simple shapes, such as a conical or ovoid vase form with undulating rim; but although the shapes may have been simple, the decoration often was complex. The fish was a popular decorative subject and sometimes appeared as a modelled feature, forming the spout of a jug. Likewise, bird-jugs, vases and candlesticks with twisting dragons applied, butterfly wall plaques, etc., were produced. Models of animals were also made, such as the wild boar, tall cats, and also many grotesques (devil jugs, spoon warmers, etc.)

During the late Victorian and Edwardian period, Brannam's decoration was generally heavy and crowded. Dark, but highly glazed colours were often used and decorative subjects were executed in a variety of ways on the same piece—sgrafitto, cut-away, applied slip, stippling, modelling, etc.

After 1918, Brannam's wares became less decorated. The decoration on some items consisted only of a monochrome glaze, such as blue, green or orange. Indeed, by the 1930s, much of the Barum Ware relied solely on the simplicity of its shape and colour. A catalogue of this period names several new colours developed, one of which was "Liberty Green." The same catalogue shows decorated pedestals, pots and large vases "suitable for drawing-rooms, halls and billiard rooms."

The 1930s saw an increase in the domestic product range, together with a decline in art wares. Wall plaques, salt cellars, candlesticks, ash trays, bulb bowls, ink pots, pen trays, butter dishes, sweet dishes, umbrella stands—all were produced to order with a choice from 40 colourings. The ornamental art wares continued to be produced, such as umbrella stands, devil jugs and other grotesques, fishmouth jugs, bird jugs, toby jugs and loving cups. Terracotta garden wares were also produced at this time.

Some light industrial wares were also manufactured, amongst which were heavy cloam ovens. Many of these ovens, which were made until 1939, are still installed in some West Country houses.

Collecting Brannam Pottery

Brannam pottery is popular with collectors, not only for the interesting articles produced (with much guesswork sometimes as to their use) but also for their decorative appeal. A wide range of small items is available for collection, in keeping with the high output, and early signed pieces are particularly sought after.

James Dewdney is certainly the most well known of the Brannam decorators, and his work exhibits an accomplished artistry. Signed pieces by him are not rare as he was fairly prolific in his work, but the quality of his ware varies significantly.

Collectors should be wary of the similarity between Brannam products and those of the neighbouring Lauder and Baron potteries. The mark is often the only discernable difference. Certain other Devon potteries also produced wares similar to Brannam, such as at Fremington. Be wary also of modern Brannam reproductions, many of which bear the mark "Kev".

Suggestions for Further Study

The Brannam pottery at Litchdon Street, Barnstaple welcomes visitors.

The Museum of North Devon, Barnstaple, has a large number of Brannam pieces on display.

Brannam, Peter. *A Family Business—The Story of a Pottery.* pub. privately, 1982.

Edgeler, Audrey. *Art Potters of Barnstaple.* Nimrod Press Ltd., 1990.

Monkhouse, Cosmo. "Some Original Ceramists," *Magazine of Art*, 1882.

James, Susan. "Barum Ware—The Work of C.H. Brannam (1855-1937)," *The Antique Collector*, August 1973.

C. H. Brannam Barum Ware, a catalogue by Harry Lyons of a display of Barum Ware at the Liberty Arts & Crafts Exhibition, Liberty, London, 1991.

Brannam Animal group. l to r:-i) cat, 275mm high. ii) seated dog, 125mm high, marked "FB". iii) cat, 210mm high.

Brannam Clock case, 300mm high, 380mm wide, deep green glaze, dated 1909.

Brannam Grotesque candlestick by Frank Thomas, 295mm high, marked "FT", "C H Brannam Barum" and dated 1899.

Brannam Specimen mark of Barum Ware, with James Dewdney's initials and date 1896.

BRETBY ART POTTERY

(1883 to present)

-earthenware
-pressed and moulded wares

Woodville, Burton-on-Trent, Derbyshire

Historical Background

In 1883, Henry Tooth left the Linthorpe Art Pottery and went into partnership with William Ault, forming the Bretby Art Pottery. The pottery began by sharing the premises of T.G.Green's pottery at Church Gresley, but in 1885 moved to the present site at Woodville.

Wares produced were initially similar to those at Linthorpe, and being of reasonable price became popular. Pieces were exhibited widely and distributed to all the main retail outlets in Britain.

William Ault did not stay long at Bretby. In 1886, he left the partnership to set up his own pottery nearby. Henry Tooth remained and was assisted at the pottery by his son and daughters, one of whom, Florence Tooth, proved to be a competent artist and later managed the modelling shop.

Tooth experimented widely, producing flambés, sang de boeuf and lustre glazes, some of which were shown at the Crystal Palace Exhibition in London in 1911.

The pottery contained costs by utilising the local clay and by producing mostly low-priced pressed and moulded wares alongside higher quality thrown art wares.

In 1912, Henry Tooth's son took over the management of the pottery which became a limited company. From this time and during the late 1920s the firm had a London showroom at the Gamages store in Holborn.

Henry Tooth died in 1918, and in 1933 the pottery came into the possession of the Parker family, and, following a period of closure during the Second World War, continues today as "Tooth & Company Limited Bretby Art Pottery" manufacturing an extensive range of wares from ornamental to horticultural.

Bretby Selection of wares. l to r:i) lustre vase; ii) small jardinière; iii) small jardinière; tall vase, 325mm high.

Bretby Umbrella stand in 'Carved Bamboo Ware'.

Bretby Jug, 253mm high, 'Nerton Ware', marked "Bretby", "1742D".

Bretby Entrance to Bretby Art Pottery.

Products

A wide range of wares was produced at Bretby, from very fine art pieces to general stock wares. Most of the stock wares were slip-cast or pressed and moulded. Plant pots, teapots and tobacco jars were produced in quantity.

The stock wares often had titles, such as:

"Ligna Ware" (c. 1905)—moulded items in biscuit terracotta resembling tree-trunks (vases, tobacco jars, ewers, jardinières, etc.)

"Copperette Ware" (1900-1915)—jugs, vases and jardinières, etc., resembling hammered copper pots

"Clanta Ware" (from the early 1920's)—vases, bowls and jardinières with black surfaces designed to resemble worked metal

"Jewelled Ware" (1900-1915)—art nouveau pots, vases, clock cases, etc., resembling metal with inlaid "precious stones"

"Pastal Ware"—items with smooth surfaces and pastel colours

"Carved Bamboo Ware" (from mid-1890's to early 1920's)—vases, umbrella stands, plaques, etc., imitative of carved bamboo in a Japanese style in beige against brown or black

"Cloisonné Ware" (late 1890's)—bird and floral scenes on a typically black ground with gilded veining imitative of Chinese cloisonné).

"Dickensian Ware" (c.1910-1930)—relief-moulded pots, plaques, figures, candlesticks, etc., portraying Dickens characters.

"Nerton Ware" (from 1920)—described below

There were other wares which were not named, but were equally imitative of metals or ethnic styles, such as a ware imitating bronze.

The stock wares proved immensely popular, especially the Nerton Ware, which was produced in 1920 in five different colourings—green, rose, Royal blue, green and yellow. It was chunky in appearance with streaked and mottled matt glazes. The full range of Bretby art wares was made available for decoration in Nerton Ware, from small urns, pitchers, vases and pilgrim bottles to umbrella stands and large jardinières.

Both colour and shape tended to be simple on the many jardinières produced, and although pieces were also plainly decorated, several bore complex moulding. Colours were frequently gaudy, even on the most artistic of pieces, with many pieces bearing two colour combinations, often oddly matched (cerise and yellow, for example.)

Bretby Selection of wares. l to r:i) pair of candlesticks, 224mm high. ii) pair of vases, 320mm high. iii) jardinière.

Bretby Plant pot, 150mm high, 'Clanta Ware', marked "Bretby CLANTA Made in England", "2327".

Bretby Two-handled vase, 255mm high, 'Nerton Ware'; blue, turquoise and green streaked glaze on cream ground.

On simple shapes "dimpling" was a frequently used form of decoration. Dimpling was the practice of depressing the sides of a pot at intervals. It was widely practised at Burmantofts, Ault and Linthorpe, and may also have been a remedy for correcting badly thrown pieces.

As at Linthorpe, some of the glazes used were multicoloured, but tended to be rather thick, such that underlying details often became obscured. Apparently the glazes employed were not of a type that would craze or crack. The test of time has generally proved this to be mainly the case.

Some garden figures were produced in limited numbers from about 1895 until the 1930s. Many were glazed in "Ivorine," a Bretby glaze also used on other wares, and comprised rustic subjects about 76cm in height.

About 1910, when the demand for oriental styles was evident, Bretby produced some brown-based vases and jardinières, with mostly bird and floral decoration in gold and pink lustre on matt black panels.

Many novelty wares were produced, such as green leaf-shaped plates with appliqué ceramic walnuts, plus or minus a nut-cracker! These lines were popular for Christmas gifts.

During the 1930s, some successful ranges of ornamental wares were produced, such as "Peasant Pottery" (with incised abstract patterns beneath a matt glaze) and "Aquarius" (comprising a fish motif modelled in outline beneath a plain glaze).

The increasing popularity of house-plants in the home and the functionality of Victorian jardinières have created a ready market for many of the Bretby art wares. Prices are therefore keen and the higher quality of the Bretby and Ault jardinières enables them to stand out from among the many hundreds of unmarked vases produced during the late-Victorian period.

The collector should be wary of some modern reproductions of earlier wares which have been produced by the factory using old moulds.

Suggestions for Further Study

Derby City Museum has a good representative collection of Bretby wares.

Bretby Art Pottery, Woodville, Derbyshire has visitor facilities.

Haslam, Malcolm. *English Art Pottery 1865-1915*. Woodbridge, Suffolk: Antique Collectors' Club, 1975.

Pinkham, Roger. "A Tale of Three Potteries." *The Antique Collectors' Fayre*, September, 1977.

Anderson, Judith. *"Bretby Art Pottery"* (museum catalogue); Derby Art Gallery, March, 1988.

BRETBY ART POTTERY

Types of Ware	Production	Quality	Availability
Art wares	High to Very High	Fair to Very Good	Abundant

Marks

Most Bretby pieces were marked, but the author has come across unmarked pieces which are without doubt Bretby. Similarities between Linthorpe and Ault occur in terms of style, shape and glaze. The collector generally has to decide between the three factories when considering an unmarked piece.

Impressed:	☼ BRETBY	1884 - c.1939 (on its own: 1884-1890)
+ ENGLAND		1891 onwards
+/- (Henry Tooth's initials)	HT (in monogram)	1883 - 1900

+/- title of ware (eg. 'CLANTA' or 'CLANTA WARE')
+/- shape number (eg. '1853E');
(the shape number followed by an alpha character denoting size)
+/- artist's mark (rare) (eg. Richard Joyce (later at Pilkington), Florence Tooth, William Metcalf (ex. Linthorpe).
+/- Registered Number (various exist)

(NB The mark "MADE IN ENGLAND" is found on later wares to the present day)

Bretby Specimen mark on dish.

—thrown earthenware
—architectural faience
—moulded wares

Leeds

Historical Background

The Burmantofts Works were established by Messrs. Wilcock & Co. in 1858 for the production of drain-pipes and fire-bricks, using a locally available grey-white clay.

From 1879, the firm was managed by James Holroyd who had previously been a woollen manufacturer. He commissioned the architect Maurice Bingham Adams in 1880 to design architectural faience, which heralded the start of the company's involvement in art pottery.

Work was exhibited at Howell & James' showroom in London in 1881, and in 1882 the company produced their first catalogue entitled "A Catalogue of Architectural Faience and Decorative Terra-Cotta." By this time a large range of wares was being produced, from tiles, panels and fireplaces to vases and jardinières.

The early success of the firm was demonstrated by the expansion of the premises from four acres to fifteen in 1885. Commissions for Burmantofts' architectural faience poured in, particularly for public buildings, notably The Metropole Hotel at Brighton (1889) and The National Liberal Club, Whitehall (1884.)

By 1888, the firm had its own showrooms in Charterhouse Street, London. During the same year the firm was renamed "The Burmantofts Company." The name "Burmantofts" had been associated with the pottery for some time, and referred to the district in Leeds where the works were situated.

In 1889, however, the firm amalgamated with other Yorkshire enterprises, and became known as "The Leeds Fireclay Company Ltd.". The same year, staff were taken on from the Linthorpe Pottery which had just closed down.

In 1890, James Holroyd died and was succeeded by one of his sons, also called James. Under the new management, pieces were more widely exhibited, and new retail outlets were established (Liberty & Co. and Harrods, particularly).

With the turn of the century, public taste for art wares was dwindling, and in 1904 production of art pottery ceased at Burmantofts. The production of architectural faience continued until 1957, however, when the works closed and the buildings were demolished.

Burmantofts Clock case, 340mm high, marked "1434 WA".

Burmantofts Vase, 390mm high, moulded with appliqué dragon chasing a dragonfly, marked "Burmantofts Faience", c. 1881.

Burmantofts Vase, 305mm high, by V. Kremer, Persian style, marked "Design 22", "BURMANTOFTS FAIENCE" and monogram for V.Kremer.

Burmantofts Vase, 315mm high, marked "BURMANTOFTS FAIENCE".

Burmantofts Model of a frog and monkey, 450mm high, marked "Lefico" (Leed Fireclay Co.).

Products

For many years, architectural faience, glazed bricks and tiles were the main source of income for the pottery. The venture into art pottery (from 1880) produced pieces which closely followed the Linthorpe Pottery in characteristics, early wares being plainly decorated with a single coloured glaze, and tending to be bulbous-shaped vases with long necks. Occasionally, minimal surface decoration was executed, such as sgraffito stars. Glazes were translucent and the colours bright.

The firm soon began to introduce more elaborate surface designs, however, such as sgraffito work and moulded decoration in relief. Most items were moulded and included bowls and large jardinières as well as vases of every size. Pieces were fired at very high temperatures, producing hard, thickish glazes and warm colours.

Some decoration consisted of appliqué work in the form of hand—modelled animals and flowers. Some early wares exhibit a heavy appliqué form of decoration, similar to the French "barbotine" technique. The appearance of vases with twisting snakes and lizards among dense foliage is reminiscent of Palissy ware. Vases with this form of decoration were made in different sizes, and frequently consisted of a two-colour background (often blue at the top and brown at the base) against which the modelled forms were applied. A dragon chasing a dragon-fly was a popular subject.

Floral motifs were also popular in Burmantofts decoration. The chrysanthemum featured on many pieces made in the 1890s as well as in copies of William De Morgan's "Persian" designs, many of which were executed by the artist V. Kremer, and which were predominantly blue-green in colour.

Tiles were also produced at Burmantofts, not only in earthenware but also in terracotta. Tiles and terracotta panels were often decorated with the popular bird and floral motifs, and the "barbotine" style was also sometimes employed for panels.

European artists were among those employed at Burmantofts, notably V. Kremer and B. Sicard, who contributed distinctive styles to many of the wares.

A series of African-style bottles and jars was produced, characterised by bold patterns and colours; gourd-shaped bottles (V. Kremer) and pilgrim bottles in particular. Moorish patterns were also evident, appearing in Burmantofts' catalogues until about 1900.

Other pieces included flower-stands, water-bottles, lamp—bases, umbrella-stands and candlesticks, as well as the architectural products such as fireplaces. As at the Ault Pottery, the coloured glazes tended to run on the surfaces. Large items, such as jardinières and umbrella-stands, particularly exhibit this feature. Production of jardinières was increased during the 1890s for what was a very buoyant market.

Non-moulded wares are popular with collectors. The colours are extremely attractive, even in their usual monochrome, and range from brilliant turquoise to warm-toned russet-browns. As with Elton's colours, they were somewhat unique.

Other glazes produced were a sang-de-boeuf (often made richer by being applied over a yellow slip) as well as some copper or silver lustres on dark red or blue grounds. The artist J. Wilcock produced some fine lustre vases with fish decoration about 1905.

Some of the early bulbous vases were dimpled in shape (compare Bretby Pottery) but generally shapes were kept simple. Some candlesticks and many of the jardinière pedestals were of an architectural style with square bases and columnar features, and were quite different from the rounded forms of other pieces. Many pieces were very large in size, reflecting the initial desire of Burmantofts to create large original wares.

After 1904, some modelled wares were produced by the Leeds Fireclay Company. These included animal figures decorated in monochrome glazes and were marked "Lefico" (for Leeds Fireclay Co.). Grotesques were also produced, sometimes as spoon-warmers, a popular model being a Chinese lion.

Suggestions for Further Study

Leeds City Museums and Abbey House Museum, Leeds have a collection of Burmantofts wares.

"Burmantofts Pottery;" catalogue of an exhibition at Cartwright Hall, Bradford; pub. Bradford Art Galleries & Museums, Nov. 1983.

Burmantofts Small vase 100mm high, by V. Kremer.

Burmantofts Umbrella stand, marked "Burmantofts Faience", "1981", c.1890.

Burmantofts Jardinière (27 cm high) and pedestal (68.5 cm high); impressed BF monogram plus "1948B JL ENGLAND".

BURMANTOFTS POTTERY

Types of Ware	Production	Quality	Availability
Thrown faience	Moderate	Good to Very Good	Common
Tiles	High	Good	Uncommon
Moulded items (also termed "faience")	High	Fair to Good	Common (some styles scarce, eg. barbotine style and decorated lustres)

Marks

Impressed	Burmantofts Faience	1880 - c.1882
Impressed	B U R M A N T O F T S F A I E N C E	1882 - 1904
	ᗺᗯᖴ or ᗺF	1882 - 1904

+ "ENGLAND" (*from 1891*)
+/- Pattern number
+/- Artist's mark, eg. V. Kremer   ⊾

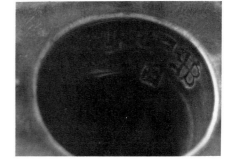

Burmantofts Specimen mark on candlestick, showing "BF" (Burmantofts Faience) mark.

The Cottage, The High Road, Bushey Heath, Hertfordshire
Historical Background

During the early 1900s, Henry Perrin acquired a large property on the main road at Bushey Heath known as The Cottage. His wife, Ida Perrin, was an accomplished painter and watercolourist, and had trained at South Kensington and had exhibited work at the Royal Academy of Art. She was a member of the Artists' Guild and Guild of Potters, and in 1921, established a pottery at The Cottage, which she later styled *The De Morgan Pottery Works*.

The pottery is noteworthy since a former partner of William De Morgan's, Fred Passenger, came to work there from 1923 until the pottery closed in 1933. Encouraged by Mrs. Perrin, Fred Passenger produced lustre pieces similar to De Moragn's lustre ware, though more thinly potted. In fact, Fred Passenger's wares were stamped "De M" within the Bushey Heath monogram, signifying that De Morgan's process was being employed.

We know very little of the operation of the pottery. Ida Perrin was an accomplished sculptress, but it is not clear whether she had any working involvement with the pottery. The Perrins were prominent in the art and music circles of the day, and Ida Perrin spent much of her time living at her second home in West Kensington. She lived to the age of 96, but her home, The Cottage, no longer exists. It was demolished in 1965, and the site is now occupied by the Colne Valley Pumping Station.

Products

Mostly lustre vases and bowls were produced from 1923 in at least two types of pottery body. Firstly, a fine white earthenware, somewhat porcelainous in texture, which produced generally thinly potted pieces; and secondly a soft, sandy coloured stoneware, with a very open structure, which produced thickly potted pieces.

The crafting and symmetry of the pots were not as fine as, say, De Morgan's Fulham period, though the decoration was usually of good quality. The lustre decorations were particularly effective and of good quality, with colours ranging from gold or ruby lustres on a cream ground to silver lustres on deep blue.

Decoration by Fred Passenger was mostly Isnik inspired, with floral and foliage motifs (often using De Morgan designs, such as the chrysanthemum and dianthus). Animals and fish were also employed as decorative subjects.

Suggestions for Further Study

Leighton House Museum, 12, Holland Park Road, Kensington, W.London has some examples of Bushey Heath pottery.

Bushey Museum Trust (details from Bushey Library, The High Road, Bushey, Hertfordshire.)

See also references under William De Morgan.

Bushey Heath Planter, 200mm diam., ruby lustre; Bushey Heath stamp and initials of Fred Passenger.

Bushey Heath Bowl, 100mm diam., purple, blue and silver lustre on porcelain, decorated inside with fish, marked "Bushey Heath DM".

Detail of above photo.

BUSHEY HEATH POTTERY			
Types of Ware	**Production**	**Quality**	**Availability**
Lustres	Low	Good to Excellent	Rare
Marks			
Stamped in black or blue: (incorporating Fred Passenger's monogram)			1923 - 1933
+/- "FP" (stamped) (Fred Passenger's initials)			

MICHAEL CARDEW, Studio potter

(1901—1983)
(fl. 1923—1983)

—slipware
—stoneware
(—earthenware)

St. Ives, Cornwall (with Bernard Leach) (1923-1925)
Greet, Winchcombe, Gloucestershire (1926-1939)
Wenford Bridge, Cornwall (1939-1942, 1949, 1965-1983)
West Africa (1942-1948, 1950-1965)

Historical Background

Michael Cardew was educated at Exeter College and at Oxford University and first learned to throw pots at the Braunton Pottery. He was no stranger to the area or to potting, since his father had frequently taken him to visit E. B. Fishley's pottery at Fremington some years before.

In 1923 he joined Bernard Leach and Shoji Hamada as the first of Leach's English pupils at St. Ives. Here he was to begin the work through which he is most associated—earthenware dishes, jugs and mugs in the English slipware tradition.

In 1926, he rented a pottery, which had been closed since 1915, at Greet near Winchcombe in Gloucestershire. Here he specifically concentrated on domestic earthenware in the slipware style with the help of a few assistants: Elijah Comfort (who had worked at the pottery previously,) Sidney and Charles Tustin (young apprentices) and Ray Finch, who was to purchase the Winchcombe Pottery from Michael Cardew in 1946.

In 1939, leaving Ray Finch to manage the pottery, Cardew decided to set up another pottery at Wenford Bridge, St. Tudy in Cornwall, building a smaller version of the wood-fired kiln at Winchcombe. He had married in 1933 and with three children the living conditions at Winchcombe had become unsuitable.

In 1942, in need of more regular income, he accepted a post as pottery instructor at Achimota College at Alajo in Ghana (formerly the UK colony of Gold Coast) as part of a scheme to develop local crafts. He replaced a previous instructor Harry Davis, who had been instructing in the making of bricks, tiles and stoneware using local materials. Cardew carried on this work.

This scheme was wound up in 1945 when its patron, H.V. Meyerowitz, died, so Cardew opted to stay in Africa and went to Vume-Dugame, a native pottery-making centre on the Lower Volta River, where he constructed his Volta Pottery in order to make stoneware.

He returned to England in 1948 because of illness and exhaustion, and spent six months earning a living making earthenware at the Kingwood Potteries at Wormley, Surrey, before returning to Wenford Bridge the following year, where he added another chamber to his kiln for the production of stoneware.

In 1950 he was appointed Pottery Officer in the Nigerian Department of Industry and Commerce, and was influencial in the construction of a Pottery Training Centre at Abuja, which opened in 1952. He returned frequently to Wenford Bridge and exhibited pieces of his own and those of his African pupils (including Ladi Kwali) at the Berkeley Galleries in London.

In 1965, he retired from his Nigerian post, was awarded the MBE and returned to Wenford Bridge. In 1968, however, he visited Australia and New Zealand on a lecture and demonstration tour, and assisted Ivan McMeekin to establish a Pottery Training Centre for aborigines in Darwin.

His son, Seth Cardew, joined him as an assistant at Wenford Bridge in 1971 and now runs the pottery. Michael Cardew continued working until his death in 1983.

Michael Cardew Group of wares. (courtesy of Christie's Images) 1 to r:earthenware charger, 360mm diameter, slip-trailed wavy line decoration in deep brown on mottled mustard coloured ground, pie-crust rim, Winchcombe mark and "MC"; earthenware bowl, 240mm diameter, toadstool motif, Winchcombe mark and "MC"; casserole dish and cover, 228mm diameter, marked "MC" and Abuja seal.

Products

Cardew's output at Winchcombe was mostly in the slipware tradition of the North Devon area, with yellow or brown lead (galena) glazes. Many pieces emulate designs produced by William Fishley Holland at the Braunton Pottery, which in turn emulated the early English slipware of Thomas Toft.

The pieces were designed to be functional—baking dishes, bottles, jugs, pitchers, cider-jars, tea-pots, cups and saucers; all at affordable prices.

Slip-trailed patterns, the art of combing the slip to produce wavy lines and sgraffito decoration, were all traditional techniques employed. Patterns were usually geometrical with some bird and other motifs.

Early Winchcombe pieces were not as fine as later ones. Late Winchcombe and Wenford Bridge slipware moved away from the traditional slipware patterns, bringing Cardew's own designs very much to the fore. The potting was more assured and a black slip was used to great effect.

The stoneware Cardew produced was frequently African inspired in shape. Oil jars and soy pots (with screw stoppers,) flower jars, plates and other functional items were produced. Decoration was often sgraffito (such as cross-banded concentric lines) or cut-away geometric forms. Little brush work was employed. Some stoneware pieces also incorporated the early slipware patterns.

Various glazes were employed, iron-red and black (tenmoku) being favourites. Wares made at the Volta Pottery were characteristically of a dark red pottery with dark glazes. Later African and Wenford Bridge wares were often brighter and lighter in tone, more colours being regularly employed, such as blue and grey-green.

Suggestions for Further Study

The Crafts Study Centre, Holburne of Menstrie Museum, Bath, houses examples of Cardew's work.

The Victoria & Albert Museum, London has an extensive collection of Cardew's work.

The Milner-White Collection at York City Art Gallery houses nine examples of Cardew's stoneware work from 1959 plus some from his African pupils.

Cardew, Michael. *Pioneer Pottery.* London: Longman Group UK Ltd., 1969.

Clark, G. *Michael Cardew.* London: Faber & Faber, 1978.

"Michael Cardew and Pupils;" catalogue of an exhibition at York City Art Gallery 1983; York City Art Gallery.

Cardew, Michael. *Michael Cardew—A Pioneer Potter. An Autobiography.* London: William Collins & Co., 1988.

Rice, Paul and Christopher Gowing. *British Studio Ceramics in the 20th Century.* London: Barrie & Jenkins, 1990.

Riddick, Sarah. *Pioneer Studio Pottery—The Milner White Collection.* London: Lund Humphries, 1990.

Watson, Oliver. *British Studio Pottery—The Victoria & Albert Museum Collection.* Oxford: Phaidon & Christie's, 1990.

MICHAEL CARDEW

Types of Ware	Production	Quality	Availability
Slipware	Moderate	Good to Very Good	Uncommon
Stoneware (UK)	Moderate	Good to Very Good	Uncommon
Stoneware (Volta)	Very Low	Very Good	Rare
Stoneware (Abuja)	Low	Good to Very Good	Scarce

Marks

Impressed	(St. Ives Pottery seal)		1923 - 1925

+ "MC" in monogram, in rectangle

Impressed	WP	(in monogram, in circle)	c.1926 onwards

+/- "MC" in monogram, in rectangle: 1926 - 1939.

Impressed:	(Volta Pottery seal)		1945 onwards

("VOLTA" in monogram)
+/- "MC" in monogram, in rectangle: 1945 - 1948.

Impressed: (at Kingwood Potteries)	K (in circle)		1948 - 1949

Impressed	"Abuja" (in Arabic)		1952 onwards

+/- "MC" in monogram, in rectangle: 1952 - 1965.

Impressed	(Wenford Bridge seal)		c.1939 - 1942 1949 onwards

+ "MC" in monogram, in rectangle: 1939 - 1983.

Michael Cardew Vase, 220mm high, Winchcombe mark.

CARLTON WARE

(1893 to 1989)

—earthenware
—porcelain
—lustres

Wiltshaw & Robinson, Carlton Works, Copeland Street, Stoke-on-Trent, Staffordshire

Historical Background

The Carlton Works were established in 1893 in Copeland Street, Stoke, by Wiltshaw & Robinson. Here "Carlton China" was produced, which was mostly of a domestic nature, but during the 1920s fine art pieces were also produced.

Wiltshaw assumed sole ownership of the company in 1911, Robinson moving on to other pottery ventures.

The art wares were well received, and the company exhibited some fine specimens at the British Industrial Arts Fair in 1920. Many of the art wares contained lustre decorations, with much use of gilding, and the company became renowned for its striking achievements with lustre glazes, particularly on porcelain.

Novelty tablewares were produced from the mid-1920s, and many imitated leaves and vegetables in shape as well as decoration. In 1932, the company merged with the china firm of Birks Rawlins & Co., thus expanding their capabilities in the production of tablewares. During the Second World War decorative ware was made only for export, with functional plain wares for the home market.

The company was renamed "Carlton Ware Limited" in 1958, and in 1967 was taken over, but continued to make Carlton Ware. In May, 1989, the company went into receivership, and the right to the Carlton name and pattern books were bought by Grosvenor Ceramics of Stone, Staffordshire.

Products

The great age of Carlton Ware was during the 1920s, when many quality earthenware jugs and vases were produced alongside delicate porcelain tea and coffee services. A great deal of brightly coloured porcelain was produced as well as many pieces with interesting glaze effects, particularly lustres.

Many of the designs were of Chinese influence, and were richly coloured with much use of gilding. A "Cloisonné Ware" was produced, for example, in yellow and black, with a gold crazed background, and decorated with a Chinese pagoda pattern. Yellow and black seems to have been a favourite colour combination on Carlton earthenwares, for floating-flower bowls were produced, decorated with a black centre and yellow rim, to match the Cloisonné Ware. Even on porcelains, much decoration was accomplished against a black background.

The discovery of Tutankhamen's tomb in 1922 prompted a range of Egyptian inspired pieces, and during the 1920s generally, a great variety of items was produced, from lamp bases to fruit bowls, wall plaques and ginger-jars. Many pieces were moulded and shapes were frequently simple, but lavish decorative treatment, sometimes verging on the gaudy, was regularly employed. Abstract hand-painted bold colour designs of zig-zags and harlequin diamonds were a striking variation from the stylised floral and foliage designs.

Carlton Coffee set in bone china.

Carlton Pair of Carlton Ware "Handicraft" vases, 260mm high, blue and yellow painted decoration. (courtesy of Christie's Images)

Carlton Porcelain box, bluebird design in enamel decoration.

In 1920, a series of rouge flambé decorated pieces was launched, some of which were also decorated with a gold dragon motif. Another ware of the 1920s was "Armand," which was a range of pale blue lustre ware. About a dozen different lustre colours were created.

Some of the lustres were deep in colour, as demonstrated by the range entitled "Rouge Royale"—a rich dark red ground against which decorative motifs were executed in gold or coloured enamels. "Bleu Royale" and "Noir Royale" were also deep shaded lustres.

The porcelain table wares were often produced with lustre decoration, such as coffee sets with bright orange lustre interiors accompanying exterior designs of delicate pastel motifs. Coffee and tea sets were often sold in silk-lined presentation boxes.

After 1925, some heavier earthenwares were produced, such as semi-grotesque jugs bearing relief moulded decoration. The "Oak Tree" design was an early relief moulded pattern, which made maximum use of a plate, jug or bowl to portray a twisted stemmed oak tree with acorns and green and brown leaves.

The product range at this time was one of contrasts; some pieces bore a high gloss glaze, whilst others bore a silky smooth glaze; some pieces were heavy and chunky in appearance, whilst others were light and delicate. Animal models and figures were also made.

During the late 1920s, blue and mauve colours were employed to good effect, and the bluebird and kingfisher motifs appeared on many items. These designs almost became a hallmark for Carlton, being so popular.

Another extremely popular line was a large range of art deco leaf-shaped dishes and plates, produced in quantity during the 1930s and early 1940s. These were often produced with appliqué fruits in bright colours (often orange) set against yellow or green embossed leaf-shaped backgrounds with a high glaze. "Lettuce and tomato" was a particular favourite. Relief moulded foxglove and rose patterns were also favourite decorative subjects which adorned the leaf-shaped wares. Most pieces were sold in attractive individual cardboard boxes and many had accompanying pottery knives or spoons.

Other novelty tablewares included flower-shaped plates and services with a buttercup pattern or water-lily pattern (both produced from about 1936 to 1940.) "Apple Blossom" and "Wild Rose" were other service patterns produced just prior to the Second World War. An interesting accessory range often accompanied the services, such as a lemon-squeezer, cruet set and egg cups.

Much domestic ware was produced, and a large proportion was of very good quality. Carlton catered well for specialist use tableware, such as salad sets and sandwich sets, and in 1929 even launched an innovatory range of oven-to-table ware.

Unfortunately, there is no information at present of artists or designers at Carlton during the 1920-1930 period. Many records, including pattern books, have not survived.

Suggestions for Further Study

Stirling, Robert. "Carlton Ware: Naturalistic Patterns of the 1930's and 1940's." *Antique Collectors' Club*, May 1984.

Spours, Judy. *Art Deco Tableware.* London, United Kingdom: Ward Lock Ltd., 1988.

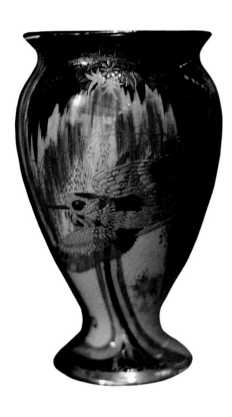

Carlton Vase, 150mm high, lustre and enamelled decoration.

Carlton Group of wares. (courtesy of Christie's Images)

Carlton Specimen mark on porcelain saucer.

CARLTON WARE

Types of Ware	Production	Quality	Availability
Earthenwares	High	Fair to Very Good	Abundant
Porcelains	High	Good to Excellent	Abundant

Marks

Printed: (usually in black)	W & R Stoke on Trent CARLTON CHINA (in circle with bird (swallow) and crown.	c.1906 onwards
(Variations exist)		
Printed or painted: +/- shape number, impressed +/- Registered Number	Carlton Ware MADE IN ENGLAND 'Trade Mark'	1925 onwards
Printed or painted: +/- shape number, impressed	Carlton China MADE IN ENGLAND	1925 - 1957
+/- 'REGISTERED AUSTRALIAN DESIGN' +/- 'REGISTRATION APPLIED FOR'		c.1935 - c.1945

CASTLE HEDINGHAM POTTERY (1837—1905)

—earthenware
—moulded wares
—terracotta

Castle Hedingham, near Halstead, Essex
Hedingham Art Pottery (1864-1901)
Essex Art Pottery Company (1901—1905)

Historical Background

Edward Bingham founded the Castle Hedingham Pottery in 1837 with the aim of satisfying a local need for domestic wares. His son, Edward Bingham junior, born in 1829, was apprenticed at an early age to a local shoemaker, but also assisted in his father's pottery for six months of every year.

When his apprenticeship ended in 1846, his only particular interest lay in pottery, such that after several false career starts he contented himself to try his hand at producing ornamental wares at his father's works. As a boy he had frequently read books and his interest in historical subjects, coupled with a visit to the British Museum and the Great Exhibition of 1851 spurred on his desire to create wares different from the utilitarian wares produced by his father.

Bingham junior created a stock of plaster moulds and first sold his ornamental wares from a shop in the village. Times were hard, however, and he was forced to run evening classes to make ends meet. His "school" became fairly successful but was upstaged by the opening of a National School, such that in 1864 he decided to set up his own pottery, calling it the Hedingham Art Pottery.

With the pottery, retail shop and various other sidelines (such as supplying ironmogery and homeopathic medicines,) Bingham produced his heavily ornamental wares alongside more useful items such as dairy pitchers, pots and pans, etc. He had married in 1853 and his wife and, later, his family, assisted at the pottery.

Bingham had developed a religious interest from an early age, and in 1865 he became a member of the Plymouth Brethren. Locals believed he lived only for his religion and his craft, and some viewed him as somewhat eccentric, for he was rarely seen without his umbrella and bowler hat, even when potting.

His wares were displayed in show-cases up the alley leading to the pottery, as well as in the shop; and orders were soon being taken for the London market. The Victorian taste for country pottery was well satisfied by Bingham's elaborate but crudely made products, which he sold at very low prices. A notice on his showcases read "Original, Quaint & Classical," and a visit by the Royal Archeological Society to Hedingham Castle in 1876 prompted approval of Bingham's wares from such worthies as Lord Lytton.

A few years after his father's death in 1872, Bingham moved in to his father's premises. His elder son, Edward William Bingham, was by now playing a more productive and creative role in the pottery.

Though the business was productive during the 1880s and 1890s, it began to dwindle rapidly by the turn of the century. In 1899, Edward William Bingham took over the ownership of the pottery from his father, but had no head for business and by necessity had to sell the works in 1901 to Hexter Humpherson & Company Ltd. Edward William then carried on as manager, moving back to the other premises where the pottery became known as the Essex Art Pottery Company.

Problems with the softness of the clay body, bad marketing, competition and poor sales, however, forced Humpherson's to close the pottery in 1905. Edward William's brother Richard had emigrated to America in 1888, so he decided to join him. A year later his father joined him in America, where the whole family seemed particularly contented.

Products

Early ornamental products included trellis-work terracotta baskets and vases which Bingham copied from a German design and which sold particularly well.

Earthenware vases, puzzle-jugs, tygs, jardinières and posset-pots[1] were also popular, and were richly ornamented with coats of arms, mottoes, cassical scenes, fruit and foliage, etc. Puzzle-vases were also made, which utilised the puzzle-jug principle, and contained a hole in the base around which was the inscription: "cork up for use, uncork for cleansing."

Castle Hedingham l to r: three-handled tyg, with inscription "Robart Shaw 1692" (copied from the Franks Collection in the British Museum) and marked "E.W.B. England No. 159" with impressed castle stamp; ewer, incised mark "England 55" with large castle stamp and words E W BINGHAM; ewer, 265mm high, catalogued by Bingham as "X-handled Tudor" (first made in 1892) with incised mark "Made in Essex=England No 37 (Bingham Ware)" and castle stamp; ewer, pattern copied from Henry I penny, castle stamp.

Bingham drew readily on classical and historical subjects for inspiration, recreating historical scenes and copying Roman, Grecian, Elizabethan and other pieces which he had seen in the British Museum (The Franks Collection, particularly). Frequently he just copied the inscriptions or dates, particularly those from the seventeenth century. His workshop was littered with prints of historical interest from which he drew inspiration.

His reproductions of early German stoneware and early English earthenware were especially noted. Many pieces were a mixture of styles, however, or merely commemorations of events or local history. His renowned "Essex jugs," for example, featured scenes of Essex history, with panels of Queen Boadicea, Essex castles and landmarks, and the ceremony of the "Dunmow flitch."[2]

The quality of potting, however, was poor, and the adhesion of the glaze to the body and the heavy decoration was such that pieces were prone to flaking. One collector described the body as being like sand!

According to Bingham's notes, various clay bodies were utilised. The early terracotta wares were obviously red-bodied, but the bulk of the ornamental output was white-bodied. A grey-white clay was used, obtained from a local outcrop of London Clay, but the "best clays" were obtained from Devon and Dorset. A white-bodied double jug in the Chelmsford and Essex Museum is inscribed "Opus Primus Materium Novum"—"the first work in the new material," and dated 22nd. July, 1874.

Whatever the quality of the clay, the primitive methods used to manufacture the wares did not do justice to the artistic and modelling skills of the Binghams. Edward William Bingham was a particularly fine modeller and pieces by him stand out from those of his father through the quality of his relief modelled work.

Wares were often colourful, though a limited palette was used. It is possible to generalise on three main colour groups: a chocolate brown ground, with yellow, brown or white decoration; an emerald green ground, with yellow decoration; a blue ground, with yellow or white decoration. Most background colours were splashed and mottled, and pieces mainly bore a thin transparent glaze.

A less common colour seemed to be a mixture of pink-brown and pale green, which the author has noted on some pieces. The colour mottling was used to good effect on agate-like wares, where mottled green or blue with brown produced an effect resembling late seventeenth century Whieldon pottery. Many pieces were quite large in stature, and ornate chargers and vases were produced up to at least 64cm in diameter or height. Modelling was particularly evident on all wares, and some standalone models were produced, such as models of the local castle. Bingham's youngest son, Richard James Bingham, also produced some miniature pieces, before he emigrated to America, which he called "Gem Ware."

[1] Posset was a popular drink in Staffordshire and Derbyshire which consisted of a brew of hot ale, milk, sugar, spices and crumbs of bread (sometimes toasted) or oatcake.
[2] A custom, no longer practised, where married couples of the village of Dunmow could compete for a side of bacon (or flitch) if they could prove their relationship lasted a twelve month period.

Suggestions for Further Study

Chelmsford Museums Service has about fifty examples of Castle Hedingham pottery (many on display) at Chelmsford & Essex Museum, Oaklands Park, Moulsham Street, Chelmsford, Essex.

Saffron Walden Museum, Saffron Walden, Essex, also has a collection (not on display).

Bradley, R. J. "Castle Hedingham Pottery 1837-1905." *The Connoisseur,* Feb., Mar, Apr., 1968.

King, C. Eileen. "Curious Pottery of Castle Hedingham." *Art & Antiques,* July 26, 1975.

Warren, C. Henry. *Essex.* London: Robert Hale Ltd., 1950.

Castle Hedingham 'Essex jug', 370mm high, incised mark "Edward W. Bingham Castle Hedingham 1883".

CASTLE HEDINGHAM POTTERY

Types of Ware	Production	Quality	Availability
Earthenwares	Moderate	Poor to Good	Common

Marks

Not all Castle Hedingham Pottery was marked, though a great variety of mark combinations was used. At present it is difficult to date pieces from the mark, but various marks that have been seen by the author are shown here.

Applied in relief:	Picture of the keep of Castle Hedingham	c.1865? - c.1901?

+/- "E. BINGHAM" in scroll below or incised "E.W.B." or "Made in Essex = England (Bingham Ware)", incised, etc.
+/- "England" incised (*after 1891*)
+/- Pattern number, incised

(various representations and sizes of the castle mark are known)

Incised:	E. BINGHAM CASTLE HEDINGHAM ESSEX	c.1865? - c.1901?

Incised:	EDWARD W. BINGHAM CASTLE HEDINGHAM ESSEX	c.1899? - c.1901?

Incised: (or variants)	ROYAL ESSEX ART POTTERY WORKS	1901 - 1905

A.J. Wilkinson Ltd., Royal Staffordshire Pottery, Burslem, Staffordshire. (1885-1964)

Newport Pottery Co., Newport Lane, Burslem, Staffs. (1920-1964)

Historical Background

Clarice Cliff trained as an artist at Burslem School of Art and joined A.J. Wilkinson Ltd. as an apprentice lithographer in 1916. Wages were low (about 28p. per week, including bus fares), and an amount was deducted for training for apprentices between the ages of 16 to 21.

The special talents of Clarice Cliff, however, were soon noticed by A. J. Wilkinson's owner, Colley Shorter, who arranged for her to study sculpture at the Royal College of Art and then to experiment freely upon her return.

A.J. Wilkinson Ltd. were operating the Royal Staffordshire Pottery at Burslem, and in 1920 acquired the adjoining Newport Pottery Company.

It was from this time that Clarice Cliff began to produce her famous art deco styles of decoration, mainly on tea services. As sales for the then unusual pottery increased, Wilkinson concentrated production of shapes on the Royal Staffordshire Pottery, whilst decoration was almost exclusively undertaken at the Newport Pottery where various areas were specially set aside for the new designs.

The number of decorative designs rose from two to seventy, reaching a maximum of one hundred and fifty by 1931, and by when Clarice Cliff had become art director of both potteries.

During the 1920s, Wilkinson had a London showroom for their wares at Holborn Viaduct, where many other pottery manufacturers had retail outlets. In 1934, the company exhibited pieces at the Harrod's Exhibition of Modern Tableware.

Many wares were produced by Wilkinson in association with the Foley Pottery, and not all production was in the art deco style. Several fine flambé pieces were produced as well as those decorated in a Chinese style.

Wilkinson managed to cater for the popular market as well as the finer art market, and during the later 1930s produced many low-priced transfer-printed wares. With the outbreak of war in 1939, however, the selling of decorated pottery for the home market was banned. This, coupled with the removal of most of the company's skilled labour, forced the closure of the pottery.

After the war the art deco market which Wilkinson and Clarice Cliff had reaped so well had almost completely vanished. Clarice Cliff had married Colley Shorter in 1940 and continued to design, though on a much smaller scale. Colley Shorter died in 1963, and the following year Clarice Cliff sold the company to a local rival pottery concern, W.R. Midwinter Ltd.. Clarice Cliff retired in 1965 and died in 1972.

Products

Clarice Cliff's early designs consisted of brightly coloured bands and diamond patterns on simple rounded shapes. When these designs were found to sell well, she added circles, squares and primitive landscapes to her pattern range. The Cubist style of painting was a strong influence on many of her early abstract patterns.

Clarice Cliff Group of wares. (courtesy of Christie's Images)

Clarice Cliff Tea-set, marked "Bizarre", "Honeyglaze Hand Painted".

Clarice Cliff Group of wares. (courtesy of Christie's Images)

Clarice Cliff Coffee-set, marked "Bizarre".

Her colour palette was mostly reds, blues, greens, orange, yellow and black, mainly executed on a characteristic pale buff-yellow ground. Her use of colour was bold, with little use of shading or toning, and many of her creations were child-like in their simplicity.

Shapes soon became more angular, but complemented well the bold styles of decoration. The "Conical" shape introduced in 1929 featured triangular handles which were solid on tea-cups and annoyingly difficult to use. The "Stamford" and later "Trieste" shapes on tea-sets were less angular, and comprised more rounded features. Style frequently sacrificed practical use, since, besides impractical handles, teapots were often bad pourers. Other early shapes were "Isis," "Lotus" and "Bon Jour."

Faults in pieces created through poor potting were liberally covered with colour, and because the painters were apparently often allowed to copy the designs in a free style (without guide tracings) every piece was slightly different.

Designs were marketed under names such as "Bizarre" (an umbrella title for many of Clarice Cliff's designs marketed from 1928), "Ravel," "Crocus," "Scarab Blue," "Inspiration Bizarre," "Biarritz," "Lodore," "Fantasque," "Caprice," "Gayday" and "My Garden."

"My Garden" was characterised by brightly enamelled flower handles on vases, jugs, etc. Other designs incorporated stylised trees and flowers, sweetcorn, geometric motifs, sailing boats, houses, etc. The "Crocus" design incorporated not only the flower, leaves and stalk of the plant, but also the roots and corm. "Crocus" was particularly popular, appeared on many articles of tableware, and ran for many years.

Designs featuring buildings in primitive landscapes were typically "Blue Windmill," "Lucerne" "(a castle in mountainous landscape,)" "Lugano" (an Italian mill,) and "Trees and House." With the exception of the last named, these designs were built up with blocks of colour.

Although many tea-sets, sandwich sets and other tableware sets were produced, ornamental wares were also made. Designs such as "Persian" and "Inspiration" were influenced by ancient styles, such as South American Aztec.

A range known as "Tibetan Ware" featured floral designs in bright colours and gold, and was well suited to large jars and ginger-jars. A later ornamental design entitled "Delecia" featured an abstract arrangement of predominantly red and green vertical streaks of colour, which displayed well on tall vases.

Some terracotta pieces were also produced and decorated in characteristic style. Other types of ware included face masks (for wall mounting,) statuettes and small models, such as a gnome reclining beneath a red spotted toadstool. With the exception of these and some moulded wares and jolleyed tablewares, a large proportion of Wilkinson's output was hand thrown, as seen particularly well in large ornamental pieces, such as "Lotus" jugs and "Isis" vases, which exhibit strong rib lines below the painted surfaces.

Some fine dinner sets and other pieces were specially commissioned from well known artists such as Frank Brangwyn, Laura Knight, Paul Nash, the London artist May J. Riach and Milner Gray.

Laura Knight's printed design "Naked Ladies" featured crowds of ladies' heads and shoulders within wavy borders in turquoise, brown and orange colours. It appeared not only on plates but also on beer mugs and other items. Her pink printed "Circus" design was another commission.

Wilkinson produced several ranges of art ware besides those decorated by Clarice Cliff. Their "Oriflamme" range, for example, which was produced during the early 1920s, was well thought of, and consisted of a multi-coloured pattern similar to marble veining on a cream coloured ground. It often featured fish in the decoration, and was executed on bowls and vases, solileur and was usually accompanied by gilding. "Oriflamme" was exhibited at the British Empire Exhibition of 1924.

Some art deco toilet sets decorated with black and white squares on a grey ground with art deco flowers (pattern no.6731) also attacted interest about this time, as did Wilkinson's imitations of Wedgwood's "butterfly lustres." Some flambé glazed vases and saki bowls were also part of Wilkinson's art wares.

Collecting Clarice Cliff Wares

The striking designs and art deco shapes have ensured a strong following for Clarice Cliff's wares among collectors, in spite of the poor quality of many of the wares and the high quantity of output. Apart from some transfer-printed wares, the majority of wares were hand-painted, and, even though this was accomplished in a mass-produced way, it had given some individuality to pieces.

Since the vast proportion of output was tablewares, ornamental pieces are less abundant and consist of items such as large jugs, vases, plaques and wall masks. The collector has plenty of choice, however, from the many tableware ranges, and, if not deterred by the high prices, can form a colourful and striking collection.

Suggestions for Further Study

Meisel, Louis K. *Clarice Cliff—The Bizarre Affair.* London: Thames & Hudson Ltd., 1988.

Watson, Howard. *Collecting Clarice Cliff.* Kevin Francis Publishing, 1988.

Wentworth-Shields, Peter & Kay Johnson. *Clarice Cliff.* L'Odeon, 1976 & 1981.

Hopwood, Gordon & Irene. *The Shorter Connection.*: Richard Dennis, 1992.

"Clarice Cliff," catalogue of an Exhibition at The Museum & Art Gallery, Brighton, 1972.

Watson, Pat. "Commercial Courage." *The Antique Dealer & Collector,* August 1988.

Spours, Judy. *Art Deco Tableware* London: Ward Lock, 1988.

Clarice Cliff Jug, 177mm high, marked "Bizarre".

Clarice Cliff Plate, with pansies on a yellow ground, marked "Bizarre".

Clarice Cliff Vases, marked "Bizarre"; red, blue, orange and black decoration.

Clarice Cliff Model of a gnome and toadstool.

Clarice Cliff Vase, marked "ISIS Bizarre", Newport Pottery, c.1925.

Clarice Cliff Jug, 250mm high, "Isis" shape, impressed mark "Isis" on base.

Wilkinson Two "Oriflamme" pattern vases, tallest 110mm high, transfer printed mark.

Clarice Cliff Honey-pot, blue design on yellow ground, marked "LODORE".

Clarice Cliff Group of wares. (courtesy of Christie's Images)

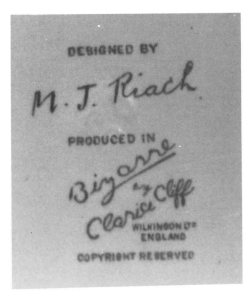

Clarice Cliff Specimen mark on plate designed by May Riach.

CLARICE CLIFF

Types of Ware	Production	Quality	Availability
All tablewares & domestic wares	High to Very High	Poor to Good	Abundant
Ornamental wares of Clarice Cliff	Moderate to High	Good	Common
Other Wilkinson's ornamental wares	Moderate	Fair to Very Good	Uncommon

(NB Quality varies even within the ranges)

Marks

Transfer printed:	Clarice Cliff WILKINSON LTD ENGLAND	c.1930 - c.1939
or:	Clarice Cliff NEWPORT POTTERY ENGLAND	c.1930 - c.1939

+/- range name (eg. 'Bizarre by Clarice Cliff')
+/- design name (eg. 'DELECIA')
+/- 'HAND PAINTED'
+/- designer's name (eg. 'M.J. Riach')
(NB. Many design names were not marked. Of the range names, 'Bizarre' and 'Fantasque' were the most commonly marked.)

Printed: with lion and crown	IRONSTONE CHINA ROYAL STAFFORDSHIRE POTTERY WILKINSON LTD ENGLAND	c.1910 - ?
Printed: with lion and crown	NEWPORT POTTERY CO LTD	c.1920 - c.1939
Printed: with crown	ROYAL SEMI-PORCELAIN A.J.WILKINSON LD. ENGLAND	c.1930 onwards

S. & E. COLLIER LTD. (c. 1861—1967)

—earthenware
—terracotta

Brick, Tile & Pottery Works, Waterloo Road, Reading, Berkshire (c. 1861—?)
Grovelands Potteries, Water Lane, Tilehurst, Reading, Berks. (1870-1967)

Historical Background

The Reading area had long been known for brick-making, because of its ample supplies of porous, red clay from the Reading Beds and grey clay from outcrops of the London Clay. A principal manufacturer of bricks and tiles in Reading was the firm of S. & E. Collier Ltd., who first established their works in Waterloo Road at the southern end of the town.

Samuel Collier and his wife Jane opened a shop in Minster Street (now gone) in 1836 to retail pottery and glass. They soon came to a decision to produce their own pottery, rather than sell the wares of others, and so, with his brother Edwin, Samuel Collier set up the Waterloo Road factory.

As business expanded, they established additional works in 1870 at Grovelands, in the north-eastern part of Reading —an extensive site, now occupied by a housing-estate.

Their principal business was the manufacture of bricks, tiles and architectural mouldings (gargoyles, cornices, etc.), much of which was exported to the United States and China; but at some stage during the latter part of the nineteenth century they embarked on the production of hand-produced art pottery. Little is known of the pottery side of the business, and much needs to be researched, but some wares bear dated inscriptions as early as 1883. The company became a limited company in 1901.

The local Reading Beds clay fired to a bright, sandy red colour, but, though admirably suitable for bricks, its porosity made it unsuitable for water-holding vessels, unless mixed with other clays and internally glazed. Nonetheless, many types of art wares were produced using the local clay, and, although wares were advertised as being available in a red or white body, by far the majority of pottery output was red-bodied.

The kilns were sited in Water Road, whilst the bricks were made in Kentwood Hill, nearby, adjacent to the clay pits. S. & E. Collier Ltd. seemed to operate from various premises in the Reading area over the years. For example, the company purchased Poulton & Son, brickmakers in Elgar Road, in 1908; and, during the 1920s the company transported clay for over a mile via a system of overhead buckets—a feature of the landscape for many years afterwards.

Information is not yet available concerning the cessation of pottery production at S. & E. Collier Ltd., but the Grovelands site closed in 1967, and the buildings were demolished soon afterwards.

Products

The earliest art pieces appear to have been "Rustic Ware" which featured various terracotta objects designed to look like tree stumps. Each piece featured colouring in mid-brown and contained protrusions resembling lopped branches, tipped with green. The remaining decoration comprised sgraffito graining, filling in any gaps that might be present.

Surpisingly, a large range of utilitarian items were produced in this rather complex ware: teapots, tobacco jars, wall bracket pots, flower containers, fern stands, crocus pots, vases and hanging flower pots, for example. Some pieces were inscribed with names and dates in relief lettering on their lids.

Another early ware consisted of small terracotta busts, though these seem to be rarely found today. The red clay, known locally as "Collier's Reading Red," produced a particularly warm, though slightly rough, terracotta. Nonetheless, Collier's architectural mouldings were often particularly creative, exhibiting an accomplished artistry.

S & E Collier Three vases: l to r: black lustre (pattern no. 218); brown matt lustre (marked "S"); brown mottled lustre 150mm high (shape no. 238). All with impressed mark S & E C SILCHESTERWARE.

The excavation of the Roman town of Calleva Atrebatum (Silchester) in the area, between 1890 and 1909, prompted the production of terracotta reproductions of pottery unearthed from the site. This led to the launch of "Silchester Ware" which became an umbrella term for a wide range of shapes, mainly connected with early styles: Roman, Medieval, Ancient Egyptian, Peruvian, etc.

Silchester Ware was generally characterised by a black or dark brown silky glaze, with no other means of decoration. Each piece was hand-thrown and simplicity of shape and design was deliberately attempted. A contemporary catalogue quotes from Christopher Dresser's "Principles of Design" regarding the simplicity of shapes, and many of the advertised shapes appeared to emulate Dresser's designs (particularly "Ancient Peruvian.")

Regrettably, we do not yet know the driving force for many of the Silchester Wares other than that significant contemporary interest in ancient styles was present and that the desire for hand-crafted studio wares was also strong. The Silchester Ware catalogue extols the craft element: "The finish is not so overdone that the articles have lost all human interest. The mark of the "Potter's Thumb" is prized, "not despised." (This latter refers to Collier's trade-mark, registered in 1906, which contained the words "SILCHESTER WARE—THE POTTER'S THUMB" in a double circle with a thumb print in the middle.) The Ware certainly had a rough, hand-made appearance. It was heavily potted, and frequently contained firing cracks.

The catalogue refers to the availability of colours in brown or "purple bronze," but some rare examples of Silchester Ware in blue, green and beige have been noted by the author. The dark colours were created using manganese, which, with the addition of lead, produced an iridescent, silky, black-brown glaze. The catalogue, however, speaks of "staining the goods previous to firing" to obtain a "dark duncolour."

Silchester Ware was also available in the natural red clay colour, though customers were warned of the lack of water-holding properties through this option. Some pieces made from the local porous clay were marketed under the name "Radynges Ware," after the Anglo-Saxon name for Reading.

A few shapes in the Silchester Ware range were titled, such as "Ancient Egyptian," "Ancient Peruvian," "Modern," etc., and some were available with silver or pewter mounts. Some pieces were marked "LB," which is believed to be the mark of a Mrs. Bowley who is mentioned in the catalogue as being a designer.

Suggestions for Further Study

Blake's Lock Museum, Gas Works Road, Reading, has a good exhibition of local industrial archaeology, plus examples of S. & E. Collier's pottery and architectural wares.

Examples of Collier's architectural ornamentation may be seen throughout the Reading area, in particularly Coley Avenue, Castle Crescent, Cholmeley Road and Oxford Raod Primary School (1882).

Reading Museum:-

"Notes on S & E Collier Ltd..." (A C Wheeler, 1981).
"Price List of Goods manufactured by S & E Collier Ltd, Edition 70" (1913).
"Decorative Brickwork in Reading & Region" (Jane Wight).

S. & E. COLLIER LTD.

Types of Ware	Production	Quality	Availability
Art pottery	Moderate ?	Poor to Good	Uncommon
Architectural wares	High	Good	Uncommon

Marks

On Architectural Wares

Impressed	TRADE MARK RR C (within oval device)	c.1870 - 1905
Impressed or printed: (NB. "RR" stands for "Reading Red")	RR C (within oval device)	1905-1957

On Silchester Ware

Impressed	S	c.1890 - c.1929
Impressed	S & SILCHESTER WARE (in oval) E C	1890 - c.1929

+ shape number, impressed (eg. 218)
(The catalogue lists shape numbers from 200 to 596, though 611 has been noted, incised, on an unusual Silchester piece)
+/- "LB", painted (Mrs. Bowley?) on shape nos. 333-336, 339 & 497
+/- "LYGON", impressed (shape name?)
(NB. Rustic Ware appears to have not been marked)

—grey and red terracotta
—"earthenware"
—gesso murals

Mary Seaton Fraser Tytler Watts
Limnerslease, Down Lane, Compton, Surrey.
(Potters' Art Guild Ltd. 1936-1954)
Aldourie Pottery, Dores, Inverness-shire, Scotland (1900—c. 1914)

Historical Background

Mary Seaton Watts, the wife of the renowned painter George Frederick Watts, established the Compton Potters' Arts Guild in 1899. She had studied at the Slade and South Kensington Schools of Art, and during her spare time at art school she often used to teach the Whitechapel shoeblacks clay modelling, a gesture commensurate with her belief in the Home Arts & Industries Association, in which she became actively involved.

She married Watts in 1886 and lived at his house in Melbury Road, London, before moving to Compton a few years later for the benefit of his health.

They named their new house "Limnerslease" (lit. "painters' place") and the discovery of a seam of clay in the grounds during the early 1890s prompted Mary Watts to commence clay modelling classes in Compton village in 1895. These proved immensely successful (up to forty people recorded as regularly attending in 1898) and were in part a reflection of the typical Victorian philanthropic desire to perpetuate local education in the applied arts (compare Elton and Aller Vale.)

When the Compton Parish Council decided to create a new burial ground, Mary Watts offered to build a mortuary chapel and set about organising local workers to construct a building to her design. The chapel took two years to build (1896-1898) but construction of the interior, which was decorated with art nouveau gesso panels also to Mary Watts' design, continued until 1906. Almost everyone in the village contributed to the work in some way, and the desire to participate was so strong that just the addition of a decorative leaf to a tile was for some villagers a satisfying contribution.

An altar for the chapel, made of terracotta, was exhibited at the Home Arts & Industries Exhibition in 1899, and during this same year, Mary Watts constructed a small pottery studio at Limnerslease, with a small wood-fuelled kiln in the garden. The potter William De Morgan gave advice on its construction.

The venture into other clay products commenced from this time, and the pottery began to produce terracotta garden ornaments and figurines. In 1900, a sub-branch of the Compton pottery was established in Mary Watts' home village of Aldourie, near Dores, on the shores of Loch Ness in Scotland. The clay for this pottery was sent up from Compton by train, and items produced were mainly garden wares, similar to those at Compton. One of the Compton workers, Louis Deuchars, was sent up to manage the Aldourie Pottery, but the venture lasted only a few years. Deuchars returned to Compton in 1903, and the Aldourie Pottery had closed by the start of the First World War.

Compton Bookends, tallest 190mm high, galleon, archer and "Sunrise",
c.1932.

Compton Large jardinière, 440mm diam. terracotta, marked "AWR". (courtesy HCMS, DA 1985.42).

Compton Owl jug, frog model and Toby Jug, tallest 200mm high, c.1925.

In contrast, by 1903 the Compton pottery was flourishing, and the Potters' Arts Guild was fulfilling regular orders. From an article written in 1903 it transpires that several "studios" existed at Limnerslease, both in the house and in the grounds, such that the whole establishment was a hive of activity.

A contemporary edition of the Pottery Gazette states that sixteen men were regularly employed at the "works" in 1912 and that the Potters' Arts Guild was essentially a benevolent organisation though conducted on commercial lines, and provided an "artistic and remunerative occupation for the villagers." In 1919 more favourable terms of business for the potters were offered, whereby they shared 50% of the proceeds of their work and put 50% back into the business. The Guild became a limited company in 1936.

The pottery might well have remained a mediocre cottage industry in terms of quality were it not for the originality of designs encouraged by Mary Watts and the Watts' connections with leading artists of their day. The designer Archibald Knox contributed several designs for garden ornaments and, in particular, a set of drinking mugs. Some Compton designs are also said to have been influenced by Alfred Gilbert, the renowned designer of the statue of Eros in Piccadilly Circus, London, and who was a personal friend of George Watts.

The well known garden designer Gertrude Jekyll contributed some designs for garden jardinières, and Compton terracotta garden vases were awarded silver medals at the Chelsea Flower Show on three occasions. Architectural work was undertaken for Sir Edwin Lutyens, Clough Williams-Ellis and Harry Goodhart Rendel.

Designers worth noting who were also employed at the pottery were Lincoln Holland (ex Macclesfield Art School,) Ralph Lindsey, George Aubertin (from 1904 and also the pottery manager from 1935,) Frank C. Payne (a co-director of the limited company) and Harry Yalden.

Queen Mary was a frequent visitor to the pottery and Queen Alexandra visited at least twice. Many pieces were made for Liberty & Co. of London.

The 1920s was a productive period for the pottery, and orders were fulfilled for customers in countries as far afield as Canada and Australia. Additional workers were taken on, and many were apprenticed from early ages. Roy Saywell was apprenticed to the pottery in 1920 at the age of 14, and a Mr. Wren is recorded as being "one of their most successful modellers" at this time. The period was only marred by the destruction by fire of the thatch roofed main studio building in 1923.

George Watts died in 1904, a year after the Watts Gallery commemorating his works was built. Mary Watts survived until 1938, but by then the potters were elderly, producing somewhat old-fashioned designs. Even so, the venture struggled on through the war, but the exhaustion of the local clay and the 100% purchase tax placed during the early 1950s on luxury goods not made for export signalled the end of the pottery. The Potters' Arts Guild was wound up in 1954, the pottery itself finally closing in 1956.

Products

The primary output of the pottery was memorials and unglazed garden wares, consisting of urns, statuary, jardinières, bird-baths and sundials, etc. Architectural items (cornices, plinths, house fronts, etc.) were made to order either to standard designs or to specific requirements (for replacement pieces, for example.) All these items were offered in either grey or red terracotta.

The porous terracotta body was an unusual construction, and was advertised as frost-resistant and particularly fine for achieving an antique look by the accumulation of moss!

The Celtic influence was strong in many of the garden wares, whilst others were entirely original creations or copies of George Watts' bronze creations (such as the bust, "Clytie.")

The "Pomona" design was popular on terracotta garden urns during the Edwardian period, and consisted of a simple garland of fruits in a classical style and shape (the "Duchess" design was a later variant) whilst the "Vine" design featured a central band of vine leaves on a typical flower-pot shape.

The most striking jardinière designs, however, were undoubtedly the Celtic and Nordic inspired creations, such as "Olaf," "Regin" (more like a font on pillars than an urn), "Freyia," "Fafnir" (featuring bold swirls, heavily incised), "Sigurd," "Asgrim," "Thrym" and "Wottan." Many simulated heavy carving reminiscent of ancient Nordic stone monuments.

Sundials were similarly decorated and included the "Ulf' design (a columnar shape with Celtic motifs and engraved brass plate bearing the motto "I mark time, God measures eternity"), the "St. Andrew" design (a similar shape, but with more ornate decoration and motto "I count no hours that are not bright") and the more elaborate "Owl" design (a Norman style trefoil columnar shape on a large stepped base, 135cm in height, owl motif and motto "Light and shade by turns, but love always.")

The output of smaller items and hollow wares was mostly in a white, chalky body, similar to plaster-of-Paris. Figurines, statuettes, plaques and other ornaments were produced, as well as sets of buttons, fruit bowls, flower vases, jugs and mugs. Early pieces were moulded, but later pieces (1920s onwards) were slip-cast.

The wood-fired kilns were incapable of achieving the high temperatures required for the production of stoneware and pieces produced had the disadvantage of not being naturally water-tight. A lacquer was therefore applied in some circumstances to overcome this.

Items were hand-coloured in tempera but the colours were unfired. A label affixed to each item warned the purchaser not to wet the piece! Difficulties with temperature control in the kilns meant that colours could not be fired. Instead, some pieces were varnished after colouring.

It is possible to recognise two distinct styles among the white-bodied wares: those wares of the pre-First World War period (such as statuettes of knights and saints) and those wares of the 1920s and 1930s (bookends, mugs, bowls, buttons, etc.)

The early statuettes exhibit a style typical of the period (knights in armour, for example) and were generally produced in sizes from between 21.5cm to 25.5cm high (though larger sizes could be had to special commission). St. George (shown with the dragon) St. Francis, St. Christopher, St. Martin, St. Michael (shown with a set of scales for weighing souls) and St. Cecilia (shown with musical pipes) were produced about 1910. Other statuettes included "The Four Seasons," Joan of Arc, Sir Galahad, Botticelli's and Luini's Madonna.

Early plaques (usually about 18.5cm by 11.2cm) featured subjects such as St.George and the Dragon or Francis of Assisi. A set of large Nursery Rhyme plaques was also produced (eg. Little Miss Muffet, Little Boy Blue) though these are rare.

Coronation mugs were produced in June, 1911, to mark the coronation of George V. One mug was given to each of the local school-children.

Archibald Knox designed the "Compton in Surrey" mug which features St. Nicholas on the Pilgrims Way.

Crude models of the Watts chapel were also made, as were other models.

During the 1920s and 1930s, handsome owl jugs were produced alongside "Tennyson" bookends, "Sunrise" and "The Galleon" book-ends in large numbers. Plaques with nativity scenes or the Tree of Life and shallow bowls such as "The Lily Pond" were also produced. Pieces produced during this period were characterised by vibrant, intense colours.

Suggestions for Further Study

The Watts Gallery, Compton, Surrey, has some pieces on display in the Gallery and around the garden. It is open most days throughout the year.

The Mortuary Chapel, Compton. Usually open to visitors.

The Mortuary Chapel, Cambridge Military Hospital, Aldershot. Interior decorated by Mary Watts.

Cecil, Victoria. "For House & Garden," *The Antique Collector,* January, 1981.

Botting, Meg. "A Wielding Force in the Shadows." *Country Life,* September 20, 1979.

Art Journal, 1900.

The Studio 17(76), July, 1899 and 14(66), September, 1898.

Boreham, Louise M. "Aldourie Pottery, Dores Inverness-shire." *Scottish Pottery Review* 9, 1984.

Watts, Mary. *The Word in the Pattern.* A rare book, which explains the symbolism of the decoration in the Chapel.

Compton Group of statuettes, talled 225mm high, representing St. Michael, St. Cecilia, St. George, "Summer" (from the Four Seasons) and St. Francis, c. 1910, impressed circular mark "PAG" and paper label.

Compton Pilgrim bottle, 95mm diam. marked "Pilgrim Bottle" on base, decorated with a medallion incorporating a Celtic knot design, circumscribed "Their work was as it were a wheel in the middle of a wheel" and the legend "Limnerslease". (courtesy HCMS, DA 1958.78).

COMPTON POTTERS' ARTS GUILD

Type of Ware	Production	Quality	Availability
White-bodied art wares	Moderate	Poor to Very Good	Scarce (pre-1920), Uncommon (1920 onwards)
Garden wares	Moderate	Good to Very Good	Uncommon

Marks

Most wares were marked.
Ornamental white-bodied wares

Impressed		c.1903-c.1914
Impressed: (in cartouche)	COMPTON POTTERY GUILDFORD	c.1920-c.1939

+/- "Made in England" (in circle)
+/- paper label printed in black "Unfired Colours DO NOT WET. To Clean, brush with a stiff brush".

+/- artist's mark:	LH	Lincoln Holland (modeller)
	RL	Ralph Lindsay (statuettes)
	GA	George Aubertin
	(this list is not exhaustive)	

Garden Wares

Impressed: (in rectangle)	Designed & Manufactured by LIBERTY & Co.	c. 1904-c. 1914
or similar (in rectangle)	DESIGNED AND MANUFACTURED FOR LIBERTY & CO.	c. 1904-c. 1914

+/- artist's mark (as above)

General
+/- impressed circular motif featuring a central Celtic knot surrounded by the words "Limnerslease Compton" and the legend "Their work was as it were a wheel in the middle of a wheel" around the outer edge. This same mark was used for Aldourie wares, with the words "Aldourie Dores" instead of "Limnerslease Compton".

Jackfield, Shropshire.

Historical Background & Products

Craven Dunnill & Company (formerly Hargreaves & Craven) was formed in 1871 and was principally a manufacturer of floor and wall tiles using similar processes to Maw & Company nearby (ref. Maw & Co.)

Craven Dunnill was well known for its copies of medieval lustred tiles for church or home, a speciality which won the company numerous commissions, not only for restorations but also for new buildings in the Gothic revival style so popular during the latter part of the nineteenth century. The Roman Catholic Cathedral at Shrewsbury was one of Craven Dunnill's commissions and is a good example of the company's encaustic tile work.

The company was known to have commissioned designs from architects such as Alfred Waterhouse, and tiles were often produced for insertion into items of furniture, such as tables and wash-stands.

The majority of tiles produced seem to have been mostly decorated with stylised floral motifs. Greens, browns, pink and yellow-ochre were commonly employed colours, often as monochrome decoration, including lustres. The colour and style of decoration varied with the process of tile production. Some relief-moulded tiles frequently bore a monochrome translucent glaze, such as green, whilst others might be underglaze printed in monochrome, on-glaze transfer-printed, or produced by a variety of processes. Designs were also hand painted, hand stencilled, lithographed or press-moulded.

Tile sizes were mostly six inches square (150mm) but some eight inch square (200mm) tiles were also made, such as a series of twelve tiles featuring animal portraits. Few pictorial tiles, however, seem to have been produced, and those that were vary considerably in subject matter and style.

Very little is known about the operation of the company and much research still needs to be done. For a short period, Craven Dunnill ventured into art pottery and some rare pieces are on display at Jackfield Tile Museum along with several examples of the company's tiles.

Art pottery produced was similar to Maw & Company's wares, with lustre decoration on blanks bought in, mainly from the Staffordshire Pottery of Thomas Forester & Sons, Fenton, Longton. Many of these blanks were moulded or slip-cast, and pieces were generally light in weight.

The quality of decoration was good, but not quite as fine as that of Maw & Co., although similar designs were employed. Mostly vases of varying shape were decorated. Many pieces were decorated in a monochrome lustre, such as beige or ruby, and applied thinly, often to reveal a pattern in relief below.

Suggestions for Further Study

Jackfield Tile Museum, Ironbridge, Shropshire.

Clive House Museum, Shrewsbury, Shropshire (tiles and vases).

The Red Lion public house, Erdington, Birmingham, exhibits much of Craven Dunnill's interior tile decoration, particularly the fine bar front.

The Roman Catholic Cathedral, Shrewsbury (tiles).

Dawes, Nicholas M., *Majolica*: Crown Publishers, Inc., New York 1990.

Messenger, Michael. *"Pottery & Tiles of the Severn Valley"* (catalogue of the Clive House Museum collections): Remploy Ltd., 1979.

CRAVEN DUNNILL & CO. LTD.

Types of Ware	Production	Quality	Availability
Tiles	Moderate to High	Good	Abundant
Art Pottery	Very Low	Good	Rare

Marks

Not all Craven Dunnill's art pottery was marked, although many pieces bear the impressed mark of Thomas Forester & Sons.

Impressed: (Tiles)	Craven Dunnill & Co.
	(plus a drawing of the factory)
	JACKFIELD
+ 'Salop'	
Transfer printed in black: (art pottery)	CRAVEN DUNNILL & CO. JACKFIELD
Painted: (art pottery) + 'FORESTER' impressed	C.D. + Co. J (with a shield)

Craven Dunnill Art Pottery. l to r:i) two-handled vase, 229mm high, heraldic beasts decoration in red lustre on a fawn ground, white body. ii) two-handled vase, 300mm high, classical shape, ruby lustre on white ground, white body, marked "C.D. & Co.J" with shield, and stamped "FORESTER".

Craven Dunnill Pair of vases, 188mm high, yellow lustre, marked with a transfer print in black underglaze "CRAVEN DUNNILL & CO. JACKFIELD".

WILLIAM DE MORGAN, artist/potter   (1839—1917)

—earthenware
—lustres
—enamels

Fitzroy Square, London (1869-1872)
Orange House, Cheyne Row, Chelsea, London (1872-1882)
Merton Abbey, Merton, South London (1882-1888)
Townmead Road, Sands End, Fulham, West London (1888-1907)

Historical Background

To many, William De Morgan was a symbol of the renaissance of British pottery, releasing it from the many dull monotonous styles that had pervaded ceramics for so long. Through relentless experimentation he contributed much to the science of ceramics as well as to its artistry, influencing potters for many years to come. His pottery is, therefore, something of an historical landmark both technically and artistically.

De Morgan himself was strongly influenced by the British arts and crafts movement. He was a founder member of the Arts and Crafts Exhibition Society, and was a close friend of other pioneers in the movement, notably William Morris the textile designer and Edward Burne-Jones the painter. Both these friends had some influence on his pottery decoration.

De Morgan was educated as an artist at the Royal Academy Schools from 1859 to 1861, upon leaving which he took up the design of stained glass. His venture into pottery began in 1869 when he constructed a kiln at the family home in Fitzroy Square, London, for the firing of tiles to his own design. He began solely as a decorator, working on biscuit blanks of vases and plates manufactured for him in Staffordshire, mainly from the firm of J.H. & J. Davis, and tiles manufactured as white blanks from Holland.

He experimented in metallic pigments and lustre colours, reviving old processes and imitating oriental and medieval designs. His lustre colours were based on copper and silver, and were produced by a complicated process of high temperature reduction in the kiln. He also developed a series of non-lustre colours from metal oxides which he termed "Persian Colours."

In 1872 he moved production to Cheyne Row, Chelsea, incorporating a showroom for his wares. Vases, plates and bottles were decorated, alongside the continued decoration of tiles. His pieces gradually became known, and the business expanded, necessitating the employment of three assistants: Frank Iles as kiln operator and Charles and Fred Passenger as decorators. Several commissions were undertaken, notably the completion of missing Islamic tiles at Lord Leighton's Arabian Hall in Kensington, the decoration of the Tabard Inn at Turnham Green, West London, and designs for steamships of the P & O Company.

In 1882, De Morgan moved to larger premises near William Morris's textile factory at Merton Abbey, South London, in order to accommodate his expanding business. He maintained the showroom at Orange House, however, until 1886, when it was relocated to Great Marlborough Street. At Merton Abbey he was able to produce his own shapes in quantity without relying on blanks bought in. This gave him greater freedom of decorative expression and control.

Wm. De Morgan Group of pieces. l to r:i) tile, 200mm square, parrot decoration, impressed Sands End rose mark (1888-97). ii) vase, 450mm high, fish decoration in ruby lustre by Fred Passenger, painted mark of "De Morgan & Co" and "FP". iii) bowl by Fred Passenger, marked solely "FP". iv) vase, lion and snake lustre decoration, impressed Sands End wings mark (1888-97).

In 1888, he moved again; this time to Townmead Road, Sands Ends, Fulham, in South-West London, where he went into partnership with the architect Halsey Ricardo. Here he developed a process of "double-lustering" which gave increased depth to his pieces, and he also succeeded in decorating wares with two tones of lustre.

Ricardo advocated, along with William Morris, that city buildings could be made to look brighter with exterior tile decoration. This prompted an increase in the production of art tiles which were used not only to embellish buildings but also furniture, such as tables and wash-stands.

The partnership with Ricardo lasted ten years during which time De Morgan created his finest pieces. Much of the high quality of output was achieved through the use of equipment designed by De Morgan himself, as well as through continual experiment with chemical processes. The pottery expanded to meet demand and additional decorators were taken on but, in spite of this, the business steadily lost money.

From 1892, De Morgan began to winter in Florence for health reasons but managed to send designs back to London by post. In 1898, the partnership with Ricardo was dissolved for financial reasons and the same year De Morgan formed a new partnership with Frank Iles and the Passenger brothers which continued until the closure of the pottery in 1907.

In 1907, De Morgan retired from ceramics, aged 68. Amazingly, he took up a new career in novel writing with which he had been toying just prior to his retirement, and he became highly successful. His novel "Joseph Vance" was published in 1906 and this was quickly followed by others. He died in 1917, having contracted trench-fever through conversing with a war witness about the fighting at the Front. Frank Iles and the Passenger brothers moved away but continued to decorate pottery until 1933 at Bushey Heath (ref. Bushey Heath).

Products

De Morgan's pottery was highly distinctive, often exhibiting great artistry in its decoration. It is thus eagerly sought after by collectors and can command very high prices. Pieces can vary significantly in quality, however, and since much of De Morgan's work was experimental, pieces of poorer quality (through potting or misfired glazes, etc.) may be found.

Early wares tended to be decorated on a plain white background and were a product of the white blanks bought in from other potteries. Later wares (of the Fulham period for example) were often decorated over a deep blue ground, which enhanced the reflective quality of the lustre colours.

Early pieces comprised mostly chargers, many of which bore wide flat rims with depressed circular centres which were often likened to Cardinal's hats. The simile was the more appropriate since many pieces were decorated with a monochrome ruby lustre produced through use of copper oxides.

A beige or yellow-ochre monochrome lustre (produced from silver oxides) was less commonly employed on these early wares, although a common characteristic was the decoration of both sides of a charger (compare the Pilkington Pottery's lustres).

Decoration was generally bright, covering the entire surface of a piece, with favourite subjects being exotic flowers and foliage, mythical beasts (dragons, snakes, etc.) medieval galleons, animals (rabbits, deer, etc.) and cherubs.

The lustre colours were more matt in finish than the mirror-like lustres of the Pilkington Pottery and exhibited an iridescence rather than a deep reflection. The Fulham period saw the production of the finest quality lustres. A silvery blue lustre with a mirror-like finish was particularly spectacular.

Not all the colours used were lustres, however. His "Persian Colours" were enamels painted on to a white crackled slip, and ranged from turquoise to red, purple, yellow and various shades of green. These colours were used on tiles as well as ornamental wares.

De Morgan used multicolours sparingly, however, and even when his monochrome lustres gave way to duochrome lustres and Persian colours, many of his wares continued to be decorated in only one or two colours. The use of a slip or enamel colour against a lustre of the same colour was a frequent means of giving depth to a piece.

De Morgan's vase and bottle shapes were characteristically rounded, though many were poorly and heavily potted from his own factory. Bowls were often deep with steeply rounded sides, and vases were sometimes gourd-like, with occasional domed covers. The potting quality varied noticeably from site to site.

Some trial wares were produced to De Morgan designs about 1911 by A.F. Wenger, his glaze suppliers in Hanley, Staffordshire. These were mostly small plates depicting De Morgan's animal designs or abstract geometrical patterns. As these pieces tended to be proofs and try-outs of glazes, they often bore the name or number of the glaze, accompanied by the impressed monogram "AFW" plus the name "Furnivals Burslem" on the base.

A great deal of tiles was produced, particularly early in De Morgan's pottery career. Favourite designs were floral, the sunflower being particularly popular, as well as carnations and pinks in enamel colours. Duochrome decoration seemed to be predominant, although many tiles were monochrome or multi-coloured.

Standard tile sizes were six inches (150mm) square, though some eight inch ranges (200mm) were produced together with larger tile panels. The similarity between many of the floral tile patterns and contemporary wall coverings was no accident. De Morgan made use of William Morris's London showroom for many years to display his tiles.

Animal subjects were commonly employed as decoration on tiles, frequently appearing in a monochrome lustre such as ruby. Rabbits, hares, fish, lions and peacocks were decorative subjects commonly used.

Wm. De Morgan Early charger, 300mm diam., decorated in ruby lustre on a Staffordshire blank, impressed mark "JH & J DAVIS", c.1872.

obverse of above.

Wm. De Morgan Vase, 125mm high, ruby lustre, Persian design.

Wm. De Morgan Vase, 200mm high, deep blue and silver lustre, by Fred Passenger.

Wm. De Morgan Tazza, 230mm diam., blue lustre by Fred Passenger, marked solely "FP".

71

Suggestions for Further Study

Lord Leighton's Arabian Hall is open to the public at The Leighton House Museum, 12, Holland Park Road, West Kensington, London.

The Tabard Inn, Turnham Green, South-West London. The public house is near the underground railway station in Bath Road. Tiles may be seen in the entrance porch and upstairs.

The Victoria & Albert Museum, London, houses an extensive collection of De Morgan's works.

Tiles may still be seen in some of the porches of houses in Chiswick Mall, and at Sand's End, near Putney Bridge, south-west London. De Morgan Road appropriately commemorates the potter.

Cardiff Castle houses a collection of De Morgan's work as does the National Trust at their properties at Standen (Sussex), Cragside (Northumberland) and Wightwick (near Wolverhampton).

The William Morris Gallery, Forest Road, Walthamstow, London E17, houses a collection of De Morgan's works.

Catleugh, J. *William De Morgan Tiles.* Trefoil, 1983.

Gaunt, W. and M.D.E. Clayton-Smith. *William De Morgan.* London: Studio Vista, 1971.

Prouting, N. "William De Morgan." *Apollo,* January, 1953.

"William De Morgan (1839-1917);" catalogue of an exhibition at Leighton House, 1972; pub. De Morgan Foundation.

Pinkham, Roger. *Catalogue of Pottery by William De Morgan.* London: Victoria & Albert Museum, 1973.

"De Morgan Wares." *Antique Collector's Club* 19(5), September 1974.

Greenwood, Martin. *"The Designs of William De Morgan;"* catalogue, Richard Dennis & William Wiltshire III, 1989. Published to coincide with an exhibition at the Victoria & Albert Museum, London.

Wm. De Morgan Specimen marks on tiles of Sands End and Merton Abbey.

WILLIAM DE MORGAN

Types of Ware	Production	Quality	Availability
Tiles	High	Fair to Good	Uncommon
Ornamental wares	Low	Fair to Excellent	Scarce

Marks

Many early wares were unmarked.

Impressed: (on ornamental wares, mostly chargers)	J H & J DAVIS	1869 - c.1882

+/- "H" or "W" impressed

(NB. These early decorated Staffordshire blanks were unsigned by De Morgan. Early tiles were often supplied and marked by the Poole and Wedgwood factories.)

Impressed: (in relief)	DE MORGAN MERTON ABBEY (in oval)	1882 - 1888
	WDE MERTON ABBEY (in large square with outline of abbey)	1882 - 1888
Impressed	W.DE MORGAN (in rectangle)	1882 - 1888
	DE MORGAN (in oval)	1888 - 1898
Impressed: (in relief)	DM (surmounting a tulip motif)	1888 - 1898
	W. DE MORGAN & CO SAND'S END POTTERY (around circular wings motif)	1888 - 1898
	WM DE MORGAN AND CO SANDS END POTTERY FULHAM S.W.	1888 - 1898

Impressed	WM DE MORGAN & CO SANDS END POTTERY FULHAM (around circular Tudor rose motif)	1888 - 1898
Impressed: (In relief)	DM	c.1898
	W.DE.MORGAN (circular within square)	c.1898
Impressed	DIP (within circle)	1898 - 1907

+/- artist names (from c.1880), painted:

FP	- Fred Passenger
CP	- Charles Passenger
JH	- Jim Hersey
MJ	- M Juster
JJ	- Joe Juster
HR	- Halsey Ricardo

(NB. Some blanks were again bought in from the Poole Pottery after 1898, and are so marked.)

DELLA ROBBIA POTTERY

(1894—1906)

—modelled and hollow wares
—tiles
—architectural wares
—ecclesiastical statuary

2A, Price Street, Birkenhead, Cheshire.

Historical Background

The Della Robbia Pottery was founded in 1894 by the sculptor Conrad Dressler and the artist Harold Rathbone (who was a former pupil of the artist Ford Madox Brown). The pottery took its name from the 15th century Italian family of Della Robbia who produced faience during the period of the Italian Renaissance.

The pottery was the main part of an enterprise which also included metal work and wood carving, and employed artists from local schools of art. About fifteen people were employed at one time in the production of pottery, and included the artist Robert Anning Bell and the Italian sculptor Carlo Manzoni.

Harold Rathbone found affinity with many of the exponents of the Arts and Crafts movement, and, although the original purpose of the pottery was to produce solely architectural wares, Rathbone's ideas in this area were not readily accepted by architects at the time. Ornamental wares were thus produced alongside the production of architectural wares.

Work was exhibited widely, however, and found favour in high places; pieces were purchased by King George V when he was Duke of York and also by Queen Victoria and Edward VII. Other famous purchasers included the musician Paderewski and the actress Sarah Bernhardt.

Rathbone was keen to promote many of the principles adopted by the Arts and Crafts movement such as the production of practical hand-made wares as a reaction against the machine age. He also took a liberal approach to his workforce, allowing them a certain freedom of expression in their work.

Pieces were sold at Liberty & Co. in London between 1894 and 1901 and also at Morris & Co. in the West End of London as well as at outlets in New York, Paris and locally in Liverpool.

In 1897, Conrad Dressler left Della Robbia to establish his own pottery at Great Marlow which he called the Medmenham Pottery. He was replaced by Carlo Manzoni who had been running his own pottery in Stoke-on-Trent (the Granville Pottery), which he closed in order to join Della Robbia.

In 1900, the pottery amalgamated with a business run by the sculptor Emile de Caluwé, which produced ecclesiastical and architectural wares, hoping to exploit a profitable market in monumental gravestones, etc. The new company was named "The Della Robbia Pottery & Marble Co. Ltd."

In spite of the popularity of Della Robbia's ornamental wares and good press coverage for the many architectural commissions undertaken, the pottery was never commercially successful and was forced to close in 1906. Rathbone's general lack of business sense seems to have been a prime cause for failure of the company.

Della Robbia Plaque, 490mm wide, marked "LJ", "102", and dated 1906.

73

Products

Ornamental wares were of good decorative quality, but the pottery body was poor. Problems with the clays resulted in the glazes flaking and crazing. The clay body was mostly red, but sometimes white, depending on the clay source.

Artists employed at Della Robbia proved to be both competent and faithful to the Italian Renaissance style. One designer, Miss Aphra Peirce, produced some noticeably original work, and the artist Annie Smith is recorded as having decorated some fine plates.

More prolific artists were Liza Wilkins, who often decorated vases with heads of figures or animals in relief, and Cassandia Annie Walker, who produced many pieces in an art nouveau style with figure and floral subjects.

Harold Rathbone himself threw and decorated many pieces and Carlo Manzoni designed several geometric patterns, many of which were similar to those he had produced at his own pottery.

Vases, ewers, plates and chargers were the main ornamental wares produced, and some were shaped as grotesques. Decoration was accomplished through an initial coating of a thin cream-white slip to the pottery body, upon which sgraffito work was undertaken accompanied by painting. A thin translucent glaze was applied to the finished decoration.

Colours were noticeably bright, with colour combinations often verging on the gaudy. Yellow and green was a favourite colour combination, as was red-brown and green. Some pieces were mounted in silver.

Apart from the Italian influence, many pieces bore elements of Middle Eastern and Islamic art. Medieval and Celtic designs were also employed, as well as the more usual European art nouveau and pre-Raphaelite styles.

Wares also included ceramic panels, modelled in high relief with figure subjects. These were frequently given titles, such as "King Alfred" or "Isaac," and were sculpted by Harold Rathbone, Carlo Manzoni, Ellen Mary Rope, Robert Anning Bell and Conrad Dressler, in particular. These architectural wares were part of a large range of items which included window-boxes, fountains, sun-dials and, from 1900, ecclesiastical statuary. The fountain for the Savoy Hotel in London, which was designed by T.E. Colcutt in 1898, was embellished with ornamental features designed and modelled by Harold Rathbone.

A regular decorative subject on ceramic panels by Ellen Rope was processions of children, and her work generally included figure subjects executed to high quality.

Quality of wares varied widely, however, reflecting the talent of the artists and throwers employed, though a single attraction of Della Robbia wares was the individual style against other potteries of the same period. The short life of the pottery, however, has meant that pieces are not found in abundance today.

Suggestions for Further Study

The Birkenhead Central Library has some examples of Della Robbia ceramic panels.

An example of the work of Carlo Manzoni can be seen as two sculpted figures above the entrance to the Midland Bank building in Charing Cross, London.

The Memorial Church, Manor Road, Wallasey, Cheshire, houses some panels by Conrad Dressler.

The Williamson Art Gallery, Birkenhead, houses a large collection of Della Robbia wares.

The National Trust's property at Standen, Sussex, has a good collection of Della Robbia wares.

Tattersall, B. "The Birkenhead Della Robbia Pottery." *Apollo*, February 1973.

Williamson Art Gallery & Museum. *Della Robbia Pottery, Birkenhead 1894-1906, An Interim Report.* Metropolitan Borough of Wirral, c.1974.

"The Birkenhead Della Robbia Pottery, 1893 (sic) -1906;" catalogue of an exhibition in 1980; Jeremy Cooper Ltd.

Della Robbia Two vases by Charles Collis. l to r:-i) vase and cover, 165mm high. ii) vase, 280mm high, dated 1900.

Della Robbia Ewer, 295 mm high, by Cassandia Annie Walker, sgraffito decoration of two figures in yellow, and flowers in turquoise and yellow on a light brown ground, dated 1897.

Della Robbia Jug, 200mm high, with silver lid, base and handle.

DELLA ROBBIA POTTERY

Types of Ware	Production	Quality	Availability
Ornamental wares	Moderate	Fair to Excellent (body poor)	Uncommon
Architectural wares	Low to Moderate	Good to Excellent	Scarce

Marks

Incised and painted:	A medieval sailing ship in outline, varying in style but usually green, with the letters D R to the left and right, usually in red.	1894 - 1906

+/- year, under the above mark
+/- thrower's monogram (usually incised)
+/- pattern number (1 to at least 1050)
+/- artist's initials, painted, eg.:
     AB - Annie Beaumont
     AP - Aphra Peirce
     AS - Annie Smith
     RB - Ruth Bare
     C - Charles Collis
   M de C - Marianne de Caluwé (wife of Emile de Caluwé)
    EMR - Ellen Mary Rope
     GR - Gertrude Russell
     HR - Harold Rathbone
     LW - Liza Wilkins
    CW (or CAW) - Cassandia Annie Walker
(NB. Carlo Manzoni and Conrad Dressler do not appear to have marked ornamental wares to their design.)

Della Robbia Specimen mark, with date 1898 and initials for Charles Collis and Liza Wilkins.

Denby, Derbyshire.
Historical Background
 The discovery of a bed of fine stoneware clay at Denby in 1806 during excavations for a new road led to the formation, three years later, of the Denby Pottery. William Bourne, a potter from Belper nearby, having obtained a lease on the clay bed in 1806 for use in his Belper Works, established the pottery at Denby for his son, Joseph Bourne, in 1809.

 Joseph Bourne set about producing quality brown salt-glazed wares featuring carved and modelled decoration. Two-handled vases, bowls, ink-wells, jugs, mugs, bottles, jars and spirit flasks as effigies of famous personalities, were among the many items produced.

 The Bournes were well connected in the area as potters. William Bourne, besides owning the Belper Works, was also a partner in Pinder, Bourne & Co, the Stoke pottery that Henry Doulton bought in 1878, whilst one of his sons, William junior, purchased the pottery at Church Gresley which was sold to T.G.Green in 1864, and which continues today.

 Joseph Bourne died in 1861, and his son took over the management of the pottery until his death in 1869. His widow, Sarah Bourne, then took over, increasing the product range and expanding the workforce to some four hundred employees. Upon her death in 1898, her two nephews carried on the business until 1907, when one of the nephews, Joseph Henry Topham, left the partnership, leaving the other nephew, Joseph Bourne-Wheeler, as sole proprietor. In 1916 the business was registered as a limited company, and Joseph Bourne-Wheeler assumed the post of Governing Director until his death in 1942.

 The company exhibited its "Vitreous Stoneware" at international exhibitions, winning medals at the Sydney International Exhibition of 1879 and the Paris Exhibition of 1881. The pottery celebrated its centenary in 1909 and could boast then that its machinery and equipment was state-of-the-art. The site stood on seven acres and contained twenty-two ovens and kilns of the latest type. Additionally, the company had a London office and showroom in the Euston Road.

Denby 'Danesby' wares with pastel decoration,l to r:-'Regent Pastel' range
'Melville' vase, with palm decoration; 'Regent Pastel' range small size 'Faun'
vase; 'Pastel Blue' range 'Bowness' vase, 250mm high, with fish decoration
and handles formed as otters, designed by Donald Gilbert, and stamped
"GILBERT"; 'Regent Pastel' range 'Catkin' jug.

After the First World War, ornamental art wares began to be produced. Until 1924, however, when the first "Danesby" ware was produced, these were fairly bland, glazed mainly in brown and deep green. The product range was also fairly mixed at this time, and included industrial wares (electric insulators, etc.)

From 1924, however, more colourful lines were introduced, both in the art wares and tablewares. In 1931, Norman Wood joined the company. He modernised much of the inefficient equipment, installing two Dressler tunnel-kilns to replace the fourteen salt-glaze kilns. This enabled glazes other than salt-glaze to be produced, significantly extending the colour range.

With greater decorative potential, Norman Wood recruited a freelance designer named Donald Gilbert who designed new oven-to-tableware ranges from 1934.

During the Second World War, only "Utility Brown" ware could be produced for the domestic market because of output restrictions. Other strategic items, such as telegraphic insulators, were made during this time. Following the war, additional designers, such as Albert and his son Glyn Colledge, added their own destinctive type of designs to ornamental and table wares.

In 1959, the company acquired the Nottingham business of Lovatt & Lovatt at Langley Mill which was also producing stoneware. Langley Mill was founded about 1863 by the Calvert family, later to be joined by the Lovatt family. From 1976, as a division of Denby Pottery Co. Ltd., it traded as Denby Tableware Ltd.. Both Denby Pottery Co. Ltd. and Denby Tableware Ltd. were taken over in 1981 by Crown House plc. The Langley Mill buildings were recently demolished and the pottery at Denby was bought out by its management in 1990.

The pottery continues today as The Denby Pottery Company Ltd., producing tablewares and ornamental wares (lamp-bases, vases, etc.) using the traditional hard-bodied, fine-textured stoneware. Many wares are still expertly hand-thrown in spite of a significant investment in new equipment.

Products

The local clay produced an exceptionally smooth-textured stoneware body which, when fired, became very tough and vitreous. Many early domestic products were sold as "British Fireproof" ware or "British Chef Ware" and so marked. Items that could be used in the oven were in particular demand. Containers of all sorts were produced—bottles for brewers, ginger-beer bottles for companies such as R. White & Sons, and ink bottles for Stephens Inks. Many of these had the customers' company names stamped on the wares. A catalogue of 1908 shows a wide variety of salt-glazed and white-glazed beer bottles, and large bottles contained in wicker baskets. Footwarmers, muff warmers and other utilitarian brown-wares were produced by the thousands.

The "Neva-drip" brown-ware teapot, launched in 1920, was a great success. So much so that a revival is being planned currently.

In 1924, the first "Danesby" ware was launched. This was an ornamental ware available in a variety of plain colours such as "Royal Blue," "Ruby," "Pewter," "Black and Yellow," etc.. Stylised floral bands were added and the wares appeared rather Edwardian in style. Items were mainly functional—vases, flower bowls and several jardinières.

These ornamental wares were either thrown or slip-cast, and the 1924 catalogue lists twenty shapes with size variations. A choice of decoration was available in some cases, such as "Belt," "Gothic," "Carnival" and "Floral." These could be applied to named shapes, such as "Oxford Plant Pot," "Balliol Plant Pot," "Grecian Bowl," "Siamese Pedestal and Plant Pot", etc.. Quality was good and items were aimed at the middle of the price range. It is interesting to note that only a year later decoration was augmented on the same range, indicating a trend towards more colour and more decoration on a single item. The same range in 1925 appeared less Edwardian in style.

In 1925, the first of a new type of Danesby ware was launched, entitled "Electric Blue." Vases, jardinières, jugs, candlesticks and flower bowls were produced in this range. Electric Blue featured no decoration save for a blue glaze with a high gloss, which formed subtle, vertically gradating streaks. The 1925 catalogue shows 27 shapes, all of which bore titles such as "Oriel" and "Sicilian," and many were named after local places such as "Crich," "Baslow" and "Birchover." Conical and tubular shapes were common, such as the "Crich jug," "Trumpet" vases and "Sweet Pea Tube." The popular "Owl jug" was included in this range and, like many of the shapes, was available in two sizes.

Electric Blue continued until at least 1935 and a catalogue of about 1930 shows an increased range with two-handled ovoid vases ("Lytton" and "Elton"), and jugs and vases featuring concentric ribbing at their necks (such as "Brassington" and "Riber"). Simplicity of shape and decoration, in order to show off the high glaze, was desired, though the 1930 catalogue shows a minor relaxation of this aim with some items bearing a floral roundel and limited geometric lines. An "Elephant Bookend" was the only item produced which was not a type of container.

Electric Blue was quickly followed by "Orient Ware" (1928), a more ambitious ornamental and tableware which featured moulded Chinese and Korean symbols with an orange-brown glaze. Many of the Electric Blue shapes were available for decoration in Orient, but some new shapes such as "Monsal" were introduced.

By 1930, "Danesby Ware" had become an umbrella term for all the non-tableware wares. "Antique Green" was the next range to be launched, followed by "Herbaceous Border" and "Floral Pastel" about 1935.

"Antique Green" continued the trend for decorating the top third of vases, jugs and bowls with ornamental bands over a plain pastel green glaze. Geometric swirls were the main decorative motif, emphasised in black, though shapes were similar to those of earlier wares with a few favourites appearing, such as the "Elephant Bookend."

Denby Pieces from the 'Orient' range, l to r:-'Brassington' vase (cylindrical); 'Lytton' urn; 'Riber' jug, 195mm high; small size 'Monsal' vase.

In complete contrast, both Herbaceous Border and Floral Pastel were decorative styles of the 1930s—deco representations of floral subjects liberally covering a piece. Herbaceous Border, however, still retained many earlier shapes and featured pastel-coloured vertical and diagonal floral streaks whilst Floral Pastel exhibited restrained art deco shapes with less stylised floral decoration—recognisable fuchsia, foxglove (a 1930s favourite), anemone, daisy and hollyhock were decorative themes. Naturally, flower containers featured strongly in this range, which also included wall vases. Curiously, all the shapes in Floral Pastel were given Scottish place-names: "Thurso," "Troon," "Peebles," "Moffatt," "Paisley," etc.—a veritable gazetteer of Scotland!

About 1935, a range of animal models was produced as giftwares. "Byngo" the dog, "Fido" (another dog), ducks, geese, cats, more dogs, penguins, fish, a giraffe, an elephant, etc., were all produced either as stand-alone models or as ashtrays, bookends, etc. Prices were reasonable, and some items could be bought in a range of sizes. The "Rabbit" model, for example, was available in seven sizes and has often been confused with its Sylvac counterpart, which was very similar.

About 1938, further ranges of Danesby Ware were produced. "Regent Pastel," "Blue Pastel," "Sylvan Pastel" and a revamped "Herbaceous Border" appeared. All these wares exhibited pastel colours over more ambitious relief moulded decoration. "Bowness," a two-handled Regent Pastel vase designed by Donald Gilbert, featured swimming fish and two otters as the handles. Birds and trees featured more strongly as decorative subjects in these ranges, and the heavy modelling created a chunky appearance. Most of these items were slip-cast, of course, in order to effect the modelled appearance; and collectors should note that quality of casting varied markedly. Some mixed options were available in these ranges, such that the "Catkin Jug," for example, was offered in both Blue Pastel or Regent Pastel.

Tableware ranges appeared from 1934 when Donald Gilbert designed "Epic" and, later, "Manor Green." The installation of the tunnel kilns in 1931 and 1932 enabled more applied glazes to be produced, and "Cottage Blue" was the first new colour for general domestic wares. Gilbert's tablewares were also available in Cottage Blue.

Some new domestic ranges were launched about 1935 in plain glazes with no surface decoration. "Gretna" (light and dark green) and "Farmstead" (cream and blue) were kitchen wares consisting primarily of harvest jugs and pitchers. Surprisingly, footwarmers were still being produced as late as December, 1938.

An important influence on some of the late 1930s designs was an Austrian refugee called Alice Teichner. She worked at Denby from 1938 to 1943, and influenced the design of ornamental wares and animal models in particular.

Collectors will come across various miniatures which were used as salesmen's trade samples during the 1920s.

Suggestions for Further Study

The Denby Pottery Company Ltd. welcomes visitors to their works on the Ripley Road (B6179), Denby. The extensive site houses a small museum of early wares, coffee-shop, visitors' shop, etc. Denby Pottery Co. Ltd., Denby, Derbyshire, DE5 8NX. Tel. 0773 743641.

Nottingham Castle Museum houses some Langley art wares, whilst others are on display at the Museum of Costume & Textiles, Castlegate, Nottingham.

Denby Pottery Co. Ltd. *The Denby Story—A Short History of Denby Pottery.*, Oct. 1990.

White, Eileen. "Retrospective Reflections." *"Tabletalk."*

Denby Wares from 'Electric Blue' range, l to r:-Two sizes of 'Swiss' jug (2 pint & half pint); 'Trumpet' vase, 280mm high; 'Goblet' candlestick; two sizes of owl jug.

Denby Selection of 'Danesby' rabbits, largest shown 205mm high; 5 sizes shown.

Denby 'Danesby' pitcher, 310mm high. (courtesy Reg Adams collection)

DENBY POTTERY

Types of Ware	Production	Quality	Availability
Ornamental wares	High	Good	Common

Marks

Impressed or printed:	DENBY CHEF WARE TRADE MARK (with cupboard doors)	c.1895 - c.1914
Impressed or printed:	BOURNE DENBY ENGLAND	c.1931 - c.1948
Printed (on unglazed base):	Danesby Ware	1924 - 1939

+/- Designer's name or mark
   (eg. "GILBERT", stamped, Donald Gilbert;
    or "AT", stamped, Alice Teichner's monogram)
+/- Range name (eg. "Regent Pastel," "Epic")
+/- "BOURNE DENBY ENGLAND" (as above)

Lower Dicker, Near Hailsham, Sussex
Boship Green Pottery (1821-1912)
Dicker Pottery (1843-1957)

Historical Background

Historical records of pottery production on Dicker Common exist from the thirteenth century, and examples of this early ware can be seen at nearby Michelham Priory which was established after the Norman conquest.

The pottery known locally as "Dickerware" was first produced by Benjamin William Bridges when he took over the Boship Green Pottery in 1890. This pottery had been in operation since 1821 and was situated across the road from the Dicker Pottery, established in 1843 by Uriah Clark and his nephew Abel.

Bridges' Dickerware was the first local attempt at art pottery production, for the Dicker Pottery opposite was still producing mainly utilitarian wares such as bowls, flowerpots, etc.

Bridges' early production of Dickerware resembled wares of the Torquay potteries and has often been confused with Watcombe greenwares through its petrol-like lustre. Early wares also included reproductions of medieval and Carolian designs, though these were clearly marked "Dicker Sussex" and not meant to deceive.

Uriah Clark died in 1904 and his nephew Abel then rented the Dicker Pottery from his widow. Uriah Clark had been a prominent citizen locally, running several undertakings besides the pottery. His brother also ran the local public house.

The Boship Green Pottery continued to prosper with Bridges' artwares, outgrowing the current premises. In 1912 the two potteries merged to form a new company known as Uriah Clark and Nephew Limited, which operated from the Dicker Pottery site.

The new company prospered until the First World War when the main workforce was called to national service, and wartime production was restricted to plain wares. Bridges died in 1916, and after the war art ware was again produced under the management of Sidney Harte.

Harte introduced many new glazes and increased the range of shapes listed in the firm's catalogue to nearly three hundred, with several sizes available for each shape. Advertisements of the time declared the firm to be "Manufacturers of Hand-Made Sussex Pottery."

The main production during the 1920s was of the famous iron lustre ware—a creation unique to the pottery. It is often compared to the Gloucestershire monastic pottery of Prinknash, though is actually quite different in form and composition.

Harte experimented widely, though one of his cold glaze effects which seemed to be a winner at the time actually proved to be disastrous—the clay body and glaze expanded and contracted at different rates causing the pots to leak and the glaze to flake off!

During the 1920s and 1930s, the pottery became a well known tourist attraction with regular summertime coach parties arriving from the nearby seaside resort of Eastbourne.

In 1935, a new circular trademark was registered and was employed as a paper label glued to the base of pots. It is ironic that the label glue adhered better than the disastrous cold glazes, since many labels still exist in situ!

At the outbreak of the Second World War, the pottery was requisitioned for use as a Royal Army Service Corps depot. In 1947, when the pottery was handed back, the company became a registered business and was known as Dicker Potteries Ltd.

Shortly afterward, the pottery was taken over by the ironmongery and hardware firm Wightman & Parish of Lewes, Sussex. This heralded the decline of the pottery, since the new owners never managed to establish a market for the wares then being produced. The pre-war style was out-of-date and competition was fierce for new styles. The company struggled on until 1956 when production ceased and the pottery closed. The property was sold a year later for development as a factory estate.

Keith and Fiona Richardson, who ran the pottery for Wightman and Parish, moved to the village of Laughton nearby and set up the Brickhurst Pottery where a few pots are still produced in old Sussex shapes.

Dicker Group of post-1940 wares,(tankard, 135mm high) (courtesy Reg Adams collection)

Dicker Group of black lustre wares (1918-1940), (tallest piece, 210mm high) (courtesy Reg Adams collection)

Products

Early wares exhibit the local red Wealden clay to good effect, being mainly greenglazed wares with minimal surface decoration of sgraffito motifs on simple shapes, the body being often revealed at the base of a piece. A lead glaze was used, which is revealed as an iridescence on surfaces.

Reproductions of medieval and sixteenth and seventeenth century wares were also made, and these mainly feature white slip-trailed motifs over a brown glaze with an overall covering of a thin tin glaze. The clay slip used was known as "Hewitt's white faience" and decoration often featured crude slip-trailed designs of faces and patterns, with or without a motto. Certainly there was some attempt to copy designs from the Franks Collection at the British Museum as well as being locally inventive.

The middle period (1918-1940) was more adventurous. Art pieces were made in a range of items, from miniature scent bottles to large jardinières on stands. Shapes were generally simple, with some attempt occasionally at a deco form. Surface decoration was almost non-existent save for a monochrome glaze, of which many experiments were made.

Harte's cold glazes stem from this period, and, in spite of the problems, many were quite impressive. An electric blue lustre was particularly outstanding and quite unlike anything produced elsewhere, and a speckled orange cadmium-like glaze was similar to one produced at the Pilkington Pottery, though with a matt finish.

The most important pieces produced during this period, however, were the well-known black lustrewares. These appeared in a great variety of forms and almost became the hallmark of the pottery. The black lustre was achieved via a glaze recipe containing manganese and sulphate of copper. This produced a fairly thick glaze which frequently obscured the impressed factory mark. The final effect was achieved through reduction firing.

Typical Sussex shapes were produced in black lustre (compare the Rye pottery) as well as some medieval styles, such as candlesticks. Miniature posy baskets, miniature vases with twisted handles (many miniatures were made), jugs, tankards, bowls, tea sets, toilet sets, etc. were made in this ware.

A noticeable variant to the black lustrewares was a splashed and mottled brown glaze speckled with aventurine which was supposed to simulate wood grain.

Wares from 1948 were noticeably different. Miniatures and Sussex shapes continued to be produced but glazes were different, though still monochrome. A turquoise glaze was effective as was an emerald green. Some wares decorated by Fiona Richardson stand out during this period.

Suggestions for Further Study

Lewes Museum, at Anne of Cleves House, Southover Street, Lewes, Sussex, has some examples of Dicker Ware.

Mainwaring-Baines, J. *Sussex Pottery* Fisher Publications, 1980; for a detailed account of the workings of the Dicker potteries.

East Sussex County Records, The Maltings, Lewes, Sussex. Papers and Sydney Harte's glaze recipes.

The author is indebted to Reg Adams for compiling the majority of this chapter from his wealth of knowledge on Dickerware.

Dicker Group of early wares (1890-1916). Tall green vase, 240mm high, incised mark "Dicker Ware 220"; Large yellow and brown planter, with legend "Robart Shaw 1692" (compare similar piece from Castle Hedingham Pottery); Small brown three-handled vase, with legend "1653 GR BV". (courtesy Reg Adams collection)

Dicker Group of middle period wares (1918-1940), showing vase with brown streaked aventurine glaze, electric blue lustre cold glaze and orange cold glaze (conical vase); large blue urn, 230mm high. (courtesy Reg Adams collection)

DICKER POTTERIES

Types of Ware	Production	Quality	Availability
pre-1940	Moderate	Poor to Good	Common

Marks

Incised:		Dicker Ware	1890 - 1912
Impressed: (upper or lower case)		DICKER SUSSEX	1890 - 1912
+/- shape number (incised)			
Impressed		THE DICKER U.C & N SUSSEX *(written as oval)*	1912 - 1916
Impressed		DICKER WARE SUSSEX	1918 - 1940

(NB If this mark is obscured, check for crystalline deposit on inside base of pot)

Paper label: (circular)		DICKER WARE MADE IN ENGLAND *(in black within black circle on white paper)*	1935 - 1940
Impressed		DICKER WARE MADE IN ENGLAND *(circular)*	1948 - 1956

(1815—present)

—saltglazed stoneware
—earthenwares
—faience
—terracotta
—bone-china
—silica stoneware
—flambé glazes

Doulton & Watts, Lambeth (1815-1853)
Doulton & Co.,* Lambeth (1853-1956)
Doulton & Co.,* Nile Street, Burslem, Staffordshire (1878-present)

(* became Doulton & Co.Ltd. in 1899 and Royal Doulton in 1901. The principal company is now Royal Doulton Tableware Ltd.)

Historical Background

Doulton began in 1815 when John Doulton and John Watts formed the firm of "Doulton & Watts" at Lambeth in South London for the production of brown saltglazed stoneware.

Wares produced were mainly drinking vessels, plaques and chemical jars, although drainpipes were manufactured as a single concern by John Doulton's brother Henry. When John Watts retired in 1853, Henry Doulton's drainpipe business merged with Doulton & Watts to form "Doulton & Company."

At the time, there were several potteries producing saltglazed stoneware in the Lambeth area and all made similar wares. It was not until much later that the production of art pottery commenced at Doulton.

After exhibiting some experimental stoneware pieces at the Paris Exhibition of 1867, and having had them well received, Henry Doulton engaged a student artist by the name of George Tinworth. Tinworth had studied with Robert Wallace Martin at the Lambeth School of Art, and his task at Doulton was to undertake stoneware plaque modelling and terracotta work to his own design, a medium in which he soon became renowned.

In 1871, another student from the Lambeth School of Art was employed as an artist, Hannah Barlow, who had previously spent a short time at the ill-fated Minton's Art Pottery Studio in Kensington. She was soon joined at Doulton by her brother, Arthur Barlow.

As the company expanded, more students were engaged for studio work, notably Hannah Barlow's sister Florence (in 1873) and Frank Butler. Arthur Barlow died in 1878, but by 1881 there were 36 artist-decorators and modellers employed at Doulton, which, together with many assistants, indicated the degree of expansion of the business at this time.

In 1878, Doulton & Co. purchased the Pinder Bourne & Company works at Burslem in Staffordshire for the production of pottery blanks which could subsequently be decorated at Lambeth. From 1884, painted china was also produced at the Burslem factory.

The 1870-90 period saw Doulton & Co. at its best in terms of artistry. The company had, after all, the cream of English decorators and modellers. In 1878, the company won the Grand Prix at the Paris Exhibition, and many similar honours have been awarded since that date.

In 1880, Mark V. Marshall joined as a decorator and modeller, having previously worked for the Martin Brothers. Whilst at Doulton he modelled many fine animal studies as well as decorative panels ("The Evangelists," particularly) and vases.

Doulton Selection of Lambeth wares. l to r:i) vase, 275mm high, by George Tinworth (monogram on body). ii) vase, 210mm high, 'Carrara Ware', by Edith Lupton. iii) vase, 287mm high, by Frank Butler.

83

Doulton Two vases designed by Frank Brangwyn, l to r: squat vase, with Royal Doulton lion and crown mark and painted mark 'BRANGWYN WARE', and incised shape no.7934; ovoid vase, 185mm high, Royal Doulton mark as above and printed 'BRANGWYN WARE' mark, and incised shape no.7973.

Doulton Selection of flambé wares. l to r:-i) vase, fish decoration, marked "Doulton Sung" "943". ii) vase, peacock decoration, marked "Doulton Sung", "Noke", "1394" and Arthur Eaton's initial. iii) tall vase, 240mm high, decoration of a John Dory fish, marked "2813", Arthur Eaton's initial, and Arthur Eaton's signature on body. iv) gourd-shaped vase, marked "Doulton flambé".

Doulton Two Lambeth wares. l to r:i) vase, 255mm high, pâte-sur-pâte decoration with three appliqué unglazed white clay medallions of heads, by Eliza Simmance, marked "Doulton Lambeth", dated 1884. ii) vase, 205mm high, early Silicon Ware on olive body, pâte-sur-pâte decoration with appliqué mosaic, marked "Doulton Lambeth Silicon", "OB" (olive body), c.1880.

Of the many women artists employed, Eliza Simmance became renowned for her art nouveau style flower and fruit paintings, and during the 1870s, Emily J. Edwards showed great artistry in her formal incised decorative style of simple geometric lines and foliage.

Technical achievements were also being made at Doulton during this time, and during he 1880s, William Rix played an important part in evolving coloured glazes which could withstand the great heat of the kilns which produced the saltglazed stoneware. The range of decorative colours was thus extended and the scene was set for further experimentation, culminating in some of the finest technical achievements in the history of ceramics. The Doulton workforce in 1898 numbered fifteen hundred, many of whom were women decorators.

During the late 1890s and early 1900s, Charles J. Noke (previously of the Worcester Porcelain Company) together with Doulton's art director at the time, John Slater, began to experiment with rouge flambé and sang-de-boeuf glazes on Chinese ceramics. The revival of early oriental glazes was technically difficult since a precise temperature control was required in the kiln.

In 1901, however, Cuthbert Bailey, assisting the team, was able to control the reducing process so that flambé wares could be produced not only with certainty but also in quantity. The work took three years before any pieces could be produced for sale. Bailey was assisted in his work by Bernard Moore who was later to produce his own distinctive style of flambé wares at his studio nearby.

The new flambé was first exhibited at the St. Louis Exhibition in the United States in 1904 and was an immediate success. Each piece was more or less unique, the streaks and mottles said to match the quality of the finest antique Chinese specimens.

Bailey and Noke also experimented with crystalline glazes, applying them to a high-temperature zinc-oxide ceramic body. Production was limited, however, as special kilns had to be used in order to maintain a steady temperature of 1400 degrees centigrade for several hours. A slow cooling was then induced to allow crystals to grow. Pieces consisted principally of small vases with a whitish background and little other decoration. Their production was discontinued in 1914, such that they now rank amongst the rarest items of Doulton pottery.

From 1907, the production of decorated saltglazed stoneware at Lambeth gradually diminished. It began to lose its appeal beacuse of its heavy appearance and colour. Doulton therefore decided on a different range of products, and so the "Lambeth Art Wares" were promoted.

Charles Noke, who had succeeded Slater as art director in 1914, was meanwhile experimenting further with flambé glazes by extending their colour range and by coating them with metallic oxides. He termed the products of this latter approach "Sung Ware" after the Chinese dynasty of the same name. It was immediately popular, was advertised extensively by Doulton during the early 1920s, and was much favoured by King George V and Queen Mary. Sung Ware was shown at the British Industrial Arts Exhibition of 1920 where it was advertised as "a revolution in ceramics."

During the 1920s, Charles Noke was joined in his experiments by Cecil Noke (his son) and Harry Nixon. Through research into high-temperature fired glazes, they produced "Chang Ware" in 1925. This had a heavier body than Sung Ware and was brightly coloured with streaked and thickly congealed glazes.

Charles Noke eventually retired in 1936, having gained much acclaim for Doulton in the field of art wares. His son Jack then took over as art director.

During the late 1920s and through the 1930s, the artist Frank Brangwyn (1867-1956) was designing pottery for Doulton. Brangwyn was once an assistant to William Morris, but produced items for Doulton under the Royal Doulton "Brangwynware" mark. He was knighted for services to art in 1941.

In 1956, production of saltglazed stoneware finally ceased and the pottery at Lambeth closed. Production of other Lambeth wares moved to Burslem where art pottery is still made today alongside the production of domestic wares.

Products

The early saltglazed stoneware was decorated in cobalt blue, but by the early 1870s green and brown colours were also used. Designs were often similar to German saltgalzed stoneware at first, but it was not long before Doulton's own individuality of style emerged. The Barlows were renowned for their animal, bird and leaf-scroll sgraffito designs, but decoration also included modelling, embossing and appliqué slip work such as beading. Artists and modellers often shared work on a piece.

Distinguished modellers included George Tinworth, who produced many animal groups and stoneware figurines, and Leslie Harradine, who later modelled some of Charles Noke's designs. Doulton figures were produced regularly from the end of the nineteenth century, with production increasing from 1913. The bone-china sets of named studies, such as "The Balloon Seller," are as popular today as ever. Charles Vyse was instrumental in designing many figure studies, and his "Return of Persephone," which was first exhibited in 1913, was a best seller.

Painting increased as a means of decoration at Doulton during the late 1880s through to the 1890s. The range of colours was increased, extending to yellows and pinks, and decoration included more surface texture work. Eliza Banks was renowned for her painting on stoneware using the pâte-sur-pâte method.

Besides the stoneware, Doulton produced many other types of ware including varieties of faience. Contemporary taste demanded less sombre decoration, and the faience consisted of bright colours painted on to a smooth pottery surface. It was fired a minimum of three times and the work was carried on separately at the Doulton Art Studios from 1874 by such artists as Minna Crawley, Mary Butterton, and Florence and Esther Lewis, who all painted classical floral designs on vases and wall plaques. The Lewises also painted landscapes and bird groups.

Between 1880 and 1912, Doulton & Co. were also producing "Silicon Ware." It was a smooth, hard form of stoneware which was liberally decorated by such artists as Elzia Simmance and Edith Lupton. Silicon Ware, a high quality production, was so successful that Doulton produced a whole series of other quality wares towards the turn of the century. These included "Carrara Ware," "Crown Lambeth Ware," "Impasto Ware," "Chiné Ware" and "Marqueterie Ware."

The Sung and Chang Wares exhibited much variety of colour and today are highly prized by collectors. Flambé wares revealed several characteristics, a typical example being "landscape flambé" in which pastoral and other scenes were set in a dark tone merging into a polished red background. Landscapes varied in decorative quality and were featured on a range of items from small ashtrays to large ovoid vases.

Many other types of ware were produced at Doulton during the latter part of the 19th century including delicately proportioned miniature vases, sporting and commemorative wares. Many models and figures were produced either in stoneware or earthenware; and flambé decorated animals, ranging from elephants to dogs and leaping fish, were modelled by Charles Noke.

In 1906, Noke introduced a "series ware" based on Ingoldsby's poem "The Jackdaw of Rheims." This was mildly successful and was produced mainly on vases, jugs, trays and other small pieces. Other series followed, including "Dickens Ware" (scenes from Dickens' novels), "Shakespeare" (scenes from Shakespeare's plays), "Bayeux Tapestry," "Old Coaching Scenes," etc. Designs were transfer-printed on to slip-cast pieces and the scenes were particularly effective on large jardinières which gave a larger expanse to view the designs. A lighter more porcelainous body was developed for series wares and mass-produced wares.

From 1933, when Noke introduced a range of Toby jugs, character jugs of all kinds became popular at Doulton.

A significant amount of tableware was produced, of course, and the opening of the new china works for domestic tableware in 1907 set the scene for Doulton's expansion into this sector of the business. A successful range was the "Bunnykins" nursery ware (1934) which has been reproduced today.

Doulton's venture into the art deco style was somewhat restrained, but during the 1930s a few deco ranges were produced. "Viridian" was a colourful range of vases and bowls; and, although the tablewares have not been closely examined in this survey, certain tableware lines are worth noting.

"Radio," launched in 1935, was a banded deco pattern for tableware which was advertised as being "fragile in motif as century old Chintz." The "Casino" shape, introduced about 1932, was characterised by semicircular lids to tea and coffee pots and also to tureens (which bore a flattened circular shape). Casino was decorated with simple monochrome bands such as green or orange. Doulton's only stark contribution to the art deco style was "De Luxe" (1932) which featured a black and platinum coloured band diagonally separating a green zone of colour from a white zone.

Brangwynware was in some ways a reaction against art deco. Its restrained rounded shapes were designed to appear hand-thrown, whilst the colourful fruit and floral motifs on cream-yellow grounds were depicted in softened outline.

Doulton Moulded figure, 200mm high, unglazed and undecorated.   **Doulton** Lemonade beakers, 150mm high, by Eliza Simmance.

Doulton Flambé models by C.J. Noke; leaping fish, 255mm high.

Survey of the more familiar wares:

All wares 1875-1890—characterised by rich colourings, modelling, carving, gilding, etc.

All wares 1890-1910—less carving; marbled effects, glaze effects; new art styles.

Brangwynware (from 1930)—designed by Frank Brangwyn; several patterns such as "Harvest" in mainly pastel pink and green colours on beige grounds: common.

Carrara Ware (1887-1896)—white marble-like stoneware usually decorated in pastel colours: scarce.

Chang Ware (c.1927)—by Charles Noke; thick bodied ware with thick, streaked glazes and appliqué figures in flambé colours; mainly vases: rare.

Character Wares (from c.1906)—by Charles Noke; Toby jugs, etc.

ChinéWare (1886-1914)—lace patterns impressed on stoneware prior to firing; also known as Slater's Patent: common.

Copper Lustre Ware or Copper Wares (1887-1912)—mainly jugs and candlesticks imitating copper.

Crown Lambeth Ware (1892-1900)—fine textured earthenware with a real ivory tint: rare.

Crystalline glazes (c.1904-1914)—by Cuthbert Bailey: scarce to rare.

Dickens Ware (from c.1906)—scenes from Dickens' plays; transfer printed: uncommon.

Holbein Ware (1895-1914)—by Charles Noke; portraits of people in low relief by Walter Nunn and other artists: uncommon.

Imitation Leather Wares (1890-1910)—stoneware jugs and bottles imitating leather.

Impasto Ware (1879-1906)—coloured slip decorated ware; various styles: common.

Natural Foliage Ware (1886-1936)—created by pressing real leaves into the wet clay, removing to expose impression, and painting in brown and orange colours; mostly vases and jardinières: common.

Marqueterie Ware (1886-1906)—a ware in which the body of the pot was built up with a mosaic of coloured clays, similar to marquetry work. This ware was rarely produced since the process involved was technically difficult, necessitating many firings in the kiln: rare.

Morrisian Ware (1901-1924)—transfer-prints of dancers or curious figures such as golfers in classical costume: scarce.

Persian Ware (1884-1900)—influenced by William De Morgan; tiles and panels, mostly painted in blue, green and orange; (revived from 1919 to 1922 for vases, bowls and plaques): all rare.

Rembrandt Ware (1898-1914)—by Charles Noke; landscapes (some-times with children or other figures) in monotones of brown, orange or blue; mainly vases and jardinières decorated by Arthur Eaton and Walter Nunn: scarce.

Sang-de-boeuf and Rouge Flambé glazes (from 1890)—by Charles Noke; general flambé made through to the 1920's and revived during the 1970s: uncommon.

Silicon Ware (1880-1912)—a hard, smooth, high-fired stoneware; jardinières, vases and flower-pots; easily recognised by its smooth beige-coloured body; usually marked; common.

Sung Ware (1907-1925)—by Charles Noke; splashed and mottled effects in flambé colours; mainly vases: scarce.

Titanian Ware (1914-1929)—transfer-printed bird-of-paradise motif or Egyptian scene (after 1922) on tablewares (eg. plates, bowls) in shades of royal blue: common. Also, hand-painted birds in landscapes or figures, in a soft, eggshell-like glaze by artists such as Harry Allen and Edward Raby: scarce.

Velluma Ware (c.1912-1914)—transfer-printed decorations painted with soft colours of landscapes and figures in landscapes: rare.

Doulton Pair of vases, 147mm high, c.1929.

Doulton Vase by Hannah Barlow.

Doulton Leaf impressed vase, 150 mm high, 'Natural Foliage Ware', brown and orange colouration.

Doulton Pomander, 120mm high, blue streaked glaze, marked "Royal Doulton England", "CA".

Doulton Vase, 425mm high, by Mark V. Marshall; green, blue and brown decoration on a cream ground.

Doulton Vase by Frank C. Pope.

Doulton Royal Doulton plate, 254mm diam.

Doulton Jardinière, 'Rembrandt Ware', blue monochrome decoration.

Doulton Gladioli bowl and cover, 85mm high, by Edith Lupton, marked
"Doulton Lambeth", dated 1884.

Doulton Selection of wares.

Doulton 'Natural foliage' jardinières. l to r:i) 290mm diam., impressd elm leaves, marked "Royal Doulton England", "2109". ii) 230mm diam., impressed chestnut leaves, marked "Royal Doulton England", "EW", "2109".

Doulton Plate, 260mm diam., designed by Frank Brangwyn, marked "D5033".

Doulton Vase, 200mm high, tube-line decoration, marked "Royal Doulton England", "BN".

Doulton Jardinière, 320mm diam., sgraffito decoration of cows in a landscape by Hannah Barlow.

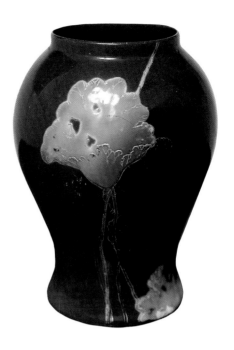

Doulton Jug, 200mm high, with incised marks "BN" and "Art Union of London", made at Lambeth, c.1900.

Doulton Vase, 220mm high, enamelled decoration with flambé glaze on porcelainous body.

Doulton Jardinière, 230mm high, 'Silicon Ware', brown and cream decoration.

Collecting Doulton Pottery

Doulton were by far the largest producers of art pottery in Britain. They built up a strong reputation for quality and artistry, such that although the range of products was extensive, each piece bears a characteristic that indicates it was made at Doulton. With few exceptions one can instinctively recognise a Doulton ware, whatever the period, and, since nearly all the wares were marked, the collector should have little trouble with identification.

The familiar "Royal Doulton" mark which was used after 1902 poses a problem, however. Since it is still used today, closer examination is sometimes necessary to discern a period of manufacture. If an identifiable artist's mark or year is present, then there is little difficulty.

The collector should be particularly wary of modern reproductions of earlier styles. Doulton have reproduced flambé glazes on wares closely resembling those of the 1920s. The only difference is often the freshness of appearance of the modern piece and the accompaniment of a title such as "Veined Flambé." The modern reproductions are nonetheless high quality products and often fairly expensive to order, but their value must be considerably less than their earlier, rarer counterparts.

Many Doulton antique wares sell at a premium, in spite of generally high outputs. Their attractiveness and high quality, together with ready availability to collectors, endorse this fact. There are also several rare, elusive Doulton wares which collectors will enjoy seeking out.

Doulton was able to keep pace over the years with public demand and taste, and the vast technical and artistic resources the company deployed has ensured that the collector is presented today with a very wide range of pieces from which to form a worthwhile and rewarding collection.

Summary of Principal Decorators

Decorator/Artist	At Doulton	Typical Work
Eliza Banks	c.1876-c.1884	carved and foliate decoration
Arthur Barlow	1871-1876	leaf scroll decoration
Hannah B. Barlow	1871-1913	sgraffito animal designs
Florence E. Barlow	1873-1909	painted birds and water fowl
Wilmot Brown	1879-1930	decorated flambé; landscape flambé
Frank A. Butler	1872-1911	foliate and art nouveau designs
Mary Butterton	c.1874-c.1894	flower painting (Lambeth)
Mary Capes	c.1876-c.1883	flower painting (Lambeth)
Minna Crawley	c.1877-c.1885	flower painting and Persian styles (Lambeth)
Arthur Eaton	1889-1932	decorated flambé
Emily J. Edwards	c.1872-c.1876	carved and foliate decoration
Louisa E. Edwards	c.1873-c.1890	carved and foliate decoration
John Eyre	c.1884-c.1897	painted figures (Lambeth)
William Hodkinson	1880-1920	decorated flambé
Francis Lee	c.1875-c.1890	pâte-sur-pâte and foliate decoration
Esther Lewis	c.1878-c.1895	painted figures in landscapes; mostly plates (Lambeth)
Florence Lewis	c.1875-c.1897	painted flowers and birds on large vases; Carrara Ware (Lambeth)
Edith Lupton	c.1875-c.1896	pâte-sur-pâte and foliate decoration
John Henry McLellan	c.1880-c.1910	tiles, murals, large vases and chargers with figures (Lambeth)
Mary Mitchell	c.1874-c.1887	children
Frederick Moore	1920-1957	decorated flambé
Harry Nixon	1900-c.1946	decorated flambé
William Parker	c.1879-c.1884	intricate carving of foliate decoration
Edith Rogers	c.1881-c.1884	intricate carving of foliate decoration
William Rowe	c.1925	slip-cast and moulded figures, vases, plaques and plates
Eliza Simmance	1873-1928	pâte-sur-pâte flowers; foliate decoration
Linnie Watt	c.1876-c.1886	painted figures in landscapes; mostly plates (Lambeth)
Charles Yeomans	1883-1936 & 1939-1951	decorated flambé; landscape flambé

Some of the Principal Modellers

Modeller	At Doulton	Typical Work
Harry Barnard	c.1880-c.1890	dragons and grotesques
John Broad	1873-1919	stoneware figures (1912-1914), eg. "The Bather"); fountains and busts
Richard Garbe (b.1876;d.1957)	c.1931-c.1932	vases, busts, figures
Arthur Leslie Harradine	1902-1914	Dickens characters; stoneware spirit flasks of politicians; moulded figures
Mark V. Marshall	c.1876-c.1912	dragons and grotesques; art nouveau animal studies; terracotta panels with religious scenes; saltglazed stoneware figures; vases and jugs in floriate designs
George Tinworth	1866-1913	

Some of the Principal Designers & Artist/Designers

Designer	At Doulton	Typical Work
Frank A. Butler	1871-1911	vases, jugs; floriate designs
Frank Brangwyn	(from late 1920s)	tableware, vases, lamp-bases, candlesticks, plaques, etc.
Joan Cowper	1937-1939	vases, bowls (saltglazed and unglazed)
Vera Huggins	1923-1950	saltglazed stoneware pots from 1933-1935
J.H. Mott	c.1910-1929	crystalline and lustre glazes (one-time art director at Lambeth)
Charles J. Noke	1895-1936	crystalline, sang-de-boeuf, flambé glazes; face jugs (c.1920) etc.
Francis C. Pope	1880-1923	slip-cast wares; gourd shapes
Edward Raby	c.1901-1929	enamel colours, eg. Titanian Ware
Harry Simeon	1894-1936	figures, vases, plates; Persian Ware; Toby series wares
John Slater	1887-1914	Art Director; Slater's Patent; Chiné ware, etc.
Margaret E. Thompson	1911-1925	art nouveau female figures on vases, plaques
Charles Vyse	1896-1919	figures, eg. "The Return of Persephone."

Suggestions for Further Study

Eyles, Desmond. *Royal Doulton 1815-1965.* Hutchinson, 1965.

Gosse, Edmund. *Sir Henry Doulton;* biography edited by Desmond Eyles; Hutchinson, 1970.

Eyles, Desmond. *The Doulton Lambeth Wares.* Hutchinson, 1975.

Eyles, Desmond and Richard Dennis. *Royal Doulton Figures Produced at Burslem 1890-1978.* Royal Doulton Tableware, 1978 (see Bibliography for new edition).

Atterbury, Paul and Louise Irvine. *The Royal Doulton Story.* Royal Doulton Tableware Ltd., 1979.

Eyles, Desmond. *The Doulton Burslem Wares.* London: Barrie & Jenkins, 1980.

Irvine, Louise. *Royal Doulton Series Ware.* Richard Dennis, Vol.1 1980, Vol.2 1984, Vol.3 1986, Vol.4 1988.

Irvine, Louise. *Royal Doulton Figures.* Richard Dennis, 1981.

Lukins, Jocelyn. *Doulton Flambé Animals.* pub. privately, 1981.

Pearson, Kevin. *The Doulton Figure Collectors' Handbook.* Kevin Francis, 1986, 1988.

Yeman, Mick. *The Lyle Price Guide to Doulton.* Lyle Publications, 1987.

Rose, Peter. *George Tinworth.* Richard Dennis, 1990.

"Catalogue of an Exhibition of Doulton Stoneware & Terracotta 1870-1925," Part 1; pub. Richard Dennis, 1971.

Edwards, Rhoda. *Doulton Ware & Products of Other British Potteries, the Woolley Collection including 'Lambeth Stoneware';* catalogue, London: London Borough of Lambeth, Directorate of Amenity Services, 1973.

"Doulton Pottery from the Lambeth & Burslem Studios 1873-1939," Part 2, Richard Dennis, 1975.

Rose, Peter. *"Hannah Barlow,"* catalogue of an exhibition at Christie's, South Kensington, Richard Dennis, 1985.

Witley, W.T. "The Arts & Industries of To-day." *The Art Journal,* 1898.

Doulton Specimen mark, showing monogram of Eliza Simmance.

Doulton Specimen mark, showing initials of Mark V. Marshall.

DOULTON

Types of Ware	Production	Quality	Availability
Saltglazed stoneware	Very High	Fair to Very Good	Abundant
Named wares, eg. 'Carrara'	Low to High	Good to Excellent	As per list
Earthenware	Moderate to High	Good to Excellent	Common

Marks

Until 1882, each example of artistic stoneware produced at Doulton was original and unique. From 1882, some designs were produced in series by assistants. These were marked 'X' followed by a number.
Almost all Doulton wares were marked, especially by the artists who decorated them. Two albums of artists' marks from 1871 to 1881 were presented to Henry Doulton by the artists themselves.

Impressed	DOULTON LAMBETH	1853 - c.1900
	Above mark within oval: within oval + year:	c.1869 - 1872 1872 - 1879
	Above mark written circular or within a circle +/- year:	c.1877 - 1880
	Above mark within rosette: + 'England' impressed:	c.1879 - 1902 1891 - 1902
	DOULTON LAMBETH ENGLAND	1891 - c.1902

+/- name of ware
+/- year
+/- artist's mark
+/- 'ART UNION OF LONDON'

Impressed	ROYAL DOULTON ENGLAND (written circular, +/- surmounted by a crown and lion)	1902 - c.1922
	ROYAL DOULTON ENGLAND (within larger circle surrounded by lion only)	c.1922 - 1956
	ROYAL DOULTON LAMBETH ENGLAND (written vertically and semi oval)	c.1912 - 1956

+/- name of ware
+/- artist's mark
+/- year
(NB The impressed marks 'IVORY' and 'OLIVE' relate to the colour of the body used.)

Artists' Marks

These are many and varied. A selection of the more important monograms are given below:-

Eliza S Banks		Agnete Hoy	
Arthur B Barlow		Vera Huggins	
Florence E Barlow		Edith D Lupton	
Hannah B Barlow		Mark V Marshall	
John Broad		Frank C Pope	
Frank A Butler		William Rowe	
Mary Capes		Harry Simeon	
Minna L Crawley (on faience)		Eliza Simmance	
Emily J Edwards		Margaret E Thomspon	
Arthur Leslie Harradine		George Tinworth	

(NB. The signature of Arthur Eaton on flambé wares often appears as part of the decoration)

Airth, Dunmore, Stirlingshire

Historical Background

Peter Gardner (1834-1902) took over the tenancy of a pottery at Dunmore Moss on the death of his potter father, John Gardner (1798-1866). The pottery was originally established by Peter Gardner's grandfather, also Peter Gardner, during the early part of the 19th. century. It was Peter Gardner junior, however, who produced the range of ornamental wares known as Dunmore Ware, and who was probably running the pottery during his father's illness.

The pottery was situated close to the River Forth on a fairly desolate stretch of moorland, four miles from Larbert railway-station. The land was owned by the Earl & Countess of Dunmore Ware, who were influential in the promotion of the pottery's wares.

Using the local red clay, supplemented by white clays exported from Devon and Cornwall, Peter Gardner transformed the previously domestic output to one of art pottery in a variety of sytles. The Earl and Countess patronized the pottery, encouraging interest from London dealers and the nobility. In 1871, Dunmore Ware gained national recognition when the Prince of Wales, Prince Albert Edward, visited the pottery.

A showroom was established at the pottery for visitors, but wares were also retailed in Edinburgh, Glasgow and elsewhere. Pieces are recorded as having been sold from the London premises of C. Hindley & Sons in Oxford Street in 1880, and there are records of Dunmore Ware having been exhibited widely.

The Alloa Journal remarked in 1876 that "Mr. Gardner, whose productions have rendered Dunmore to be known throughout the globe, has already sold the whole of his pottery ware at the Philadelphia Exhibition...Orders are pouring in and no doubt Mr. Gardner's world-wide reputation is envied by his brothers in trade." This latter remark may be particularly pointed at the large Alloa pottery of W. & J. A. Bailey, who were known to be envious of Gardner's success.

The following year, James Paton, the curator of Glasgow Museums and Art Gallery, made a far-sighted purchase of over a hundred pieces of Dunmore Ware, direct from Peter Gardner.

Dunmore Pair of vases, 204mm high, impressed mark "DUNMORE" on side.

Dunmore Ware earned Gardner a medal in 1886 at an exhibition in Edinburgh, which also featured wares from Linthorpe, Doulton and Burmantofts. Queen Victoria visited this exhibition and is known to have purchased several Dunmore pieces.

Dunmore Ware was also exhibited at the Glasgow International Exhibition of 1888, which James Paton reviewed for the Glasgow Herald newspaper, describing Dunmore as "an excellent example of what can be done by judicious taste to give really artistic decoration by inexpensive processes to cheap materials."

The demand for Dunmore Ware, spurred on by the royal patronage, placed an increasing burden on production. A catalogue of about 1886 gives an insight into the production processes, by describing a visit to the pottery by an unknown person, guided round by someone connected with the pottery. The account describes a potter seated at his wheel, which is turned and regulated by a woman. A lathe-turner is mentioned, who finishes the pots ("a tall, fine looking, old man"), and a girl, who makes spouts and handles, etc. ("up to 288 spouts in a day")! The account explains that after biscuit firing, wares are decorated by "ladies who wish to paint upon them." The number of paintresses is not given, but was probably at least three. "A cheery old man" was employed as a glaze-dipper, and stated to be the father of the guide giving the tour. The kiln is mentioned, which was a brick-built bottle type, and the tour ended at the showroom, where various pieces are described, such as a large bronze-green vase "in the new crackled ware."

Peter Gardner died in 1902, and a former employee, Thomas Harrison, returned to take over the tenancy in 1904. Harrison operated the business as the Dunmore Pottery Company until 1912, when he died. The pottery dwindled on, managed by his widow, until about 1917, when the land was sold. The catalogue of the *Sales of Dunmore Park Lands* on 20th. September, 1917, itemises the Dunmore Pottery as comprising "a six-bedroom house, two cottages, stable, barn, kilns, potter's shop, etc.." The house remains, currently run as a hotel.

Products

Prior to 1866, the pottery produced mainly garden wares and brown-glazed domestic wares using a red clay body. Peter Gardner introduced new shapes and the use of richly coloured glazes, such as orange, crimson, yellow, brown, various shades of blue and sea-green. A turquoise glaze and a dark blue "mazzarine" glaze were thought particularly noteworthy. Running glazes were a hallmark of the Dunmore Wares, frequently striated, and usually tones of a single colour.

Articles ranged from large, classical vases (in the Grecian style) and classical jugs (featuring figures of the Bacchanal) to models of dogs, fish, crabs and hens. Sometimes these latter took the form of wall-vases, and animal forms featured regularly in functional items, such as teapots, tazzas and fern vases (eg. "The Dunmore Toad"). Much pottery was moulded, and a huge variety of designs was created, from the simply traditional to the bizarre. Umbrella stands, candlesticks, tea-sets, medallions and even garden seats, were amongst the wide range of articles produced.

Relief moulding was commonly employed on articles such as plates, baskets and vases, patterns often being figures or foliage. Leaf-shaped plates were also produced. Some pierced work was undertaken, as shown on a stock item referred to as "The Lady Dunmore Bowl," and imitation wicker-baskets were made, using fine strands of clay squeezed through a special box.

Busts and figures were less commonly produced, but included busts of personalities, such as Robert Burns, Sir Walter Scott and General Gordon. Tiles were also produced, often heavily embossed with bird, animal and floral subjects depicted in rich colours.

Suggestions for Further Study

Glasgow Museum & Art Gallery, Kelvingrove, Glasgow, houses a collection of Dunmore Ware (the Burrell Collection).

Huntly House Museum, 124, Canongate, Edinburgh, houses a large collection of Dunmore Ware, together with the "Dunmore Room," a room decorated with Dunmore tiles.

Catalogue by Robin Hill of an exhibition of Dunmore Pottery at The Kippen Gallery, 1979. (unpublished)

Morrison, Oonagh. 'Dunmore—An Old Pottery in the Carse of Stirling.' *Scotland's Magazine,* August, 1966.

Olding, Simon & Zoe Capernaros. 'A Remarkable Dunmore Plague.' *Scottish Pottery Historical Review* (SPHR) 7, 1982.

Kinghorn, Jonathan. 'Scottish Ceramics at Glasgow's International Exhibition of 1888.' *SPHR* 12, 1987/88.

The author is indebted to Katherine Dickson of the Scottish Pottery Society for her generosity in making available extensive research material on the Dunmore Pottery.

DUNMORE POTTERY			
Types of Ware	**Production**	**Quality**	**Availability**
Dunmore Ware	Moderate	Good	Uncommon
Marks			
Impressed		DUNMORE (within POTTERY double circle) PETER GARDNER + (written circular)	1866 - 1902
+/- "PETER GARDNER", impressed (NB. the mispelled mark "DUNMOR" has been noted)			
Impressed		DUNMORE POTTERY CO	1903 - 1911

Sir Edmund Elton, artist/potter (1846-1920), Sunflower Pottery, Clevedon Court, Clevedon, Avon.

Historical Background

In 1883, upon succeeding to the title of eighth baronet, Sir Edmund Harry Elton and his wife took up residence at the family home of Clevedon Court, a splendid manor house dating from the 14th century and situated near the Bristol Channel in Somerset (now Avon).

Sir Edmund had become interested in pottery making about the year 1880, and, being of a highly inventive nature, decided to learn all he could about ceramic art and chemistry. By 1884, after many exhausting attempts at kiln design, glaze recipes and clay firings, he believed he had developed a "sound and marketable ware," such that he was able, with the help of two servant assistants (George Masters and Charlie Neads) to establish his "Sunflower Pottery" in the grounds of Clevedon Court.

Sir Edmund had a firm belief in the value of the crafts. He frequently showed pieces at international exhibitions, but never undertook any serious business venture for his pottery, and, although pieces were sold at prestigious establishments such as Tiffanys, New York, many were given away as presents to friends, relations and estate workers.

Until 1902, the output of the Sunflower Pottery consisted entirely of slip-decorated ornamental earthenware. From 1902, Sir Edmund began experimenting with liquid gold and platinum, producing metallic glazes which were coated onto wares over a coloured primary glaze, and which crazed during firing. This "craquèle-ware," as Sir Edmund called it, was not only a major technical achievement, but was also an international success.

Sir Edmund also produced items of Church furniture in Elton ware, not only in slip-ware but also in crackle ware. These ecclesiastical items are still to be found in some churches today, and consist mostly of candlesticks, sanctuary crosses and plaques depicting religious subjects.

Sir Edmund died in 1920, and his son, Sir Ambrose Elton, tried to carry on the pottery. In 1921, he approached the potter William Fishley Holland who agreed to come to Clevedon and throw pots to Sir Ambrose's design on one day a week, and using the rest of the time for his own pottery production in one of the Court's stables (ref. "Fremington Pottery.")

However, George Masters (Sir Edmund's premier assistant) died in 1921, and without his knowledge, Sir Ambrose found it difficult to continue. The demand for Elton Ware's particular style had also fallen off and William Fishley Holland recommended not to continue production. The pottery therefore closed in 1922.

Elton Group of slip wares. (tall vase, centre, 340mm high).

Elton Selection of unusual shapes. l to r:—early crude bulb vase; teapot with trumpet handle; candlestick.

Elton Two teapots, (left, 190mm high).

Elton Sir Edmund Elton, George Masters and Charlie Neads at the Sunflower Pottery.

Elton Group of crackle wares, gold and platinum crackle. (tall vase, centre, 230mm high).

Elton 3 tygs. l to r:—i) tyg, 160mm high, sunflower decoration with gargoyle-like heads on handles. ii) commemorative tyg in gold crackle. iii) tyg, inscribed "Eureka" with sunflower on one panel, and tulips on two further panels (commemorating the discovery of a gold field in South Africa).

Elton Vase, 215mm high, combined gold crackle and slip decoration.

Elton Large vase, 440mm high, with kingfisher and hedge-parsley decoration.

Elton Group of gold crackle wares, tallest 280mm high.

Products

Wares were mostly vases and jugs, but there were also tygs (three-handled loving cups), teapots (of unusual form), ewers, bowls (scarce), jars, candlesticks, plates (scarce), jardinières (scarce) and plaques (scarce).

Shapes were either simple or highly complex, and relief moulding or bossing were common decorative devices employed. Much use was made of twisted handles to jugs and vases, and some pieces exhibited quite complex structures with several twisted handles. Cutaway decoration was also employed to a certain extent, and some vases, for example, exhibited a thick lattice work at their rims.

The most common form of decoration was stylised floral motifs, which were modelled from clay slips and applied in relief. The sunflower was a favourite subject, each flower head containing individually modelled seeds which Sir Edmund often scattered about a piece or formed as geometrically placed groups of three, five or seven raised dots.

The applied slip decoration might or might not be accompanied by sgraffito decoration, which was used as a low relief embellishment very much in the background. Sgraffito was frequently used to depict outlines of grass or coral, against which the floral motifs could be applied, though it was also used as part of the floral motifs themselves.

Combined use of sgraffito, applied slip and bossing gave considerable depth to pieces, which was further enhanced by light on dark colour combinations and a high gloss glaze. Sir Edmund was clearly able to convey many of his talents as a watercolourist to the ceramic medium, and any observer of his slipwares will find that pieces often require more than an instant appreciation, because of the depth of decoration.

The earliest wares produced (prior to 1885) were crude in shape and decoration. They were characterised by a thin tin glaze over sgraffito and applied slip decoration in exaggerated relief. Shapes resembled the early English slipware tradition, and some early decorative devices were also employed, such as piecrust rims. The colour palette was also somewhat different from later wares. Early wares tended to have bolder, brighter colour combinations, such as yellow on black or pink or green on pale blue.

From about 1885, wares became more refined. Colours became more subdued with a strong predominance in the blue/brown/green range. Red was a difficult colour for the pottery to produce and so was used sparingly. Some all-over red wares were produced, however, though many of these were early wares. All later slipwares were characterised by a high gloss glaze.

Quality of potting was generally poor since it was necessary to throw the red clay body thickly, and this made large wares extremely heavy in weight. Shapes became more symmetrical over time, however, though never lighter in weight. Bowls were only scarcely produced, partly because of this, and because they did not present as suitable an area to show off external decoration as did, for example, vases.

Elton A selection of slip wares.

Elton A selection of slip wares.

Elton Ecclesiastical plaque, 280mm high, of David the Good Shepherd (after Donatello).

In design, Sir Edmund was influenced by many styles. Some wares were distinctly South American in style, with Pre-Columbian shapes and human grotesques. Others were influenced by Mediterranean, African and Oriental styes. Exotic handles, contorted spouts, squashed rims and ovoid or gourd-shaped bodies were common expressions of these many influences.

Many of the floral designs were drawn from specimens in Sir Edmund's own greenhouses. Cattleya, poinsettia, fuchsia, carnation and various types of rose were just a small part of his subject material. A common decorative characteristic was to portray a flower, buds, stem and leaves as a single sprig, with the leaves being given scant attention. The decoration might be completed by scattered sunflower seeds or a butterfly, for example. Most applied decoration was executed against a background of marbled slip, created by trickling coloured slips over a piece while held upside down.

Occasionally a floral motif might take the form of a decorative medallion or be reduced to an almost abstract representation. Sir Edmund was able to adapt his designs readily to the shape of a piece, creating a symmetry which only the combination of artist and engineer could accomplish.

Motifs other than floral subjects were less commonly employed, although birds and lizards, for example, were depicted. Animal and fish subjects were more likely to be employed as part of the shape of a piece (such as a fish-mouth jug). Mask-head decoration was also used, which, when applied to the lips of tygs, often resembled gargoyles.

The cracklewares generally featured less surface decoration, relying more on the lustrous effect of the metallic glazes. Sometimes the gold crackle would appear as a copper colour, the firing producing subtle variants. Likewise, the platinum crackle could take on a silvery appearance. All the crackle wares exhibited a primary glaze colour through the metallic craze. This colour was usually yellow, green or blue. Occasionally the crackle would be a double crackle (crackle within crackle) which might also be crystalline in appearance, yielding a particularly sparkling effect.

The most spectacular wares were probably the crackle and slipware combinations, of which less were produced than straight crackle wares. These combined wares were unique in their decorative form, often employing all the features of Sir Edmund's decoration toolkit.

Some commemorative items were made including tankards and jars commemorating Kitchener, Queen Victoria's Golden Jubilee (1887), the Coronation of Edward VII (1902), the Coronation of George V (1911), and wares celebrating the end of the First World War (inscribed "Pax 1918"). There were also some special commissions.

After 1920, Sir Ambrose completed Sir Edmund's unfinished pieces and also produced wares to his own designs. Wares of this period were also made by Fishley Holland, though these were generally very simple in shape (eg. bowls) and devoid of embellishment.

Suggestions for Further Study

See the spectacular collection at Clevedon Court, open through the National Trust. The collection is in the Tea-Room, and the Court is situated close to Junction 20 of the M5 motorway.

Other collections are held at The Victoria Art Gallery, Bath; the Reference Library and Guildhall, Bath; Somerset County Museum, Taunton Castle, Taunton; Exeter Museum; and Reading Museum. Sir Edmund Elton made several bequests to Museums throughout the country.

The Clock Tower in Clevedon's "Triangle" (the centre of the old village) contains panels of Elton Ware, and Tickenham Church nearby (permission to visit required) boasts many examples of Elton ecclesiastical ware, including altar columns.

Haslam, Malcolm. *The Story of Sir Edmund Elton.* Richard Dennis, 1989.

Holland, William Fishley. *"Fifty Years a Potter."* Pottery Quarterly, 1958.

Monkhouse, Cosmo. *"Elton Ware." The Magazine of Art,* 1882.

Ruck, Pamela. "A Victorian Squire & His Eccentric Pottery." *Art & Antiques,* March 27, 1976.

Elton, Julia. "Eltonware at Clevedon Court." *National Trust Magazine,* 1980.

Bartlett, John. "Elton Ware Rediscovered." *Antique Collector Magazine,* July, 1985.

Bartlett, John. "Elton Ware." *Bristol Illustrated Magazine,* Nov. 1986.

Bartlett, John. "Elton Ware—The Genius of Sir Edmund Elton, Potter-Baronet." *Antique Collectors' Club* 21(9), Feb. 1987.

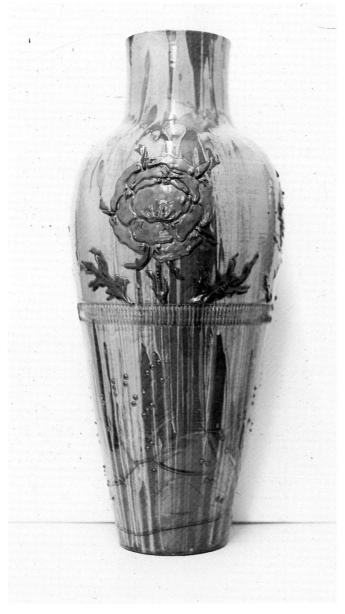

Elton Early vase, 120mm high, marked "Elton Clevedon,1881".

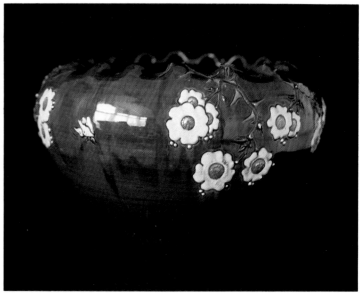

Elton Large vase, 560mm high. (courtesy Hoddell Pritchard Salerooms)

Elton Jardinière, 200mm high, with applied slip decoration of butterflies, flowers, roots and sgraffito decorated grass, dated 1884.

Elton Vase, 255mm high, c. 1921.

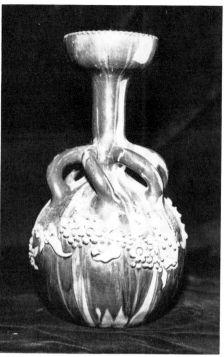

Elton Vase, 212mm high, floral motif on deep blue

Elton Jug, 200mm high, with applied decoration of a carnation flower, and sgraffito decoration of grass.

ELTON WARE

Types of Ware	Production	Quality	Availability
Slipware prior to 1885	Low	Poor to Good	Rare
Slipware post-1885	Moderate	Good to Very Good	Uncommon to Scarce
Crackle wares	Low	Good to Excellent	Scarce
Combined slip and metallic glazes	Very Low	Very Good to Excellent	Rare
Commemoratives	Low	Poor to Good	Scarce
Ecclesiastical	Low	Poor to Very Good	Scarce to Rare

Marks

Generally all pieces were marked. The presence of the year or date is rare. Marks prior to 1885 were varied. A single painted sunflower has been noted on a vase without the name Elton, for example. From 1920 to 1922, the signature "Elton" was accompanied by a cross, signifying pieces decorated after Sir Edmund Elton's death.

On the base of each piece were usually unglazed marks left by the clay supports in the kiln. These reveal the red earthenware body below the glaze. Pieces with a totally unglazed base were probably products of Sir Edmund's very early kilns, whilst pieces with a totally flat glazed base (i.e. no kiln support marks) were probably very late wares from Fishley Holland's involvement. Pieces with a white earthenware body are extremely rare, and represent Sir Edmund's experiments using other than local clay materials, such as a white ball-clay.

Pieces comprising more than one part, such as a vase and cover, were usually marked with a matching letter or number, either painted or on a paper label.

Painted: (in black or turquoise)	E.H. Elton Clevedon	1881 - 1884
(plus variants) +/- year	Elton Clevedon	1881 - 1884
Incised:	E	1881 - 1884
Impressed:	.. ELTON ..	1881 - 1884
Painted signature: (in black or turquoise)	Elton	1884 - 1920
(generally on smaller pieces) +/- year (rare)	E (also written as a Greek "E")	1884 - 1920
Painted:	Elton (plus cross)	1920 - 1922

Elton Large vase, gold crackle, with appliqué parrots. (courtesy Hoddell Pritchard Salerooms).

Bridgend Road, Ewenny, Bridgend, South Wales

Historical Background

A biblical inscription in old Welsh beside the wheel in the Ewenny Pottery translates as "Hath not the potter power over the clay, of the same lump to make one vessel unto honour, and another unto dishonour?" (Romans, 9.21) whilst over the door another reads "Better a craft than gold."

Such epithets give an insight into some of the country pottery traditions which Bernard Leach sought to revive and teach at St. Ives.

Ewenny had been famous for its potteries since medieval times on account of its deep deposits of good workable clay and its position close to an abundant supply of coal for fuel and galena ore for the manufacture of lead glazes.

The most important potteries at Ewenny concerning the period covered by this book were Ewenny and Claypits, which were situated opposite each other on the Bridgend Road. About the year 1900, Hernston and Corntown Potteries were also operating in the area, but these had closed by about 1920.

Evan Jenkins (1791-1856) founded the Ewenny Pottery in 1815 after serving a five-year apprenticeship with his relation, John Williams, at the Claypits Pottery across the road. Claypits had been going at least since the early 18th century and possibly long before then.

Evan Jenkins bequeathed the *Ewenny Pottery* to his two eldest sons, John Jenkins (1822-1888) and David Jenkins (1824-1905), though David sold out to John in return for a waged employment at the works. When John died in 1888, one of his sons, Edwin Jenkins (1860-1919) took over the pottery. At some stage Edwin Jenkins' son, Edwin John Jenkins, took control and in 1922 the pottery passed to his cousin David John Jenkins (the son of Edwin Jenkins' brother David). Ewenny continues today under the management of Alun Jenkins.

The *Claypits Pottery* was owned and managed by the Williams family until 1884. It then passed to Evan Jones, who had come from another family of potters in the area and had married into the Williams family. In 1907, William Jenkins (1869-1955) took over the management of Claypits, acquiring the ownership of it in 1912 when Evan Jones died. William Jenkins retired in 1939. His nephew Thomas Jenkins took over until his own retirement in 1972. The pottery then passed out of the family and continues today.

The families connected with the potteries did not necessarily confine themselves to a single undertaking, particularly as the potteries themselves were also small farms. Through marriage and inheritance or just by choice, individuals became associated with more than one pottery, such that any attempt to unravel the family connections with the businesses is complicated. The author, therefore, urges the interested reader to consult the excellent volume on the Ewenny Potteries produced by the National Museum of Wales, which details family trees and connections.

Output from the two potteries was mainly utilitarian and domestic wares. This was the pattern until the influence of the Arts and Crafts Movement during the 1880s which prompted the production of more decorative wares.

Most of the clay was provided from the claypit adjoining the two potteries, which yielded a variety of clays, the finest being "clai coch bach" (little red clay) which was found about a foot (30cm) below the surface. This clay was reserved for ornamental wares. Other rougher clays were used for the domestic wares.

The potter, W. Fishley Holland (ref. Fremington), on a visit to Ewenny, described the kiln as "primitive as could be, yet they got excellent results." Contemporary photographs show a ramshackle site, typical of many country potteries at the time.

Both potteries employed local men as well as members of the family, and frequent visits by journeymen potters, particularly from the Bristol area, complemented the workforce.

From the turn of the century most of the output was distributed via Neath, where once a week dealers would collect it. Pottery was also sold at shops in nearby towns and, later, at stores of F.W. Woolworth in Neath and other local towns.

Ornamental wares, however, were given a more national audience through the intervention of Horace Elliott, a London entrepreneur and member of the Arts and Crafts Exhibition Society, who paid annual visits to Ewenny from 1880 to 1913. Elliott would today be branded as somewhat eccentric. He craved for what he termed as "the simple joys of peasant life" and seemed quite at home in Ewenny as in Bayswater, London, where he had a crafts shop (circa 1885).

Elliott epitomised the growing interest in country potteries, and on his annual trips would visit each of the potteries buying for his showroom. Without doubt he was a major influence on the Ewenny Pottery particularly, for he produced his own pieces there as well as bringing new designs (many of which he registered at the Board of Trade). In one extended six months stay at Ewenny in 1908, he executed various ceramic commissions for his own clients.

The wares that Elliott made at Ewenny and that which he purchased were occasionally exhibited at the Arts & Crafts Exhibition Society. He usually added his own mark to pieces. In 1893, he made a vase with elaborate nautical motifs as a wedding gift for the Duke and Duchess of York.

After about 1930, there was a decline in the demand for the heavy utilitarian wares since milk-churns were being replaced by metal containers and wash-bowls were going out of fashion. The potteries also had difficulty competing with the mass-producing Staffordshire potteries for domestic wares, white china becoming more fashionable and desirable. As country potteries, Ewenny and Claypits survived, however, continuing today.

Products

Apart from the utilitarian and domestic items, some highly decorative ornamental wares were made at the potteries almost as a tradition. Money-boxes, puzzle-jugs, tygs, posset pots and wassail bowls were regularly produced. These latter bowls related to the New Year celebrations of wassailing, which was commonly practised in Wales during the nineteenth century. Groups of wassailers, armed with wassail bowls filled with spiced ale, toured houses in a district, dispensing New Year greetings.

The wassail bowls were extremely elaborate, characterised by a bowl section with up to eighteen loop handles plus a domed cover heavily ornamented with crude appliqué figures or animals in relief (a hen often being the crowning feature). Sgraffito decoration of names, dates, floral or geometric motifs (such as interlocking circles) would complete the ornamentation.

Such ornamental wares were usually glazed with a thin yellow glaze over a white clay slip, the sgraffito decoration revealing the red clay body below. The glaze palette was very limited and the yellow lead-based glaze was extensively used by the Ewenny potteries. Occasionally blue and black glazes were used, and later, during Horace Elliott's involvement, some glazes were brought in from suppliers such as Wenger in Staffordshire.

Many domestic wares were also highly decorated, such as flower-pots, bread crocks and shaving-mugs. The money-boxes were particularly distinctive, with elaborate decoration in relief of hens, chickens and other birds perched on globular, thrown bases.

Most pottery at Ewenny was thrown, but Horace Elliott introduced mould-making to produce objects such as commemorative plaques and medallions (featuring such subjects as Gladstone).

Other designs of Elliott's which he either produced himself or were executed on his behalf at the Ewenny Pottery included vases with leaf impressed designs (similar to Doulton's Natural Foliage Ware), a series of sanctuary candlesticks made in 1908 for St. Matthew's Church, Pontypridd, and a jug in the form of a pig, inscribed "Y Mochin," (the pig)—a design which he registered at the Board of Trade in 1890.

At the Claypits Pottery, Evan Jones produced his own form of art wares in the form of tygs, jugs, vases and candlesticks which emulated Roman and medieval styles. Pieces were just as crudely made as at Ewenny, but less elaborately decorated. Tall candlesticks emulating early coiled ware were characteristic. A mottled green glaze was widely used and many pieces had motto inscriptions either in English or Welsh.

Collectors should note that cohesion between the glaze and body was poor, such that wares tend to easily flake or chip.

Suggestions for Further Study

The National Museum of Wales, Cardiff, has an extensive collection or early and later wares.

The Welsh Folk Museum, St. Fagans, Cardiff has an old brick-built kiln which was removed from the Ewenny Pottery in 1980, plus other artefacts.

Both the Ewenny and Claypits Potteries continue on the same site but mostly in modern buildings.

Lewis, J.M. *The Ewenny Potteries*. National Museum of Wales, 1982.

EWENNY POTTERY
CLAYPITS POTTERY

Types of Ware	Production	Quality	Availability
Art wares: Ewenny Pottery	Moderate?	Poor to Good	Common
Art wares: Claypits	Moderate?	Poor to Fair	Common

Marks

Ewenny

Incised:	Ewenny Pottery	c.1805 - ?
+ variants		
+/- Horace Elliott's Fleur-de-lys stamp (in lozenge)+/- "ELLIOTT" stamp. (c.1893-1913)		
Incised:	E l l i o t London	c.1887 - c.1913
+ year		
+ variants		

Claypits

Incised:	Clay Pits Pottery Ewenny	c.1884 - ?
Incised:	Jones Bridgend	c.1884 - c.1912
Incised:	Jones Ewenni	c.1884 - c.1912

Ewenny l to r: jug, 140mm high, with motto "Gwr dieithr y w Foru" and incised mark "Jones Bridgend"; bowl, 140mm diameter, with motto "Rhosynau" (Roses) and incised mark "Claypits Pottery Ewenny"; jug with motto "Dwfr Pur. Rhodd Rhad Duw" ("Pure water. God's free gift") and mark as for bowl.

Clay Hill, Wrecclesham, Farnham, Surrey.

Historical Background

In 1873, Absalom Harris set up a pottery at Clay Hill, Wrecclesham, near Farnham, having previously maintained a pottery at Charles Hill, Elstead, Surrey (1860-1866), and also in Alice Holt Forest (1866-1872) on the Surrey/Hampshire border.

The local deposits of Gault Clay were utilised, and red bodied wares were produced, consisting of drain-pipes, tiles, plant pots, chimney pots and other domestic items.

After 1880, however, a different type of ware was produced, which became known as "Farnham Greenware." The name "Greenware" was derived from the lead glaze used, which was made green by the use of copper oxide.

The ware developed through requests for copies of medieval and Roman pieces, which sprang from an initial request by the artist Miles Birket Foster, who lived nearby and who wanted a badly weathered antique garden vase copied.

Absalom Harris became quite adept at reproducing earlier pottery styles, and freely imitated Tudor and Roman pieces. The trade in copies grew, and through the many commissions received, this work became quite profitable in relation to the more mundane work of producing red plant pots. Pieces were retailed through Heal's and Liberty's stores from 1892 through to the 1920s, and at Liberty, the ware was advertised in their catalogue as "Green Ware."

From 1880 to 1939, art pottery at Farnham was made in conjunction with Farnham School of Art, where art pieces were exhibited by Harris in 1890. The local artist W.H. Allen was instrumental in establishing the connection with Farnham School of Art, where he was art master, and for arranging to provide designs for the pottery from his students. The students' designs were executed by the pottery, and the resultant pots returned to the students for decoration prior to being fired—a co-operation which proved both beneficial for the school and the pottery.

The publicity brought by the Greenwares enhanced the reputation of the pottery, such that additional buildings had to be erected to cater for the expansion in trade. The domestic and horticultural side of the business also expanded, and the workforce increased.

Absalom's two sons and two daughters became involved in the running of the pottery, as well as producing pieces in their own right.

Two world wars caused an inevitable downturn in business, but the pottery survived. With the fall in demand for art pottery during the 1940s, the pottery survived on the production of its horticultural wares. The pottery continues today, making horticultural wares, but is no longer involved in the production of art pottery.

Farnham Selection of 'Green Wares'. l to r:-i) vase, 230mm high, marked "Green" on base, dated 1929. ii) ewer, 325mm high. iii) two-handled vase, 203mm high. (courtesy HCMS, ACM 1957.63/2; ACM 1936.89/7; ACM 1936.89/3).

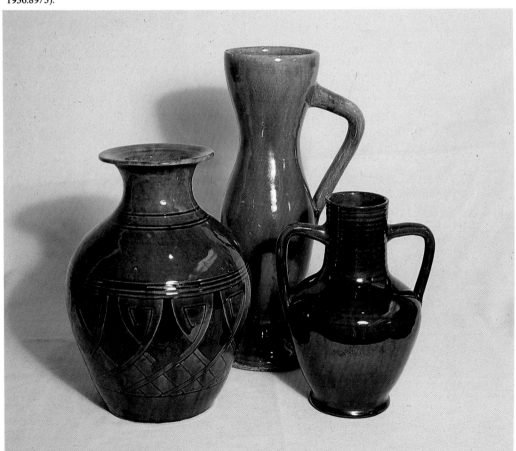

Farnham Selection of wares. l to r:-i) owl jug, 157mm high, blue glaze. ii) candlestick, 145mm high, green glaze. iii) globular vase with handle, 250mm high, blue glaze. (courtesy HCMS, ACM 1936.89/6; ACM 1936.89/2; ACM 1936.89/8).

Products

Most art pieces prior to 1914 were of simple shape, decorated with a single green glaze, and bore little or no pattern. After 1914, brighter glazes were introduced in colours such as yellow or blue (although still generally monochrome). Some simple decoration in black, such as a zig-zag frieze, was occasionally employed. The words "yellow" and "green" were often incised on the base of a piece, to indicate the glaze colour to be used.

Many designs were taken from pieces in the Victoria & Albert Museum, and included Medieval and Roman styles; other designs were supplied by students at the Farnham School of Art. Owl pitchers, amphora and "rustic fern pots" were regular stock items, but pitchers and vases of many shapes were produced.

From 1905, some sgraffito designs were produced, and during the 1920s, Barbra Daysh created sgraffito patterns at Farnham School of Art, as well as the reproduction of Spanish and Moorish styles.

The sgraffito designs were often effected on a cream glaze ground, and the red earthenware body frequently showed through the glaze. Patterns tended to be much more decorative and intricate than those executed for the standard Greenwares, and some large chargers seem to have provided a suitable canvas for some spectacular work.

Agnes Hall, who was assistant Art Mistress at Farnham School of Art during the 1920s, also used the sgraffito technique of decoration to produce some pieces in an art deco style.

W.H. Allen was associated with the pottery from 1889 to 1943. Apart from designing the more general Greenwares, he worked with William Freemantle Harris (one of Absalom's sons) to produce press-moulded birds, animals and architectural wares. The modelled pieces bear some resemblance to the work of the Martin Brothers.

Absalom's daughters, Gertrude and Nellie Harris, also worked at the pottery, and undertook both architectural and Greenware work.

Another significant artist at Farnham School of Art (c.1897/8) was Ada K. Hazell, who is recorded as having sold pieces at Heal's and Liberty's stores under the name of "Farnham Sgraffito Pottery."

The more decorative pieces were usually marked, but the plainer Greenwares were often unmarked. As an aid to identification, Farnham wares exhibit a particular iridescence of glaze, owing to the high lead content. The iridescence is particularly noticeable on the base of Greenwares.

Suggestions for Further Study

The Curtis-Allen Gallery, Alton, has a good representative display, which includes a bequest from W.H. Allen. W.H. Allen's sketchbooks are housed in the collections of Hampshire County Museums Service at Chilcomb House, Chilcomb Lane, Winchester, Hants.

The Farnham Pottery, Pottery Lane, Wrecclesham.

Brears, P.C.D. *Farnham Pottery.* Phillimore & Co.Ltd., 1971.

Farnham Large charger, 460mm diam. "Miranda", yellow slip decoration on a red body, marked "Yellow" on base, c.1929.(courtesy HCMS, ACM 1966.165).

Farnham Large charger, 480mm diam. orange slip decoration on a brown ground, dated 1928. (courtesy HCMS, ACM 1957.64).

Farnham Owl jug, 157mm high, blue glaze.(courtesy HCMS, ACM 1936.89/6).

FARNHAM POTTERY

Types of Ware	Production	Quality	Availability
Garden ornaments and architectural wares	Moderate	Poor to Good	Common (but difficult to identify)
Art wares	Low to Moderate	Fair to Very Good	Uncommon (highly decorative pieces ` rare)

Marks

Many pieces were unmarked, but marks noticed so far are:-

Impressed	HARRIS HAND MADE FARNHAM SURREY ENGLAND (enclosed in a square)	c.1880 - c.1939
Incised: (Farnham Sgraffito Pottery)	F.S.P. (written circular, plus 3 hazel nuts)	c.1897/8
Impressed	(figure of an owl)	?
Impressed	(symbol)	?
+/- artist's mark, eg.	(B symbol)	(Barbra Daysh) during 1920s

+/- "yellow" or "green", incised

THE FOLEY POTTERIES

—earthenwares
—bone china
—lustres

Wileman & Co (1872-1925)
Shelley Potteries Ltd. (1925-1966)
Fenton, Longton, Staffordshire.

Historical Background

The Foley Potteries, named after a local family, were set up by John Smith of Fenton Hall around 1827. Blue printed earthenwares and plain white china were manufactured until 1872, when the potteries were taken over by James F. Wileman, in partnership with Joseph Shelley, and known as Wileman & Co.

When Joseph Shelley's son, Percy, joined the business in 1881, he began to improve designs and increase business. Reports of 1893 talk of an expanding trade in rich and varied tea-sets and table decorations, in spite of a somewhat depressed market. Showrooms were established in London together with agencies in Australia, Canada and the USA.

When Joseph Shelley died in 1896, Percy Shelley took over and set about recruiting reputable artists, such as Rowland Morris, who designed one of the most successful wares of the pottery—the "Dainty White" range of tea-ware. Production of this ware continued through to 1966 when the pottery closed. Morris's untimely death in 1898 was thus a significant loss to the pottery.

The well-known designer Frederick Rhead joined Wileman & Co. as art director about 1897, and was influential in creating new pottery lines such as sgraffito decorated pieces in coloured parian ware, and a large range of wares painted underglaze.

Many of Rhead's new lines were given Italianate names, the most popular of which was "Intarsio," although this name referred only to a style and not to a particular pattern or motif. Other ranges were "Urbato," "Faience," "Primitif," "Pastello" and "Spano-Lustra."

In 1905, Walter Slater (of Doulton) took over as art director, and Frederick Rhead left to concentrate on writing, illustrating and other design work. Rhead went on to become art director of Wood & Sons in 1912, a position which lasted until 1929, during which time he wrote many articles on pottery, becoming highly respected throughout the trade. He died in 1933.

In 1910, the name "Shelley China" was promoted because of a conflict with other potteries using the name "Foley China" (ref. E. Brain & Co.).

Wileman & Co. regularly exhibited at British trade exhibitions, and some Shelley wares which were shown at the British Industries Fair at Crystal Palace in 1920 and also at the British Industrial Arts Exhibition in Knightsbridge the same year, proved successful.

The Shelley range became so successful that a separate company was set up in 1925 as Shelley Potteries Ltd.. Prior to this date, most of Wileman's wares had been marked "Foley Art China."

The company went from strength to strength. Percy Shelley's two sons had entered the business before the Great War and continued to expand production into the 1920s.

In 1925, the employment of Hilda Cowham heralded the launch of a highly successful venture into nursery ware under the name "Playtime." A year later, the illustrator Mabel Lucie Attwell was engaged. Her extensive ranges of nursery ware were designed in all shapes and sizes.

The popularity of these wares brought competition from other potteries such as Doulton, who launched their "Bunnykins" range in 1934. Equally popular, however, were the Shelley jelly moulds, of which more than 50 shapes were produced in thick white china until 1939.

Percy Shelley retired from the company in 1932, and by 1938, Walter Slater had also retired. The company lasted until 1966, however, when it was taken over by Allied English Potteries (now part of the Doulton Group).

Foley (Wileman & Co.) Group of Shelley wares. (courtesy of Christie's Images)

Foley (Wileman & Co.) Designs for the first "Intarsio" series, from an original Foley pattern book.

Foley (Wileman & Co.) Jardinière on stand, 1000mm high, "Intarsio" pattern (first series), transfer printed mark "The Foley, Intarsio, England" with monogram for Wileman & Co. and pattern no. 3161.

Foley (Wileman & Co.) Jardinière on stand, 1000mm high, transfer printed mark "The Foley" with monogram for Wileman & Co.

Foley (Wileman & Co.) Group of Intarsio wares. (courtesy of Christie's Images)

Products

The popular "Intarsio" range included many genre studies (such as characters from plays by Shakespeare and caricatures of Lord Roseberry on teapots), as well as animals and birds (cats, geese and peacocks, for example). The decoration of these subjects was accomplished by painting onto underglaze transfer prints. Colours were bold and bright, and designs were often painted against a brown or green background.

Pieces exhibited many influences, of which one of the most recognisable was a Dutch style, both in shape and decoration. Wares in the "Urbato" range were tube-lined, whilst "Spano-Lustra" was characterised by the use of pale lustre glazes over Spanish style shapes. The "Pastello" range was similar to Intarsio, though recognisable by the use of pastel colours over a dark ground, and the "Faience" range featured decoration by the use of coloured slips.

Some grotesques were also made, mostly animals and mythical beasts. In 1911, a new range of Intarsio ware was introduced. This was followed by numerous other new ranges, some of which adapted well to the increased demand for toilet sets. "Etruscan," "Alexandra" and "Cloisello" were some of the patterns which appeared as jug and basin sets.

From about 1913, bone china was also produced, much of which appeared under the Shelley mark. From 1915, Wileman & Co. introduced some interesting ranges entitled "Roself" (a stencilled rose motif mainly on a matt black ground), "Violette" (similar to Roself but with violets), "Roumana." "Rosata" and "Vinta" (a bird and vine pattern), all of which were exhibited at their London showroom. The designs were classically inspired, with vivid colourings, and many had lustre and gilt finishes. They were executed on tea sets, floating-flower bowls, spill vases, plates and other articles.

During the early 1920s, the commemorative and souvenir trade proved particularly lucrative, and various moulded miniatures were produced with heraldic motifs, and ranged from models of cars, boats and trains to shaving mugs and comical animals.

The first real art pottery to be produced by Wileman & Co. after the Great War appeared from 1920 as Shelley lustre wares. These wares were particularly spectacular, although initial experiments produced poor quality lustres. Once the technique had been perfected, however, fine vases, bowls and plates were produced with both lustre and enamel decoration.

The Shelley lustrewares are popular with collectors, commanding high prices at auction. The appeal is in the rich decoration and attractive colour combinations. Designs included animals, birds, fish, butterflies and other insects (often in a Japanese style), and the pieces are comparable to the Mackeig-Jones lustres produced by Wedgwood.

The 1930s saw new ranges of bone-china tea-sets in typical art deco syle. The "Mode" (1930), "Vogue" (1930) and "Eve" (1934) shapes were distinguished by triangular handles, and appeared in a wide variety of bright deco patterns, such as "Sunray" and "Butterfly Wing." The "Regent" shape was distinguished by circular handles, and also appeared in deco patterns.

In 1932, Shelley launched "Harmony Artware," which was a range of high-fired wares, characterised by streaks of bold colours, mainly duochromes of purple, green, orange, pink or blue. The effect was produced by mixing turpentine with the glaze, and spinning the pots on the wheel while the glaze was still wet. Harmony Artware was very popular, and produced in great quantity.

Suggestions for Further Study

Rhead, Frederick & George. *Staffordshire Pots & Potters* London: Hutchinson & Co., 1906 (reprinted by EP Publishing, 1977).

Watkins, Chris, William Harvey & Robert Senft. *Shelley Potteries, The History & Production of a Staffordfshire Family of Potters.* Barrie & Jenkins, 1986.

Hill, Susan. *The Shelley Style—A Collectors' Guide.* Jazz Publications Ltd., 1990.

Spours, Judy. *Art Deco Tableware.* London: Ward Lock, 1988.

"Mabel Lucie Attwell," catalogue by A. Packer of a centenary exhibition at Brighton Museum, 1979.

"Shelley Potteries," catalogue of an exhibition at the Geffrye Museum, 1980.

Foley (**Wileman & Co.**) Charger, 300mm. diam., blue and yellow lustre with gilding, marked "Shelley England".

Foley (**Wileman & Co.**) Vase, 200mm high, yellow transfer decoration of flying geese on a painted dark green ground.

Foley (**Wileman & Co.**) Ginger-jar, 120mm high, 'Harmony Artware', marked "Shelley, England".

Foley (**Wileman & Co.**) Vase, applied slip floral decoration in yellow and brown, marked "Foley Faience".

Foley (Wileman & Co.) Group of wares, l to r: Spano-lustra ware candlestick, 310mm high, marked "The Foley Faience England"; ewer, similarly marked plus pattern no. 14007 and incised "E"; Spano-lustra ware vase, marked with pattern no. 10013 and incised "B"; double-gourd shaped vase with iridescent glaze pattern no. 11003; vase, marked "The Foley Faience, England", pattern no. 11062 and incised "E".

THE FOLEY POTTERIES

Types of Ware	Production	Quality	Availability
Named wares by Frederick Rhead	Low to High	Fair to Very Good	Common (except Urbato and Spano-Lustre which are scarce, and Primitif and Pastello which are rare)
Other wares pre-Shelley	Moderate to High	Fair to Good	Abundant
Shelley wares (except lustres)	High	Fair to Good	Abundant
Shelley lustres	Low to Moderate	Poor (early) to excellent	Uncommon

Marks

Printed:	W & Co. (in monogram surmounted by a crown)	1872 - 1890
	THE FOLEY W & Co. (as above)	1890 - 1910
	THE FOLEY CHINA ENGLAND	c.1872 - c.1920
	FOLEY ART CHINA	c.1920 - 1925
	SHELLEY ENGLAND (in capitals in shield)	c.1912 - 1925
	Shelley England (in signature in shield)	1925 - 1940
	Shelley CHINA ENGLAND	1930 - 1932

+/- 'FINE BONE CHINA' (1945-1966)
+/- name of ware
+/- pattern number
+/- registered design number

Foley (Wileman & Co.) Jardinière, Intarsio pattern, 1220mm high, (courtesy of Christie's Images)

Robinson & Son (1881—1903)
E. Brain & Co. (1903—1967)
Fenton, Longton, Staffordshire.

Historical Background

The Foley Pottery, which was established by Robinson & Son in 1881, came under the ownership of E. Brain & Co. in 1903. The pottery was situated across the road from Wileman & Co., and used the local name "Foley," as did Wileman and many other potteries in the district. Brain, however, objected to Wileman's owner, Percy Shelley, attempting in 1910 to register the name "Foley China", and a resulting court case decided that Wileman & Co. had no exclusive right to the name "Foley China."

Brain produced fairly plain bone-china wares noted for their simplicity of design and domestic usefulness, such as tea and breakfast sets. E. Brain died in 1910, but his son, William Henry Brain, who was in partnership with him, took over the ownership and management of the company, and introduced more decorative wares. The impact of the First World War, however, meant a rough passage for the company during the post-war period, as many markets had been lost.

In 1920, E. Brain & Co. were exhibitors at the British Industrial Arts Exhibition, and during the 1930s much work was produced in association with the Royal Staffordshire Pottery of A.J. Wilkinson Ltd., some of which was exhibited at the Harrods Tableware Exhibition in 1934. The designer, Freda Beardmore, who joined E. Brain & Co. in 1930, assisted in organising this landmark exhibition.

In 1931, William Brain's son, Eustace Brain, joined the company, and a year later, Thomas Acland Fennemore joined Brain & Co. as Managing Director, bringing with him previous sales skills in the pottery industry. Fennemore increased the company's product ranges by launching new designs specifically aimed at mass-production.

Also, between 1932 and 1934, work was commissioned from contemporary artists, such as George Logan, Vanessa Bell, Frank Brangwyn, Gordon Forsyth, Laura Knight, Graham Sutherland, Clarice Cliff and Fanny Rhead (who was known to have submitted a series of six Egyptian designs). The association of such well-known artists with mass-produced wares seems ironic, but, as it happened, their work was sold at a premium in small limited editions, which were quickly snapped up by discerning collectors.

The Harrod's Tableware Exhibition, entitled "Modern Art for the Table," at which much of these artist commissions was aimed, was well received, though it failed to fulfil its commercial objectives consequently, and Clarice Cliff remarked that it was "the closest thing to a flop" in which she had been involved.

E. Brain & Co. acquired Coalport China Ltd. in 1958, and became part of the Wedgwood Group in 1967.

Products

Prior to 1905, wares were simple, with neat, individual lines of decoration. The pottery body was heavy and hard-wearing, all pieces having a characteristically curved interior base to avoid dirt collecting.

From 1905, a range of decorative wares entitled "Peacock Pottery" was produced, which was well received in the trade. Small giftwares were also made, as a response to a growing souvenir trade.

The main product of Brain & Co., however, was tablewares, especially tea-sets. The company produced its contribution to the many ranges of art deco bone-china tea-sets during the 1930s, and Brain's "Foley Mayfair" range of 1932 was similar in style to Shelley's "Vogue" and "Mode" ranges. Some tea-sets were also produced in a cubist style, with square cups and tea-pots. Decoration was fairly restrained, however, and styles such as "Cubist Landscape" and "Cubist Sunflower" featured decoration only on part of a piece, such as the rim.

In 1930, the strongly curved "Pallas" shape was launched for tableware, and was decorated in a variety of deco styles. More traditional shapes were also made in the 1930s, and "Devon," "Perth" and "Avon" typically bore floral scenes. A successful design was "Clovelly," which utilised blue, green, yellow and pink colourations.

In 1933, Brain & Co. launched six designs for tea-ware, which comprised floral motifs in a conical shape with angled handles, entitled "Langham." Again, this shape was similar to Shelley's "Regent" shape, but was distinguished by handles containing the outline shape of a diamond. In the same year, a polka-dot range was produced for the mass-market called simply "Spot," again similar to a Shelley design.

Suggestions for Further Study

Spours, Judy. *Art Deco Tableware*. London: Ward Lock, 1988.

Buckley, Cheryl. *Potters & Paintresses—Women Designers in the Pottery Industry 1870-1955*. The Women's Press, 1990.

Foley (Brain & Co.) Bone china part tea and coffee set designed by George Logan. (courtesy of Christie's Images)

THE FOLEY POTTERY (E. Brain & Co.)

Types of Ware	Production	Quality	Availability
All wares	High	Fair to Good	Abundant

Marks

Impressed	R. & S. L.	1881 - 1903
Printed:	ESTABLISHED R & S L. (in rope motif, plus '1850')	1881 - 1903
Impressed	E B & CO F.	1903 - c.1905
Printed: (plus variants)	ESTABLISHED E B & CO F. FOLEY CHINA (in rope motif, plus '1850')	1903 - 1967
	FOLEY ART CHINA PEACOCK POTTERY ENGLAND RD. (in peacock picture)	1905 - c.1914
	FOLEY E B & CO CHINA	1930 - 1936
	ENGLISH BONE CHINA	

+/- artist's signature

Foley (Brain & Co.) Teapot, 100mm high, design attributed to the Glaswegian artist George Logan. Transfer printed mark "Foley Art China, Peacock Pottery, England. Rd. Copyright, 29".

Combrew, Fremington, North Devon (c.1805-1915)
    (The Fishley family: c.1805-1912)
    (Ed Sadler: 1912-1915)
William Fishley Holland
    The Braunton Pottery, Braunton, North Devon (1912—1921)
    The Pottery, Clevedon, Avon (1922—1969)

Historical Background

The Fremington Pottery was established about 1805 by George Fishley (1771-1865), in the North Devon hamlet of Combrew. It seems that George Fishley had established pottery-making facilities intially at Muddlebridge, close by, in 1800. The rich local clay with its typical deep red Devon colour has ensured a long line of potteries in the neighbourhood of Fremington from earliest times to the present day.

For many years the output was mainly cheap domestic wares: jugs, cooking pots, cups, dishes, etc., which were very coarse and plain in appearance. During the 1840s more ornamental wares were made using red and white Devon clays, including some stained with manganese. Jugs and highly decorated ornaments for mantelshelves were also produced, characterised by extensive sgraffito and appliqué decoration.

About 1839, George's eldest son, Edmund (1806-1860) took over the management of the pottery, and when he died as the result of an accident in 1860, his son, Edwin Beer Fishley (1832-1912), assumed control. Edmund's brother Robert (1808-1887) also worked at the pottery.

Edwin was keen to diversify the output of the pottery, and during the 1880s began to introduce art wares. Local patrons encouraged his venture and enabled him to study national collections of classical and ancient pottery in London.

In 1902, Edwin's grandson, William Fishley Holland joined the pottery as an apprentice, and in his later autobiography, "Fifty Years a Potter" (1958), he noted that there were eight staff including himself at the pottery when he joined.

The production of art wares continued alongside the production of domestic and tourist wares, of which there were many. Journeyman potters could apparently turn out as many as one thousand pots a day, and certainly the skilled throwers and drawers of handles for cups and jugs could keep up with the heavy local demand.

Every Friday, wares were taken to Barnstaple market and sold from a stall. Apart from the local interest, however, there was little national patronage or recognition for the wares. The Cardew family were acquainted with the pottery, and the potter Michael Cardew remembered visiting as a boy and admiring the many pots that his father purchased from Edwin Beer Fishley. The potter Bernard Leach was also an admirer and often upheld the pottery at Fremington to his students as an example of a pottery run to traditional lines.

When Edwin died in 1912, the pottery was sold to Ed Sadler, a Staffordshire potter, who produced wares under the title "Devonia Art." He sold out to C.H. Brannam Ltd. in 1915, who closed the pottery and used the premises for the manufacture of Cornish bread ovens into the early 1930s, when the buildings were demolished.

Fremington l to r: harvest jug, 215mm high, with motto:-"Fill me full of liquor sweet For that is good when friends do meet When friends do meet and liquor plenty Fill me again when I.B.M.T. " incised mark "E.B. Fishley Fremington"; beaker, with motto:-"From rocks and sands and barren lands Kind fortune keep me free And from great guns and womens tongues Good Lord deliver me" "1896" incised mark "E B F 7".

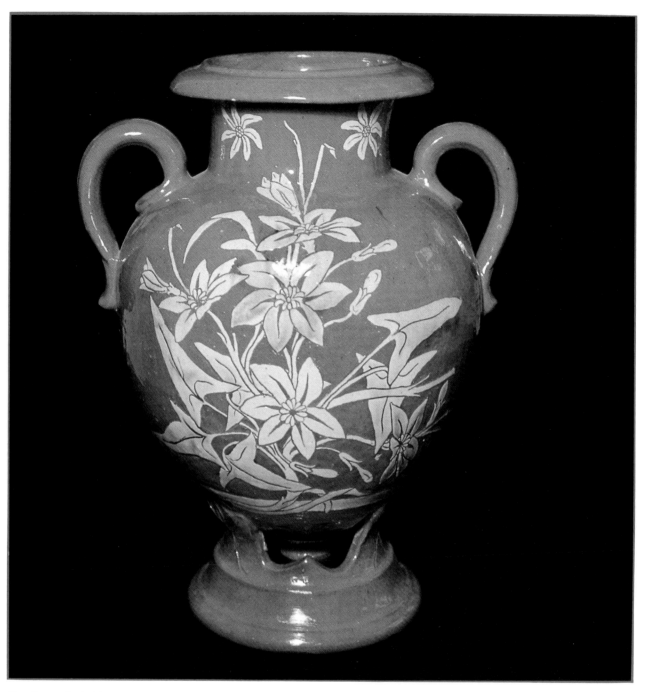

Fremington Urn by E.B. Fishley, 400mm high.

William Fishley Holland found employment as the manager of a pottery at Braunton, having turned down an offer to work with Bernard Leach at St. Ives. The pottery was able to continue throughout the First World War, although many staff left to join the forces. William Fishley Holland was himself called up to the Royal Air Force in 1916.

At the end of the war he returned to Braunton, but when in 1921 his employer ran into difficulties, he went to Clevedon Court, Avon, to join Sir Ambrose Elton, who required assistance in keeping the Sunflower Pottery open following Sir Edmund Elton's death.

William Fishley Holland's throwing skills were particularly sought after, and a suitable arrangement was entered into whereby he threw pots to Sir Ambrose's designs for one day a week, working on his own wares the remainder of the week. Sir Ambrose also allowed him to set up his own kiln and workshop in the grounds of Clevedon Court, but in 1922, he wisely purchased a cottage with outbuildings opposite the Court and set up his own pottery, which he called simply "The Pottery."

The Sunflower Pottery closed the same year, but his own pottery thrived, continuing for many years. His principal assistant at The Pottery was George Manley (who had been with him at Braunton), and his chief designer was Bill Janes. His son, George, was also associated with the pottery, and his daughter, Isabel Fishley Holland, is known to have produced pieces.

After William Fishley Holland's death in 1969, George Manley and Bill Janes continued at the pottery. On George Manley's death, Bill Janes set up a pottery with a partner in Clevedon town.

Products

A great range of wares was produced, from domestic and tourist items to ornamental and art pieces. The wares of Braunton and The Pottery were in many ways similar.

Some of the domestic output is quaintly summarised by William Fishley Holland in his book "Fifty Years a Potter": "pipkins, owlsheads, gallipots, butterpots, baking dishes and pans for scalding Devonshire cream."

Harvest jugs (with or without mottoes) were a popular product, not only for tourist use, but also for ornamental and domestic use (on local farms, for example). The sgraffito decoration through a yellow or white glaze to the brown body of the jug was characteristic, as was much use of "thumbing," slip trailing and scalloping as decorative means.

Edwin Beer Fishley also produced some green glazed wares about 1900.

The art vases of Edwin Beer Fishley were much finer by comparison than the rougher harvest jugs and other wares, and tended to display classical subjects by means of painted decoration on dark grounds. The subjects were either copied from museum pieces or freely composed in similar vein.

A characteristic of all wares, though, was a coiled finial to handles (on vases, jugs and tygs particularly).

Puzzle jugs were an important traditional output, and invited the bearer to drink whilst attempting to cover up all the holes in the rim, spout and neck with particular dexterity. A typical motto inscribed might be "Within this jug there is good liquor, Fit for parson or for Vicar, But how to drink and not to spill, Will try the utmost of your skill."

William Fishley Holland employed a wider variety of glazes at The Pottery, some of which were lustrous in appearance. He continued the tradition of combed patterns on dishes and plates, however, which he had practised at Fremington.

His son, George, worked at The Pottery for a while, before setting up his own pottery at Dunster on the North Devon coast. His daughter, Isabel Fishley Holland, also worked at The Pottery, and is known to have decorated tiles and figures (such as "Beatrix Potter" animal figures).

Suggestions for Further Study

The Museum of North Devon, Barnstaple, has some examples of the work of Fishley Holland on display.

Holland, William Fishley. *"Fifty Years a Potter."* Pottery Quarterly, 1958.

Edgeler, Audrey, *Art Potters of Barnstaple.* Nimrod Press Ltd., 1990.

"By Potters Art and Skill: Pottery by the Fishleys of Fremington;" catalogue by Emmeline Leary and Jeremy Pearson of an exhibition at the Royal Albert Memorial Museum, Exeter, 1984.

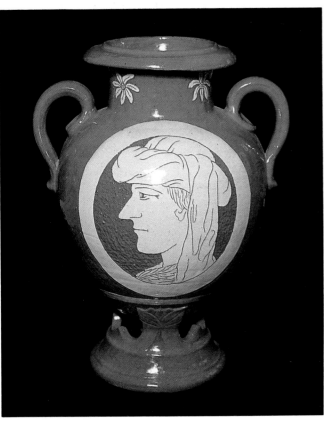

Reverse side of urn on page 119.

FREMINGTON POTTERY

Type of Ware	Production	Quality	Availability
non-domestic wares (motto jugs, etc.)	High	Poor to Good	Common
E.B. Fishley art wares	Low	Good to Very Good	Scarce

Marks

E.B. Fishley

Incised: +/- pattern number		EBF	1861 - 1912
Incised:		E B Fishley Fremington (+/- N. Devon)	1861 - 1912
+ variations:		E B Fishley maker (or "potter") Fremington (+/- ND)	
+/- date			

Ed. Sadler

Incised:		ED Sadler Devonia Art Fremington Barum	1912 - 1915
+/- pattern number			

W.F. Holland

Incised:		W Holland Fremington N Devon	c.1910 - 1912
Incised: +/- pattern number +/- date		Braunton	1912 - 1921
Incised:		W F Holland	1922 - 1969
		W F H	1922 - 1969
+/- date Incised:		I Holland	1929 - 1942

Hanley, Stoke-on-Trent, Staffordshire.

Historical Background

The Granville Pottery was founded in 1895 by the Italian sculptor, Carlo Manzoni (1855-1910). Manzoni was a gentleman of private means, who was skilled in anatomy, languages, sculpture, mosaics and wood-carving.

It seems that he maintained close contact with Harold Rathbone and Conrad Dressler, the co-directors of the Della Robbia Pottery, so much so that when Dressler left Della Robbia, Manzoni closed his own pottery and joined Rathbone (ref. Della Robbia), moving his family to Birkenhead.

Manzoni clearly brought his own style of pottery to Della Robbia, since early Della Robbia pieces were similar to those he produced at the Granville Pottery. He was, however, more competent in sculpture, and his architectural wares exhibited a higher quality of design.

When Della Robbia closed in 1906, Manzoni continued to produce architectural wares from his home in Birkenhead until his death in 1910.

Products

Vases, jugs, bottles, plates and dishes, strongly influenced in design by the Italian Renaissance period, were the main output of the Granville Pottery. Wares were similar to those produced by Manzoni at Della Robbia, and were characterised by incised and thickly painted decoration on a red pottery body. Pieces were generally much cruder in appearance than those produced at Della Robbia, however.

A thin translucent glaze was employed, and pieces could easily be damaged if knocked. (Care should be taken with cleaning, as for Della Robbia wares). Colour combinations were fairly gaudy—bright green, red-brown and yellow frequently occurring together on a piece.

The majority of designs were geometric patterns, floriate in style. Painted scenes were rarely executed, but consisted mainly of classical subjects. There is evidence of Persian patterns in some wares, and also Mediterranean influences, such as Moorish designs.

Suggestions for Further Study

As for Della Robbia.

Granville Plate, 260mm diam., by Carlo Manzoni, marked "No.46 P14", dated 1897.

Granville Two pieces by Carlo Manzoni. l to r:-i) jug, 134mm high; ii) bottle vase, 190mm high.

GRANVILLE POTTERY			
Types of Ware	**Production**	**Quality**	**Availability**
All wares	Very Low	Poor to Good	Rare
Marks			
Painted: (usually in red-brown) + "Hand drawn and painted"	CM.	(in monogram plus year)	1895 - 1898

121

A.E. GRAY & CO. LTD.

(1907—1961)

—porcelain
—earthenwares
—stoneware
—lustres

Glebe Works, Hanley, Staffordshire (1907-1933)
Whieldon Road, Stoke-on-Trent, Staffs.(1934-1961)
Susie Cooper, artist/designer (b. 1902)
    at A.E.Gray & Co. Ltd. (1922-1929)
    at Chelsea Works, Burslem, Staffs. (1930-1931)
    at Crown Works, Burslem, Staffs. (1932-1961)

Historical Background

Albert Edward Gray (1871-1959) established his business as a decorating studio in 1907, having previously been a glass salesman in a Manchester retail shop. Gray was conscious of the demand for colourful hand-painted pottery, and employed high calibre designers at his studio, which quickly came to specialise in hand-painted decorations on a variety of items.

Wares were brought in from other potteries as undecorated white-ware, much of it coming from Johnson Brothers, and varied from porcelain to earthenware and stoneware.

In 1922, a student artist by the name of Susie Cooper (b.1902) was taken on from the Burslem School of Art, where she had studied under the artist Gordon Forsyth (ref. Pilkington Pottery). She was paid on a "time-work" basis, and given free rein to create her own designs.

In 1929, Susie Cooper left Gray to set up on her own, and for a short period she had a decorating studio at the Chelsea Works in Burslem. From 1932, however, she was designing tableware for her own company in premises offered her by H. Wood & Sons, an arrangement which enabled her to be in command of the shape of her pieces as well as the decoration.

Her early work was exhibited at the British Empire Exhibition in 1924, and in Paris in 1925. Later designs were shown regularly at the British Industries Fair from 1932, and at the Festival of Britain in 1951. She was awarded the OBE in 1979.

In 1936, A.E. Gray & Co. Ltd. secured an interest in another Staffordshire Pottery, the Kirklands Pottery, which allowed them to produce shapes to their own design, which could then be decorated at the studio.

The Crown Works merged with the Royal Tuscan China Company in 1961, and this company became part of the Wedgwood Group in 1966. Susie Cooper continues to design today on a freelance basis. After 1961, A.E. Gray & Co. Ltd. also became part of the Wedgwood Group. Albert Gray retired in 1947.

Susie Cooper Jug, 215mm high, modelled decoration of a ram, monochrome green glaze.

Susie Cooper Jug, 215mm high, modelled decoration of a ram, cobalt blue glaze. (courtesy HCMS, DA 1976.40).

Susie Cooper Vase, 215mm high, "Moon & Mountain" design. (courtesy of Christie's Images)

Products

A.E.Gray's early wares were hand-painted, and designs by Susie Cooper for the company were initially floral or as bright geometric bands. She also produced several high quality pieces in silver or copper lustres, as tea-sets and other tableware. These lustres were generically known as "Gloria Lustre," and were developed in collaboration with Gordon Forsyth.

Lustre patterns were mostly geometric motifs with foliage, and were later reproduced on porcelain from 1930 to 1933. Some colourful red and gold lustres were employed to good effect on ornamental wares, such as vases and ginger-jars, but the lustres tended to be thin, and thereby easily subject to damage through scratching. Lustres were therefore less suited to tablewares.

Susie Cooper's non-lustre pieces at Gray's studio often contained bright enamel colours of orange, brown or green, but during the 1930s her colours became more pastel, and the patterns smaller and more delicate. A running deer pattern was popular, as were designs featuring small floral motifs.

Heavy sgraffito decoration on earthenware was a particular Susie Cooper hallmark. Jugs and vases of rounded form displayed well outlines of animals, such as squirrels and goats, in simple landscapes. A smooth, matt, monochrome glaze completed the decoration, and the same scene would be produced in different colours, such as royal blue, jade green, beige, pink or orange. Sgraffito floral designs were similarly produced.

Art deco tableware designs comprised simple monochrome concentric lines, as in the "Crayon Lines" pattern, which was executed on rounded deco shapes. "Kestrel" (1931) and "Curlew" (1935) were typical of these shapes. Pastel green, grey and brown were predominant colours used in Susie Cooper patterns of the 1930s.

Painted decoration gave way to experimental lithographic decoration on Susie Cooper's wares from 1935 to 1939. "Dresden Spray" was a particularly successful lithographed pattern, though there were several hundred other patterns.

From 1936, a range of nurseyware was produced by Susie Cooper, exploiting the market opened up Mabel Lucie Attwell's designs for Shelley (ref. Foley, Wileman).

The ornamental wares of Gray's studio were attractive and generally of high quality. During the 1920s, the studio decorated some fine art vases, jugs and bowls in stoneware, with sgraffito decoration. V-shaped wall-vases were popular items during the 1930s, and were produced by the studio in a variety of sizes, with gilded rims and with designs such as acanthus leaves in soft graduated colours. Some animal models were also decorated.

Many of Gray's porcelain tea-sets bore English style shapes, though styles from the Eastern Mediterranean often influenced the decoration.

Suggestions for Further Study

Niblett, Paul. *Hand Painted Gray's Pottery.* Stoke-on-Trent: City Museum & Art Gallery, Stoke-on-Trent, 1982, 1983; new edition 1987.

Casey, Andrew. *Susie Cooper Ceramics—A Collector's Guide.* Stratford-on-Avon. Jazz Publications, 1992.

Spours, Judy. *Art Deco Tableware.* Ward Lock, 1988.

"Elegance & Utility 1924-1978: The Work of Susie Cooper, A Tribute from Wedgwood;" catalogue by Adrian Woodhouse of an Exhbition at Sanderson's Showrooms, London, 1978.

"Susie Cooper Productions;" catalogue by Ann Eatwell of an Exhibition at the Victoria & Albert Museum, London and the City Museum & Art Gallery, Stoke-on-Trent, 1987.

Crossingham-Gower, Graham. "Susie Cooper—Pride of the Potteries." *Art & Antiques*, April 12, 1975.

Eatwell, Ann. "A Bold Experiment in Tableware Design." (1934 Harrod's Exhibition) *Antique Collector's Club*, 19(6) November, 1984.

Fletcher, Neil. "Sixty Glorious Years—The Work of Susie Cooper, OBE." *Antique Collector's Club*, 19(5) October, 1984.

McDonald, C. Haig. "Excellent in its Simplicity." (Susie Cooper); *The Antique Collector*, July, 1987.

Peake, Grahm. "In the Advance Spirit" (Susie Cooper); *The Antique Dealer & Collector*, July 1987.

Snodin, Su. "Susie Cooper, Diverse Designer." *The Antique Collector*, August, 1982.

Winstone, Victor. "As Fresh as 50 Years Ago" (Susie Cooper); *Art & Antiques*, June 10, 1978.

A.E. Gray Ltd. Part of a tea-set in silver lustre, c.1933.

Susie Cooper Coffee-set in 'Kestrel' shape, Crown Works, Burslem.

A.E. GRAY & CO. LTD.

Types of Ware	Production	Quality	Availability
Designs by Susie Cooper	Moderate to High	Good to Very Good	Common
A.E. Gray ornamental wares	Moderate to High	Good to Very Good	Common

Marks

A.E. Gray & Co. Ltd.

Transfer printed: (galleon on water   1912-1931
            plus legend:
            A E GRAY & CO LTD
            HANLEY ENGLAND)
(two galleon styles have been noted; one without a square border is an earlier mark of the above period)

Transfer printed: (ocean liner on water   1930-1933
            plus legend:
            HAND   PAINTED
            GRAY'S   POTTERY
            HANLEY-ENGLAND
            in square frame or square outline)

+/- "Designed by Susie Cooper"   c.1925 - 1929
    or "Susie Cooper Ware"
+/- artist's signature, eg. 'Susie Cooper'
    or monogram, eg. 'S.V.C.' (Susan Vera Cooper)
    (NB. From 1930, Susie Cooper worked for herself)

Transfer Printed: (clipper ship on water   c.1931 - 1961
            plus 3 wavy lines & legend:
            HAND PAINTED
            GRAY'S POTTERY)
+/- "MADE IN STOKE-ON-TRENT ENGLAND" or variations.

Susie Cooper (1930-1961)

Stamped: (in black triangle)   A   1930 - 1931
            SUSIE
            COOPER
            PRODUCTION

Transfer printed   A   1932 - 1939
 overglaze: SUSIE COOPER
(surmounted by a   PRODUCTION
 leaping deer)   CROWN WORKS
            BURSLEM
            ENGLAND

            Susie Cooper   1952 - 1953
            England

+/- pattern name and number
(NB. Many variations exist)

A. E. Gray Wall vase, 205mm high, stamped 'Gray's Pottery, Stoke-on-Trent' and ancient ship mark.

125

34, Bristo Street, Edinburgh (1917-1918)
Boroughloch, Buccleuch Street, Edinburgh (1918-1927)

Historical Background

The Holyrood Art Pottery was established by Henry Wyse in 1917, in financial partnership with a Mr. Isles. Henry Taylor Wyse (1870-1951) came to Edinburgh in 1904 to take up a part-time teaching post as Art Master at George Watson's Ladies' College. He had previously been an Art Master in Arbroath, and his artistic talents also extended to furniture design and etching. After a couple of other art teaching appointments in the city he took up a post as Lecturer in Art at Moray House Training College in 1922.

Wyse was active all his life in art, becoming president of the Scottish Art Teachers Association. He was also co-founder, with Robert MacLauren, of the Scottish Guild of Handicraft Ltd., about 1900. The Guild was run on similar lines to that of the English Guild of Handicraft, and operated a shop in Glasgow at 414, Sauchiehall Street, for sale of members' work. Pottery was specifically promoted by the Guild, which included among its members, Hugh Allan of the Allander Pottery (Glasgow, 1904-1908), whose art wares bore some similarity to those of Wyse. Wyse was certainly influenced by Allan.

Wyse established his pottery at 34, Bristo Street, but soon moved to larger premises south of Princes Street on the site of the old Boroughloch Brewery, adjacent to Archers' Hall. There was an amusing story that his kiln was causing a nuisance at the Bristo Street premises, and that a neighbour living in an appartment above the kiln room complained that her cat's paws were getting too hot!

The pottery became known for ceramic buttons and inserts for jewellery, which were particularly individual in design. A large range of art pottery was also made, however, for domestic and ornamental use.

The pottery welcomed visitors and regularly gave demonstrations of pottery making. Clay and glaze materials were also supplied, together with tools and instructions for "The Making and Decorating of Simple Pottery." The pottery advertised the sale of biscuit wares for amateur decorating, and the availability of a firing service.

The pottery was a centre for other crafts besides pottery. Articles such as table runners, tea-cosies and ladies' purses were fashioned out of livery cloth and suede, with applied "china stones" and silk embroidery. Serviette and finger rings were also produced, in sterling silver, with inset ceramic "stones." These other crafts demonstrated the application of ceramics to other uses, an interesting alliance of which was the output of calendars in pottery and suede.

Wares were exhibited at the 1924 and 1925 Wembley Exhibitions, and retailed by outlets such as Green & Co.; Jenner & Co. and Ford & Co. in Princes Street, Edinburgh; and Rankine & Co.. Pieces were also exported to North America and Australia. The business, however, became uneconomic and was hit by the recession during the late 1920s. Wyse had always tried to run the pottery more as a hobby, and during this period his daughter, Helann, became involved in the management of pottery.
In 1927, the business was sold. Wyse continued teaching, and retired in 1935.

Products

All hollow wares were thrown, using a white Cornish clay body, and some 68 shapes were listed in a catalogue of about 1923. Wyse was conscious of the dangers of lead glazes, and used coloured leadless glazes for his wares, substituting instead, copper and iron to achieve some interesting mottled effects. Although the mottled glazes were much admired, the majority of output seems to have been produced using flat, monochrome glazes. The catalogue lists Laburnam yellow, crimson, Cobalt blue, Madras green, Apple green, Victoria green, turquoise, Dove grey and purple as some of the colours available. Glazes were quite thick, with a silky finish of a high sheen.

The recruitment of an accomplished thrower, George Griffiths, from Buchan's Pottery in Portobello, nearby, enabled more hollow wares to be produced. Wyse's daughter, Helann, later recalled that fluctuations in the gas supply to the large gas-fired kiln, owing to local demands for gas-lighting, created a reducing effect on the copper oxide glazes used, which provided some initially unexpectedly pleasing results. It was found that the kiln could thereafter be regulated to the gas-lighting timetable to recreate the reducing effects!

A variety of hollow wares was produced, which were sold as "Holyrood Wares." Cruet sets, candlesticks, bowls, plates, vases, tea-sets, "fern pots," marmalade pots, tobacco-jars and ash-trays, etc. were produced in simple shapes. Many shapes were typically Edwardian in style, others were emulations of primitive styles or early Chinese. Apart from the glaze, most of the Holyrood Wares appeared to contain no further embellishment.[1]

By contrast, the ceramic jewellery produced, which was marketed as "Waverley Ware," comprised moulded designs, demonstrating clear Celtic influences. Ceramic "stones," buttons, beads, buckles, hair tidies, etc., were available, as well as what the pottery advertised as "unique pottery necklaces," featuring sometimes grotesque faces.

The ancient Egyptian influence was evident in some wares, particularly the Suede and Pottery Calendars. Highly ornamented glazed medallions of figures, birds, animals and Celtic symbolism were mounted on suede pendants, with a calendar attached.

---

[1] Since the pottery made available all its stock wares for amatuer decoration the collector may come across Holyrood shapes with very different forms of decoration.

Suggestions for Further Study

Huntly House Museum, 124, Canongate, Edinburgh, houses a collection of Holyrood wares.

Wyse, Henry T. "Some Arts & Crafts;" unpublished pamphlet (c.1946); plus other publications by Wyse from the archives of Huntly House Museum.

Wannop, Helann. "Henry Taylor Wyse—The Holyrood Pottery;" journal article by Wyse's daughter; *Scottish Pottery Historical Review* (SPHR) 9, 1984/85.

Kinghorn, Jonathan & Gerard Quail. "The Holyrood Pottery." *SPHR* 10, 1985/86.

Kinghorn, Jonathan. "The Allander Pottery 1904-1908." *Antique Collector's Club* 21(1), May, 1986.

The Studio Yearbooks for 1925-27 show illustrations of Holyrood art wares.

Holyrood Vase, 130mm high.

HOLYROOD ART POTTERY

Types of Ware	Production	Quality	Availability
Art pottery	Moderate	Good	Uncommon
Waverley Ware	Moderate ?	Good	Scarce

Marks

Impressed:	HOLYROOD (around Celtic Cross)	1917 - 1927	
+/- "MADE IN SCOTLAND"			
Incised or painted: (mainly on small items)	WYSE	1917 - 1927	

127

30, High Street, Honiton, Devon.

Historical Background

Charles Collard, well known among the Devon and Dorset pottery fraternity as an artist and pottery owner, purchased a rather run-down pottery in 1918 in Honiton High Street, which he proceeded to renovate and develop into a business which continues today.

Prior to this, Collard had owned and operated the Crown Dorset Art Pottery (Charles Collard & Co. Ltd.), which he had founded in 1905 in Poole, Dorset, and was forced to sell for financial reasons in 1917.

The local red clay was used at first, then mixed with white Cornish clay to produce a beige coloured body. Collard adopted a practice of painting over a glazed white slip ground, which involved pre-firing to fix the white ground and a main firing to fix the decoration. This technique was also employed at the Poole Pottery, resulting in similar matt finishes.

The similarity with Poole did not end there, for there were also decorative similarities, especially in the 1930s. A prime difference, however, between the output of Poole and Honiton during the 1930s was one of quality. Whereas Poole would exact a high standard of quality control over pieces offered for sale, the Honiton Pottery was not averse to releasing misshapen or misfired pieces for sale on purely economic grounds.

The position of the Honiton pottery in the High Street was to be of particular importance for the tourist trade, since Honiton was conveniently located on the main route west to Devon and Cornwall and ideally positioned for travellers as a rest point.

About twelve persons were employed at the pottery, which reached a peak of maturity during the late 1930s. Visitors to the pottery were welcomed and shown round the works by Collard's daughter Joan, who became a partner in the Pottery and also decorated some of the wares. Today she is President of the Honiton Pottery Collectors' Society.

Some wares were exhibited in the late 1930s in department stores and at County Shows. The onset of the Second World War, however, prevented the continuous production of anything other than undecorated utility wares, so the pottery closed for the duration of the war, reopening in October 1945.

Government restrictions, however, were still in force, and for a while most of the production was made for export. In 1947, Charles & Joan Collard sold the pottery to Norman Hull and Harry Barratt, both Staffordshire potters, who re-registered the business as Honiton Art Potteries Ltd. The current owners are Mr. & Mrs. Reevers.

Charles Collard retired to Torquay in Devon with Joan, and died in 1969, aged ninety-five.

Honiton Selection of typical wares, all with HONITON ENGLAND mark; l to r, back to front row:-jug, Celtic knot decoration, shape no. 30; vase, 200mm high, shape no. 87; ovoid vase, shape no. 19; circular box for false-teeth; tile, 100mm square, 'Woodland' pattern; pair of scent bottles; small jar and cover.

Honiton 'Woodland' pattern, l to r: vase, marked "COLLARD HONITON ENGLAND HAND MADE"; vase, 250mm high, shape no.8; rope-handled cup with saucer, marked COLLARD HONITON ENGLAND; ewer with leaping deer on a pink ground, marked COLLARD HONITON ENGLAND.

Products

The wares Collard produced at Honiton were generally very different from those he produced at Crown Dorset, although similarities of decoration and design can be seen which he obviously transferred and stylised. At Crown Dorset, heavy and richly coloured naturalistic painting was a characteristic (as at Aller Vale), whilst at Honiton, the decoration was less rich, more detached and frequently executed on a ubiquitous cream-white ground.

The general range of tourist wares was produced, but Collard disliked the almost obligatory Devon and Dorset motto wares and so used mottoes sparingly.

Although many domestic wares were produced (tea-sets, cruet sets, etc.) there was no production of heavy utilitarian wares such as milk-churns, bread pancheons, etc., as at some other country potteries. The clay was clearly not suited to heavy wares, being delicate in consistency, but ideally suited to the ornamental, tourist and commemorative wares which were produced in quantity.

The first ranges of wares produced were mainly tourist wares, featuring painted cottage and windmill decoration and scent bottles with painted Devon violets and appropriate legends. These wares were similar to those Collard had produced at Crown Dorset.

By the mid-1920s much larger more ornamental wares were being produced, mainly as jugs and vases. A 1930s catalogue lists over a hundred shapes and styles, which collectors today can cross-reference through the shape number, which was frequently marked on the base of a piece.

An early pattern featured a Celtic knot design, but a pattern known as "Jacobean" soon became popular and found favour with the craze for reproduction Jacobean furniture during the late 1920s. The Jacobean pattern featured colourful stylised floral motifs, reminiscent of Jacobean needlework designs (hence the pattern name). This pattern was developed and produced for many years, with not only colour variants but also design variants.

A pattern of the 1920s demonstrated a clear Persian influence and was a stylised version of De Morgan's chrysanthemum design, with the flower being depicted in pink and blue.

A pattern developed in the mid-1930s was known as "Stuart" after the decorator Vera Stuart and featured a greater coverage of colour over the surface of a pot with typically a wide emerald green band at the rim and base. The decoration was mainly geometric bands with a heavily stylised central floral motif.

Both the Stuart and Jacobean patterns were well suited to larger pieces such as shape number 8 (250mm. high). Another pattern of the mid-1930s was known as "Woodland" and consisted of a leaping deer decoration in an emerald green.

The shapes of the ornamental wares were not strikingly innovatory but rather plain. It could be said that the bold colour decorations did not require elaborate shapes. Certainly the more domestic and tourist wares bore functional shapes: ink-wells, scent bottles, candlesticks, pipe-holders, even false-teeth containers!

A less usual form of ornamentation employed was sgraffito decoration, since overglaze painting was the most preferred method of decoration. The sgraffito outlines were complemented by painting, but the glaze on such pieces seems to have been different, exhibiting a gloss finish rather than the more usual matt finish.

Another less usual decorative device was the use of handles resembling twisted rope, which was common to sgraffito decorated wares.

A common characteristic of Honiton wares was the use of coloured dashes painted around the rims of vases, jugs, cups, etc. It was almost a hallmark, it occurring so frequently.

A few tiles were decorated, mainly four-inch square (102mm), which were believed to have been brought in originally as blanks for making tea-pot stands.

Other wares included small animal models. These were made from plaster moulds and were a popular line with children. Lamp-bases were another popular line and were often produced with matching linen or parchment shades.

Honiton Group of wares, stylised chyrsanthemum motif, l to r:-ovoid vase, marked HONITON ENGLAND, shape no.9; jam pot, marked COLLARD HONITON ENGLAND, shape no.13; jug, 210mm high, marked COLLARD HONITON ENGLAND, shape no.33; jug with sgraffito and painted decoration, marked COLLARD HONITON ENGLAND, shape no.29.

Honiton Wares showing trefoil design, all marked COLLARD HONITON ENGLAND; l to r:-jug, 150mm high; vase; squat jug; jug, shape no.29.

Suggestions for Further Study

The Honiton Pottery Collectors' Society, 112, Sylvan Avenue, London, N22 5JB, welcomes new collectors and produces a regular newsletter.

"The Honiton Potteries," 30, High Street, Honiton, Devon. Opposite the current pottery is a local museum with a small display of wares.

Cashmore, Carol and Chris. *Collard the Honiton & Dorset Potter;* pub. privately 1983, contains a wealth of contemporary accounts of life at the pottery.

Cashmore, Carol. "Honiton—A Neglected Pottery." *The Antique Dealer & Collector's Guide,* May, 1987.

(The author is indebted to Carol Cashmore and Carl Rosen for permission to draw freely on their knowledge of the pottery.)

Honiton Wares showing De Morgan influence; l to r:-small vase, shape no.6; charger, 310mm diam., marked HONITON ENGLAND; large vase, shape no.9; jug, shape no.64, marked HONITON ENGLAND.

THE HONITON POTTERY

Types of Ware	Production	Quality	Availability
Ornamental wares	High	Poor to Good	Abundant

Marks

Impressed	HONITON ENGLAND		c.1920 - c.1929
+/- shape number (painted)			
Impressed	COLLARD HONITON ENGLAND	(small)* (large)	c.1927 - c.1937 c.1935 - 1947

* (both a large and small version of this mark was used)

+/- shape number (painted)

Other marks are rare.

Honiton Three vases showing Jacobean pattern, all with COLLARD HONITON ENGLAND mark, l to r:-vase, 250mm, one of a pair, shape no.8; smaller vase, centre, shape no.9.

131

Gunville, Carisbrooke, Newport, Isle of Wight.

Historical Background

Samuel Edgar Saunders established his Isle of Wight Handcraft Pottery in 1926 at Gunville, Carisbrooke, having obtained a brickworks from Pritchett & Co. Ltd. about 1920.

The "Carisbrooke Brick, Tile & Pottery Works" had a Head Office and Showrooms at 110, High Street, Newport, Isle of Wight, but hand-made pottery was advertised as Isle of Wight Handcraft Pottery.

Apparently the Brickworks Manager, Frederick Joseph Mursell was impressed by the suitability of clays on the island for ceramics, and suggested the making of glazed pottery.

The clay utilised was a red clay from Afton in the west of the island, and the kilns used were modelled on kilns at the Ceramic Works in Devres, France.

Mursell visited the Staffordshire Potteries and took on a potter by the name of Laye to supervise the establishment of the Handcraft Pottery.

It seems that several people were employed in the making of Isle of Wight Handcraft wares. It is recorded that in 1930 Mr. Laye was in charge of glazing, and a potter from Stafford by the name of Jackson was in charge of potting, whilst the painter and designer was a Mr. Reg Davies. The manager of the pottery at this time was Edward Jervison Bagley, who had sole charge of the operation.

A great variety of shapes and patterns was created, and because each piece was hand-made no two pieces appeared exactly alike, although many bore a similar decorative motif. "The keynote" was "simplicity and grace of outline combined with softness of colour," exclaimed the first catalogue of wares.

Pieces were said to have been purchased by Queen Mary, and Princess Beatrice was said to have taken a keen interest in the pottery. A London Showroom is recorded as having been at 15, Gamage Buildings in the "pottery mecca" of Holborn, EC1; but in spite of any prestige by this outlet or Royal patronage, the pottery never made a profit, and according to a newspaper report of 1938, the enterprise was carried on more "out of sentiment, fulfilling a useful purpose on the island."

Samuel Saunders lived at Padmore House in Whippingham, Isle of Wight, but there is little information at present as to his involvement in the pottery. He also owned the firm of Saunders Ltd., boat builders and seaplane manufacturers, which was also based on the island (later becoming Saunders-Rowe Aviation).

Samuel Saunders died in 1933, and ownership of the pottery passed to his son, Hulbert Samuel Saunders. In 1938, the pottery Manager, Edward Bagley, was found guilty of theft, through making and selling ceramic roundels without Hulbert Saunders' knowledge or consent. As a result of this case, and because he had no knowledge of the intricacies of pottery manufacture, Hulbert Saunders decided to close the Handcraft Pottery. The Brickworks, however, continued for some time afterwards.

Isle of Wight Selection of wares in "mottled glaze".

Products

Mostly vases were produced, sometimes two-handled, of smallish stature and simple shape (the tallest being 375 mm. high), but other wares included bowls, plates, candlesticks, jugs, egg-cups, lamp-bases, lemonade sets, tea and coffee sets, jars, cake stands and ash trays. Some pieces had external decoration in pewter.

Pieces were of good quality, with silky or high, leadless glazes, which tended to be thickish in consistency, not always covering the base of pieces.

On early wares, a range of ground colours was used, such as black, beige, pink, pale and deep blue, jade and olive green. A characteristic form of decoration was a single band of wavy or zig-zag lines, or instead, a covering of streaky coloured glaze at the top of a piece which was allowed to drip down.

A rare decorative motif was an owl painted centrally on a cake-stand, and any recognisable subject other than abstract was rare.

Pieces were mainly produced in monochrome colours, and a favourite colour on later wares appears to have been a bright mottled turquoise-green—a colour which extended across the product range. The turquoise-green wares were often tinged with pink, forming an attractive colour combination.

Later patterned wares were sometimes decorated in an art deco style with simple geometric lines executed in blue, black, brown, red or colour combinations.

The similarity of some early Isle of Wight pieces to some early Poole Pottery pieces is remarkable, and both were known as "Handcraft Pottery." Perhaps some of the Poole artists assisted at Carisbrooke.

Suggestions for Further Study

Carisbrooke Castle Museum, Newport, Isle of Wight.

Isle of Wight Selection of wares. l to r:i) shallow bowl, 245mm diam. ii) two-handled vase, 210mm high iii) lustrous bowl, 231mm diam. (courtesy of HCMS, DA 1984.114/7; DA 1977.157; CRH 1950.10/42).

ISLE OF WIGHT HANDCRAFT POTTERY

Types of Ware	Production	Quality	Availability
Handcraft wares	Moderate	Fair to Good	Uncommon

Marks

Incised or printed:	SES (in monogram within two concentric circles containing the words ISLE OF WIGHT POTTERY CO.)	incised: 1926-c.1933, printed: c.1933-1938

+/- letter and number codes. (On early pieces the numerals indicate the number of the glaze and the letters the shape, in the format numerals/letters. On later wares the first letter indicates the size (M=Medium, S=Small, L=Large), the numbers indicate the shape (up to 229), and the final letter or number indicates the glaze, eg. M/185/4.

(NB: Early wares bearing the incised mark have unglazed bases; later wares bearing the printed mark have glazed bases.)

Some later ware glaze codes:-
  Mottled Glazes: C.4, D.4, O.4, P.4, Q.4 (4 on its own appears to have been turquoise-green).
  Plain Glazes: E = Natural Semi-Matt
        S = Rose Du Barry
        A = Green
        B = Dark and Light Blue
        D = Blue Green
        J = Yellow
        K = White

Isle of Wight Specimen marks.

Brick & Tile Company, Pottington, N. Devon (1876-1914)

Historical Background

Alexander Lauder was educated in Edinburgh, and studied art and architecture, returning to his home town of Barnstaple in North Devon just prior to the death of his brother in 1860. His father operated a lime kiln at Pottington, which Lauder took over on his father's death. Lauder occupied much of his time with art and as a practising architect, designing many local buildings, chapels and schools in particular.

He had a strong interest in local affairs, and was elected Mayor of Barnstaple for two consecutive terms in 1885. He was particularly concerned for the full employment of the town's inhabitants, and encouraged local craft trades, through his own strong interest in the arts and crafts.

Quite when he became interested in pottery is not known, but it is logical to assume that his architectural work and special interest in the ornament and embellishment of buildings with terracotta and brick features led him to launch his "Devon Art Pottery" wares. He had established a business with his brother-in-law, William Smith, in 1876 to manufacture bricks and tiles, and it seems that within a few years he was also producing decorative art wares.

The brick business dovetailed well into art pottery production, since Lauder specialised in the manufacture of artistic brickwork and architectural tracery, including busts and decorative terracotta medallions designed to order. The clay onsite, however, proved not to be suitable for art wares.

The partnership of Lauder and Smith was dissolved in 1889, but Lauder was able to save a nearby brickworks from threatened closure (owing to bankruptcy of the owner), by buying shares in the business. This deal provided him with the source of a more suitable clay for his art pottery venture, which appeared to really get off the ground during the early 1890s.

In spite of his obvious artistic talent, his personal involvement in the day-to-day running of the pottery must have been limited, however, since he continued to be heavily involved in his architecture practice.

The pottery closed with the onset of the First World War in 1914.

Products

Early art wares seem to have been terracotta flower vases, many of which were substantial pieces several feet in diameter, and clearly stemmed from the production of architectural wares.

Later wares were often similar to Brannam's in shape and decoration, though several of Lauder's pieces were small in stature, and many miniature vases and jardinières were made. The similarity to Brannam's wares and the use by Lauder of the word Barum in his mark caused Brannam to consider legal action, though this was never carried out.

Shapes were generally simple, but the rich all-over decoration was often bold and colourful. Fish, floral and bird subjects were popular, usually executed in relief against cut-away stippled backgrounds of a lighter colour. Sgraffito decoration was also employed to good artistic effect, and there seems to have been little venture into the motto wares so characteristic of the Devon tourist market.

Some modelling was also undertaken, particularly on pots and vases. Coloured slips were liberally employed and some interesting pieces were produced with stylised floral and swirl decoration.

A wide range of art wares was produced, though vases were a predominant output. Umbrella stands, tobacco jars, fishmouth jugs, bird jugs, puzzle jugs, jardinières, etc, were made in considerable variety.

Lauder's architectural wares were often richly embellished with extensive modelling and coloured glazes, such as the fireplaces in his later Barnstaple home at "Ravelin" (not open to the public). The twin pediments above the Squires building in Tuly Street are rare surviving examples of his external workmanship.

Suggestions for Further Study

The Museum of North Devon, Barnstaple, has some Lauder pieces on display.

Edgeler, Audrey. *Art Potters of Barnstaple*. Nimrod Press Ltd., 1990.

Lauder Jardinière, 350mm diam.

Lauder Two vases, l to r:vase, with crane bird and flower decoration, inscribed mark "Lauder Barum"; vase, twisted handles with bird and foliage decoration, 210mm high, impressed mark "LAUDER BARUM".

Lauder Two vases, marked "LAUDER BARUM". l to r:i) 263mm high; ii) 328mm high.

Lauder Jug, 100mm high, fish motif in dark green, marked "Lauder, Barum".

ALEXANDER LAUDER

Types of Ware	Production	Quality	Availability
Art wares	Low to Moderate	Poor to Very Good	Common

Marks

Incised:	Lauder & Smith Barum	c.1880 - 1890
+/- date in full (eg. "17/8/89")		
Incised: +/- date in full (as above)	Alex Lauder Barum or A Lauder	1890 - c.1914
Incised:	Lauder Barum	c.1890 - c.1914
Impressed	LAUDER BARUM	c.1906 - 1914

(NB. Other variants exist, plus marks relating to "Lauder & Smith, Devon Art Pottery, Barnstaple")

BERNARD LEACH, artist/potter (1911-1979)

—stonewares
—porcelain
—slipware
—raku
—tiles

St. Ives, Cornwall (1920-1972)

Historical Background

Bernard Leach erected his pottery at St. Ives in December, 1920, with the object of producing a blend of Western and Eastern pottery designs, using his knowledge of Japanese and Oriental pottery styles. He was initially assisted by Shoji Hamada, from Kyoto, Japan, and, using local materials, he set about producing hand-crafted pieces, often emulating the Sung and Korai Celadons.

The Far East was not new to Leach—he had lived there since the age of ten, and by 1920, on his return to England, he had acquired a valuable knowledge of the cultures of China, Korea and Japan. In 1911, whilst in Japan, he had become apprenticed to the Japanese potter, Ogata Kenzan, and was able to learn centuries old skills, which set him in good stead for his later work at St. Ives.

At St. Ives, Leach and Hamada constructed the first traditional Japanese kiln in Western Europe, and two years later, the pottery was in full production, producing both high and low temperature stoneware, together with Japanese "raku" wares (porous, fragile stonewares). He employed student apprentices, such as Michael Cardew, Katherine Pleydell-Bouverie and Norah Braden, who were all to become accomplished potters in their own right. The early wares were not successful commercially, however, as they were too dull and monotonous for the British public.

In 1928, after Hamada had returned to Japan, Leach published a pamphlet entitled "A Potter's Outlook." This was the forerunner to his famous "A Potters Book," first published in 1940, in which he set out the standards of description for ceramic pots. His interest in English slipware was spurred on by successful sales in Japan, where it was highly acclaimed; but exhibitions in England could not boost the rather poor sales at home.

Pieces were shown at Paterson's Gallery in London in 1925, where his English slipware attracted particular interest. This was inspired by early English potters and their slipwares, such as the 17th. Century dishes of Thomas Toft. Leach was perhaps best known for his stoneware, however, and from 1930, when Leach's son, David, joined the St. Ives Pottery, stoneware tiles were also produced.

Bernard Leach Group of stonewares. (courtesy of Christie's Images), l to r:oviform vase, pale mushroom glaze over grey glaze, with mountain and cloud decoration in lavender blue and olive-green glaze; small jar in mushroom glaze, 87mm high; pear-shaped vase, 161mm high with deep brown glaze over mushroom glaze, incised willow pattern decoration.

Bernard Leach was a great admirer and friend of Howson Taylor, of the Ruskin Pottery; and he generally admired the work of many English slipware studio potters, including that of the Fishley family at Fremington in North Devon (ref. Fremington Pottery).

In 1934, Bernard Leach returned to Japan for a year's tour of working and lecturing with Shoji Hamada, Soetsu Yanagi (the philospher), and the potter and architect, Kenkichi Tomimoto. The same year, Harry Davis was employed as thrower at St. Ives.

After the war, David Leach took over most of the production management at St. Ives, giving his father more time to concentrate on new styles.

Bernard Leach made several further visits to Japan, and exhibited in Northern Europe (1949), the United states (1950, 1958, 1961), New Zealand and Australia (1961) and South America (1966). In 1977, the Victoria and Albert Museum, London, staged a retrospective exhibition of his work, which encouraged dealing in Leach's early wares in the antiques trade.

Bernard Leach continued potting until 1972, and died in 1979. His elder son, David, continues to pot at the Lowerdown Pottery, near Bovey Tracey, Devon, and his other son, Michael, runs the Yelland Pottery at Fremington, North Devon. Production of general wares ceased at St. Ives in 1979.

Products

Early wares at St. Ives were very much in the Japanese style, exhibiting an earthy appearance, local unrefined materials having been used for the pottery bodies.

Experiments in slipware gave way to more decorative pieces, using slip-trailed and sgraffito decoration, birds and leaping fish being predominant subjects. Red and brown on beige were predominant colours employed, with a yellow galena glaze over a white slip. Many vases and jugs were produced, though chargers and plates gave a broad canvass for the slipware designs, which often bore titles, such as "The Mermaid of Zennor," "Willow & Ducks" and "The Fish." The traditional use of wide borders, with a slip-trailed criss-cross pattern, was employed on plates and chargers, which ranged from about 305 to 510mm in diameter.

Some pieces bore mottoes, in the English slipware tradition. A globular vase made about 1930, with three handles, bears the motto "God with us" in sgraffito work, emphasised in a dark brown colour.

The potter, Michael Cardew, was particularly fond of Leach's slipwares, and wrote: "It is surely permissable to consider them (the dishes) as created purely for their decorative value, in places where such is spiritually necessary and desirable, as, for example, the living-room of an English home."

Colours on stonewares were generally browns and pale greens. Celadon glazes were employed, as well as Japanese glazes such as "tenmoku black" and "khaki iron red."

Colours were generally subdued and never gaudy. Pale blue was the brightest colour employed with any regularity, and occasionally a light green was used. Many designs on stoneware gave more the impression of being executed by colour wash, because of the subdued hues and indefinite outlines. Wax-resist decoration was also employed on some stonewares, however, and this, when accompanied by sgraffito decoration gave a more solid outline and appearance.

Landscapes and tree scenes featured strongly on some pieces of the late 1920s and early 1930s, and tree motifs such as "The Tree of Life" occurred throughout the pre-war years.

Medieval pitchers and pots often formed the shapes of Leach's pieces during the 1920s, and the Japanese glazes and designs combined to produce a hybrid style.

Slipware and stoneware were made by Bernard Leach until the late 1930s, after which porcelain and porcelainous stoneware were produced almost exclusively.

Models were rarely produced, but some sculpted horses were created during the early 1930s. Tea-sets and coffee-sets were produced during the mid-1930s, and tiles (usually no more than 100mm square) and tile panels were produced generally from about 1929.

Collectors should note that whilst the bulk of Bernard Leach's pots were made at St. Ives, some were made on visits abroad at different potteries. From 1911 to 1919, all his pieces (some were only *decorated* by him) were made at potteries in Japan, but all were marked with his monogram.

Suggestions for Further Study

The Holburne Museum in Bath houses a collection of pieces by Bernard Leach, and York City Gallery houses thirty-four pieces as part of the Milner-White Collection. The Victoria & Albert Museum, London, also houses a sizeable collection.

Leach, Bernard. *A Potter's Book.* London: Faber & Faber Ltd., 1940, revised 1976.

Leach, Bernard. *A Potter's Portfolio.* Lund Humphries, 1951 (reissued as *The Potter's Challenge.* New York: E.P. Dutton, 1975 & London: Souvenir Press, 1976).

"The Art of Bernard Leach;" retrospective exhibition catalogue; London: Victoria & Albert Museum, 1977.

Rice, Paul and Christopher Gowing. *British Studio Ceramics in the 20th. Century.* Barrie & Jenkins, 1989.

Riddick, Sarah. *Pioneer Studio Pottery—The Milner White Collection.* Lund Humphries in assoc. with York City Gallery, 1990.

Birks, Tony R. and Cornelia Wingfield Digby. *Bernard Leach, Hamada & Their Circle.* London: Phaidon Press Ltd., 1990.

Wateson, Oliver. *British Studio Pottery (The Victoria & Albert Museum Collection).* Oxford: Phaidon & Christie's, 1990.

Bernard Leach Bowl, 203mm diameter, white bodied earthenware

Bernard Leach Shallow dish, 160mm diam., earthenware with yellow slip decoration on a brown ground, c.1930.

Bernard Leach Dish, 163mm diam., painted mark "BL" and impressed monogram.

Bernard Leach Obverse of dish, 163mm diam, showing painted mark "BL" and impressed monogram.

BERNARD LEACH

Types of Ware	Production	Quality	Availability
Art wares	Low to Moderate	Good to Excellent	Uncommon

Marks

Painted:	B.H.L.	1911 - 1913
Trailed slip:	B.H.L.	1917
Incised:	BL	1913 - 1919
Coloured slip:	BL	1923 - 1933
Impressed	BL (in circle)	1917 - 1919
	BL SI (in circles)	1921 - 1942
	BL (in rectangle)	c.1925 - 1942
	SI (in circle)	c.1925 - 1942
+/- name of Japanese pottery		
+/- date		
Impressed	BL SI (in rectangles)	1943 - c.1946
	BL SI	c.1945 - 1972

(NB. Various permutations of the above marks have been recorded.)

Linthorpe, Middlesbrough, Teesside

Historical Background

The Linthorpe Art Pottery was established in 1879 by John Harrison in a brickyard known as the "Sun Brick Works," where deposits of a fine clay could be found.

The establishment of the pottery was at the suggestion of the renowned art designer, Dr. Christopher Dresser, who visited Middlesbrough in 1874. Dresser (1834-1904), who had published "The Art of Decorative Design" in 1862, was one of the first European designers to visit Japan, where, in 1877, he had gathered much useful information concerning Japanese art and culture, which he later put to good use in his designs for Linthorpe and elsewhere.

Dresser, as well as producing designs for ceramics, glass and metalwork, was also a botanist. He was retained as Art Director at Linthorpe, though probably never visited the works. He was also a close friend of Arthur Lasenby Liberty (of Liberty & Co.), and was manager of the Art Furnishers' Alliance in Bond Street, London, from 1880 until it went into liquidation in 1883.

The running of the pottery was undertaken by Henry Tooth, an enthusiastic artist and stage designer, who shared Dresser's interest in Japanese art. Dresser was thus left free to submit designs to the pottery, as well as to undertake work in other media, though it is believed that his designs for Linthorpe were considerable in number.

Many of Dresser's designs were considered avant-garde at the time. Utilitarian wares bore unusual shapes, often reflecting primitive South American and other styles. A contemporary advertisement speaks of "eastern colouring," reflecting the Oriental influence of Dresser's designs.

Henry Tooth had no previous pottery-making experience, but by 1883 he had become competent in throwing wares as well as decorating them. From quite early on in the life of the pottery, he specialised in the use of multi-coloured glazes, and managed to imitate the brilliant colour glazes found on 17th. and 18th. Century Chinese porcelains. He also experimented with streaked and mottled glazes, and produced some striking crackle glaze wares.

In 1882, some Linthorpe pieces were exhibited at the Society of Arts Exhibition in London, and from 1883 to 1885, Linthorpe wares took their share of prize-winning medals at various world exhibitions.

Henry Tooth left Linthorpe in 1882 to go into partnership with William Ault, and establish the Bretby Art pottery at Woodville, Derbyshire, the following year. He was succeeded as manager by Richard Patey. It is noticeable that Linthorpe designs became less avant-garde after 1882, and that more conventional designs were used. John Harrison, however, was always conscious of the need for pieces to be produced in accordance with the highest principles of art.

Certainly, output was of high quality, and although pieces were inexpensive to purchase at the time, those bearing Dresser's signature command high prices today.

Working conditions at Linthorpe were reported as excellent for the period, and, at one time, almost 100 people were employed at the pottery. The pottery used gas-fired kilns, and was the first in Europe to do so. Production lasted only ten years, however. Competition was strong, and, in 1887, prices had to be reduced.

The pottery closed in 1889, when John Harrison died, bankrupt. Christopher Dresser opened up a design studio in Barnes, West London, in 1889, employing ten assistants, one of whom was Archibald Knox, who became renowned for his designs in silver.

Linthorpe Vases designed by Christopher Dresser, "C.Dresser", "HT" (Henry Tooth), and "Linthorpe". l to r:-i) l.front: 200mm high, pattern no."200". ii) l.back: 200mm high, pattern no."336". iii) centre: 120mm high, pattern no."440". iv) r.front: 150mm high, pattern no."2JL". v) r.back: 165mm high, pattern no. "342CP".

Linthorpe Biscuit barrel, 200mm high, silver plated top, marked "1532" and Linthorpe squat vase mark.

Linthorpe Vase, 180mm high, designed by Christopher Dresser, sea-urchin shape, marked "C.Dresser", "HT", "312".

Products

Owing to the variety of glazes available, no two pieces were made exactly alike, and no single style predominated. Pâte-sur-pâte was used as successfully as sgraffito in decoration, and on some of the wares a form of impasto decoration was used, the ornamentation being placed on the item in the biscuit state. Most wares were slip-cast, though early wares were thrown.

Items produced at Linthorpe consisted of flasks, plaques, flower-pots, tazzas, salad-bowls (often complete with matching ceramic handles for salad-servers), fruit-bowls, large jardinières, jugs and vases (of which there were many). Ranges of domestic wares were also produced.

Shapes were generally simple, often bearing characteristic depressions or dimples. Many pieces bore similarities to the later Ault and Bretby Pottery wares, which is not surprising, considering the influence of Henry Tooth at all three potteries.

Painting was much utilised as a form of decoration, and the painted designs included flowers, animals, birds and insects. Colours varied from bright reds to deep blues, and nearly always occurred in monochrome or bichrome combinations, the latter often being a primary colour with a secondary tone (red and orange, for example).

Many of the glazes exhibited a highly polished effect, especially those used over streaked and mottled designs. Glazes were also fairly thick, and often formed a congealed ridge on the base of pieces. The quality of the pottery body was low, and the body was occasionally revealed through unglazed portions on the base of pieces.

The streaked effects complemented the asymmetrical shapes of Dresser's designs, though after 1882, shapes became simpler and more symmetrical. Sea-green, shades of brown, and burnt orange were predominant colours on Dresser's streaked and mottled wares. Some pieces also incorporated metal work, such as silver-plated rims and handles.

Aesthetically, collectors are often drawn between the two faces of Linthorpe. The one is attractive, stylish and decorative, the other mundane and unstylish. Current auction prices reflect this dichotomy, and Dresser-designed wares of unusual form command considerably more than other Linthorpe wares.

Suggestions for Further Study

A good selection of Linthorpe wares may be seen at the Dorman Memorial Museum, Middlesbrough.

Hart, Clive W. *Linthorpe Art Pottery.* Guisborough: Aisling Publications, 1988.

Halen, Widar. *Christopher Dresser.* London: Phaidon Press Ltd., 1990.

Le Vine, J. *"Linthorpe Ware;"* catalogue of an exhibition at Billingham Art Gallery, Jan. 1970; pub. Teesside Museums & Art Galleries.

Dennis, Richard and J. Jeffe. *"Christopher Dresser 1834-1904;"* illustrated catalogue of an exhibition at the Fine Arts Society, 1972; Richard Dennis, 1972.

Collins, Michael. *"Christopher Dresser 1834-1904;"* catalogue of an exhibition held at Camden Arts Centre (1979) and the Dorman Museum, Middlesbrough (1980); Arkwright Trust.

Tilbrook, Andy. *"Christopher Dresser Phd;"* catalogue of an exhibition by Andy Tilbrook and Dan Klein at The Halkin Arcade, London, Autumn, 1981.

"Christopher Dresser 1834-1904;" catalogue of an exhibition at The Fine Art Society, London, 1990; The Fine Art Society and Haslam & Whiteway Ltd.

Bracegirdle, Cyril. "Linthorpe the Forgotten Pottery." *Country Life*, 1971.

Pinkham, Roger. "A Tale of Three Potteries." *The Antique Collectors' Fayre,* September, 1977.

Wade, Hilary. "Christopher Dresser & The Linthorpe Potteries." *The Antique Collector*, February, 1984.

Linthorpe Selection of vases designed by Christopher Dresser.

LINTHORPE ART POTTERY

Types of Ware	Production	Quality	Availability
Art wares signed by Dresser	Low	Very Good to Excellent	Scarce
Other art wares	Low to Moderate	Fair to Very Good	Uncommon

Marks

Impressed	LINTHORPE (sometimes with the outline of a vase)		1879 - 1889
+/- Henry Tooth's initials or monogram, impressed:	H T (large or small)		1879 - 1882
+/- pattern number, impressed (up to 4196)			
+/- Christopher Dresser's signature (up to pattern number 1700), impressed, incised or painted	Chr. Dresser		1879-1882

+/- artist's initials, monogram or signature, eg.:

Fred Brown	FB
William Davidson	WD
Arthur Fuller	AF
Thomas Hudson	TH
Emily Leary	EL or Emily Leary
William Metcalf	William Metcalf
Florence Minto	F.M.
Clara Pringle	CP or C.A.P.
Arthur Shorter	AS or APS or A Shorter
Rachel Smith	RS or R:Smith
Lucy Worth	LW

Linthorpe Specimen mark on vase, showing Henry Tooth's monogram and pattern no. "811".

North Hylton, Sunderland, Co.Durham (1762-1817)
Ouseburn Bridge Works, Tyneside (1815-1859)
Ford A Pottery, Tyneside (1859-1926)
Ford B Pottery, Walker, Tyneside (1878-1963)

Historical Background

Christopher Thompson Maling (1741-1810), together with his brother John Maling (1746-1823) were appointed by their wealthy father, William Maling, a Huguenot refugee, to manage the newly established North Hylton Pot Works near Sunderland in 1762.

John Maling's son, Robert (1781-1863), moved the business to Ouseburn Bridge in 1815, and the successful production of brown wares, cream wares and blue-and-white transfer-printed white wares, begun at North Hylton, was enhanced in the rapidly expanding industrial area of Newcastle-upon-Tyne.

Robert Maling's son, Christopher Thompson Maling II (1824-1901), assumed control of the pottery in 1853, and continued the expansion programme, so much so that in 1859 a new pottery was constructed closeby. The "Ford A Pottery," as it was known, went into massive production of domestic white wares, with a heavy commercial bias. The pottery apparently accounted for production of almost ninety per cent of commercial jam-jars in the UK!

With the huge profits accumulated, Maling invested in the building of another pottery nearby, the "Ford B Pottery" at Walker, in 1878, which was to become probably the largest single site for ceramic production in the British Isles. The two Ford Potteries were run concurrently, producing a wide range of industrial and commercial containers in very high output.

The company became C.T. Maling & Sons in 1889, when C.T. Maling's three sons joined as partners (John Ford Maling (1858-1924), who managed Ford A; C.T. Maling III (1863-1934) and Frederick Theodore Maling (1866-1937), who managed Ford B).

A slump in trade and the miner's strike of 1926 forced the Ford A Pottery to close. The other pottery struggled on, however, in spite of a continued slump in trade and mounting debts; and about this time, the Mintons and Sèvres trained designer, Lucien Boullemier, was appointed art director at Maling. He remained until 1936, when his son, also Lucien, assumed the post of art director, a position he retained until 1963. Frederick Maling's son, C.T. Maling IV, entered the business in 1929, remaining until 1947.

The war took a considerable toll on production, and the Maling family were forced to sell the business in 1947 to a furniture removals business, Hoults Estates Ltd. The name of C.T. Maling & Sons was retained, however, and, thanks to the enterprise of Frederick Hoult the business was revived. New equipment was installed and many wares were successfully exported. Hoult's death in 1954, though, marked the beginning of the end, and the pottery closed in 1963, following the loss of Antipodean markets to Japanese competition.

Maling Flower bowl, lustre glaze, 280mm long, transfer-printed castle mark.

Products

Although the vast majority of output was for industrial and commercial use, transfer-printed decorative wares, such as commemoratives, dinner and tea services, had been produced since at least the beginning of the eighteenth century. Ornamental wares were almost a by-product of the early days of the Ford Potteries, and it was not until the 1920s, that they, together with colours other than the traditional blue-and-white, featured more strongly as output.

Without doubt, the influence of Boullemier was markedly demonstrated through the use of multicoloured and lustre decorated wares of the 1920s and 1930s. Deep salad bowls of a semi-porcelain body with bright, crowded floral decoration and colour washes were typical of the ornamental output. Many of the floral patterns were named, and appeared usually against a green or pink colour wash background.

Vases and flower holders of various shapes were often decorated solely with a bright iridescent lustre, and some fine painted art deco plates and services were produced during the 1930s. The body used for much of these wares was named "CETEM" (a corruption of C.T.M.), and so marked. Some undecorated porcelain was bought in, however, from European potteries, and this often bore the impressed mark of the factory of origin.

Maling's early obsession with blue-and-white transfer printed designs naturally extended to significant use of the Chinese "Willow Pattern" for domestic wares. Tea-caddies and various jars and containers were typically decorated with versions of this pattern, which continued to be used into the 1930s. Much of these latter wares were the result of a long-running association with the tea-merchants, Ringtons Ltd., from 1928. Other Chinese patterns included dragons or "Asiatic Pheasant," a favourite of many manufacturers of blue-and-white wares.

Suggestions for Further Study

The Laing Art Gallery, Higham Place, Newcastle-upon-Tyne, has some examples of Maling pottery in their collections (though not on display).

Bell, R.C., L. Dixon & S.H. Cottle. *Maling, A Tyneside Pottery.* Tyne & Wear County Council Museums, 1981 & 1985.

Bell, R.C. *Maling & Other Tyneside Pottery.* Shire Publications Ltd., 1986.

Moore, Stephen and Dr. Catherine Ross. *Maling, Trademark of Excellence.* Tyne & Wear Museum Services, 1989.

C.T. MALING & SONS

Types of Ware	Production	Quality	Availability
Ornamental wares	High	Good	Common

Marks

Impressed	MALING	c.1817 - c.1875
	C. T. MALING	c.1859 - c.1870
or	C. T. M.	
Printed:	C.T.M. & SONS (plus picture of Newcastle castle keep) ENGLAND	c.1891 - 1900
Printed:	CETEM WARE	c.1900 - 1925

+/- "ENGLAND" or "MADE IN ENGLAND"
+/- new picture of castle keep.

Printed:	MALING NEWCASTLE-ON-TYNE (plus castle keep, new picture)	c.1924 - 1963

+ either "ENGLAND" or "MADE IN ENGLAND" or both!
+ "EST. 1762" (*from c.1929*)
+/- name of pattern (eg. "Japonica")

(NB. Much early Maling wares were unmarked, and all Maling marking practices were inconsistent, with many variations evident.)

Pomona House, Fulham, S.W. London (1873-1877)
Southall, Middlesex. (1877-1914)

Historical Background

The four Martin Brothers commenced production of saltglazed stoneware in 1873 at their Pomona House studio in Fulham, firing their work at the Fulham Pottery nearby. They moved their workshop to Southall in 1877. Production was based on Doulton techniques, but designs at Southall were clearly their own.

Charles Martin (1846-1910) kept a shop and gallery in High Holborn, London, which acted as the retail outlet for the pottery. Robert Wallace Martin was deemed head of the firm, and was concerned mainly with modelling the wares. Walter Frazer Martin was the principal thrower, whilst Edwin Martin's role was as principal decorator. The brothers often interchanged roles, but also relied on outside help. The artist, Mark V. Marshall, assisted them at one time as decorator, before moving on to Doulton; and an artist by the name of Walter Edward Willy was also employed.

Both Walter and Edwin Martin had previously worked as assistants in Doulton's Art Studios, and had attended evening classes at Lambeth School of Art from 1872 to 1873. During the late 1890s, the Martin Brothers came under the patronage of the architect Sydney Greenslade. The "vegetable" designs of this period resulted through one of his commissions. He proved influential to the brothers' business, persuading them to accompany him to the Paris Exhibition of 1900, where they collected many new ideas.

After 1900, however, business began to fall steadily, resulting in the closure of the pottery in 1914, the shop closing not long afterwards. Robert Wallace's son, Clement Wallace Martin, made wares similar to Martinware through to the 1930s. The workshop buildings were destroyed in 1942.

Products

Early pieces at Fulham contained elements of early Doulton stoneware in design, whilst early wares at Southall consisted of carved and modelled wares, often with a Medieval Gothic-like appearance.

Apart from some early terracotta ware and a short-lived venture into painted earthenware, production was exclusively saltglazed stoneware. Pieces were often heavily carved and incised, and output consisted primarily of vases and pots.

From about 1883, sculpted models of birds, animals and reptiles were introduced. Many of the birds had detachable heads, for use as tobacco jars, and featured curious expressions. These "Wally Birds," as they became known, were produced in a variety of guises and sizes, from baby owls to large birds with human attitudes.

Many of the animal and bird models were grotesque in shape, and were often the results of errors in modelling the clay, rather than any deliberate design. The practice of using thrown rejects for modelling into grotesques not only reduced waste, but was also profitable.

The contemporary writer, Cosmo Monkhouse, wrote in 1882 of the Martin Brothers' grotesques: "A strangely human jug completes a group of creatures like many things, and yet like nothing on this earth." Concerning the brothers' vases, he wrote: "there is scarcely any variety of decoration which is not employed."

Vases might be square shaped, cylindrical, columnar or globular; symmetrical, or assymmetrical. Certainly many of the vases were extremely beautiful, yet many were quite awkward in shape, leant at unusual angles and stood lopsided. This confirms the two faces of the brothers' work, which so often influence the collector—the rough, earthy type of wares as opposed to the smooth, delicate and symmetrical wares.

Martin Brothers Three pieces, marked "Martin Bros London & Southall", l to r:Cylindrical vase, 260mm high, with fish decoration, dated "9-1911"; Renaissance style vase, dated "6-1898"; Four-sided vase, with sea creatures, dated "8-1898" and incised faint mark "Queer".

Martin Brothers Writing set. (courtesy of Christie's Images)

Martin Brothers Photo of the Martin Brothers in their studio and two
examples of their work. (courtesy of Christie's Images)

Martin Brothers Vase, 340mm high, with sea creatures, dated "10-1898" and "Martin Bros London & Southall".

Early "renaissance" or "medieval" style wares featured mainly symmetrical floriate designs on chargers, jugs and vases. Decoration was mainly a buff coloured design on a brown background, which often exhibited the inlaid effect that was produced by medieval workers in encaustic tile production.

Other wares bore generally brown based decoration or occasionally cobalt blue on early wares. Floral motifs were common, with subjects such as foxglove, the designs being incised with often a single glaze covering. Multi-coloured designs were unusual, the colour palette being usually restricted to two or three colours per piece. Sea-scenes were often depicted, with sea-creatures (fish, jelly-fish and squid, for example) as well as dragon motifs and other animals. Sgraffito designs were often accompanied by modelling, and wares were made in all shapes and sizes, from finely detailed miniatures to pieces of substantial size.

The late 1890s saw the brothers producing textured vases and pots resembling vegetables and natural forms. These exhibited fine texturing and modelling, and were made in a variety of shapes, and frequently resembled a Japanese style known as "Mishima." This involved the creation of an incised pattern, which was filled in with clay paste of a different colour to the body of the ware. Other textured wares were also made, such as bamboo-like vases.

About the same period, the brothers produced their well-known "face jugs" (jugs modelled with grinning faces). These were usually in brown salt-glazed stoneware, without additional colouring, and bore either a single face or one opposite the other. Doulton later produced their own colourful version of this type of jug in earthenware, as well as vegetable shaped vases, similar to those of the brothers. Faces were also modelled on to portions of vases.

Other wares consisted of fountains and large garden ornaments, cornices, mantel-pieces, plaques and bas-reliefs, tiles, miniatures (mostly by Edwin Martin), figurines, clock-cases, and even chess-men and oil-lamp bodies. Many items were sold privately, and were costly in comparison to other studio pottery of the time. Ten guineas was not an unusual price to pay for a Martin Brothers vase of say only eight inches high (205mm).

Between 1896 and 1898 an attempt was made to produce painted earthenware, but this was soon abandoned. Later potting in stoneware was noticeably more rounded and thinner than the heavily potted early wares.

The brothers' stoneware is highly valued by collectors, particularly for its craftsmanship and individual style. The brothers were firstly modellers and throwers, and although decoration was only a secondary skill it was always accomplished well. One has only to see the expressions on the face-jugs and Wally birds to appreciate the skill of the brothers' work in clay modelling.

Collectors should note that some pottery marked "Martinware" was made until the 1930s by Robert Wallace Martin's son, Clement Wallace Martin; but this is of poorer quality than the brothers' ware.

Suggestions for Further Study

Pitshanger Manor Museum, Walpole Park, Ealing, West London, houses the Sydney Greenslade bequest (the largest collection on public display).

The Heritage Museum, Kingston-upon-Thames, Surrey, houses a small, but fine representative collection, the result of a local bequest.

The Victoria & Albert Museum, London houses several examples of Martinware.

Southall Library, South London.

"Some Recent Developments in the Pottery of the Martin Brothers." *The Studio* 42, 1908.

Haslam, Malcolm. *The Martin Brothers, Potters.* Richard Dennis, 1978.

Summerfield, Angela. "The Martin Brothers." *The Antique Collector*, November, 1987.

Martin Brothers Vases. l to r:i) 150mm high, signed "R W Martin, London 9/9/1880". ii) 240mm high, signed "R.W.Martin Bros,London & Southall 21/4/1883".

Martin Brothers Stoneware examples. l to r:i) 'Wally bird' jar and cover, 200mm high, marked "R.W.Martin & Brothers London & Southall 10-4-1903". ii) vase, 306mm high, incised decoration of sea creatures, marked "R.W Martin & Brothers 8 1891 London & Southall".

Martin Brothers Selection of wares.

Martin Brothers Selection of wares.

THE MARTIN BROTHERS

Types of Ware	Production	Quality	Availability
Modelled birds, animals, face-jugs, grotesques	Low	Good to Excellent	Scarce
Vases	Low to Moderate	Poor to Very Good	Uncommon
Plaques & architectural items	Low	Poor to Very Good	Scarce

Marks

Impressed: (with variations)	R W MARTIN, FULHAM	1873/4
	R W MARTIN fecit	1874 - 1877
	R W MARTIN LONDON	1874 - 1877
	R W MARTIN SOUTHALL	1877 - 1878
Incised signature: + "London" or "Southall"	R W Martin Sc	1877 - 1878
	R W Martin London & Southall	1879 - c.1883
+ month and year (eg. "7-1882")		
	R W Martin & Brothers London & Southall	1883 - 1914
	Martin Bros. London	1883 - 1914
+ month and year (eg. "4-1906")		
+/- artist's initials and/or thrower's initials:	EBM - Edwin Bruce Martin RWM - Robert Wallace Martin WFM - Walter Frazer Martin	

Martin Brothers Specimen mark on vase, with date July, 1889.

(1850—1967)

—earthenware
—tiles
—lustres
—pâte-sur-pâte

Benthall Works, Broseley, Shropshire (1852-1882)
Benthall Works, Jackfield, Shropshire (1882-1967)

Historical Background

Originally established by George & Arthur Maw at Worcester in 1850, Maw & Company transferred their encaustic tile-making business to Ironbridge Gorge at Benthall, Shropshire, in 1852.

From 1851 to 1857, output was mostly tiles, plainly decorated with geometric patterns. From 1857, new colours were introduced, which gave greater pattern flexibility.

In 1861, Maw & Co. began to produce small tesserae for use in pictorial mosaics, either as wall or floor decoration. Not long after, coloured enamels were produced for majolica tiles, and, in 1867, Maw & Co. exhibited their renowned turquoise blue enamel at an exhibition in Paris. The company advertised some tiles as "faience furniture inlays," for inclusion into pieces of furniture, such as wash-stands. A cast-iron radiator cover at the Ironbridge Gorge Museum features a group of colourful Maw's majolica tiles as a ceramic grille.

In 1882, a new enlarged "Benthall Works" was established at nearby Jackfield, but tiles remained the principal output of the firm, the production of which was facilitated by ample clay supplies from pits adjacent to the factory.

Art pottery began to be made, the production of which increased significantly from the late 1880s. Designs were commissioned from well-known artists, not only for art pottery but also for tiles. The artists Lewis Day (1845-1910) and Walter Crane (1845-1915) contributed many designs, and tiles designed by them were exhibited at the Royal Jubilee Exhibition in Manchester in 1887.

Maw & Co. won many medals at international exhibitions, including Dublin, Paris, Oporto and Melbourne (1888/9). They also exhibited in Glasgow (1888) and at the Chicago World's Fair (1893), the trade-stand of which was designed by Charles Henry Temple, their chief designer. His monogram appeared on several wares from about 1885 to 1901.

Maw & Co. established a world-wide reputation, and undertook several commissions for decorative work, notably the Maharaja's Palace at Mysore in India.

The company ceased trading as Maw & Co. in 1967, and the Benthall Works at Jackfield is now a crafts centre.

Maw & Co. Vases designed by Walter Crane. (courtesy Clive House Museum, Shrewsbury: photo G.T. Prince).

Maw & Co. Tiles, 130mm square, designed by Walter Crane, 'Nursery Rhymes', c.1874. (courtesy HCMS, 1969.129/1-6).

Maw & Co. Ruby lustre tiles. (courtesy of Christie's Images)

151

Products

During the late 1870s, Maw & Co. produced a range of lustre decorated wares, similar to those of William De Morgan, and, like De Morgan's wares, a common decorative subject was a galleon. Lustre glazes were used to good effect on vases, jugs and tazzas, but sgraffito decoration and pâte-sur-pâte were also employed as methods of decoration.

Charles Henry Temple's favourite decorative subject seems to have been the draped classical female figure, but he also designed wares with relief-moulded floriate patterns, some of which were on a green ground with a brown lustre glaze.

Decorative themes of Walter Crane were Grecian ships or naked female figures with foliage. Crane often used a simple gold or ruby lustre on a white ground in his designs. About 1885, he designed some vases, ewers and plates in a Mediterranean style, reminiscent of Italian pottery of the Renaissance period. These also incorporated the decorative themes described above, often in monochrome lustres on a white ground. Shapes were in keeping with the Mediterranean style, and sometimes featured relief-moulded swan's head handles on vases and ewers. These wares were produced until about 1915.

A catalogue of "Maw's Decorative Pottery" for 1900 lists a variety of ornamental wares and decorations, viz:-

1) Rich Persian Glazes: "beautiful colours" on modelled surfaces; "marbled" or "splashed" colours, intermixed or layered "after the manner of the Oriental potters." These glazes were available across the product range.

2) Polychrome Enamel Decoration: combined with painting on modelled features, "after Palissy or Della Robbia." Mostly on urns and heavily moulded items.

3) Underglaze Painting: on plain surfaces, sometimes with enamel painting or gilding.

4) Barbotine, or Clay Painting: "impasto" painting on vases in a floriate Persian style.

5) Incised Ware: intricate sgraffito work on vases, covered with transparent glazes.

6) Oiron, or Henri Deux: as for Incised Ware but "the indentation is filled in with coloured clays, and the whole is covered with a transparent colourless glaze."

7) Sgraffito: decoration incised through a layer of different coloured clay, producing a cameo effect.

8) Lustre Ware: lustre colours available across the product range.

Items for decoration ranged from large urns and jardinières to chargers and vases, many featuring heavy use of modelling. A series of moulded plates and chargers was advertised as "subjects adapted from designs of fine antique silver." These subjects included 17 personalities from 1491 to 1653, including Henry VII, Mary Queen of Scots, Lord Darnly, Shakespeare and Cromwell. Many of the other items imitated classical or antique pottery styles.

Tiles, however, were the principal output of the company, and, with the increase in colours and the introduction of enamel colours, they became an attractive medium for the attention of competent artists. Walter Crane designed a nursery-rhyme series for tiles about 1874, featuring characters such as "Little Boy Blue" and "Little Brown Betty." The designs were similar to his illustrations with music for "The Baby's Opera" (1877).

About 1890, Maw & Co. produced a range of dust-pressed, hand-painted, ruby lustre tiles in art nouveau floriate designs. The "dust-pressed" technique was a quick and easy method of producing tiles from dry "dust" clay, using a steam press. It was also used to produce "mosaic effect" tiles; and the collector will come across trade tiles which advertise the many finishes and sizes available from the company.

The "encaustic sandwich" method was also used, particularly for floor tiles, whereby an outline was pressed into a block of clay, which was then inlaid with strips or blocks of clay of different colours. This method was utilised by medieval craftsmen, and was particularly suited to heavy wear on church floors, for example, since the design was pressed some way through the thickness of the tile. Maw & Co. utilised the opportunity to reproduce medieval patterns for replacement tiles, as well as satisfying the Victorian demand for Medieval Gothic. Maw & Co. also employed a similar process called the "plastic clay" method, where clay of one colour was pressed into clay of another, and smoothed down. Tube-lining was also used on tiles, a method of decoration which gave a relief outline to a design.

From 1905 to about 1915 colourful embossed tiles were produced, many of which featured the galleon theme; and about the same time Lewis Day designed many embossed tiles with richly decorated floral motifs.

During the 1930s, many tiles in the art deco style were produced (small four inch (102mm) tiles in particular). These bore strong geometric patterns with low-relief "eggshell" glazes which exhibited a metallic sheen.

Maw & Co. Tile, 150mm square, 'The Old Man & His Sons' (courtesy HCMS, 1971.410/6).

Suggestions for Further Study

Clive House Museum, Shrewsbury, Shropshire.

Kensington Palace Gardens, West London. (Maw commission, c.1862)

Jackfield Tile Collection, Ironbridge Gorge Museum, Ironbridge, Shropshire.

Arthur Maw's House (now the Valley Hotel), Ironbridge.

Various churches have examples of floor tiles. St. Martin's, East Horsley, Surrey, has good examples of Maw's early floor tiles in plain Medieval Gothic style (1868/9), produced via the encaustic sandwich method, plus their renowned turquoise-blue enamel on a few plain tiles.

Beaulah, Kenneth. *Church Tiles of the Nineteenth Century.* Shire Publications, 1987.

Messenger, Michael. *"Pottery & Tiles of the Severn Valley."* (catalogue of the Clive House Museum collections) Remploy Ltd., 1979.

Maw & Co. Tiles in porch at St. Martin's Church, East Horsley, Surrey.

Maw & Co. Vase, 304mm high, marked "No 1".

MAW & CO.

Types of Ware	Production	Quality	Availability
Tiles	High	Fair to Good	Abundant
Art pottery	Low to Moderate	Good to Very Good	Scarce

Marks

Impressed	FLOREAT MAW SALOPIA (in circle)	c. 1880 - 1914

+/- "BROSELEY SALOP" (on tiles)
+/- the words "DOUBLE" and "GRIP", enclosed in separate circles, on tiles
+/- "ENGLAND" (after 1891)

Printed and later moulded:	MAW	c. 1850 onwards
	MAW & CO	c.1885 - 1915

+/- artist's mark:

Walter Crane (died 1915):	CW (in monogram + crane bird)	
Lewis F Day	LFD (in monogram)	
C H Temple	CHT	c.1885 - 1901

153

THE MINTON FACTORIES

(1793—present)

—earthenware
—pâte-sur-pâte
—majolica
—tiles
—reduced glazes (from 1914)

South Kensington Art Pottery Studio, London, (1871-1875);
Stoke-on-Trent (1793-present);
Minton, Hollins & Co. (Ltd., from 1927) Patent Tile Works, Stoke-on-Trent (1868-1962)

Historical Background

Mintons began in 1793, when Thomas Minton set up the first works. From 1845 to 1872, the firm was known as Minton & Co., whilst from 1873 to 1968 it was known as Mintons Ltd.

From 1845, Michael Daintry Hollins, a partner in the company, undertook the production of tiles through the subsidiary firm of Minton, Hollins & Co.. Although some tiles were produced under the title "Minton & Co.," the majority were produced and marked by Hollins' subsidiary company. The partnership ceased when Minton, Hollins & Co. became a totally separate manufacturing operation in 1868.

In 1870, the French artist Louis-Marc-Emmanuel Solon (1835-1913) was employed at Minton & Co. as a designer and modeller of the pâte-sur-pâte process which he had studied at the Sèvres Porcelain Factory in France. Pâte-sur-pâte was a Mintons success story, and Solon's work is recognised from the familiar designs of cherubs and female figures in white pâte-sur-pâte on blue-grey backgrounds. Solon's work was shown at the Paris Exhibition of 1878. The process was expensive and time consuming, but the results were often spectacular. Solon retired from Mintons in 1904. One of his sons, Léon Victor Solon (1872-1957) became art director at Mintons in 1901.

The establishment of an Art Pottery in South Kensington, London, was prompted by the success of a collaboration between the artist Edward J. Poynter and students of the National Art Training Shcool, in the decoration of the tiled grill-room of the South Kensington Museum (now the Victoria & Albert Museum). In 1871, a studio was set up near the Royal College of Music, South Kensington, under the directorship of William Stephen Coleman (1829-1904). Here, mainly tiles and plaques were produced, with several plaques by Coleman himself which sold from £30 upwards.

Hannah Barlow was a decorator of the Studio, prior to her joining Doulton; and there were several competent artists engaged in work during the Studio's lifetime, notably John Eyre (a member of the Royal Society of British Artists) and Edmond Reuter (connected with Mintons from 1874 to 1895).

The Studio was never a successful venture, however. Coleman left in 1873, and the Studio was not re-opened after fire broke out in 1875. The closure of the South Kensington Studio did not end the production of art pottery at Mintons, though. The company saw the rest of the century out with many fine ornamental creations, thanks to the skill of its art directors and artists.

The art directors are worth listing, since each contributed some special talent to the pottery:-

Art Director	Period as Art Director
Léon Arnoux	1849—1895
(French chemist and potter)	
Louis Jahn	1895—1900
Léon Victor Solon	1901—1909
John William Wadsworth	1909—1914
Walter Woodman	1914—1930
Reginald Haggar	1930—1935
John William Wadsworth	1935—1955

In 1902, Léon V. Solon and John Wadsworth introduced a new ware based on Viennese art nouveau designs, which became known as Secessionist Ware. The striking use of colour combinations (such as crimson against green) and the stylised art nouveau floral patterns ensured the success of this ware for several years.

Today, the name "Mintons" continues as a trade-mark of Royal Doulton Limited, but the indiviudal style of their tablewares has been assured. Minton, Hollins & Co. Ltd. was absorbed into H & R Johnson-Richards Tiles in 1962.

Mintons Vases in the 'Secessionist' style. l to r:-i) 290mm high, marked "Mintons Ltd.",."3537", plus date code for 1904. ii) 130mm high, marked "T542", plus date code for 1905. iii) 250mm high, marked "3334D". iv) 160mm high, marked "Mintons Ltd. No.46", "3548". v) 290mm high, marked "Mintons Ltd. No.39", "3505", plus date code for 1907.

Products

Tableware was the principal output of Mintons during the Victorian period, although production of ornamental wares increased after 1868, (tiles and architectural ceramics having been legally declared to be the sole business of Minton, Hollins & Co.).

Although tiles were produced in quantity by Minton, Hollins & Co., they were also part of the output of Minton & Co.'s South Kensington Studio. During the early part of 1871, W. S. Coleman produced an initial series of tiles and other items, decorated by means of underglaze painting, but later on, tube-lining became a favoured method of decorating tiles. Tube-lining consisted of creating raised lines of trailed slip, using a tubular tool, and, with the application of coloured glazes, gave a greater depth to pieces.

Some fine tile designs were created by the artists Edward J. Poynter and Walter Crane (1845-1915) during the South Kensington Studio period, and about 1880, the designer John Moyr Smith designed a popular series of tiles with scenes from Shakespeare's plays (one of five series designed for Minton, Hollins & Co.).

Many tiles were produced for insertion into pieces of furniture, and the designer and architect Augustus Pugin contributed many tile designs for Mintons in this respect, as did the designer John Moyr Smith. A large tiled stove designed by Pugin was a centre-piece at the Great Exhbition in 1851.

Mintons Jug and basin set, 360mm high, in the 'Secessionist' style.

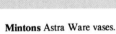

Mintons Astra Ware vases.

Mintons Astra Ware vases.

Under the direction of Léon Arnoux, a range of so-called "majolica ware" was produced, decorated in relief by Arnoux's "majolica glazes." The items produced in this range (fountains, jardinières and other garden ornaments) bore litle relation to actual majolica ware in composition, but were similar in appearance. The range proved popular, however, and sold well into the turn of the century.

From 1870, printed and painted dinner services were produced at Mintons, and the more important pieces were signed by such painters as Herbert Wilson Foster (1848-1929) (portrait and figure designs plus animals and birds) and J.E. Dean (d. 1935) (animal designs).

Perhaps the most spectacular example of decoration at Mintons during the mid-Victorian period was Louis M. Solon's pâte-sur-pâte. The pâte-sur-pâte process (literally "paste on paste") involved building up layers of white clay slips—a technique developed by Solon whilst at the Sèvres factory in France. The decoration was then cut into the piece before firing.

Solon's styles were mainly classical, and from the time he joined Mintons (1870), the company was greatly influenced by the rich colourings of items produced by the Sèvres porcelain factory. So much so, that Mintons employed several continental artists in an attempt to emulate some of the Sèvres styles. Pâte-sur-pâte was successful at Mintons, and was revived by Alboine Birks (Louis Solon's best apprentice) as a means of decoration during the 1920s, continuing until 1937.

The production of earthenware art nouveau vases was undertaken at Mintons during Léon Victor Solon's directorship. The most noticeable range was the Secessionist Ware, which appeared on may vase forms as well as jardinières, candlesticks, etc. Colours were bright and often duochromes, and were usually executed against a cream ground. Most items were cast.

In 1896, a range of high-glazed ornamental pieces known as "Byzantine Ware" was launched. Vases, jardinières, etc. were produced in a classical style, with dark, streaky glazes.

After 1909, under John Wadsworth's direction, many fine art nouveau floral motifs were executed on vases and tablewares.

During the Edwardian period, some Mintons pieces were cast from models by French sculptors, but generally pieces were still hand-thrown. A common colour combination of this period was green, yellow and pastel blue, which appeared across a wide range of articles.

Six inch (150mm) square tiles were still being produced in quantity, with some four inch (100mm) square and ten inch (252mm) square tiles in limited production. The artist G.E. Cook designed some fine monochrome portraits on four inch tiles.

During the First World War, Minton, Hollins & Co. departed from their normal tile production and produced a range of ornamental ware under the umbrella title "Astra Ware." This ware originated through a slump in the tile trade as a result of the war, and was first advertised in 1917. It proved so successful that production continued after the war until 1934. It sold at a moderate price, and consisted of mainly vases, with variegated glazes, created by reduction during firing. The variegations ranged from bright reds to sea-greens with black, sometimes with bubbles of coloured glaze in relief.

The texture of glazes on Astra Ware varied considerably, as did the shapes and sizes of the pieces, which ranged from small buttons and medallions to bowls, flasks and vases. Shapes were mainly simple, but stylish, designed to show off the reduced glazes. A sang-de-boeuf, smooth streaky glaze was particularly effective, as was a similar turquoise glaze. Some pieces were thrown, but most were cast.

During the early 1920s, the craze for floating-flower bowls was admirably satisfied by Mintons, who produced a wide range of pieces for this purpose.

A general characteristic of Mintons wares was the richness and brightness of colour used. Under the direction of Reginald Haggar (from 1930) more modern designs began to appear, which were widely reflected in the ranges of tableware. Stylised landscapes were depicted in the "Landscape" pattern, but the more typical deco, geometric patterns were also produced.

Under John Wadsworth's second period of direction, new ranges of earthenware were launched, such as "Solano Ware" (from 1937) and a bright art deco pattern called "Byzantine" (1938).

Suggestions for Further Study

The Minton Museum, Stoke-on-Trent.

The Jackfield Tile Museum, Ironbridge, Shropshire, has a splendid collection of Mintons tiles.

Osborne House, Isle-of-Wight (Queen Victoria's summer retreat) houses the largest pâte-sur-pâte vase ever produced by Mintons.

Atterbury, Paul. *Dictionary of Minton.* Woodbridge, Suffolk: Antique Collectors' Club, 1988.

Beaulah, Kenneth. *Church Tiles of the Nineteenth Century.* Shire Publications, 1987.

Lemmen, Hans Van. *Tiled Furniture.* Shire Publications Ltd., 1989.

Dawes, Nicholas M., *Majolica.* New York: Crown Publishers Inc., 1990.

"Minton 1798-1910;" catalogue of an Exhibition by E. Aslin & Paul Atterbury at the Victoria & Albert Museum, London, 1976; London: Victoria & Albert Museum, 1976.

"Minton Tiles 1835-1935;" catalogue of an Exhibition, edited by D. Skinner & Hans Van Lemmen; Stoke-on-Trent City Museum & Art Gallery, 1984.

Mutler, Grant. "Minton Secessionist Ware." *The Connoisseur*, August, 1980.

Weaver, Cynthia. 'The "Astra" Ware of Minton, Hollins & Co.' *Antique Collector's Club* 26(6), November, 1991.

Minton Two tiles, 200mm square, marked "Minton China Works" (the tiles featuring flying storks were probably designed by Christopher Dresser).

Minton Jardinière, 970mm high, yellow and green "secessionist" decoration on a red ground, marked "No. 72".

Minton Jug, 288mm high, in the 'Secessionist' style.

Minton Specimen mark of South Kensington Studio on dish.

Mintons Vase, 210mm high, by John Wadsworth, c.1937.

MINTONS

Types of Ware	Production	Quality	Availability
Tiles	High to Very High	Fair to Very Good	Abundant
Pâte-sur-pâte	Low	Very Good to Excellent	Scarce
Earthenwares	Moderate to High	Good to Very Good	Common

Marks (from 1870)

Printed:	MINTON'S Art Pottery STUDIO Kensington Gore (in circle)	1871 - 1875
Impressed	MINTONS ENGLAND	c.1890 - 1910
Printed:	MINTON LTD (in signature)	c.1900 - 1908
(in black)	Mintons No.1	c.1910
Impressed or printed:	MINTON HOLLINS & CO	1868 onwards
	M.H. & CO.	1868 onwards
Printed:	(Globe surmounted by a crown, and legend: "Mintons England")	1873 - 1912
	(as above, but with laurel leaves, and legend: "Mintons Est 1793")	1912 - 1950

+/- artist's mark
+/- year mark (1842 - 1942)

Astra Ware (1917-c.1934)

Moulded:	(Crescent and Star; M.H. within crescent)	c.1917 - ?
Printed in black: (rarely in green)	MINTON HOLLINS & CO. STOKE-ON-TRENT (written circular, within double circle)	c.1917 - ?
	(ASTRA WARE or "ASTRA" WARE in centre of circle)	

(NB. the scale of this mark varies)

Impressed	ASTRA WARE (within MADE IN ENGLAND double circle) (M.H. in centre of circle)	c. 1917 - ?
	ASTRA WARE ENGLAND	c. 1917 - ?
Printed:	ASTRA WARE (within circle)	c.1917 - ?

(NB. "X ... ::" etc. are assumed to be decorators' marks)

Minton Jardinière on stand.

159

WILLIAM MOORCROFT, artist/potter   (1872-1945)

James MacIntyre & Co., Washington Works, Burslem, Staffs. (1898-1913)
W. Moorcroft Ltd., Sandbach Road, Cobridge, Burslem, Staffs. (1913-1945)

Historical Background

William Moorcroft was born at Burslem in Staffordshire, the son of a gifted artist. He was educated at the Wedgwood Institute, Burslem, and later at the South Kensington School of Art, London, (founded by Prince Albert), where he came under the influence of the styles of William Morris and of the artist Walter Crane. In 1897, he gained his Art Master's Certificate, but instead of starting work as a teacher, he took up a job as designer with the established pottery of James MacIntyre & Co.

1) At James MacIntyre & Co., Washington Works, Burslem(1898-1913)

Historical Background

From 1898, William Moorcroft was in charge of the Art Pottery Department at James MacIntyre & Co., who manufactured mainly good quality tea-wares and domestic wares (such as finger-plates for doors). Moorcroft replaced Harry Barnard, who had established the Art Pottery Department at MacIntyre, and was responsible not only for the decoration of the wares, but also for their production. He formed a group of decorators, working on art wares designed by Moorcroft on MacIntyre shapes, many of which were made for Liberty of London.

Liberty also marketed "Florian Ware," which proved so popular that market outlets were also established by MacIntyre at Tiffany of New York and Rouard of Paris.

In 1904, Moorcroft was awarded the gold medal for pottery at the St. Louis Exhibition—the first of many awards throughout his lifetime.

In 1913, MacIntyre's art pottery department closed, as a result of the company's desire to capture the potentially lucrative market in ceramic electrical insulators. For a while, the company had been testing this market; and Moorcroft was able to prepare for the closure by making plans for the establishment of his own pottery. In 1912, Moorcroft had married Florence Lovibond, the local factory inspector, who had assisted him to design his own factory to a, not surprisingly, high safety standard.

Moorcroft effected, therefore, what was almost a seamless transfer to his own factory, which was constructed through a debenture from his friend Alwyn Lasenby of Liberty & Co., and was situated not far from MacIntyre & Co.. He took several staff with him from MacIntyre, and production of his art pottery continued initially along similar lines to wares he had produced at MacIntyre.

Products

At MacIntyre, Moorcroft drew all his own designs, which were slip-trailed on to the pots. The main ware produced by Moorcroft at MacIntyre was entitled "Florian Ware," and consisted of art nouveau floral designs of cornflowers, poppies, violets, etc.

The colours were derived from metallic oxides, and were applied under the glaze, except on some gilded pieces—gilding being used only for a short period, before being abandoned. The ware was fired at least twice at very high temperatures.

From 1902, Moorcroft evolved a landscape pattern with "mushroom headed" trees, which was named "Hazledene," whilst the following year saw the development of a pattern of fungi in raised outline, which was called "Claremont," after the wooded locality near Esher in Surrey.

In 1910 a colourful design termed "Spanish" was introduced, which featured a William Morris style of red-orange stylised flowers against a yellow-green background.

The familiar "pomegranite and berries" theme was not introduced until 1911; and generally all the floral themes, whether natural or abstract, were executed against a white or cream background, the outlines being mainly blue or green in colour. Many straight floral designs were produced from about 1908, such as wisteria, cornflowers, prunus blossom, harebells, iris, most of which were on cream grounds, with a thin lustrous glaze.

From 1905, Moorcroft produced some red and green flambé wares, which he termed "Flamminian." These comprised a plain glaze on simple shapes, with a decorative roundel bearing a trefoil motif. The glaze was usually loaded on the roundel so that it streaked downwards. Flamminian was made for Liberty & Co., and so stamped. It appeared as varyingly shaped vases, boxes, pin-trays, candle-sticks, etc.

About the same time, Moorcroft produced a ware entitled "Aurelian," which utilised ornately classical shapes for a richly decorative pattern of stylised foliage and floral motifs in blue and rust-red against a cream ground. Pieces were generally also heavily gilded, and occasionally a brown colour was added to the normal colour range.

In his designs, Moorcroft was strongly influenced by Persian and Turkish decoration, and in his potting, the simple shapes of 5th. Century Grecian wares attracted him. He was able to combine the two styles admirably on a range of products, which consisted of such items as flower-pots, flower-vases, tobacco-jars, jugs and biscuit-barrels. Some of these pieces (such as biscuit-barrels and tobacco-jars) were mounted in silver, whilst other pieces (such as tazzas and some vases) were mounted in "Tudric Pewter," and so marked. Tudric Pewter was a brand name of Liberty & Co. (1903 to 1938) for pewter with a high silver content, which was inspired by Celtic designs. Many of the silver mounts were made by Francis Arthur Edwardes, who also produced mounts for Doulton.

Moorcroft A selection of early wares made at Macintyre & Co.

Moorcroft Two-handled vase, 200mm high, green and gold 'Florian' pattern on a deep blue ground, design no. "404017", c.1903.

Moorcroft Vase, 270mm high, pomegranites and berries decoration.

Moorcroft A selection of later wares made at Macintyre & Co. (1902-1913).

Moorcroft A selection of wares made at Cobridge (post 1913).

2) At W. Moorcroft Limited. (1913-1945)

Historical Background

Having founded his own firm, Moorcroft continued to produce his own individual brand of pottery. He took on some of the redundant potters and decorators from MacIntyre & Co., working alongside them until 1937, when he was joined by his son Walter Moorcroft.

During the First World War, Moorcroft supported the war effort by producing a tooth-brush holder in white (known as "Officer's Mark One"), plus white tableware for the Armed Services. The factory was expanded in 1915 to accommodate this additional work. His daughter, Beatrice, was born in 1914 and his first son, Walter, in 1917.

From 1919, Moorcroft began to develop his famous flambé glazes, using a specially built kiln. He pioneered the search for a wider range of underglaze colours that would withstand high temperatures, and his knowledge as a chemist proved invaluable in this task. For Moorcroft, his flambé glazes were his finest achievement, and they were acclaimed throughout the world.

Pieces were exhibited annually at the British Industries Fair, Olympia, London, from 1915 to 1939, and regularly at other trade fairs. At the British Empire Exhibition, Wembley, in 1924, the company manned a prestigious exhibition stand, "befitting art wares de luxe." Queen Mary made a purchase from the Moorcroft Stand at the British Industrial Arts Exhibition of 1920. In fact, Queen Mary admired and purchased Moorcroft pieces for some years, and, in 1928, William Moorcroft received the Royal Warrant as "Potter to Her Majesty the Queen." The title appeared as part of the mark on all the company's wares made since then until 1953 (the Warrant was reaffirmed to Walter Moorcroft in 1947).

In 1926 Moorcroft's wife died, and in 1928 he married Alwyn Lasenby's niece, Hazel Lasenby. The recession at the end of the 1920s had its effect on the company. Moorcroft had no interest in the art deco style, and even wrote to The Times complaining of the "new bad designs."

During the 1930s, however, the demand for Moorcroft's type of decorated studio pottery dwindled on the home market, but in spite of the fact that many of the well known pottery departments were closing down, Moorcroft continued to produce ornamental decorated wares, and evolve new techniques and designs. The overseas market was still healthy, though, and Moorcroft was careful to keep alive his contacts abroad, particularly in Australia. Consequently, there was more pottery exported during this time than was produced for the home market.

163

During the Second World War, when much of the overseas market had disappeared, William Moorcroft just managed to keep the business going by making plain "austerity" wares and military inhalers. In October, 1945, however, William Moorcroft died, aged 73. His son, Walter, obtained special leave to return from the forces and take control of the works, keeping the business going.

In 1962, William Moorcroft's younger son, William John Moorcroft (b.1938) joined the company in a marketing position. During the 1980s, however, the company, as a high exporter, was finding it difficult to compete on price, and in 1986 the company was saved from liquidation when new owners bought into the business.

Walter Moorcroft retired in 1987, but the company continues actively today, managed by John Moorcroft and a wide range of new exciting designs has been launched.

Products

Pieces made from 1913 show an improvement in the quality of the pottery body. MacIntyre & Co. were, after all, selecting clays primarily for the manufacture of tablewares. Now, Moorcroft could select his own clays, and continue his floral designs pioneered at MacIntyre.

Additional designs were created, however, the first of which was "Wisteria." Fish designs were also produced, as were trees in landscapes, and many types of fruit and floral motifs, particularly the pansy.

Many early designs were painted over a white ground (such as the first Pansy design and "Persian"), but Moorcroft soon made widespread use of a pale celadon green background, which contrasted well with the rich colours of many of his designs. Chrysanthemum (similar to Spanish) was a typical example of this type of design.

With the development of richer colours of decoration, a deep blue was also employed as the background colour—a colour which predominated much of Moorcroft's output until the 1930s, when there was a general trend towards a paler colour palette. One of the rare non-floral designs, besides fish, was the peacock feather design (from about 1918), which was set against this deep blue ground.

In 1913, Moorcroft produced a popular range of plain tableware for everyday use in a "powder blue" glaze. Shapes were generally unassuming, but each piece was hand-thrown, and production continued for fifty years. Liberty used the ware in their basement Tudor Tea-Room.

Other tea-wares followed, many of which were decorated in the same designs as the art wares. Muffin dishes, biscuit barrels (some with screw-thread lids which were extremely difficult to make), tankards, cruet sets, etc., were all part of the tea-ware range.

From 1919, flambé decorated pieces were produced of exceptional quality. These were mostly existing patterns on vases and plates (such as fish, toadstools, vine leaves and berries), which were given a partial or complete flambé covering. Early flambé wares were often dark red in tone, because of the rich underlying colours, whereas later pieces were brighter, because of paler underlying colours. On many flambé pieces, the flambé glaze overlapped the undecorated base, giving a red, sprayed appearance. Because of the uncertainty of the process, no two flambé pieces were made exactly alike.

Moorcroft also produced some lustre ware in pale monochrome colours, such as pink, yellow, green, orange and blue. Occasionally, the lustre glaze would be applied over printed motifs, but usually lustre wares bore no additional decoration. The lustres were thin, wore badly, and often misfired. They were not successful commercially, and were discontinued during the early 1920s.

The 1920s saw some particularly spectacular evolutions of the Hazledene design. "Moonlit Blue," shown at the British Empire Exhibition in 1924, featured yellow-green trees in a landscape against a deep blue ground, with an all-over blue glaze; and "Eventide," (c.1925), which was similar but with an orange-red glow.

During the 1930s, patterns became bolder and more distinct, marking a departure from the earlier crowded, all-over decorations of fruit and flowers. Pastel colours were utilised, such as in the waving corn design, and tube-lining featured on many designs, such as "Honesty."

A range of rather unassuming monochrome glazed wares was produced from the mid-1930s until 1939, characterised by concentric ribbing. A few were decorated with bird designs, though most were plain.

Collecting Moorcroft Pottery

William Moorcroft's pottery was virtually unknown to the antiques trade twenty years ago, but a surge of interest sprang up after the 1973 exhibition of his work at the Victoria & Albert Museum, London. It is now extremely popular among collectors, commanding high prices at auction, in spite of the high output.

Although much Moorcroft pottery was mass-produced, its quality and artistry equated to that of other high quality mass-producers, such as Doulton, making it emminently collectable and desirable.

Modern Moorcroft is distinctly different from either that of William Moorcroft or his son, Walter Moorcroft, although collectors occasionally have difficulty discerning William's later wares to Walter's. There is still much Moorcroft of the 1950s being sold as of the 1936 to 1945 period, often quite unintentionally. John Moorcroft readily admits that the system of marking during this period was somewhat confusing.

Moorcroft Two 'Flamminian Ware' vases, 190mm high, c.1905.

Moorcroft Vase by William Moorcroft, blue and green fish with brown seaweed on a pale cream ground, satin glaze.

Moorcroft Group of Aurelian wares, tallest 310mm high.

An alarming new facet, which is bringing greater confusion, and which has evolved because of the current high auction prices, is the art of the expert restorer. Since most Moorcroft wares lend themselves readily to restoration, collectors must now be particularly on their guard against restored pieces being passed off as perfect.

During the 1920s, various imitations of Moorcroft's style of decoration were effected by other potteries. Royal Stanley's "Jacobean Ware," for example, featured mostly berries and leaves in dark colours, whilst Hancock & Co.'s "Morris Ware" often imitated the MacIntyre Florian style. These wares are well recognised as being sufficiently different, however, and are collectable in their own right.

Suggestions for Further Study

W. Moorcroft, plc, Sandbach Road, Burslem, Stoke-on-Trent, Stafforshire, ST6 2DQ, welcomes visitors.

The Moorcroft Collectors' Club, above address.

Atterbury, Paul. *Moorcraft Pottery.* Richard Dennis & H. Edwards, 1987, 1990 & 1993.

Miller, Fred. "The Art Pottery of Mr. William Moorcroft." *The Art Journal*, 1903.

Bemrose, John. "William Moorcroft—A Critical Appreciation." *Pottery & Glass*, June, 1943.

"William Moorcroft & Walter Moorcroft (1897-1973);" catalogue of an exhibition at The Fine Arts Society, 1973" pub. Richard Dennis, 1973.

Tharp, Lars. "William Moorcroft: Master Potter of the 20th. Century." *Antique Collector's Club* 24(6), Nov. 1989

Moorcroft Specimen mark of J. Macintyre & Co., Burslem, on jug.

Moorcroft Specimen mark on pewter base of tazza.

WILLIAM MOORCROFT

Types of Ware	Production	Quality	Availability
Wares at MacIntyre	Low to Moderate	Good to Very Good	Uncommon to Scarce
Art wares 1913 onwards	Moderate to High	Good to Excellent	Common (some ranges rare)
Domestic wares (incl. Powder Blue)	High	Fair to Good	Common

Marks

Printed:	James MacIntyre (*) & Co Burslem (in brown within circular motif)		1898 - 1913

+ William Moorcroft's signature, painted in green.

Transfer Printed:	FLORIAN WARE (in brown in motif)		1898 - 1904

+ William Moorcroft's signature, painted in green.

(*) This mark, with variations, occurred on pottery made at MacIntyre from 1860 to 1930 without Moorcroft's signature. Only those pieces in which Moorcroft had a hand were marked with his signature.

Painted underglaze (in green or red):	W Moorcroft (in signature)		1898 - 1913

+/- "Made for Liberty" (c.1903-1913)

Painted underglaze: (in green until early 1920's, thence in blue, except on flambé wares)	W Moorcroft (in signature)		1913 - 1945
(on smaller articles)	WM (signed in blue)		1913 - 1945
+/- impressed:	W Moorcroft Potter to HM The Queen		1928 - 1948
+/- year, painted (rare)			1913 - 1945
+/- removable paper label: (circular)	By Appointment W Moorcroft Potter to H.M. The Queen. (plus Royal Coat of Arms)		1930 - 1953

+/- stamped or incised lettering and numbers, eg.:-
    "O" impressed: turner's mark, prior to the installation of power-driven lathes in 1926.
    "X" impressed: tube-liner's mark.
+/- shape number (eg. M16)

+/- impressed:	MOORCROFT		1913 - 1921

+ "BURSLEM" (1913-1916)
+ "ENGLAND" (c.1916-1921)

+/- impressed:	MOORCROFT MADE IN ENGLAND		1921 - 1930

+/- Registered Number (1897-1920, patent dates)
(NB. Walter Moorcroft's initials and signature are very similar to William's. The Royal Warrant circular paper label declared "Potter to the late Queen Mary" after 1953.)

BERNARD MOORE, artist/chemist   1850-1935   —decorated earthenwares
                                                                          —decorated porcelain
                                                                          —flambé
Moore Brothers, St. Mary's Works, Longton, Staffordshire (1870-1905)   crystalline & other glaze effects
Wolfe Street, Stoke-on-Trent, Staffordshire (1905-1915)

Historical Background

Bernard Moore was born in 1850, the elder son of a Staffordshire potter called Samuel Moore.

In 1870, Bernard, together with his brother, Samuel Vincent Moore, took over the running of their father's china works at Longton, which became known as Moore Brothers. Bernard also worked as a consultant in bone-china for several pottery firms, but it was not until many years later that he set up his own decorating studio in Stoke-on-Trent.

At Moore Brothers, richly coloured Victorian china and porcelain were produced, particularly tablewares, and styles frequently imitated those of the Orient, with a high degree of modelling.

The company exhibited widely, winning a gold medal at the Sydney International Exhibition in 1879, the Melbourne International Exhibition in 1881 and the World's Columbian Exhibition at Chicago in 1893.

From 1901, Bernard Moore began to experiment with flambé glazes and other reducing glaze effects, using imported Chinese blanks. His experiments were conducted on a part-time basis, in collaboration with Cuthbert Bailey, at Doulton & Co., thus giving him access to Doulton's modern laboratory. The experiments were successful, and both Moore and Bailey were acclaimed as having rediscovered the secret of the ancient Chinese flambé glazes. These early pieces were certainly influenced by Oriental styles and shapes, and reflected the popular interest at the time in ancient Oriental styles, the Chinese Sung period in particular.

Moore's brother Samuel died in 1890; and by 1905, Bernard had sold the china business in order to set up his own decorating studio at Wolfe Street. In establishing his studio, he engaged local art school graduates, as well as pupils from the Royal College of Art. Pottery bodies were bought in from mainly Mintons and Wedgwood, and many pieces bore the stamps of these potteries.

Bernard Moore produced many fine examples of his distinctive rouge flambé at the studio, and exhibited at international exhibitions. Some of his best pieces were lost, however, at the Brussels International Exhibition of 1910, when the British Industrial Hall housing the exhibits was totally destroyed by fire. Moore was able to exhibit the following year, though, at the Turin International Exhibition in Italy.

Moore's highly individual creations were costly to produce, and therefore expensive to purchase. They were, however, popular with the Royal Family and upper classes; and Queen Mary (who frequently patronised Moorcroft's wares) was known to have purchased pieces by Moore at the British Industrial Arts Exhbitions, as well as visiting Moore's showroom on her tour of the Staffordshire Potteries in 1913.

It seems that production at the studio ceased in 1915, although Bernard Moore exhibited pieces at the British Industrial Arts Exhbition of 1920. Whether much had been produced since 1915 is not clear, although some pieces in existence show a Minton date code for 1920.

In later life, Moore concentrated on the science of ceramic production, publishing several papers in technical journals and acting as adviser to many pottery firms. He died in 1935, aged 84.

Bernard Moore Selection of flambé wares. l to r:-i) vase, 145mm high, with enamelled decoration of stylised dragons. ii) tall vase, 210mm high, flambé glaze, by Evelyn Hope Beardmore. iii) miniature vase, 50mm high, with enamelleddecoration of stylised dragons. iv) vase, 175mm high, with enamelled Chinese inspired decoration.

Products

With the exception of some experimental wares (1901-1905), pieces produced at the china works of Moore Brothers differ completely from those produced at Moore's studio.

At the studio, both plain and decorative flambé were produced, most pieces having a high glaze. Recurring subjects were ships, Oriental dragons, fish, fruit and floral motifs; but the collector will come across many other subjects, particularly animals and birds, such as owls and ducks, and even flying bats in a starry setting.

Among the artists employed by Moore at the studio were Evelyn Hope Beardmore, Hilda Carter, Dora Billington (who later became Head of Department at the Central School of Arts & Crafts), Reginald Robert Tomlinson, Annie Ollier, Hilda Lindop, Edward R. Wilkes, Cicely H. Jackson and John Adams (later to become director of the Poole Potteries).

In all, eight "glaze effects" are listed in a Moore's publicity booklet: "Peach Blow" (pink and pale green, resembling the skin of a peach fruit), "Haricot," "Rouge Flambé," "Lustre," "Sang-de-boeuf," (produced by using copper oxides fused in a reducing-kiln), "Gold Flambé," (produced by dissolving liquid gold with gold chloride and fusing in a reducing-kiln), "Hispano-Moresque" and "Transmutation Glazes."

Some crystalline glazes were also produced, as well as "Persian blues" and aventurine glazes. Pâte-sur-pâte decoration was also employed, particularly on pilgrim bottles, and was often accompanied by lavish gilding.

Several small pieces were also used for flambé decoration, such as miniature vases and bowls. Shapes were generally simple, ranging from deep bowls to shallow plates, and were chosen to show the glaze effects to their best advantage.

Because all pieces for decorating were bought in, a mixture of pottery bodies was used, from thinly-potted porcelainous wares to thickly potted earthenwares.

Modelled figures were also decorated, mainly of small animals, fish and birds, such as frogs, ducks, cats, rabbits, mice and monkeys. The origin of the models is not clear, however, though many contained Oriental motifs and were known to have been imported from the continent of Europe.

Collecting Bernard Moore Studio Pottery

Bernard Moore is perhaps better remembered for his rouge flambé vases and ginger-jars, which, in the full panoply of their densely streaked glazes are spectacular examples of the potter's art. Unfortunately, many of the finest pieces are in the possession of Moore's heirs and descendants, and so are not readily available to public view.

The short life of the studio and the relatively low production of Moore's work, together with its distinctive individually, have made it popular with collectors. The flambé wares were of good quality, but easily subject to scratching. Scratches appear white, considerably detracting from the appearance of a piece,

Some of the glazes utilised by Moore were supplied by Wenger of Burslem; and the collector may come across proof-pieces of Moore's designs, marked "A.F. Wenger." The pottery bodies may also be marked on the base with a variety of factory marks, indicating their origin.

Suggestions for Further Study

The George Salting Collection in the Victoria & Albert Museum, London.

Plymouth City Museum & Art Gallery houses a small collection.

Dawson, Aileen. *Bernard Moore Master Potter (1815-1935)*. Richard Dennis, 1982.

Bernard Moore Bowl, 255mm diam., decorated in flambé with flowers and holly on a Mintons blank, interior inscribed "WITH THE SEASONS GREETINGS", marked "Bernard Moore" and Mintons date code for 1907

Bernard Moore Two flambé pieces. l to r:—i) Plate, 305mm diam., peacock decoration on Crown Ducal blank. ii) Bowl, 255mm diam., decorated with flowers and holly on a Mintons blank, interior inscription "WITH THE SEASONS GREETINGS", marked "Bernard Moore" and Mintons date code for 1907.

BERNARD MOORE

Types of Ware	Production	Quality	Availability
Flambé wares (red)	Low	Good to Very Good	Uncommon
Crystalline & other glazes	Very Low	Good to Very Good	Rare
Models	Low to Moderate	Good to Very Good	Scarce

Marks

Painted, printed or incised through the glaze: +/- "England" or "Made in England" +/- year	Bernard Moore	1905 - 1915
Impressed:	MOORE	1905 - 1915
Impressed: +/- "England" or "Made in England"	MOORE BROS	
Painted in red or incised through the glaze: (sometimes with two wavy lines underneath) +/- year +/- artist's mark	BM	1905 - 1915

(NB. On flambé pieces the mark is often red on red, therefore difficult to see)

+/- factory mark (from a variety of potteries, but mainly Wedgwood and Mintons)

Bernard Moore Unusual stoneware vase, l90mm high, "BM" mark with two wavy lines.

42, Upper Richmond Road, Mortlake, London, SW14

Historical Background

There have been potteries at Mortlake since 1742, and most are well documented. Little is known, however, of George Cox's pottery, established at Mortlake about 1910, although several well-produced earthenware designs were created during the four short years or so of the pottery's existence.

It is known that George Cox studied art at the Royal College of Art, and was particularly interested in pottery as an expression of art. "The best in his (the potter's) craft has been produced by men that were artists rather than chemists," he wrote in 1914, emulating Christopher Dresser's quote that "it is the art which gives the value, and not the material." Certainly, the technology of ceramics was not ignored by Cox, as demonstrated by some of the glaze effects which he utilised, and he was clearly interested in giving others instruction in all aspects of the potter's craft.

In 1914, Cox left Britain for America, and took up a post as "Instructor in Pottery and Modelling" at Teacher's College, Columbia University. He published a book during the same year, entitled "Pottery for Artists, Craftsmen & Teachers," which was a handbook for students and teachers alike, and was concerned with the artistic creation of ceramics. In his book, Cox shows his own designs for figurines, such as "Saint George;" but basically the book is an instruction manual with a strong artistic bias.

The pottery at Mortlake was fairly obscure, and little information is readily available about its operation. Kelly's Directory for 1911 lists Cox as being resident at 11, South Worple Way, Mortlake, and there are no entries after 1914, when he left for America. The pottery is presumed to have been located at 42, Upper Richmond Road, Mortlake.

His work, during the short life of the pottery, was well received, and The Studio magazine reviewing an exhibition at The Artificers' Guild, London, in 1914, bemoaned the fact that Cox was no longer potting, considering the high standard and quality of his work.

It is thought that Cox incurred a financial loss in excess of one thousand pounds from the Mortlake Pottery. Whether he produced any art wares in America is not clear, but it is known that he produced several industrial designs, such as ceramic facades for buildings. An exhibition at the South London Art Gallery in 1922, which was intended to show wares produced in London between 1872 and 1922, included some of Cox's wares.

Products

Vases seem to have been the main output of the pottery at Mortlake, which, together with jars and pitchers, were often fairly large in size. All were thrown, and many bore smooth, monochrome glazes. Shapes were generally simple, designed to make the best feature of the glazes, and were mainly inspired by early Chinese styles. Surface decoration was scarce, occasionally comprising slip-trailed symbols or abstract motifs. Some modelling was also occasionally employed, as a cover for a vase, for example.

A large variety of monochrome colours was used, ranging from brown, pastel grey-blue, turquoise, magenta, to pink and deep blue. Pieces were generally thickly potted using a variety of bodies, such as terracotta, white earthenware and stoneware. Quality of throwing varied, and many pieces were rather heavy in appearance, lacking good symmetry.

Glazes were often thickly applied. Some fine crystalline glazes were produced alongside the more usual smooth glazes. Cox experimented widely with high temperature glazes, producing a range of effects.

Suggestions for Further Study

Cox, George, ARCA. *Pottery for Artists, Craftsmen & Teachers.* New York: Macmillan, 1914.

Mortlake Group of wares on variety of bodies, tallest 405mm high.

Mortlake Vase, 380mm high, by George Cox.

Mortlake Vase, 350mm high, by George Cox.

171

Mortlake Stoneware vase by George Cox, tube-lined 'ying-yang' decoration, incised mark "MORTLAKE GJC 1911 Z 2" and tube-lined mark on body "GJC".

Mortlake Specimen mark of George Cox.

Mortlake Vase, 135mm high, flambé glaze, by George Cox.

MORTLAKE POTTERY

Types of Ware	Production	Quality	Availability
All wares	Very Low	Poor to Good	Scarce

Marks

Incised: (occasionally printed in black)	MORTLAKE	c.1910 - 1914
or	M	

+/- monogram of George Cox: GJC

+/- year

+/- dagger symbol

+/- monogram as part of the decoration: COX 1911

+/- various symbols, as part of the decoration, eg.:

WILLIAM STAITE MURRAY, artist/potter   (1881—1962)   —earthenware
—stoneware

(fl.1912—1939)
Yeoman Pottery, 18, Yeoman's Row, London (1915-1918)
42, Lower Road, Rotherhithe, London (1919-1924)
13, Wickham Road, Brockley, London SE4 (1924-1929)
Court Cottage, Bray, Berkshire (1929-1939)

Historical Background

Born in London, Murray's early education involved extensive travelling, studying art in Paris (c.1900) and a two year visit to North America. His interest in ceramics grew after his marriage (1905), helping his wife to start an antiques business, and from his enrolment at the Camberwell School of Arts to study pottery from 1910 to 1913.

During the First World War, he joined Cuthbert Fraser Hamilton at his Yeoman Pottery, making painted earthenware. Murray had a strong interest in the Orient and embraced Buddhism, such that he set up his own pottery at his brother's engineering works in Rotherhithe, London, to concentrate on making stoneware pots in the Sung style.

He was introduced to Bernard Leach at an exhibition in 1921 and visited both Leach and Shoji Hamada on several occasions at St.Ives, comparing notes. They had, however, many differing attitudes to pottery (particularly regarding price), and later their relationship soured when Murray was offered a teaching post at the Royal College of Art instead of Leach (1925).

In 1924, Murray moved his pottery to an outhouse in the garden of his house in south-east London, where he constructed an oil-fired kiln. The same year, he exhibited at Paterson's Gallery in London, and then annually there until 1929, when he switched to Lefevre's Gallery.

During the late 1920s Murray was achieving considerable success, selling his pots for high prices at exhibitions. Many were given intriguing titles, such as "Starry Jacinth" and "Cadence" (a rather plain pot the Rev. Milner-White paid the exceptional sum of one hundred guineas for in 1927, but which Murray considered a masterpiece).

In 1929, he moved to a house he had purchased in Bray, near Maidenhead, Berkshire, and built a larger kiln. Here he produced his well known tall pots, with titles such as "The Bather," "Madonna" and "Purple Night."

Murray continued teaching at the Royal College of Art, and among the more famous of his students in the early 1930s were Henry Hammond and Sam Haile.

With the recession of the 1930s, however, Murray found it more difficult to sell his pots, particularly at high prices. In 1939, on a visit with his wife to relatives in Rhodesia, war broke out. In effect they stayed and decided to settle permanently in Rhodesia, during which time Murray undertook no potting, effectively giving up the craft. He died at Umtali in 1962.

Wm. Staite Murray Vase, 205mm high. (courtesy of Christie's Images)

Products

Murray's earthenware pieces made during the First World War were mostly bowls decorated with brushed motifs on a white slip ground. Production was low, since Murray was called for war service during this period.

Murray's early stoneware pots were strongly influenced by Sung styles, with thick monochrome glazes, a favourite being copper-red. His desire to produce individual works of art rather than functional pieces caused him to concentrate on vase and bowl shapes. He sought to place pottery on the same level as sculpture in this respect.

Murray's stoneware vases of the late 1920s characteristically had small apertures with thick neck rims. Many were globular in shape. Bowls and tea-bowls were simple in shape with narrow foot-rings.

Murray experimented widely with glazes and produced some interesting flambé, tenmoku and iron glazes. A characteristic clay body used was a beige stoneware with iron flecks, prominently displayed when a translucent glaze was used.

Whether against a dark or light ground Murray frequently applied simple, but colourful, brush decoration of floral or geometric shapes. Some pieces were undecorated save for a coloured glaze. Others included particular subjects as painted outlines or sgraffito and inlaid work, such as "The Roundabout" (featuring a carousel) and "Birdcage."

From 1929, Murray was able to make larger pots, of which the tall, slim, medievally inspired creations such as "The Bather," "Madonna" and "Purple Night" are well known examples. His most creative period was probably about this time.

Towards the late 1930s his pots became heavier in style, with characteristic thick foot-rings to bowls and thick necks to vases.

Murray's creations are somewhat scarce on the market. His output was generally low, named creations being well documented and accounted for. The quality of potting and firing was not excellent, though very good results were often obtained. Collectors should note that the range of quality was large, but even where poorer quality occurred, the decorative subjects were often highly individual.

Suggestions for Further Study

The Milner-White Collection at York City Art Gallery houses probably the finest collection of Murray's pots.

The Victoria & Albert Museum, London, has an extensive collection of Murray's works.

The Crafts Study Centre, Holburne of Menstrie Museum, Bath, also houses some examples of Murray's work.

Haslam, Malcolm. *William Staite Murray.* Crafts Council, 1984.

Digby, G. Wingfield. *The Work of the Modern Potter in England.* John Murray 1952.

Rose, Muriel. *Artist Potters in England.* London: Faber & Faber Inc., 1955 (reprinted 1970).

Rice, Paul and Christopher Gowing. *British Studio Ceramics in the 20th. Century.* Barrie & Jenkins, 1990.

Riddick, Sarah. *Pioneer Studio Pottery—The Milner White Collection.* Lund Humphries, 1990.

Watson, Oliver. *British Studio Pottery—The Victoria & Albert Museum Collection.* Oxford: Phaidon & Christie's, 1990.

Haslam, Malcolm. "Some Vorticist Pottery." *The Connoisseur,* Oct.1975.

Rackham, Bernard. "Mr. W.S. Murray's Flambé Stoneware." *The Studio* 88, Dec. 1924.

Marsh, Ernest. "W. Staite Murray, Studio Potter of Bray, Berkshire." *Apollo* 39, 1944.

Wm. Staite Murray Vase, 320 mm high, entitled "Maggie".

WILLIAM STAITE MURRAY			
Types of Ware	**Production**	**Quality**	**Availability**
Stoneware	Low	Fair to Very Good	Scarce
Marks			
Incised or painted:		W S Murray (in signature)	c.1912 - 1924
		London	
+ year			
Impressed		M (in pentagon)	1924 - 1939

Alexander Pottery, Stoke-on-Trent (1898-1902)
Cobridge, Stoke-on-Trent, Staffs. (1902-1947)
Hanley, Stoke-on-Trent, Staffs. (1947-1986)

Historical Background & Products

In 1898, Myott & Son took over the Alexander Pottery at Stoke-on-Trent, which had been producing earthenware since 1880. The firm moved to Cobridge in 1902, thence to Hanley in 1947. From the early 1900s, Myott & Sons were producing art pottery, often similar to Carlton Ware, but generally considered by collectors not to be of such high quality.

Many sets and combination pieces were produced, such as ewers and jugs, sandwich-sets, candlesticks and dressing-table sets; and some pieces were moulded. Shapes were usually simple, and much use was made of underglaze painting. Decoration tended to be bright and gaudy, such as large geometric patterns or exaggerated leaves in red, orange or black, often on a yellow-ochre ground.

At the 1920 British Industrial Arts Exhibition, Myott & Son exhibited a bold, blue-banded ware and an "Indian Tree" pattern (No. 6514), which were both recorded as being well thought of by visitors. There is little detail at present, however, of the names of many of Myott & Son's wares.

During the 1920s, some semi-porcelain tea and dinner sets were produced, as well as many toilet sets. Although the decorations tended to be bright, many of the designs were remarkably original.

During the 1930s, more exaggerated shapes were produced in an art deco style, such as fan-shaped vases. The Pottery Gazette described Myott's decorations during the 1930s as being "free, colourful treatments, much in demand."

Prints and enamels were widely used on Myott's tableware designs during the 1930s, and the company registered almost 500 different patterns between the years 1933 and 1935.

Typical of the Myott patterns of this period was a range of tableware decorated with pencilled bands, and a hand-painted decoration of autumn leaves in silver and green. Modernistic designs were also produced, such as "Swallow" and "Acorn," and a Cubist pattern was launched in 1935, reminiscent of a checkered table-cloth, which was available in three colour schemes: green and black, orange and black, or blue.

Original shapes at this time included a "Jubilee" cider set with cider jug, and a flying-saucer shaped posie bowl, available in three sizes.

Suggestions for Further Study

Spours, Judy. *Art Deco Tableware.* London: Ward Lock Ltd., 1988.

Myott Tazza, crocus pattern, 220mm diam., transfer printed mark in gold
"Myott, Son & Co., Made in England, Hand Painted" with pattern no. 9244.
Chrome base.

Myott Jug and basin set with candlesticks, painted orange and black on a yellow ground.

Myott Jardinière, orange and green decoration on a crean

Myott Jug and basin set, painted decoration in orange, black and yellow on a cream ground.

MYOTT & SON LTD.			
Types of Ware	**Production**	**Quality**	**Availability**
Earthenwares	High	Fair to Good	Abundant
Marks			
Printed: (usually in black, but often in gold)	MYOTT, SON & CO ENGLAND (plus crown)		1907 onwards
	M S & CO ENGLAND (plus crown)		1900 onwards

176

OXSHOTT POTTERY (1920-present)

—earthenware
—stoneware

Oakshade Road, Oxshott, Surrey. (1920-1978)   Denise Wren, artist/potter
Mill Cottage, Lustleigh, Newton Abbott, Devon. (1978-1989)   Rosemary Wren, artist/potter, and Peter Crotty.
Nutwood House, Strathpeffer, Ross-shire (1989 to present)

Historical Background

The Oxshott Pottery was established in 1912 by Denise Tuckfield (later Wren), who had studied design at Kingston School of Art from 1907 under the direction of the designer and painter Archibald Knox (1864-1933).

Knox was well known for his revival of Celtic designs, designing many art nouveau pieces for Liberty & Co. in their "Cymric" silver and "Tudric" pewter ranges. His teaching at Kingston School of Art, however, was criticized as being too advanced, and he resigned his post in 1912.

Knox's resignation from the Art School prompted the departure also of his students, who wished to continue to keep in touch with him and to work according to his principles.

Many of his jewellery and silver designs were salvaged, and Denise's elder sister Winifred Tuckfield promptly established the Knox Guild of Design and Crafts at 24a, Kingston Market Place to accommodate his students.

Denise established herself as a potter in the Guild rooms, whilst other members concentrated on jewellery making, embroidery, raffia work, spinning and weaving. Exhibitions were held in the Art Gallery above Kingston Library and at Whitechapel Art Gallery. Although the rooms were relinquished upon the outbreak of war, the Knox Guild continued to exhibit until the 1930s.

In 1915, Denise married Henry Wren, who had also been a student of Knox at Wimbledon School of Art. His father had worked as a stained-glass painter for William Morris at Merton Abbey.

In March, 1920, the Wren's purchased a plot of land at Oxshott on which they built an unusual bungalow to a design by Denise, naming it "Potter's Croft." The Knox Guild made various contributions to the furnishing of the interior through curtains and stained-glass.

Denise was not only the designer of Potter's Croft but also "clerk of the works," her husband, brothers and a friendly builder being the workforce. Here they established the Pottery, working together each according to his or her own abilities.

Between 1925 and 1939, Denise designed many coke-fired kilns at Oxshott, the plans of which were regularly sold to other potters. Henry Wren wrote numerous articles on the role of the crafts "as individual fulfilment in an industrial society."

Students often came to the Pottery for short courses, and Denise also undertook some teaching and examining (having obtained her Art Masters Certificate at Kingston). Denise and Henry's book "Handcraft Pottery" was published by Pitman in 1928, and included some drawings similar to Denise's early pottery decoration.

Pieces were exhibited at the British Empire Exhibition, Wembley in 1924 and 1925. Work was also taken to agricultural and horticultural shows, such as the Chelsea Flower Show. Both Denise and Henry also organized an exhibition of about thirty leading craftsmen at the Central Hall, Westminster in 1925, which ran annually every Autumn until 1938, and was known as "The Artist Craftsman."

During the mid-1930s, Denise also designed textiles, some of which were sold at Liberty & Co.

Henry Wren died in 1947, but Denise carried on the Pottery, employing a thrower by the name of Douglas Zadek (up to 1950). Denise's daughter, Rosemary (b.1922) took over her father's workshop when she had completed art school training in 1950, and both Denise and Rosemary embarked on new pottery styles from then on.

The Pottery moved to Lustleigh in Devon in 1978, where Denise Wren died in 1979, aged 88.

Oxshott l to r: cylindrical vase, 200mm high, blue-green glaze, incised mark "OXSHOTT"; tall jug, brown streaked glaze, incised mark "Oxshott"; jug, pale blue glaze, incised mark "Oxshott Made in England"; vase, green glaze, incised mark "Oxshott"; jug, blue glaze, incised mark "OXSHOTT"; vase, deep blue glaze, unmarked; jug, blue-green glaze, incised mark "Oxshott ".

Products

The first wares produced at Oxshott were candlesticks, plates and vases. Some items were coiled, others thrown or press-moulded.

Between 1920 and 1939, decoration was primarily of animals or patterns created using cut and incised slips, or lines incised into the clay. Some slip-trailed decoration was also executed.

Designs and shapes tended to be simple, the influence of Knox's "Celtic art" often being evident.

Many pieces were undecorated, relying on shape and a single colour glaze (often blue, yellow, orange or green) for effect. However, the accentuated ribbing created in the throwing frequently allowed the clay to show through the glaze.

Some interesting glaze effects were created through over-firing, such as an orange "stormy sunset" uranium glaze, or through high-firing, such as a turquoise "majolica" glaze.

From the mid-1920s, containers for flower arrangements were a popular product of the Pottery, such that Denise Wren came to be known as "the producer of pots for flowers" (a theme which she was to develop later in her career (1958-1968) by making containers for Japanese flower arrangements).

Some figures were also produced, notably "St. George and the Dragon" (1928).

After 1968, Denise Wren concentrated on making models of elephants, working until she was 84 years of age.

Suggestions for Further Study

The Holburne Museum, Bath, houses some Oxshott pieces, as well as photographs and records in their Crafts Study Centre. *

The Museum and Heritage Centre, Kingston upon Thames, also houses some Oxshott pieces and early records.

Weybridge Museum, Weybridge, Surrey, has examples of work post 1960, plus photographs, records and equipment from the early Pottery.

Wren, Denise & Henry. *"The Oxshott Pottery."* Crafts Study Centre, 1984.* (catalogue of retrospective exhibition).

Rosemary Wren continues her Pottery at Strathpeffer, Ross-shire, Scotland, with her partner, Peter Crotty.

(The author is indebted to Rosemary Wren for providing the bulk of the information for this chapter)

Oxshott Jug by Denise Wren. (courtesy Rosemary Wren & Weybridge Museum).

Oxshott Pot by Denise Wren, orange uranium glaze, 1930's. (courtesy Rosemary Wren & Weybridge Museum).

Oxshott Jug and mug by Denise Wren, turquoise glaze, 1930s. (courtesy Rosemary Wren & Weybridge Museum).

Oxshott Vase, 110mm high, heavily potted stoneware.

OXSHOTT POTTERY

Types of Ware	Production	Quality	Availability
Earthenwares (1920-1935)	Low	Fair to Good	Scarce

Marks

Incised: +/- incised initials:	OXSHOTT	1920 - present
Henry Wren	HW	(1920 - 1947)
Denise K. Wren	DKW	(1920 - 1975)
Denise K. Wren	DKW (plus bird) (where space allowed)	(1920 - 1975)
Rosemary Wren	Bird impressed	(1945 - present)
Rosemary Wren	Bird impressed + 'Oxshott'	(1950 - c.1960)
Items made by Rosemary Wren, and decorated by Peter Crotty	Bird impressed + monogram for Peter Crotty	(1979 - present)

PILKINGTON TILE & POTTERY CO.   (1892-1938)   —earthenwares
                  —tiles
                  —lustres

Clifton Junction, Manchester

Historical Background

In 1892, pottery studios were set up by the Pilkington Glass Company at Clifton Junction, Manchester, following the discovery of a red marl suitable for the prodution of tiles and quality ornamental wares.

The Pilkington Tile & Pottery Company was formed, and William Burton was appointed its manager in 1893. He had previously worked for Wedgwood as a chemist, and shared, with his friend Bernard Moore, a like interest in glaze effects.

From 1892 to 1897, tiles were the main output of the company, but from 1897 to 1903, the decoration (but not production) of art pottery was also undertaken. The company maintained a high standard of decoration, and rejected pieces of inferior quality.

Some of the tiles produced were decorated under commission by well-known artists and designers, such as Lewis F. Day (1845-1910) and Charles Annesley-Voysey (1857-1941), whilst spectacular lustrewares were designed by the artists Walter Crane (1845-1915) and William Salter Mycock (1872-1950), and decorated by competent artists, such as Richard Joyce (1873-1931) and Charles E. Cundall (b. 1890).

William Burton's brother, Joseph, joined the firm in 1895. He became Managing Director of the company, and, according to the Pottery Gazette, was the guiding light in the years to come.

In 1903, a potter's wheel was installed, and pottery was thrown as well as decorated. A good pottery thrower by the name of Edward Thomas Radford was engaged (remaining until 1936), and in 1906, the artist Gordon Forsyth (1879-1952) joined the firm, contributing significantly to the production of lustre-painted wares in the following years.

The Paris Exhibition of 1900 greatly influenced the production of lustreware, and Pilkington launched their first range in 1903. The lustres were a technically difficult process, and because of the high cost of production, output was relatively low. The wares were much admired, however, and pieces were sold by Liberty & Co. from about 1903.

From 1913, Pilkington's lustrewares were marketed as Royal Lancastrian, following a visit by King George V and the granting of his royal warrant, though lustres were not the only type of pottery to be produced under this mark. The Royal Lanacastrian wares continued until well into the 1920s, and included such styles as Gwladys Rodgers' Lapis Ware (from 1928).

William Burton retired in 1915, and in 1919 Forsyth left Pilkington to become Principal of Stoke-on-Trent Schools of Art (although, in spite of this, Pilkington continued to produce lustrewares until 1927).

Richard Joyce died in 1931, and Joseph Burton died in 1935. When Edward Radford retired in 1936, it seemed that production of the art wares could hardly continue, because of the loss of so many people important to their production.

The last firing of art wares at the pottery was in March 1938, the directors having decided that because of the depression in trade they could not bring themselves to manufacture cheaper wares of lower quality. As "Pilkington Tiles Ltd.," the company continued to produce tiles, merging with the Poole Pottery in 1964.

The Royal Lancastrian pottery was revived, however, for a short period from 1948 to 1957, when wares were produced designed by William Barnes, and thrown by John Brannan and Eric Bridges, who had worked at the pottery before the war.

For another short period (1972-1975) a revival attempt of old pottery styles was made by Pilkington at Blackpool, under the name "Lancastrian Pottery." Pilkington Tiles Ltd. continue to produce tiles today.

Pilkington l to r: i) heraldic lustre plate by Gordon Forsyth. ii) vase, 150mm high, silver lustre, by Gwlayds Rodgers. iii) squat vase in blue streaked glaze. iv) 'Lapis Ware' vase, 255mm high, by Gwladys Rodgers.

Products

Some wares were manufactured as pressed and cast shapes in 1897, thrown wares only being introduced from 1903. The early wares were sometimes decorated with flecked or crystalline glazes developed by the chemist Abraham Lomax. These were termed "Sunstone," "Starry Crystalline" and "Fiery Crystalline." Mottled and curdled glaze effects were achieved through transmutation, and considerable depth was achieved on many of these glazes thanks to the technical abilities of Lomax.

In 1903, William Burton developed a range of scarlet and tangerine orange glazes using uranium. This latter glaze became known as "uranium orange," which was later developed as "orange vermilion" (an orange glaze with red specks). Together with the matt glaze, "ultramarine blue" (later known as "Kingfisher Blue"), these glazes led to the development of the celebrated lustrewares, which encompassed a wide range of brilliant colours, in particular ruby and silver lustres.

Mostly vases, bottles and plates were produced as lustrewares, but up to 1914, some excellent smaller items were also produced, such as circular boxes and trays.

Some decoration was in the classical style, such as tall covered vases with Grecian or Egyptian scenes, the outline being depicted in silver lustre on a red or blue ground, with often a crazed effect underglaze. Other pieces were decorated with animal scenes, or heraldic devices with Gothic lettering, depending on the speciality of the artist.

Richard Joyce decorated some fine vases with fish scenes on a dark green ground, and many of the Pilkington lustrewares exhibit this characteristic of detail against a dark background. Richard Joyce also modelled animals and birds with lustre decoration.

The lustre plates tended to be deep and heavily potted, with internal ribbing much in evidence, but shapes were kept simple, the main impact being that of the decoration.

Generally, the lustres were glazed all over, such that there was no indication of the pottery body below. This often gave the appearance of pieces being made out of glass rather than pottery.

Vases were also produced in non-lustre glazes, and, about 1911, designs included short-necked vases (after the Ruskin manner), with streaked monochrome glazes, which sometimes revealed the red body beneath. Some flambé wares were also produced, but these are scarce.

Complete picture panels of tiles were produced for floors, walls and fireplaces. The designers, Lewis Day and John Chambers, designed several Persian scenes, whereas Voysey frequently contributed bird and leaf studies. Walter Crane's designs often featured female figures in floriate surrounds. Some nursery themes were also produced on tiles, notably a series of nursery rhymes designed by Margaret Pilkington, using tube-line decoration. From 1927, tiles and pottery were also decorated with mottled-effect matt glazes, produced using titanium oxide.

In 1928, Gwladys M. Rodgers introduced her range of "Lapis Ware." This consisted of wares of simple shape, having a thick, smooth, matt glaze (similar to that of Poole) and abstract decoration in pastel streaks of blue, green or grey. The name "Lapis" related to the resemblance of the pre-fired colours to lapis lazuli, which after firing produced diffused tones of mostly greyish-green. The ware was rather unassuming, being either plainly decorated or with abstract representations of foliage.

About the same period, further interesting non-lustre glazes were evolved. An all matt black glaze was produced for bottle-like vases and jugs (similar to Wedgwood's "Basalt Ware"), and W. S. Mycock decorated some heavy plates bearing an orange Cadmium glaze.

The quality of the later wares was somewhat variable, although artist-signed pieces were always of good quality at Pilkington. During the 1930s, Richard Joyce was responsible for some interesting slip-cast pieces (mostly vases) with modelled designs, featuring subjects such as fish, mermaids and animals. These usually bore a glaze of single colour.

Some rather nondescript domestic items were also produced during the 1930s, which often resembled Ketih Murray's designs for Wedgwood, though with a mass-produced appearance.

The lustrewares, however, were by far the most impressive of Pilkington's output, and command high prices today at auction. The quality and artistry of many of these wares have rarely been equalled by modern ceramists, even though some exciting achievements have been made in modern lustres to-date.

Suggestions for Further Study

Manchester City Art Gallery houses a representative collection of Pilkington's wares.

Lomax, Abraham. *Royal Lancastrian Pottery 1900-1938.* pub. privately, 1957.

Cross, A.J. *Pilkington Royal Lancastrian Pottery & Tiles.* Richard Dennis, 1980.

Thornton, Lynne. "Pilkington's Royal Lancastrian Lustre Pottery." *The Connoisseur,* May 1970.

Cross, A.J. "Pilkington's Royal Lancastrian Pottery 1904-1957." *The Antique Dealer & Collector,* September, 1973.

Cross, A.J. "Pilkington's Tile & Pottery Co. Ltd." *Antique Collector's Club* 15(2), June, 1980.

Mortimer, Tony L. "The Royal Lancastrian Pottery." *Antique Collector's Club* 20(4), September, 1985.

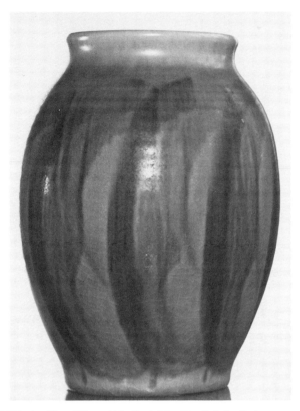

Pilkington Vase, mottled turquoise glaze, 160mm high, impressed pattern no. 2843, Bees mark for 1911 and painted "P".

Pilkington Vase, 255mm high, 'Lapis Ware' by Gwladys Rodgers, green feldspathic glaze, marked "ETR"(Edward Thomas Radford), "157", c.1927.

Pilkington Vase, 230mm high, ultramarine blue glaze, dated 1913.

Pilkington Lustre vases, l to r:-vase, bulbous base, cylindrical neck, l90mm high, pattern no.2522, monogram for Gwladys Rodgers and Royal Lancastrian mark; vase, pattern no. 2535, monogram for W.S. Mycock, Bees mark for 1906.

Pilkington Vase, 150mm high, silver lustre decoration, by Gwladys Rodgers.

Pilkington Vase and cover, 280mm high, in ruby and silver lustre, by Gordon Forsyth.

Pilkington Vase, 500mm high, orange/brown "sunstone" glaze, c.1910.

Pilkington Charger, 290mm diam., orange and gold lustre, by W.S. Mycock, heraldic inscription "Virtus Sola Nobilitas", date code for 1930.

Pilkington Lustre wares. l to r: baluster vase, 218mm high, by W.S. Mycock in golden lustre with flowers and heraldic lions on an amber ground, dated 1910; oviform vase, 164mm high, by Richard Joyce in gold and ruby lustre with classical warriors on an amber ground, dated 1925; charger, 323mm diam., by W.S. Mycock with birds and berries in gold lustre on a dark blue ground, dated 1927; bowl, 216mm diam., designed by Walter Crane and decorated by W.S. Mycock in gold lustre on a ruby and yellow ground, dated 1913; oviform vase, 164mm high, in yellow lustre with medieval figures in conversation and the inscription *They half said. O that saie they, Let them saie* on a ruby ground, dated 1906; elongated oviform vase, 191mm high, by W.S. Mycock of a galleon in full sail in silver lustre on a dark green ground. (courtesy of Christie's Images)

Pilkington 'bees' mark with Dordon Forsyth's monogram and date code for 1906.

PILKINGTON TILE & POTTERY CO.

Types of Ware	Production	Quality	Availability
Artist-signed Tiles	Low	Good to Very Good	Scarce
Other art tiles	High	Good	Common
Lustrewares (pre-1914)	Low	Very Good to Excellent	Uncommon
Lustrewares (post-1914)	Low to Moderate	Good to Excellent	Uncommon to Common
Other art wares	Low to Moderate	Good to Very Good	Common (certain types scarce)

Marks

Pilkington's pottery was well marked, the mark often being a work of art in itself. Sometimes the mark was incorporated in a small scene on the base of a piece, depending on the whim of the artist. On plates and items with large bases, the base was often decorated. Nearly all Pilkington wares bear the characteristic three-point stilt marks on their base.

Incised:	P (in italics)	c. 1900
Impressed:	P (with bees)	1901 - 1904
+/- 'ENGLAND'		1905 - 1914
+/- year in Roman numerals		1906 - 1914
(eg. VI = 1906)		
	P (with Tudor Rose)	1914 - 1938
	ROYAL LANCASTRIAN	

+/- thrower's mark, incised: E.T.R.   (Edward Thomas Radford)
(common on post-1928 wares)

+/- artist's mark:

Richard Joyce (c.1904-1931):	JR (in monogram)
(animals and fishes, particularly)	
Gordon Forsyth (1906-1919):	circular arrangement of four scythes
(lettering and heraldry, particularly)	
Charles Cundall (1907-1914):	CEC (in monogram)
(peacocks, deer, particularly)	
William Mycock (1894-1938):	WSM (in monogram)
(galleons, particularly)	
Lewis F. Day, freelance:	LFD (in monogram)
(Persian scenes, etc.)	
Gwladys F. Rodgers (c.1907-1938):	R (in shield)
(Lapis Ware, particularly)	
Walter Crane, freelance:	CW plus crane bird (in monogram)
(animals, flowers, galleons, female figures, etc.)	
Edmund Kent (1910-1939):	EK (in mongoram)
John Spencer (1936-1938):	JLS (in monogram)
Dorothy Dacre (? to c.1908):	DD (in monogram)
John Chambers:	JC (in monogram)
(Persian scenes, etc.)	
Jessie Jones (? to c.1909):	reversed J's within thistle (in monogram)
Albert Barlow (from 1903):	AB (in monogram)
Albert Hall:	AH (in monogram)
Thomas Evans (1894-1935):	TE (in monogram)

Pilkington Vase, 245mm high, lustre decoration by W.S. Mycock, dated 1912.

+/- artist's year code:

(1) William Mycock:

fleur-de-lis motif	1914		
crossed swords	1915		
floral circlet	1916		
※	1928	∀	1929
∴	1930	※	1931
半	1932	半	1933
半	1934	半	1935
半	1936	多	1937

(2) Gordon Forsyth:

flaming torch motif	1914
bird, passant gardant	1915
a swan	1916
pair of wings	1919

(3) Richard Joyce:

sickle and corn	1914
a fish	1915
a lyre	1916
a cross	1917
'R' in circle	1918
a crown	1919

Pilkington Vase, 120mm high, uranium glaze, by Richard Joyce, marked "Royal Lancastrian ENGLAND".

KATHARINE PLEYDELL-BOUVERIE
Studio potter

(b.1895—d.1985)
(fl.1924—1985)

—stonewares
—red-bodied earthenware

St. Ives, Cornwall (with Bernard Leach) (1923)
Mill Cottage, Coleshill House, Coleshill, Berks. (1924-1940)
Kilmington Manor, Warminster, Wilts. (1946-1985)

Historical Background

Katharine Pleydell-Bouverie was born of wealthy parentage at the 17th. century family mansion known as Coleshill House on the Berkshire/Wilktshire border. Her interest in ceramics is recorded as being fostered from observing the work of Roger Fry at the Omega Workshops, which he founded in London in 1913.

She enrolled for evening classes at the Central School of Arts & Crafts in Southampton Row, London, in 1921, converting to full-time study there in 1923. It was at a visit to Bernard Leach's exhibition at the Paterson Gallery, London, in 1923 that she met Bernard Leach and asked to join him at his pottery in St. Ives. His initial rebuff on the grounds of her inexperience prompted her to convert to full-time study at the Central School, where Dora Billington (late of Bernard Moore's studio) was Head of Department.

She was eventually accepted by Leach as a pupil in 1924 and went down to St. Ives to join him and Tsuronoske Matsubayashi (the Japanese ceramist who returned with Leach from his visit to Japan). Also at St. Ives at that time were Michael Cardew, George Dunn and Edgar Skinner.

"Matsu" (as Matsubayashi was nicknamed) taught her how to build and use a kiln and introduced her to the use of wood-ash glazes. Her particular interest in these glazes prompted her to return to Coleshill early in 1925 to set up her own experiments, and to this end Matsubayashi designed a wood-fired kiln for her.

She returned to Coleshill with an ex-Central School sculpture student and colleague from St. Ives, Ada ("Peter") Mason. Together they established the pottery in Mill Cottage on the Coleshill estate, an area rich in wood and plant varieties from which to make the ash glazes. There were good clays to be had on the estate, although Dorset ball clay was also used, and often an ash and potash feldspar was combined with it as a slip to make a particular glaze.

Mason produced very little herself and, three years later, gave up pottery and emigrated to America. In 1928, Norah Braden, also ex-St.Ives, joined Katharine Pleydell-Bouverie at Coleshill and remained there sporadically until 1936 when she left for a teaching post at Brighton School of Art in Sussex.

This partnership was to be the epitome of their achievement with wood ash glazes, and they exhibited their work in galleries in Manchester and London (the Paterson Gallery in particular) during this time.

Norah Braden was especially adept at understanding the science of these glazes, whilst Katharine Pleydell-Bouverie made meticulous notes of the recipes.

After Norah Braden left in 1936, Katharine Pleydell-Bouverie worked alone until 1940, when blackout restrictions prevented the use of her wood-fired kiln. Her mother died in 1936 and the estate passed to her. After the war, she resumed potting, but decided to sell Coleshill, purchasing Kilminster Manor in Warminster in 1946. Coleshill House, renowned for its interiors by Inigo Jones, was regrettably destroyed by fire in 1952.

Katharine Pleydell-Bouverie Group of stonewares. (courtesy of Christie's Images) (large bowl, 190mm diameter)

At Kilminster, she was again often assisted by Norah Braden, who would spend her teaching leave there. An oil-fired kiln was installed, which in 1960 was replaced by an easier to use electric kiln.

Katharine Pleydell-Bouverie continued to pot until her death in January 1985. The contents of Kilminster House, including many of her pots, were sold the same year.

Products

A prime influence in Katharine Pleydell-Bouverie's work was the work of William Staite Murray, rather than her early tutor Bernard Leach, but she was also strongly influenced by styles from the Sung dynasty. Most of her output was thus in stoneware, but some red-bodied earthenware was also produced.

Her pots were often simple in shape, representative of a Sung style, and mostly undecorated save for a monochrome glaze. She confessed that painting was not her strong-point, so brush decoration was scarcely employed. This and the extensive use of ash glazes was an essential difference between her work and that of her tutor Bernard Leach.

The ash glazes were certainly her hall-mark. These were many and varied, and her notes reveal successes and failures with materials such as box ash, laurustinus ash, scotch pine ash, ilex ash, rose ash, chrysanthemum ash and even peat ash.

The typically matt finishes of the ash glazes were characteristic, and though frequently monochrome in blue, pale grey, white, green or brown, they were beautifully textured. Cutaway decoration was sometimes employed, though usually restricted to a simple panel or fluted appearance at hardly noticeable depth.

Vases, bowls and bottles were the primary output, and Katherine Pleydell-Bouverie had a particular love of creating pots for flowers and plants. These were often made in an unglazed red or grey stoneware.

The stoneware bodies were generally fairly coarse and the foot of a piece would frequently be left unglazed. Though typical of Sung stoneware this enables one to appreciate the thickness and consistency of some of the glazes.

Not all glazes used were ash created, though many of the ash glazes emulated other glaze types. Some tenmoku glazes were produced in black or rust-red as well as pale green celadon glazes. Some thick crackle glazes were also produced which were particularly attractive in white.

Suggestions for Further Study

The Crafts Study Centre, Holburne of Menstrie Museum, Bath, has the largest collection of pieces together with KPB's notebooks and list of glazes and clay bodies used.

The Victoria & Albert Museum London, has several pieces.

The Milner-White Collection at York City Art Gallery houses about five pieces.

Roscoe, Barley. *Katharine Pleydell-Bouverie: A Potter's Life 1895-1985.* Bath: Bath University Press, 1980.

Rice, Paul and Christopher Gowing. *British Studio Ceramics in the 20th. Century.* Barrie & Jenkins, 1989.

Riddick, Sarah. *Pioneer Studio Pottery—The Milner White Collection.* Lund Humphries, 1990.

Watson, Oliver. *British Studio Pottery—The Victoria & Albert Museum Collection.* Oxford. Phaidon & Christie's, 1990.

Catalogue of a sale of contents of Kilmington Manor, 1st. May, 1985; Phillips Auctioneers, Sherborne, Dorset.

"Katharine Pleydell-Bouverie," catalogue of an exhibition at the Crafts Study Centre, Holburne Museum, Bath, 1980.

KATHARINE PLEYDELL-BOUVERIE

Types of Ware	Production	Quality	Availability
Stonewares to 1940	Moderate	Good to Very Good	Uncommon

Marks

(NB. It is uncertain how many pots were made by Katharine Pleydell-Bouverie during her year at St. Ives, but thought to be few in number)

Impressed in relief or incised:	KPB (in rectangle)	1925-1928
Impressed in relief or incised:	COLE (in rectangle, or rarely in a triangle)	1925-1928

(The above two marks may occur together)

Impressed in relief:	KPB (in monogram, in rectangle or lozenge)	1928-1984
	KPB (in circle)	c.1958- ?

+ incised letters or numbers or both, relating to the body used.*
+ painted Roman numerals referring to the glaze type.*
+/- painted year
* The Crafts Study Centre at the Holburne Museum, Bath, has the reference index for deciphering these codes.

Katharine Pleydell-Bouverie Globular vase, ash glaze, 190mm high, c.1958, with KPB monogram in circle.

East Quay, Poole, Dorset.

Historical Background

In 1873, the East Quay Works at Poole was acquired by Jesse Carter (1830-1927), an ironmonger and builder's merchant from Surrey, who, utilising the local deposit of Dorset Ball Clays, set about producing floor tiles for the domestic market. "Carter's Red" floor tiles soon became well established, such that by the end of 1883, production was supplemented by the making of glazed, modelled and painted wall tiles.

About this time, Jesse Carter was assisted by his two sons, Charles and Owen, and the business was known as Carter & Company. In 1895, Carter purchased the Architectural Pottery at nearby Hamworthy, for the production of architectural faience and floor tiles.

In 1908, Carter & Company became a limited company. The pottery premises were expanded along the quay, in the form of bottle kilns and workshops, which survived until 1945. A new factory was constructed at Hamworthy, specifically for the production of white and cream wall tiles.

When Jesse Carter retired in 1901, Owen Carter took over the running of the pottery. Owen was a close friend of William De Morgan and William Burton, both pioneers of art pottery, and Jesse had supplied De Morgan with tile blanks and, later, undecorated bowls, for lustre decorations. Owen tried to emulate both De Morgan's and Burton's work, producing lustre glazed ware in a reducing kiln. This was the beginning of art pottery as such at Poole, and in 1912, the Poole (East Quay) works became the centre of studio work in the Carter Group of Companies, the other works concentrating on domestic and architectural ware.

Poole Selection of wares. l to r:-i) bowl, 200mm diam., monochrome decoration, ii) vase, 175mm high, 'bluebird' decoration. iii) early bowl, 175mm diam.

As the output of Owen Carter's "Handcraft Pottery" increased, so did the employment of women artists, who were encouraged to produce their own patterns and attend evening classes at Poole Art School.

With the decline in trade at the outbreak of war in 1914, a specialised production of pottery buttons and beads was commenced, alongside the production of limited amounts of lustre ware.

After the First World War, the London stores of Liberty and Heals sold Poole wares (as did many local retailers), and pieces were advertised as being "suitable for country cottages and bungalows." So much interest was aroused over the manufacture of the ware that, about 1920, the works were made open to visitors.

Upon Owen Carter's death in 1919, Charles Carter invited the well-known gold and silversmith, Harold Stabler, to advise him. Harold and his wife Phoebe were also accomplished ceramic modellers, and contributed much to the style of Poole Pottery from this time. In 1920, Harold introduced to the pottery, John Adams, who had been a painter in Bernard Moore's pottery studio; and other talented workers were taken on as the business expanded. Harry Davis trained as a thrower at Poole, before joining Bernard Leach at St. Ives in 1934.

In 1921, the company of Carter, Stabler & Adams was formed as a subsidiary of Carter & Co., and by 1922, the workforce had doubled from that of two years ago, and Poole Pottery was in popular demand. The firm exhibited in Paris in 1925, and annually at the British Industries Fairs.

Meanwhile, Carter & Co. continued to produce tiles, virtually dominating the market during the 1920s. They fulfilled commissions for London Underground stations, restaurants, department stores and many public buildings.

In 1936, Carter, Stabler & Adams produced their first tableware sets, and domestic production of quality pottery took a major step forward. The onset of war, however, changed the market. Harold Stabler died in 1944, and during the war much undecorated Utility Ware was produced.

In 1963, the Carter, Stabler & Adams company changed its name to Poole Pottery Limited, although it had been known unofficially as Poole Pottery since at least 1914. In 1964, Carter & Co. Ltd. merged into Pilkington Tiles Ltd., and in 1971, became part of the Thomas Tilling Group along with Poole Pottery Ltd.. The Poole Pottery continues today as an autonomous enterprise, with a craft section that is vigourously alive, and carrying on the fine tradition and principles that Owen Carter founded.

Products

Owen Carter developed the production of tube-lined tiled panels, together with a form of mosaic and modelled majolica ware. His experimental ware of the First World War consisted of vases, tiles, bowls, dishes and candlesticks, with lustre glazes, both plain and decorated, glazed and unglazed. Celtic style plant pots, sold by Liberty, fountains and other large garden ornaments were also produced.

In 1914, a skilled thrower by the name of James Radley Young was appointed Works Designer at Poole. He produced a series of beaker vases, bowls, jam-pots and butter-dishes in a buff, vitreous body, with a decoration in brown of geometric lines, which gave the appearance of Neolithic pottery. This design proved popular, and by the end of 1915, a new ware had been launched, consisting of items with a reddish body, coated with grey or cream slip, and having a thin glaze. Again, geometric patterns were employed, painted over the glaze in pastel shades of blue, yellow, pink and green, such that on firing the colours fused into the glaze. This process is still employed today in producing Poole wares.

Young had been associated with Poole on and off since 1893, and was also a skilled artist. He experimented independently with lustre glazes, which were occasionally used on Poole wares, and he remained at Poole until just before his death in 1933.

The Carter, Stabler & Adams partnership concentrated strictly on studio pottery at the East Quay Works, and it was Truda Carter who introduced the traditional style of Poole pottery familiar to most collectors. Production of Owen Carter's lustre ware was quickly dropped, and the traditional designs of multi-coloured geometric patterns on a cream or white ground, with or without the famous "Blue-bird" design, were quickly launched. The glaze was silky in finish, smooth to the touch and thin in consistency.

The "Blue-bird" design became the hallmark for Poole pottery for many years, and was often accompanied by a dazzle of multicoloured swirls and stylised flower-heads. Generally, the overall colour effect was mauve, though subtle greens, reds and yellows were also present in the design.

Vases, bowls and jugs bearing the blue-bird design were produced mainly in either simple or classical shapes, such as two-handled squat urns. Occasionally, the decoration misfired, and the collector will notice pieces with patchy or broken-up decoration.

Poole Tiles from the series 'Water Birds' by Harold Stabler, 1921-29, marked "Carter, Stabler, Adams".

Poole Vase, deer motif.

Poole Vase, 120mm high, 'bluebird' pattern, marked "Poole, England".

POOLE POTTERY

Types of Ware	Production	Quality	Availability
Early art wares (except tiles)	Low to Moderate	Poor to Good	Scarce
Lustres and reduced glazes	Low	Good	Rare
Wares from 1921	Moderate to High	Good to Very Good	Common
Wares from 1925	High	Fair to Good	Abundant
Tiles	High to Very High	Good	Common

Marks

Incised, impressed or printed	Carter Poole	1873 - 1921
	Carter Co Poole	1873 - 1921
(within concentric circles, with dolphin in centre)	CARTERS POOLE	1873 - 1921
Impressed (within lozenge):	CARTER STABLER ADAMS	1921 - 1925
	POOLE ENGLAND	
+/- 'Ltd' (1925-c.1935)		
Impressed or printed: (within lozenge)	POOLE ENGLAND	1921 - 1952

During the early 1920s, John Adams launched some special colour glazes, with names such as "Chinese Blue," "Vellum White," "Zulu Black," "Sylvan" and "Tangerine," which were used to decorate ash-trays, candlesticks, vases and bowls. Some modelled items were produced, such as animals and fish, which were decorated in monochrome or bichrome colours.

A nursery toilet-set decorated with medallions of birds, fish and animals was particularly attractive, and, following the success of the experimental glazed and unglazed pottery produced cheaply during the First World War, several other designs quickly followed into the 1920s. A series of "Portuguese" designs based on the earlier styles was launched, decorated with a predominantly dull, blue stripe on a brownish earthenware ground.

In 1920, a range of semi-dull green ware was produced with a simple decoration in black, entitled "Monastic Ware," but the main product of the 1920s was the traditional multi-coloured style.

About 1925, John Adams' "Persian Stag" design appeared, and, in this style, the geometric patterns were often punctuated with animal or floral motifs. Some modelling was also undertaken by John Adams, and items such as small trays were part-modelled (usually the handles).

A range of figures was produced by Phoebe Stabler, but these are rare. Harold and Phoebe Stabler also designed and modelled facades for buildings and monuments, which were marketed as "Constructional Della Robbia," and included such commissions as portions for a War Memorial at Rugby School.

E.E. Strickland, working about 1925 to 1930, produced a "Farmyard" series of tiles (pattern code FY4), using printed patterns of turkeys, hens and other farm animals. During the late 1920s, the red body used for wares was replaced by a cream body, which was supplied from Carter's tile works.

In 1935, the "Sylvan" series was launched, characterised by broken colour effects on a matt glaze. Floriate designs with swirls and geometric lines were executed in brown, yellow and grey, green, blue and grey, in particular. In the same year, a range of nursery ware designed by Dora Batty was produced.

For collectors, certain individual lines of Poole art ware are rare, but generally Poole wares were widely disseminated. Quality was good, as quality control was widely practised.

Suggestions for Further Study

The Poole Pottery welcomes visitors, and besides the "Seconds Shop" there is a small museum of early wares.

McKeown, Jo. *Poole Pottery—The First 100 Years.* Poole Pottery, 1973.

Hawkins, Jennifer. *The Poole Potteries.* Barrie & Jenkins, 1980.

Crossingham-Gower, Graham. "The Potters of Poole." *Art & Antiques*, March 22nd, 1975.

"The Poole Potteries;" catalogue of an exhibition at the Victoria & Albert Museum, London, 1978; pub. V & A.

Poole Specimen mark of Carter, Stabler, Adams Ltd.

Poole Vase, 350mm high, c.1923.

at H.J. Wood Ltd., Alexander Pottery, Burslem, Staffordshire. (c.1919-1930)
at Radford Handcraft Pottery, Amicable Street, Burslem.(c.1930-c.1940)

Historical Background

Edward Thomas Brown Radford was the son of a skilled pottery thrower, Edward Thomas Radford (ref. Pilkington Tile & Pottery Co.). He worked initially for Pilkington as a thrower, like his father before him, then as a salesman. After the Great War he joined H.J. Wood Ltd. as a designer/salesman, managing his own decorating studio.

About the year 1930, he left H.J. Wood to work as a sales representative for other potteries, before establishing his own business in Burslem as the Radford Handcraft Pottery.

The factory was requisitioned during the Second World War, but re-opened for pottery manufacture after the war for a brief period. In 1948, Radford left Burslem to run a church holiday home with his wife. He died in 1968.

Radford Group of moulded wares, showing cottage inn scene and Butterfly Ware. Tall ewer, 275mm high. (courtesy Sharon Morris, private collection).

Radford Vase, 125mm high, stamped "E.Radford, Burslem" with pattern no. 8/F.

Radford Vase, 'Sgraffiato Ware', blue on white ground.

Radford Vase, 175mm high, painted decoration in purple, orange, yellow and green on a honey-coloured ground.

Radford i) Two-handled vase, blue on silver lustre decoration, stamped E Radford, Burslem, with painted marks. "#", "221" (shape no.), "EHN" (pattern no.). ii) Plate, stamped "E Radford, England" and painted mark "1741 A." (courtesy Sharon Morris, private collection)

Radford Group of typical floral pattern wares, showing ranunculus, anemone, etc. Tallest ewer, 345mm high. (courtesy Sharon Morris, private collection).

Products

Many vases were produced, generally of simple shape, but with decoration varying from sgraffito ("Sgraffiato Ware") to hand-painted. Radford's glazes were thin with a smooth finish, the colours being fused into the glaze (similar to the process at Poole). The general style was of soft, delicate decorative lines on thickly potted shapes, and many pieces exhibited a restrained art deco approach, both in shape and decoration.

As for decoration, floral subjects were predominant, foxgloves, lupins, ranunculus and anemones being popular. Abstract patterns involving bands of colour were also developed, but art deco geometric designs were not among the principal forms of decoration used, the floral patterns being more typical.

The flowers depicted were decorated in pastel colours, such as mauve, blue or pink, mostly on a honey-coloured ground, though pale pink or pale green grounds were also used. Some mottled backgrounds were also used, such as pastel green. Apparently, the paintresses employed at the pottery would often work from bunches of real flowers or designs from seed packets, and were given much freedom of choice in their painting style.

The pottery body was white, and is usually revealed on the base of pieces. The quality of throwing was good, as was to be expected from the son of an expert thrower.

Quality of decoration and glaze was also good, and decorative motifs tended to be simple and uncluttered. They were often well suited to a functional purpose; for example, a tall conical shaped vase decorated with lupins for lupin flowers, and an African Violet decorated plant-pot for an African Violet plant!

Shapes were chosen for their simplicity, and ranged from typically art deco reversed cone vases to tall, slim ewers, posy-holders and Grecian style bowls.

Ware marked "Sgraffiato Ware" tended to consist of incised floral motifs, such as leaf patterns, with a single outline colour under a smooth glaze, reminiscent of the "Lapis Ware," thrown by Radford's father at Pilkington.

At H. J. Wood, several ranges of moulded wares were also produced, in particular Butterfly Ware. This increased the shape range to items such as wall-vases, tea-wares, candle-holders and novelty wares.

Later wares produced by H. J. Wood (post-1959) tended to feature more stylised flowers depicted on a white ground.

Suggestions for Further Study

Northern Ceramics Society Newsletter No.36, December 1979, by Maureen Leese.

The Gentle Art of E. Radford; magazine article by Pat Watson in *The Antique Collectors' Fayre,* 2(10), April 1988.

Radford Vase, 130mm high.

EDWARD RADFORD

Types of Ware	Production	Quality	Availability
All wares	Moderate to High	Good to Excellent	Common

Marks

(at H.J. Wood, Ltd.)

Impressed:	E. Radford Burslem	c.1919 - c.1930
Stamped:	E. Radford England	c. 1919-c. 1940

± name of ware, eg. Sgraffiato Ware, BUTTERFLY WARE
(the mark BUTTERFLY WARE E Radford MADE IN GREAT BRITAIN has been noted by the author)
± shape number, impressed or painted (eg. 258 L - tall ewer)
± pattern number, painted
± Registered number (eg. Rd. 788373)
± Hand painted   c. 1946-c. 1980 (*)

(*) Apparently, H.J. Wood Ltd. continued to use this backstamp until about 1980 for wares decorated in the Radford Studio, but not necessarily designed by Radford. Some wares were stamped H.J. Wood Ltd. Burslem England, without Radford's name, plus or minus "Hand painted".

(at Radford Handcraft Pottery)

Stamped in black:	E. Radford Burslem	(in signature)	c. 1930-c. 1940

± pattern number, painted (the author has noted the following consistencies:-
        JN -anemones
        UM -ranunculus
± shape number, painted

T & R Boote Ltd., Burslem, Staffordshire (c.1906-1913)
Wood & Sons Ltd., Burslem, Staffordshire (1913-1920)
Bursley Ltd., Crown Pottery, Burslem, Staffordshire (1920-1926)
Burgess & Leigh, Middleport Pottery, Burslem, Staffs. (1926-1931)
A.G. Richardson, Gordon Pottery, Tunstall, Staffs. (1931-1934)
A.G. Richardson, Britannia Pottery, Cobridge, Burslem.(1934-1943)
H.J. Wood Ltd., Alexandra Pottery, Burslem, Staffs. (1943-1947)

Historical Background

Charlotte Rhead was the daughter of the renowned ceramic designer, Frederick Rhead. Born in 1885, she started her pottery career decorating tiles at the firm of T & R Boote in Burslem. Here she learned the art of tube-line decoration, which was to be her hallmark in later years.

In 1913, she moved to Wood & Sons Ltd. where her father had been made Art Director in 1912. Both Harry Wood and Frederick Rhead were keen on promoting art wares, so in 1920 a separate company, Bursley Ltd., at the Crown Pottery, Burslem, was formed specifically for this purpose. Charlotte moved to the Crown Pottery, continuing with her tube-lining, whilst her father concentrated on the production of tablewares. She also did work for an associate firm, Ellgreave Pottery Co. Ltd.

In 1926, she moved to Burgess & Leigh at the Middleport Pottery, Burslem, in order to train a team of tube-liners. The practice of tube-lining, or the squeezing of wet clay from a small, hand-held rubber bag to form raised tubular lines, was an immense success. It was a form of decoration that could be freely and easily applied, as opposed to the more costly and time-consuming pâte-sur-pâte method. Moreover, the raised outlines acted as a convenient guide for paintresses to fill with colour, guaranteeing greater accuracy where a repetitive design was required. Although tube-lining a repetitive pattern was a form of mass-production, potteries could still claim that pieces were hand-painted.

Burgess & Leigh produced many of their art wares under the title "Burleigh Ware." Some pieces were sold through the retail outlet of Lawley's, and featured the mark "Lawley's Norfolk Pottery, Stoke."

From 1931 to 1943, Charlotte worked for A.G. Richardson in Cobridge, who manufactured "Crown Ducal Ware." Initially, Richardson's premises were at the Gordon pottery, Tunstall, but in 1934, the Britannia Pottery at Cobridge was acquired and rebuilt to modern standards.

Charlotte's designs were copied by teams of decorators using a method known as "pouncing." This consisted of producing a pattern on paper outlined with pin-prick holes. The paper was placed on the pot, and charcoal rubbed over the pattern, which left a black outline on the pot which could then be tube-lined.

In 1943, Charlotte left Richardson and joined the firm of H.J. Wood Ltd., an associate company of Wood & Sons. Harry Wood set aside a part of the Alexandra Pottery, Burslem, for her to continue her tube-line work and experiment in lustre glazes. Her death in 1947 cut short her experiments in this field, though some wares were produced with a lustre glaze finish.

Charlotte Rhead Charger, 370mm diam., foxglove tube-line decoration, marked "Crown Ducal", "4953".

Charlotte Rhead Charger, 440mm diam., 'Golden Leaves' tubeline decoration, marked "Crown Ducal", "4921L"

Products

Charlotte Rhead's products range from large plates to small bowls and hollow lamp-bases. Much of her decoration was of characteristic style, being tube-line and "stitch" decoration on heavy-bodied wares. The stitch decoration was often applied around the edge of pieces, and on some, the whole surface was worked, giving a textured appearance.

Her colours tended to be pastel shades, often pink or pinky-brown. A favourite decoration of plates and vases was of falling leaves in a rust-brown colour on a pale cream background. Fruit and floral motifs were generally common subjects employed.

Charlotte's most renowned designs were carried out between 1931 and 1943 when she worked for A.G. Richardson. Various standard patterns are recognisable, such as "Palermo," a simple decoration resembling the head of a globe artichoke; "Manchu," an oriental dragon motif; "Persian Rose;" "Foxglove;" "Wisteria;" "Byzantine;" "Pomegranite" and "Hydrangea."

Sometimes the decoration was effected on simply shaped vases or chargers, other times on pieces with a pronounced deco style of ribbed and stepped vases, mugs and jugs, often with multiple handles.

At H.J. Wood Ltd., a "Trellis" pattern was popular on plates, whilst a pattern of oranges and leaves featured well on vases and jugs. There was a noticeable increase in the use of lustres on later wares, which were characterised by a silky finish.

Charlotte Rhead's creations are much admired by collectors. The style was very individual, the quality of decoration was good, and the lines were soft-textured, with warm colours. The pottery body was often similar to and as good as that produced by the Poole Pottery, and complemented the decorative styles produced. An interesting balance was thus achieved between decoration, shape and body, which was somewhat rare in art pottery of this period.

Suggestions for Further Study

Bumpas, Bernard. *Charlotte Rhead, Potter & Designer.* Kevin Francis, 1988.

Bumpas, Bernard. "Pottery Designed by Charlotte Rhead." *The Antique Collector*, January, 1983.

Bumpas, Bernard. "Tube-Line Variations." *The Antique Collector*, December, 1985.

Bumpas, Bernard. *"Rhead Artists & Potters 1870-1950;"* catalogue of an exhibition at the Geffrye Museum, London, 1986 (touring exhibition).

Bumpas, Bernard. "Cheerful Charlotte Rhead." *The Antique Dealer & Collectors' Guide*, August, 1988.

Charlotte Rhead Vases, 200mm high, red and black decoration on a cream ground.

Charlotte Rhead Charger, 315mm diam., green dragon tube-line decoration, 'Manchu' pattern, marked "C.Rhead" with Crown Ducal mark.

Charlotte Rhead Specimen mark on Bursley Ware (c.1943-1960).

CHARLOTTE RHEAD			
Types of Ware	**Production**	**Quality**	**Availability**
All wares	Moderate to High	Good to Excellent	Abundant

Marks

1. Printed:	Bursley Ware England	c.1921 - c.1929	
	Ellgreave Pottery Co. Ltd. Lottie Rhead Ware Burslem England	c. 1923	
2. Painted signature: (Lottie Rhead)	L Rhead	1926 - 1931	
+/- name of pottery			
+/- name of ware, printed			
eg. Bursley Ware		(c.1926-1931)	
Lottie Rhead Ware		(c.1926-1931)	
Burleigh Ware		(c.1926-1931)	
Lawley's Norfolk Pottery, Stoke		(c.1927-1930)	
+/- decorator's marks and pattern numbers			
3. Painted signature:	C Rhead	1931 - 1943	
+/- 'Crown Ducal			
Made in England' (printed)		(c.1931-c.1938)	
4. Printed mark:	Bursley Ware Charlotte Rhead England	c.1943 - 1960	
5. Printed mark:	Wood's Arabesque by Charlotte Rhead	c.1943 - 1960	

(Refer to the numerous publications by Bernard Bumpas for detailed information on the confusing array of marks used.)

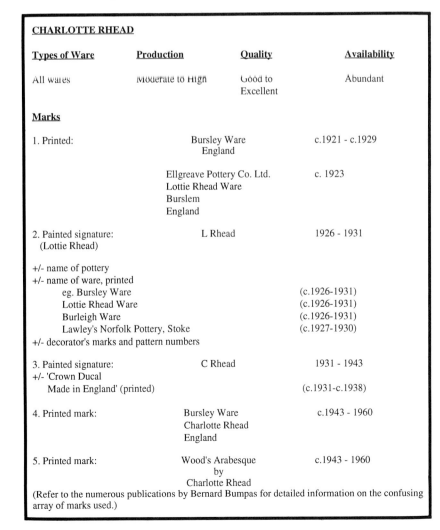

Charlotte Rhead Specimen signature of "L Rhead" (Lottie Rhead), with decorator's mark "F".

(1898-1933)

—earthenware
—reduced glazes
—crystalline & lustre glazes

West Smethwick, Birmingham

Historical Background

The Ruskin Pottery was established by Edward Richard Taylor and his son William Howson Taylor(1876-1935) in 1898, and was named after the artist John Ruskin. Edward Richard Taylor was Principal at the Birmingham School of Art, and his son was a pupil at the same School.

With the help of craftsmen from Wedgwood the Taylors experimented in high-temperature glazes and lustres, the recipes of which were kept a closely guarded secret. Apparently, William Howson Taylor destroyed his notes when he retired from the pottery in 1933.

The glazes, however, were much admired, and the flambé glaze won a prize at the St. Louis Centennial Exhibition of 1904. Other notable prizes were won at Milan, and in New Zealand; and the pottery exhibited pieces at the British Industrial Arts Exhibition of 1920. Praise came from all quarters, and the pottery was patronized by Queen Victoria and members of the Royal Family.

Edward Richard Taylor died in 1912. His son, carried on the business, and became the guiding influence on the products that we see and admire today. Howson Taylor maintained meticulous standards, and no "seconds" were allowed to be sold. Seconds were either destroyed or given to the workforce for personal use.

The potter Bernard Leach was a frequent visitor to the pottery, and also a personal friend of Howson Taylor. The two pottery styles, however, could not have been more diverse, though Leach must have been particularly interested in the Ruskin Orientally influenced shapes and glazes.

Ill-health forced Howson Taylor to close the pottery in December, 1933. He retired to Devon with his wife, and died in September, 1935.

Products

By far the most interesting of the pottery's products were the high-temperature glazes. Some fine vases and bowls of simple shape were produced, decorated with coloured speckles in a matt finish, or with interesting flambé and sang-de-boeuf glazes.

Flambé pieces were often speckled with viridian (bright green) spots, which were produced by the use of copper salts. Howson-Taylor also produced a "soufflé ware" (which consisted of a mottled glaze in a single colour), various crackle glazes, and, from 1929, some crystalline glazes.

The mottled glazes were produced in many different colours: greys, celadons, dark blues, greens, mauves and pinks. Often the glaze itself was the only decoration, but on some pieces plant forms were painted on a coloured ground. Of the lustres, predominant were a pink lustre and a pearl lustre with a kingfisher blue glaze. In 1927, Ruskin advertised "Peach Bloom" and "Crushed Strawberry" as high temperature glazes.

The high-fired pieces were more heavily potted than the normally fired pieces, and were produced using a Cornish clay, obtained through Wenger, the clay and glaze suppliers. Presumably, the thinly-potted pieces using a local clay would not withstand the high temperatures of the kiln.

Ruskin Examples of high-fired vases. l to r:-i) vase, 225mm high, with blue speckled glaze, dated 1907. ii) vase, 240mm high, with beige and pale mauve speckled glaze, dated 1906. iii) vase, 301mm high, with sang-de-boeuf glaze, dated 1907.

Ruskin Jar and cover, 149mm high, lustre glaze, dated 1919. (compare similar vase by The Ashby Potters' Guild).

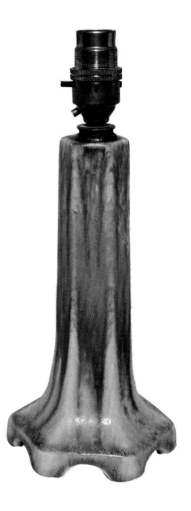

Ruskin Lamp-base, 200mm high, moulded, with mottled glaze, c.1925.

Ruskin Vase, 200mm high, by W. Howson-Taylor, yellow crystalline glaze on orange soufflé glaze, signed "W.Howson-Taylor".

A special kiln known as the "Secret Red Kiln" was apparently used to fire the flambé and sang-de-boeuf pieces, the colour being achieved by firing a copper glaze in "reducing" conditions.

Vases decorated with reduced glazes tended to be Chinese inspired. Some bore covers and specially produced ceramic stands. Other items produced included egg-cups, bowls, jars, candlesticks, lamp-bases, ink-pots, brooches, cuff-links and hat-buttons; and some pieces were mounted in silver. The collector will occasionally come across trade samples, which resemble domed brooch centres.

From the early 1920s, a cheaper moulded ware was produced in answer to the demand from those who could not afford the fairly expensive high-fired pieces. This bore stronger lines and more angular shapes, and, like the high-fired wares, tended to be undecorated save for the glaze. Yellow, orange, blue and green were colours regularly used on these wares, and glazes were often streaked and bi-coloured, some being crystalline.

The bulbous shapes and small necks of the orientally inspired vases achieved a pleasing balance visually. Mottled glaze wares possessed a chunky appearance, with a smooth, matt finish. On other pieces the pottery body sometimes appeared egg-shell in texture, with the hardness of stoneware, but with the thinness of porcelain.

Ruskin wares are today keenly collected, particularly the high-fired wares, which achieve substantial prices at auction.

Summary of Wares

Red Kiln: Sang-de-boeuf, rouge flambé and special colours with flecks. Heavily potted pieces.

Soufflé : Monochromes, with marbled or mottled gradations. Thinly potted and representative of the majority of Ruskin output.

Eggshell : Almost porcelain; lightweight and delicate pieces.

Lustres : Generally monochromes; hard lustre and soft lustre glazes, the latter tending to wear off.

Moulded wares : Mass-produced, eg. lamp-bases, candlesticks, ink-pots, vases, etc.

Egyptian Ware : Vases, jugs and jardinières in a rather heavy Egyptian inspired ware.

Suggestions for Further Study

A collection of Ruskin pottery was presented by Howson Taylor to the County Borough of Smethwick, and may be seen at the Central Library, High Street, West Smethwick, Birmingham.

Ruston, James H. *Ruskin Pottery.* Metropolitan Borough of Sandwell, 1975 and 1990 with significant corrections.

Bennett, I. *'Ruskin Pottery and the European Ceramic Revival;'* catalogue of an exhibition at Ferneyhough, 1981.

Bennett, Ian. 'Ruskin Pottery & The Ferneyhough Collection;' *Antique Collector's Club* 27(1), May 1992.

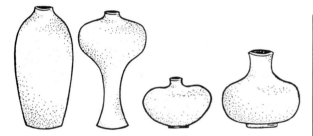

Some typical Ruskin shapes, orientally inspired.

Ruskin Vase, 225mm high, flambé glaze, dated 1925.

THE RUSKIN POTTERY

Types of Ware	Production	Quality	Availability
High-fired & lustre glazes	Moderate	Very Good to Excellent	Uncommon
Crystalline & crackle glazes (not on moulded wares)	Low	Good to Very Good	Scarce
Moulded wares	Moderate	Good to Very Good	Common
Other art wares	Moderate	Good	Common

Marks

Impressed	RUSKIN		1899 - 1904
	RUSKIN POTTERY WEST SMETHWICK	(within oval)	1904 - 1915
	RUSKIN ENGLAND		1904 - 1933 *
	RUSKIN MADE IN ENGLAND		1920 - 1933
Printed:	W. Howson Taylor RUSKIN ENGLAND		1920 - 1933

+/- year (most non-moulded pieces are dated)
+/- 'W Howson Taylor' (in signature) (1899-1903)
+/- 'HW/S/'

(NB.   1) Most of the early wares (1898-1904) were not marked.
2) An outline of scissors, painted underglaze or incised, was also commonly used as a mark until 1920.
*3) The impressed mark 'RUSKIN ENGLAND' has been noted used in conjunction with the incised signature 'W Howson Taylor', with the year impressed.)

Cadborough Pottery, Udimore Road, Rye, Sussex (c.1809-c.1890)
Belle Vue Pottery, Ferry Road, Rye, Sussex (1869—present)

Historical Background

There have been potteries in the Rye area since medieval times, when potters found a ready source of clay, timber and water. In later years, two potteries, the Cadborough Pottery and the Belle Vue Pottery, attained pre-eminence in the area, particularly during their association with the Mitchell family.

The Belle Vue Pottery was established in 1869 when Frederick Mitchell formed a partnership with his father, William Mitchell, to produce decorative pottery on leasehold land in Ferry Road. Frederick installed a brick-built kiln, from his own design.

William Mitchell had operated a pottery at Cadborough, closeby, which produced ornamental and domestic earthenware. He was assisted for a while by his two sons, Frederick and Henry. When the new Belle Vue Pottery was established, William and Henry carried on working at Cadborough. After William's death in 1871, Henry carried on, eventually selling Cadborough to George Russell, who used the pottery to make architectural brown wares.

At Belle Vue, Frederick Mitchell set about producing art wares, which were initially marketed as "Sussex Rustic Ware." William Mitchell died in 1871, and when Frederick Mitchell died in 1875, his widow, Caroline, took control of the business, producing pottery imitative of early Mediterranean styles. Production of the Rustic Ware recommenced in 1882, however, when her nephew, Frederick Thomas Mitchell, joined the firm. On her death in 1896, he assumed complete control of the pottery.

When F.T. Mitchell died in 1920, his widow took over the business, appointing one of the employees, Edwin Twort, as manager. Wares produced from this date were sold as "Sussex Art Ware." In 1930, the works were sold to Ella Mills, who continued production of Sussex wares until the outbreak of war in 1939, when the pottery closed. The pottery reopened in 1947 under new ownership, and continues today, having had several owners since then.

Rye Jug, 214mm high, 'Sussex Rustic Ware', marked "F.Mitchell". (courtesy HCMS, DA 1978.37, 'Coysh Collection').

Rye Posy vase, 94mm high, inscribed "Sussex Ware, Rye".

Products

Mitchell's earliest and most famous art pieces consisted of brown and green glazed jugs, bowls, vases, candlesticks, money-boxes, pilgrim-bottles and flower-baskets, which came under the generic title "Sussex Rustic Ware." Decoration was usually in the form of hops and foliage, (also known as Hop Ware), with handles resembling tree branches, though some pieces (particularly flower-baskets) featured handles and flower-holders as twisted rope. These latter pieces often featured squashed and contorted shapes, or pierced and latticed bodies. Other wares were also made, such as jardinières, which were similar to those produced at the Cadborough Pottery.

Quality of the Sussex Rustic Wares was good, and pieces exhibited heavy dimpling and appliqué work, with a high lead glaze, a common feature of which was a mottling effect. Plain light-brown glazes with darker flecks (manganese) were commonly employed, often as the only colour on a piece. A white clay was used for the bodies, and many pieces were light in weight, having been slip-cast. Thrown pottery was also produced, and this tended to be heavier in weight.

From 1875, Caroline Mitchell produced a variety of ornamental wares, such as copies of early Mycenean pottery, which were advertised as "Trojan Ware." These wares were topical, since Schliemann had been excavating the ancient city of Troy at this time, and there was particular interest in the finds unearthed from this site. Vases and urns in Trojan Ware were heavily ornamented and were similar to some Castle Hedingham wares, which also emulated Trojan designs. Caroline Mitchell also produced clay models of such items as Sussex pails and carpenter's bags.

From about 1882, miniature vases, jugs and urns were produced in simple classical shapes. Decoration was usually in green, but sometimes in brown or blue-green, or, more unusually, in blue with white stripes. The miniatures were produced from a white clay body and bore a high glaze. Many were not more than half an inch (10mm) in height, and were simply marked "Rye" or "Rye Ware," scratched on the unglazed base.

Some lustre ware was also produced, a gold-blue in particular, but production was limited to small items, and total output was low. Many traditional Sussex wares were also produced by F.T. Mitchell, including ale jugs in the shape of pigs, which had also been made at his uncle's pottery in Cadborough. F.T. Mitchell's modelling was more sharply defined than his uncle's, as can be seen in examples of his Hop Ware.

During the late 1930s, some interesting bowls and tea-wares were produced in a plain uranium orange glaze, similar to a glaze used at the Dicker Pottery.

Collectors should note that Frederick Masters at the Bognor Regis Pottery also produced Hop Wares similar to those produced at Belle Vue. These, however, were usually marked "Art Pottery Bognor" or "F.Masters, Bognor." Frederick Masters had been employed at Belle Vue previously.

Suggestions for Further Study

Lewes Museum at Anne of Cleves House, Southover Street, Lewes, Sussex, has some fine examples of Sussex Rustic and Sussex Art Ware.

Rye Museum has examples of all the Rye kilns since medieval times.

Hastings Museum also has examples of Rye wares.

Baines, John Manwaring. *Sussex Pottery.* Fisher Publications, 1980.

RYE

Types of Ware	Production	Quality	Availability
'Sussex Rustic Ware'	Moderate	Good	Uncommon
Miniatures	Low to Moderate	Fair to Good	Uncommon
Other art wares	Low to moderate	Good	Uncommon

Marks

Impressed or incised:		S	1869 - 1920
(Sussex Rustic Ware)	R	W	
		Rye	
+/- artist's initials, eg. 'F.T.M.' (Frederick T. Mitchell)			
+/ year			
(Sussex Art Ware):		S	1920 - 1939
	A	W	
		Rye	
Incised: (often on wares with small bases)		Rye	c.1869 - 1939
Incised:		Rye Ware	1882 - 1920
		Sussex Art Ware	1920 - 1939
+/- clay code, incised, (eg. 'WM', meaning, William Mitchell's preparation; or a "Five-bar gate" symbol)			
Impressed or printed: (John C. Cole & Walter V. Cole)		Rye	1947 onwards

(NB. 'Old Sussex Ware' and 'Rye Pottery' relate to William Mitchell & Sons' Cadborough Pottery.)

Benthall Pottery Co., Benthall, Broseley, Shropshire (1772-1982).

Historical Background

The Benthall Pottery was established in 1772 by John Thursfield, who had previously been producing stoneware at Jackfield nearby.

The Pottery went through various stages of ownership, merging with the Haybrook Pottery opposite in 1845. From this time, stoneware and brown "Rockingham" wares were produced, and about 1862, the Pottery came into the possession of the Allen family, and William Allen is recorded as being the manager from 1870 to 1907.

William Allen decided to venture into the production of art pottery, and in 1882 art wares were produced alongside the existing wares, though differentiated by the name "Salopian Art Pottery."

Little is known about the Pottery or its products, even though a considerable variety of wares was produced. Jewitt records that almost 300 shapes were advertised in 1883, though many were "ordinary yellow and other common wares."

A local advertisement of 1882 boasts a variety of wares imitating classical styles (Egyptian, Grecian, etc.) and mentions a London agent as a retail outlet. The artist Francis Gibbons is also mentioned, and at least one vase has been found with his initials recorded on the base.

An unsuccessful attempt in 1907 by William Allen's son, William Beriah Allen, to send some of the Pottery's employees to South Kensington School of Art led to the Company concentrating on the production of more domestic and industrial wares, such as electrical fittings and black lamp-bases, together with coarse terracotta wares, such as drain-pipes, garden ornaments and funerary items.

It seems, however, that art pottery was made on and off until about 1920, the Benthall Pottery Company continuing until 1982, manufacturing drain-pipes and other industrial items. The site today is used for the storage of agricultural machinery.

Salopian Selection of wares. l to r:-i) vase, 202mm high, mottled glaze. ii) double gourd-shaped vase, 222mm high, streaked glaze. iii) small vase, 109mm high, 'Scandy' pattern. iv) coffee-pot and decorated stand, 235mm high, 'Scandy' patern.

Products

Local clays were used and pieces were made in both white and brown clays, occasionally mixed.

Glazes were primarily lead, thickish in consistency, but some early pieces were decorated with a tin glaze, and later wares had unleaded thin glazes.

The majority of wares were thrown, but some were press-moulded, slabbed and modelled.

The range of wares produced is amazing as are the similarities to other potteries' styles and designs. Given the diversity of styles it is possible, however, to group the art wares into recognisable types.

An early group of wares were known as "Rhodian" and consisted of brightly coloured painted decoration on a terracotta body with a tin glaze. Colours were predominantly yellow, but variations of the same designs were produced in different colours. The Rhodian range consisted of floriate designs around a stylised Cross of St. John and featured particularly well on large and small plates. This range is remarkably similar to some of Carlo Manzoni's designs for the Granville and Della Robbia Potteries, but almost certainly pre-dates these latter.

Another range of wares was advertised as "barbotine" (compare Aller Vale Art Pottery) and featured thickly painted impasto decoration of recognisable flowers on a monochrome (often green) ground, and covered by a thick lead glaze. Vases featuring this form of decoration were similar to those produced at Aller Vale, though whether one influenced the other is difficult to say.

Another range produced was similar to the Aller Vale "Scandy" pattern, and featured brightly coloured swirls similar in decoration to painted "barge ware." Some domestic items, such as coffee-pots were also produced in this pattern.

The Salopian wares, though similar to wares of other Potteries, were often of a higher quality, and this is noticeable particularly with the Della Robbia and Aller Vale similarities.

A significant range of ware featured sgraffito work by the artist James Arthur Hartshorne, and bears some resemblance to Doulton's Silicon Ware. Precisely turned plant pots and jardinières were produced in a hard white or brown body, and featured a thin monochrome slip covering (usually blue), through which designs of birds, flowers, ferns and grasses were scratched. The quality of potting and decoration was good across this range, which was clearly designed to be functional as well as decorative.

Other wares featuring similarities to other potteries can be seen through gourd-shaped vases with streaked and mottled glazes similar to those designed by Christopher Dresser at Linthorpe, oriental glaze effects and shapes similar to Ruskin and splashed and dribbled glazes similar to Bretby.

Many Salopian creations, however, were unique, such as the heavily modelled and brightly coloured clusters of fruit, either as centre pieces for table decoration or adorning flower baskets or jardinières. A large creation (for want of a better word!) may be seen displayed in the Clive House Museum, and features modelled tortoises and lizards.

Suggestions for Further Study

Jackfield Tile Museum, Jackfield, has a few Salopian wares.

Clive House Museum, Shrewsbury, has a good representative collection of Salopian wares.

Messenger, Michael. *"Pottery & Tiles of the Severn Valley"* (catalogue of the Clive House Museum collections) Remploy Ltd., 1979.

Ironbridge Gorge Museum archaeologists' reports.

Salopian Examples of 'Rhodian' ware. l to r:-i) plate, 281mm diam., inscribed "Salopian Rhodian 2B". ii) small dish, 191mm diam., inscribed "Salopian Rhodian I".

Salopian Selection of vases. l to r:- i) 'barbotine' style, 293mm high, marked "SALOPIAN". ii) large vase, 280mm high, sgraffito decoration by Hartshorne. iii) small plant pot, 78mm high, sgraffito decoration, marked "SALOPIAN".

SALOPIAN ART POTTERY

Types of Ware	Production	Quality	Availability
Salopian art wares	Moderate	Good to Very Good	Uncommon

Marks

Most Salopian pottery is marked, the impressed mark often occurring near the base or on the foot of a piece.

Inscribed: + name of ware, eg. 'Rhodian 2B'	Salopian	1882-c.1890 ?
Impressed:	SALOPIAN	1882-c.1920 ? *
	SALOPIAN (within a diamond frame incorporating a butterfly and flower)	
Printed in black:	SALOPIAN (within a large diamond frame incorporating a butterfly and flower plus 'TRADE MARK' and 'ENGLAND')	c.1900?-c.1920 ?

BENTHALL POTTERY
BROSELEY   (in circle)
(* NB: Earlier porcelain wares from the Caughley factory used a similar mark.)

Salopian Jardinière, 196mm high, slab construction and press-moulded.   (courtesy HCMS, 1972.599).

Vine Street, Hanley, Staffs.

George Cartlidge (1868—?), artist/decorator

Historical Background & Products

Sherwin & Cotton produced mainly majolica tiles decorated with flowers, animals and portraits in relief. Colours were generally browns and greens, and the glazes were high. The tiles were characterised by "Sherwin's Patent Lock," a device comprising indentations on the reverse of tiles so that they could adhere to a wall more strongly.

Portraits were the speciality of the firm, and portrait tiles featured personalities such as Gladstone (1898), Abraham Lincoln (1909), General Booth of the Salvation Army (1904), Queen Victoria (1897), and many others, including two Maori chiefs (Tuari Netana and Matene Te Nga) and their Queens (Bella and Sophia).

The portraits were the work of George Cartlidge, who was apprenticed to the firm in 1882. He tended to work from photo-graphs, although the tiles themselves were modelled to such fine detail that they were often thought to have been produced by a photographic process, particularly as many were also glazed in a deep sepia colour. The debate continues as to the exact method of production.

Cartlidge was a graduate of Hanley School of Art, and received his Art Master's Certificate in the same year that Sherwin & Cotton produced his first portrait tile, that of Queen Victoria in 1897. Besides well-known personalities, Cartlidge also modelled on tiles such subjects as children, dogs and landscapes.

Although the portrait tiles were seen as a successful venture, Sherwin & Cotton's Works closed in 1911. George Cartlidge managed to continue designing portrait tiles, however, from 1916, when he was engaged by J.H. Barratt & Co. at the Boothen Works, Stoke. Here further tile portraits were produced, including several First World War personalities, such as Field Marshal Sir Douglas Haig, General Smuts and Admiral Sir John Jellicoe; and Prime Ministers, such as David Lloyd George; and Presidents, such as Abraham Lincoln.

Cartlidge continued to design tiles for Barratt's until about 1927, his later portraits extending to personalities of the Staffordshire Potteries, such as the sculptor Conrad Dressler, who worked at the Della Robbia Pottery for a time.

Prior to working for Barratt & Co., Cartlidge produced a series of ceramic designs for Sampson Hancock & Sons in Stoke, entitled "Morris Ware." This ware consisted mainly of vases, with painted floral decoration (such as harebells) over a mottled ground (which was usually green).

Suggestions for Further Study

City Museum, Hanley, Stoke-on-Trent, has a collection of Cartlidge's portrait tiles, plus original photographs from which he worked.

Knowles, Eric. "Photographic Portrait Tiles." *The Antique Collector,* August, 1977.

SHERWIN & COTTON

Types of Ware	Production	Quality	Availability
Tiles	High	Good to Very Good	Uncommon

Marks

Embossed: (A Staffordshire knot enclosed within a double triangle) 1877 - 1911
+/- 'Sherwin & Cotton'
+/- 'Sherwin's Patent Lock Back'

Impressed: (on tiles by Cartlidge; various permutations)	Made by SHERWIN and COTTON at their WORKS in HANLEY, in the County of Stafford 1898	1897 - 1911 (plus acorns, impressed)
or, similarly:	MADE BY • SHERWIN • & C℃TT℃N •	1897 - 1911

EASTWOOD TILE WORKS, HANLEY
STAFFORDSHIRE

+/ Cartlidge's monogram on the tile face.

Sherwin & Cotton Two panels of 150mm square tiles, tube-line floriate decoration in brown and green on blue.

Sherwin & Cotton 'Photographic Tiles' by George Cartlidge. l to r:- Gladstone, dated 1898, 223mm long by 148mm wide; General Booth, 230mm long by 150mm wide (courtesy HCMS, DA 1977.100/1-2).

The Torquay Pottery (c.1908-1939)
Hele Cross, Torquay, Devon.
Historical Background
The Torquay Terracotta Company was set up in 1875 by a Dr. William Gillow, a local man, in order to exploit the red clay deposits in the Torquay area. The clay was lighter in colour and more brittle than the clay used in the nearby Watcombe Pottery, but the resultant wares were often similar.

The enterprise set out to produce quality wares from the start, and two kilns were constructed along with purpose-built pottery buildings.

Among the decorators at Torquay Terracotta were several accomplished artists, such as Alexander Fisher, Holland Birbeck, his son Alexander Birbeck, and several Italian artists. Styles were clearly influenced by the latter, and some very fine painting was accomplished by Fisher and Birbeck.

Wares were exhibited for sale at retail outlets in Oxford Street and New Bond Street, London, and apparently sold well. The company also exhibited at the Paris International Exhibition in 1878, where their wares were well received.

The Torquay Terracotta Company closed about 1905, finding it difficult to continue as a profitable business, but the pottery soon reopened as The Torquay Pottery (c.1908), the premises having been acquired by Enoch Staddon, a former employee of the Bovey Tracey Pottery. Production at the new pottery was along different lines, and consisted initially of moulded and thrown wares with printed scenes, and, later, various types of tourist wares. The pottery finally closed in 1939.

Products
Fewer art wares were produced at Torquay Terracotta than at Watcombe, although there were many similarities between the two potteries in terms of output. A similar underglaze painting technique was employed, where designs were painted directly on to the terracotta body; and the practice of leaving large areas of body undecorated was also similarly employed at Torquay Terracotta.

The characteristic large bands of turquoise enamel frequently used for decoration at Watcombe did not seem to be as commonly employed at Torquay Terracotta. Here, early wares tended to be classical in shape and decoration, with a prevalence for simple Grecian shapes and motifs. Later wares were often characterised by a rich, painted all-over surface decoration.

Mainly vases, urns, jugs and plaques were made, and pieces were usually slip-cast or turned, with sharply defined outlines being produced from the fine, smooth body. Other items made included candlesticks, tobacco-jars, spill-jars and many domestic wares.

Alexander Fisher produced some fine colourful and detailed painting in enamel colours, featuring mainly birds and flowers in landscapes. The decoration often appeared dark against the orange-red body, resembling an old oil-painting. This "barbotine" style of decoration was popular among the South Devon potteries.

Holland Birbeck mostly painted realistic flower studies, which were equally detailed and particularly colourful. White colours stood out especially well against the smooth terracotta body, and convolvulus or daisies were striking subjects in this respect.

During the 1890s, some unusual vases were made with streaked and mottled, high gloss glazes, resembling, and in some cases identical to, some of the Christopher Dresser designed glazes from the Linthorpe Pottery. Decoration was typically in duochrome streaks, such as red and yellow, green and grey, or purple and blue, and was advertised as "Stapleton Ware." This ware and the resemblance of some Torquay Terracotta shapes to Dresser designs implies that some connection was established with either Dresser or Harrison at Linthorpe.

Also about this time, a range of vases and domestic items was advertised as "Crown Devon Ware." Pieces from this ware were characterised by decoration in thickly painted flowers, such as apple blossom.

Some reproductions of work by 19th. Century sculptors, such as John Gibson and C.B. Birch, were also made. Busts and figures of children and animals were produced in quantity, often in plain, unglazed terracotta.

Jugs, vases and other shapes were also produced in unglazed terracotta. A simple sgraffito line or motif might be the sole decorative embellishment, and some pieces were mounted in pewter or silver.

Collectors should note that undecorated blanks (particularly plates) were sold for amateur painting, and advertised as such in 1882. Quality of painting on these blanks varies considerably.

After 1908, production was of lesser quality tourist wares, comprising transfer-printed scenes of landscapes, birds and flowers. Most notable after the First World War were the painted souvenir wares on a blue ground, the king-fisher being a favourite decorative subject.

Suggestions for Further Study (see also under Watcombe)
Torquay Museum has a small representative collection of Torquay Terracotta.

Lloyd, D & E. *The Old Torquay Potteries.* Stockwell, 1978.

Catalogue of an Exhibition of Torquay Marble and Terracotta Ware at Sotheby Bearne, Torquay, 1979; Sotheby & Co.

"Torquay Pottery 1870-1940;" catalogue of an Exhibition at Bearne's & Bonham's in Knightsbridge, London, August, 1986; Torquay Pottery Collectors' Society.

Cashmore, Carol. "Ceramics for Gentlemen of Taste: The Torquay Potteries & Their Products." *The Antique Dealer & Collectors' Guide*, August, 1986.

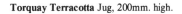

Torquay Terracotta Jug, 200mm. high.

Torquay Terracotta Two vases designed by Alexander Fisher with painted birds; l to r: vase, 345mm high, painted initials AF in body, impressed mark TORQUAY plus symbol for Wilmot (the turner) and impressed duck's feet mark.

Longpark Vase, 235mm high, painted underglaze, marked "Longpark Torquay", "701".

TORQUAY TERRACOTTA CO.

Types of Ware	Production	Quality	Availability
Art wares	Moderate	Poor to Very Good	Common (fine pieces scarce)

Marks

(NB. Most pieces were marked, but few bore an artist signature.)

Impressed	TORQUAY	1875 - c.1905
Impressed or printed:	TORQUAY TERRA COTTA C° LIMITED	1875 - 1890
(with variations)	TTC (in monogram, within oval)	1875 - c.1905
	TTC Trade Mark	c.1900 - c.1905

(in circle, surrounded by the words "Torquay Terra Cotta Co. Limited", written circular)
+/- artist signature or initials, painted (often within design), eg. "AF" (Alexander Fisher)
+/- decorator's symbols
+/- name of ware (eg. 'STAPLETON')

(NB. Impressed, painted and stamped marks such as "Hele Cross Pottery, Torquay" and "Torquay Pottery" relate to the Torquay Pottery period (c.1908 to 1939).)

Rainham, Kent.
Historical Background

The Upchurch Pottery was established in 1913 at Rainham in Kent by Seymour Wakeley. Seymour and his brother Sidney were brickmakers, and operated the firm of Wakeley Brothers at the time, but the operation of the Upchurch Pottery passed quickly to William and James Baker.

George Payne, a local antiquarian, remarked in 1915: "My friend Mr. Seymour Wakeley of Rainham has recently, at considerable cost, revived the pottery making industry upon the ancient site, selecting a spot to begin with a mile north of the parish church, and has met with marked success in the production of glazed ware suitable for table and decorative purposes. The clay used is found 2 or 3 feet below the surface of the marsh" (Archaeologia Cantiana, Vol.XXXI,1915, p.285).

The Wakeley Brothers continued in business as agricultural merchants, operating from the old chalk pit in Seymour Road, producing oven tiles, drainpipes, flower pots and chimneys.

At the Upchurch Pottery, thrown wares were produced of the type described by George Payne. Many were designed by Edward Spencer (b.1872, d.1938), the designer and metalworker who established the Artificers' Guild with Montague Fordham in 1903. Spencer was also a member of the Arts and Crafts Exhibition Society, along with Walter Crane, Lewis Day, Charles Voysey, William Morris, Edward Burne-Jones and other notable persons. At Upchurch, Spencer was retained as artistic director.

Upchurch wares were sold through retail outlets of the Artificers' Guild in London, Oxford and Cambridge until 1938, and Liberty of London, as well as locally from the Tudor Showroom in Rainham High Street. Some wares were included in the Paris Exhibition of British Decorative Arts in 1914, and pieces were exhibited at the annual British Industries Fairs from about this time. Favourable reviews were given by The Pottery Gazette through to the late 1920s.

In 1936, two years before Spencer died, the Pottery was purchased by Oscar Caradoc Davies with his wife, Grace Barnsley Davies, who was an accomplished ceramic decorator. The pottery became known as Rainham Pottery, and was managed by Ted Baker, who had worked at the pottery from 1938 until his retirement in 1975.

In 1956, Ted Baker purchased the pottery, renaming it Rainham Potteries Ltd, and specialised in commemorative wares (wall plaques and ash-trays, etc. for births, weddings and anniversaries; and trophies for sports and commercial organisations). The pottery closed in 1975, the site being taken over by Otterham Caravans. (The Tudor Showroom was demolished when the caravan site was extended).

Today the existence of Wakeley Road is a remembrance of the Wakeley Brothers.

Upchurch Group of wares, tallest 190mm high, all with incised mark
UPCHURCH.

Products

Wares produced at Upchurch were mostly plain pieces of simple shape. Surface decoration was kept to a minimum, and colours were mostly monochrome. A pale blue colour was used to good effect, with subtle plum coloured splashes, but other colours utilised included pale green, lavender, "aubergine plum," "peach blossom red," "lard white," "singed rose petal," buff and brown. Most colours were pastel shades. Spencer experimented widely with colours, attempting to emulate 10th. Century Chinese hues.

Pieces were generally thickly potted using a red clay, and glazes were predominantly silky matt in finish. Some crystalline glazes were developed, but these are scarce.

Styles were strongly influenced by early Chinese, Korean or Roman forms. The Roman connection with the area was a significant influence in some of the Upchurch shapes.

Most pieces were small in size, ranging from vases, jugs and bowls to teapots and tazzas, and several items were fairly crudely potted. Shapes designed by Spencer often included handles of rounded angular form on pieces emulating his pewter or silver wares. Designs other than by Spencer were in traditional domestic shapes.

Little is known of the wares designed by Grace Barnsley Davies prior to the Second World War, suffice it to say that they were completely different in style to the pre-1936 wares.

Collectors may come across wares marked "Claverdon," which appear to be Upchurch. These wares relate to the artist Alice Bourne Claverdon, who worked at Upchurch, and later at her own studio in London from 1947.

Suggestions for Further Study

Maidstone Museums & Art Gallery, St. Faith's, Maidstone, Kent. An Upchurch tankard is housed in the museum collections.

The library of The Goldsmiths' Company, London, to whom Edward Spencer's designs were bequeathed by his widow.

Upchurch Vase, 175mm high, impressed mark "UPCHURCH".

Upchurch Vase, 125mm high, impressed mark "UPCHURCH".

UPCHURCH POTTERY

Types of Ware	Production	Quality	Availability
Art wares to 1936	Moderate	Poor to Good	Uncommon

Marks

Incised:		Upchurch	1913 - 1936
Impressed		UPCHURCH	1913? - 1936
		UPCHURCH SEEBY	c.1946 - c.1961
Incised:		R (in monogram)	c.1937 - c.1939

(NB: "Seeby" was the name of the retail outlet in Reading, Berks. "RAINHAM" marks relate to post Second World War period.)

Doulton & Co. (1896-1919)
14A, Cheyne Row, Chelsea (1919-1940)

Historical Background

Charles Vyse was born into a family much associated with pottery, such that in 1896 at the age of fourteen, he found himself apprenticed to Doulton & Co. as a ceramic modeller and designer.

He studied sculpture from between 1905 and 1910 at the Royal College of Art and was elected a member of the Royal Society of British Sculptors in 1911. He also attended the Camberwell School of Art & Crafts the following year.

At Doulton he modelled many successful ceramic figures, production of which continued long after he left. He married Nell Vyse and together they decided to set up a pottery (July, 1919) at Cheyne Row, Chelsea to produce figures. Her knowledge of chemistry coupled with his modelling artistry set the scene for a long-running partnership of ceramic production and experimentation.

Their figure work was very popular in the United States of America, but from about 1928 they decided to branch out into making vases and bowls emulating early Chinese styles (the Sung dynasty especially). This in turn led to the production of other wares, such as decorative mugs and cat models.

Nell Vyse was particularly adept at accomplishing the intricate painting of the figures as well as modelling the almost minute flowers which frequently made up the figure subjects, and although she continued to undertake this work she was also able to transfer this skill to the decoration of the vases and bowls.

Charles's meticulous precision and accuracy in throwing resulted in some pots which could easily be confused with machine made wares. Others were highly accurate copies of the early Chinese styles or clever variants. Either way, their output was appreciated by several great collectors of the time, such as the Reverend Eric Milner-White and George Eumorfopoulos (who was also their neighbour at Cheyne Row and who allowed the Vyses to handle his own representative collection of Sung pieces).

From 1919 to 1928 the figures were regularly sold through various London retailers such as Walker's Galleries, which also later exhibited and sold the pots (1928-1938).

In 1940, the Vyse's studio was badly damaged by enemy action and all pottery production had to cease. It seems that after the war the Vyse's parted company and Charles took up a position as modelling and pottery instructor at Farnham School of Art. Here he continued to produce and exhibit pots, though production was only small in quantity.

Charles retired to Deal in Kent in 1963 and died in 1971. Nell Vyse died in 1967.

Charles Vyse Stoneware vase with rare 'fern leaf' decoration, 125mm high,
painted over incised mark "CHARLES VYSE CHELSEA".

Charles Vyse Bowl, in form of open lotus flower, 165mm diameter, incised mark VYSE 1936.

Products

Whilst at Doulton, Charles Vyse modelled several figures and figure groups with titles such as "The Return of Persephone" and "Darling" (one of his most popular figures created in 1913 and of which several thousand copies were made).

The first two figures produced at Cheyne Row were entitled "The Balloon Woman" and "The Lavender Girl," of which 100 copies each were made.

Most of the figures were studies of contemporary life and modelled from observations of flower sellers and other trades people around London. The realism of the 1920s and 1930s costumes and attitudes was particularly well captured.

Each figure was constructed from several separately made moulds, which were fitted together seemlessly, painstakingly painted and embellished with other decoration such as tiny individually made flowers. A thin white glaze was applied to the finished figure, and occasionally wood ash glazes were employed to give a different finish. Some figures were mounted on wooden stands which bore the title of the subject.

Whilst the number of copies made of any one figure subject was relatively high at first, output was soon limited to smaller numbers, often less than twenty. More than fifty subjects were produced.

Nell Vyse's interest in chemistry and Charles's interest in early Chinese stoneware led to their joint experiments in glazes, culminating in a pioneer piece of work in which they successfully reproduced an ancient Chinese blue glaze (Chun glaze) from a glaze recipe containing iron. This almost certainly led to their widening their creative range to the production of stoneware pots.

Vases, bowls and dishes were produced in a variety of Chinese and Korean styles, mainly emulating those of the Sung dynasty. Glazes ranged from celadon (pale green), tenmoku (brown-black), t'ang (various), chun (pale blue), t'zu chou (pale grey crackle), to various wood ash glazes (such as elm or poplar) and transmutation glazes (such as copper or flambé).

Shapes were particularly varied, ranging from modelled exteriors and interiors to open lotus flower shapes (from the mid 1930s). Decoration was either a simple glaze effect or in the form of painted or incised animals, fish or flowers; splashed and geometric motifs; cut-away, modelled or applied decoration.

Many pieces were of smallish stature (about 150mm in height or diameter), whereas the figures were frequently between 200mm and 290mm in height.

Some rare models of cats were made by Charles Vyse, often decorated in a figured tenmoku glaze to resemble a tabby cat.

A series of jugs, mugs, bowls, vases and goblets, painted in blue or iron-red on a grey ground with a thin wood ash glaze was produced during the early 1930s. They were characterised by motto inscriptions and depictions of simple floral motifs or circus and fairground folk. A particular artistic characteristic of these wares is the way the decorated figures bend into the shape of a jug or vase, as if to render a third dimension to a simple two-dimensional drawing.

Suggestions for Further Study

The Milner-White Collection at York City Art Gallery, York.

The Victoria & Albert Museum, London, has some fine examples of figures and stoneware pots.

Blunt, Reginald. *The Cheney Book of Chelsea China & Pottery.* EP Publishing, 1973.

"Charles Vyse 1882-1971," catalogue of an exhibition by Richard Dennis at The Fine Art Society, London, 1974; pub. Richard Dennis.

Riddick, Sarah. *Pioneer Studio Pottery—The Milner-White Collection.* Lund Humphries, 1990.

Rice, Paul and Christopher Gowing. *British Studio Ceramics in the 20th. Century.* Barrie & Jenkins, 1990.

Watson, Oliver. *British Studio Pottery—The Victoria & Albert Museum Collection.* Oxford: Phaidon & Christie's, 1990.

Rackham, Bernard. "The Pottery Figures of Mr. Charles Vyse." *The Studio* 81, 1921.

Marsh, Ernest. "Charles & Nell Vyse, Studio Potters of Chelsea." *Apollo*, May, 1943.

CHARLES VYSE

Types of Ware	Production	Quality	Availability
Figures	Moderate	Very Good	Uncommon
Stonewares	Low to Moderate	Very Good to Excellent	Uncommon
"Circus" wares	Low	Good to Very Good	Scarce

Marks

Various combinations have been noted and most wares are dated.

Figures

Painted:	CV CHELSEA	1919 - c.1927
+ year		
Incised:	C. Vyse	c.1924 - 1963
+/- "Chelsea"		
+/- year		
Incised:	Charles Vyse	c.1919 - c.1932 (rare mark)
Incised or painted:	Vyse (in signature)	c.1934 - c.1938
+/- year		

Pots

Incised:	C. Vyse	1928 - c.1931
+/- Chelsea"		
Painted or incised:	CV (in monogram)	c.1931 - c.1935
+ year		
Painted or incised:	Vyse	c.1931 - c.1939
+ year (sometimes within mark, eg. "19 Vyse 34")		
Incised:	Charles Vyse Chelsea	c.1932 - c.1963
+ year		

Charles Vyse Vase, 220mm high, incised mark 'VYSE 1939'.

Charles Vyse Two figures, l to r:-"Mid Day Rest", 1931, 205mm high; "Boy and Turkey" by Harry Parr, 1931, 263mm high excluding stand. (courtesy of Christie's Images)

WARDLE & CO. (c.1854—1935) —earthenwares

Hope Street, Shelton, Staffordshire (c.1854-1859)
James Street, Shelton, Staffs. (1859-1863)
William Street, Hanley, Staffs. (1865-1881)
Washington Works, Victoria Road, Hanley, Staffs. (1881-1910)
Wolfe Street, Stoke-on-Trent, Staffs. (1910-1924)
Cauldon Potteries Ltd.,Cauldon Place, Shelton, Staffs.(1924-1935)

Historical Background

James Wardle, was born the son of a potter, William Wardle, about 1820. He established a business for the manufacture of Parian and majolica wares about 1854 in premises at Hope Street, Shelton in Staffordshire.

In 1859, he went into partnership with George Ash and moved to James Street, Shelton. Here similar wares were produced until the partnership was dissolved in 1865. Wardle then moved to premises in William Street, Hanley, where he manufactured somewhat indifferent majolica wares both for the British and American markets.

When James Wardle died in 1871, his wife Eliza took over the business, trading under the name "Wardle & Co." She was helped initially by Thomas Forester, of a well known Staffordshire family of potters, and in 1881 as a result of increased trade with the American market they moved to a new, larger factory at Washington Works, Hanley. Eliza Wardle appointed David Jones as manager of the new factory. Her two sons, William Wallace Wardle and Frederick Charles Wardle acted as assistants.

The year 1885 proved to be a significant one in the history of the firm: Wardle & Co. introduced art pottery to their range of wares, and the first efforts included barbotine wares and slip decorated wares. T. Dean (from a family of artists) is known to have decorated and signed some of the barbotine wares.

In 1899, David Jones (James Wardle's son-in-law) took over the company and appointed a new, dynamic art director, Frederick Hurten Rhead. He was only nineteen years of age when appointed, but became responsible for a significant improvement in the production of artistic pottery at the factory. He introduced a number of striking designs, many of which incorporated tube—lining and slip decoration. His sister, Charlotte Rhead, joined the factory as a tube-liner in 1901, but the following year Frederick Hurten Rhead left for America, his brother Harry taking over as art director.

In 1903, Wardle & Co. became a limited company, with David Jones as manager, G.G. MacWilliam as chairman, and F.T. Maling and C.T. Maling (from the Newcastle pottery of the same name) as directors.

In 1904, Wardle & Co. was one of twenty pottery concerns representing Britain at the St. Louis International Exhibition in America. The catalogue of the British Section noted: "Some tasteful decorative pottery, well designed and varied in contour, form and pattern, were shown by Messrs. Wardle & Co." Nothing outstanding, but Wardle & Co. Ltd. received a bronze medal for pieces designed by David Jones and Harry Rhead.

The Rheads left the company in 1905, but Rhead-style designs continued to be produced. Trade began to decline, however, and in 1908, when David Jones died, the business went into receivership.

The next owners were J.A. Robinson & Sons Ltd., and in 1909 the business was re-registered as "Wardle's Art Pottery." Under the directorship of Herbert Forester the firm was reorganised and new designs were launched. Forester's reign was brief, however, and the same year he resigned from the company.

In 1910, the company moved to Wolfe Street, Stoke-on-Trent, and for the next few years production increased, but mainly plain glazed wares were produced with little for the overseas markets. In 1924, Wardle's Art Pottery amalgamated with Cauldon Potteries Ltd., and during the 1930s it is probable that designs were again created by members of the Rhead family: Frederick Alfred Rhead (father of Charlotte Rhead, Frederick H. Rhead and Harry Rhead), Frederick Hurten Rhead and Harry Rhead.

Wardle finally went into receivership in 1935.

Wardle Group of grotesques, 1 to r: spoon warmer, impressed mark "WARDLE ENGLAND" and "ENGLAND" separately plus pattern no. 1480; egg cover, in shape of duck's head, unglazed inside, impressed mark "WARDLE ENGLAND REGISTERED"; jug, 180mm high, impressed mark "WARDLE ENGLAND" and pattern no. 2153; armadillo, impressed mark "WARDLE ENGLAND".

Wardle Group of monochrome glazes, l to r, back row: pale green vase, 208mm high, impressed mark "WARDLE WARE" and pattern no. 1920; pink bulbous vase, incised mark "WARDLE" and pattern no. 3755; blue globular vase, impressed mark "WARDLE ENGLAND" and pattern no. 2007. l to r,—front row: blue vase, incised mark "WARDLE 7 Reg." and pattern no. 1925; pink vase, impressed mark "WARDLE ENGLAND" and pattern no. 1923; dark green vase, impressed mark "WARDLE ENGLAND" and pattern no. 3586.

Wardle Group of late decorative painted wares, l to r: vase, incised mark "WARDLE" and pattern no 8 with painted mark "301 H"; vase, 265mm high,incised mark "WARDLES" and pattern no. 218; bowl,INDUS design,painted mark "WARDLE INDUS".

Wardle Group of vases, 'Night on the Sea' range, all with impressed mark "WARDLE ENGLAND" and impressed pattern number. l to r: vase showing ships silhouetted against a daytime sky, pattern no. 2006; jardinière showing ships silhouetted against a sunset sky, pattern no. 39; vase, ditto, 320mm high, pattern no. 29; vase showing ships against a green sky, signed "S.Cooper" in body, pattern no. 2381

Wardle Transfer printed wares, l to r: vase in "Georgian" design, impressed mark "WARDLE ENGLAND" and pattern no. 2050 plus transfer-printed mark "GEORGIAN WARDLE & CO. COPYRIGHT"; plate, painted over transfer print impressed "WARDLE ENGLAND"; two-handled vase, (one of a pair), 255mm high, "Elizabethan" design, impressed mark "WARDLE ENGLAND" and pattern no. "1918 WI" with transfer printed mark "ELIZABETHAN WARDLE & CO."

Wardle Group of slip trailed and tube-lined wares showing Frederick Rhead influence, all with impressed mark "WARDLE ENGLAND", l to r: vase, stylised trees, 315mm high, pattern no. 2386; vase, similar, pattern no. 2125; vase, stylised tree and roots, pattern no.7; candlestick, pattern no. 81; small bottle vase, lined decoration; globular vase, fox and vine decoration.

Wardle Crocus pattern, all impressed "WARDLE ENGLAND" l to r, back row: trumpet shape vase, pattern no. 51; vase, flat top, 240mm high, overstamped with faulty mark "WADRLE ENGLAND" and pattern no. 84; vase, pattern no. 73. l to r, front row: two-handled vase, pattern no. 7; small vase, pattern no. 37 and mark "HA"; inkwell and cover, pattern no. 38 and mark "F.L."; small bottle vase, pattern no. 40.

Products

Wardle & Co. produced a vast amount of wares which ranged from the exotic to the mundane. They imitated the styles of many other pottery manufacturers (compare Salopian in this respect) as well as being quite inventive in their own right.

1854-1885

Mostly Parian and majolica wares, intended primarily for the American market. Parian busts of Lincoln were advertised during this period. Majolica designs included "Sunflower," "Bamboo and Fern," "Bird and Fan" and "Pineapple." These early wares are scarcely found in the UK.

1885-1910

The art pottery period saw barbotine wares of average quality appearing on the market. Then, in 1896, following a visit to the factory by the Duchess of Teck (mother of Queen Mary), three new lines were introduced: "Royal Teck," "Royal Guelph" and "Hispano Ware."

"Royal Teck" (marked "Teck Ware" below a crown) was particularly high quality, with thinly applied slip decoration of a high standard and designs of delicately slip-trailed flower sprays or landscape scenes, sometimes signed by the artist responsible. Slip decorated "Royal Guelph" had affinities with Doulton's "Kingsware," whilst "Hispano Ware" could easily be mistaken for the South Devon "Scandy" wares (see Aller Vale), and, like the Devon products often included an inscribed motto.

The next decade could be described as the golden age of art pottery at Wardle. With Frederick Hurten Rhead as art director and the recruitment of highly skilled painters, the factory produced a range of fine quality slip-decorated, tube-lined and sgraffito wares, including vases and jardinières of varying shapes and sizes.

Rhead's influence was seen in the utilisation of stylised trees as a decorative motif. Many of the pieces were individually signed, either with the surname in full (as "R.Dean") or with initials. Pieces bearing Harry Rhead's signature are rare, though other artist signed pieces are not uncommon. Little is currently known of many of the artists employed at Wardle.

In 1901, Wardle introduced a series of grotesques which included frogs, cats, dogs, ducks, etc., and in 1903, "Miss Vulliamy's Novelties" were advertised. Blanche G. Vulliamy was a free-lance artist operating from a studio in the King's Road, Chelsea. Queen Victoria is known to have purchased a number of her works, and in 1898 she had exhibited a water-colour at the Royal Institute. Prior to her designing for Wardle she had carried out design work for Foley (Wileman & Co.) and the Baron Pottery. Between 1898 and 1904 she had registered at least 29 designs for pottery, much of which was retailed at Liberty and T. Goode & Co.

'Miss Vulliamy's Novelties' featured snails, snakes, owls, bats, and even penguins, all depicted in a grotesquely humorous way. Besides these, she also designed character jugs for Wardle, and, in 1905, she designed a small pot bearing a raised moulded shape of a dinosaur, which commemorated the presentation by Andrew Carnegie of a model of the Pittsburg museum dinosaur, Diplodocus Carnegii, to the London Natural History Museum.[1]

Other wares introduced by Wardle in 1905 included a series of transfer-printed pots with hand-painted colours. These were probably designed by Frederick Alfred Rhead, and bore various titles: "Elizabethan" and "Georgian" wares which depicted various characters in period costume; "Farmyard Scenes" which depicted ducks, pigs, hens, etc.; "Country Life" which depicted characters often dressed in Dutch costumes.

[1] This is illustrated in The Pottery Gazette for November 1905 (p. 1187).

Also in 1905, Wardle supplied two series of wares for Liberty & Co. of London. These were "Hadcote Pottery," a series of slip-applied floral designs in turquoise blue on a royal blue background, and "Heros Pottery," which comprised incised shell-fish designs on a green background. These wares were simply marked "MADE FOR LIBERTY & CO.," without a Wardle stamp but with a shape number.

Several other wares were introduced before Wardle was bought out by J.A. Robinson & Sons Ltd. The most striking of these was named "Night on the Sea," depicting skilfully painted designs of sailing boats in black silhouette against a dark red background, particularly on tall cylindrical vases or large ovoid vases. The same pattern was also executed against a dark green background.

1910-1935

After 1910, Wardle appears to have concentrated on the mass production of plain glaze wares. During the late 1920s, following the amalgamation with Cauldon Potteries Ltd., a series of high quality designs with titles such as "Burma," "Ceylon" and "Indus" were produced on semi-porcelain, together with lesser quality designs such as "Lagos" and "Portland Valda." These do not seem to have been produced in large quantities.

About 1932, a range of rather striking art deco designs called 'Swansea Ware' was introduced. This ware was of a good quality, with pieces decorated in bright colours, featuring silver as one of the colours. The designs were probably by F A rhead, who was working for the Cauldon group of potteries at the time. Each shape within the series was given a title, eg. 'Van Dyke' (lotus shape), 'Classic,' 'Irena.'

Suggestions for Further Study

The author is indebted to Patrick Beasley for compiling this chapter from his wealth of knowledge on Wardle pottery.

Wardle Vase, "Hadcote" pattern, 365mm high, applied slip and tube-lined decoration on uneven surface, impressed mark "MADE FOR LIBERTY & CO." and incised pattern no. 2.

WARDLE & CO.

Types of Ware	Production	Quality	Availability
art wares, post-1885	High	Good to Very Good	Common (some wares scarce)
'Made for Liberty'	Low	Good to Very Good	Scarce
Semi-porcelain	Low to Moderate	Good to Very Good	Scarce

Marks

Impressed: (Wardle & Ash)	W. & A.		1859 - 1862
Printed:	W	(monogram with mailed fist)	c.1885 - 1890
Printed:	ENGLAND W	(in shield surmounted by a crown)	c.1890 - 1935
Impressed:	WARDLE		c.1871 - 1891
Impressed:	WARDLE ENGLAND		1891 - c.1925
Impressed (rare mark mistake):	WADRLE (sic) ENGLAND		c.1907
Printed:	WARDLE FAIENCE ENGLAND	(in double circle beneath neck of a vase)	c.1902 - 1909
Incised (various styles): +/- overstamped "Royal Cauldon" 1930-1935	WARDLE		c.1910 - 1935
Painted:	WARDLE		c.1925 - 1935

NB 1: +/- shape number
Most wares bear shape numbers, impressed or incised, up to about no.3800. Pattern numbers, which are more rarely found, are usually three digits and mainly painted.
NB 2: +/- decorator's initials or signature (usually painted, on the side or base), eg. E. Bagley, F.Butler, J. Cooper, R.Dean, T.Dean, W.Murray, H.Rhead, T. R. Ruskin, Charles Collis. Unknown: A, AHS, CM, E, FL, H, M, S, SP, WI
NB 3: +/- ware name
eg. 1896-1900 : Teck Ware (under crown, impressed); Royal Guelph (raised mark); Hispano Ware (under crown, impressed).
c.1905-1907 : Elizabethan; Georgian; Stuart; Farmyard Scenes; English Hunting Adventures; Motor-Car Ware, Rhodian Rose. (all printed)
late 1920's : BURMA; CEYLON; DELPHI; INDUS; TURIN (painted, often in blue)
late 1920's, early 1930's : LAGOS; VALDA or PORTLAND VALDA; SPARTA (painted in blue or impressed)
c. 1932: SWANSEA WARE
NB 4: +/- a variety of small marks:
single cross in oval (impressed), hatched lines in hexagon (impressed); two dots (incised); eleven dashes making a circle (impressed); a cross (incised).

Teignmouth Road, St. Marychurch, Torquay, Devon.

Historical Background

During the late 1860s, deposits of red clay were discovered around Torquay, and a company was set up in 1869 by G.J. Allen, a local resident, to exploit them. The company was initially known as The Watcombe Terra-Cotta Clay Company, and commenced the construction of buildings from 1870, going into full pottery production during 1871. The company took on local workers, assisted by skilled workmen from the Staffordshire potteries, under the direction of Charles Brock.

An initial desire was to reproduce classical wares as pottery or ceramic sculpture, the business apparently being somewhat of a philanthropic venture, giving local employment, rather than endeavouring to make a handsome profit.

The firm earned a high reputation. Pieces were exhibited locally, and in London (1872), Philadelphia (1876), and Paris (1878), in particular.

By the late 1870s, six kilns were in operation, and the workforce totalled almost one hundred. By 1883, however, the company had got into financial difficulties. Charles Brock had returned to Staffordshire in 1881, and G. Allen had died a few years previously. The pottery was revived, however, when new owners, Evans & Co., assumed control in 1884.

In 1901, the Watcombe Pottery Company, as it was then known, was acquired by Hexter, Humpherson and Company and amalgamated into the Aller Vale Pottery Company (which had been acquired in 1897) to form the Royal Aller Vale & Watcombe Art Potteries.

Pottery continued to be made at Watcombe, though the types of product were virtually identical to those produced at Aller Vale. Often the factory mark is the only difference. The Works closed in 1962.

Products

The Watcombe Terra-Cotta Clay Company at first produced terracotta vases, jugs, bottles, candlesticks, plaques and figures. Designs were classical, the decoration often comprising enamelling on the smooth red-brown terracotta surface. Few pieces were thrown, most wares being slip-cast and turned.

Many classical figures and busts were produced, as well as busts of politicians and other personalities. During the 1870s, Samuel Kirkland was noted as having modelled terracotta flowers and flower-baskets.

Turquoise seems to have been a favourite enamel colour, though black and white enamels were also used to good effect. Pieces tended to rely on simplicity of shape for effect, in the true classical tradition, and surface decoration was often minimal. A common characteristic was a single band of turquoise enamel on the neck or base of vases, with either no additional decoration or hand-painted classical scenes on the body.

Since the terracotta was porous, all water-holding pots had to be internally glazed. Plain or simply decorated pieces usually revealed the smooth texture of the terracotta body, whilst more decorative pieces revealed the body through a transparent, shiny (but thin) glaze.

From about 1879, the pottery began to produce art wares, alongside the production of classical busts and figures of earlier styles. Surface decoration increased with the art wares, with a trend towards underglaze painting. Flowers, birds, butterflies, landscapes and seascapes were typical of the decorative subjects chosen.

Shapes became more interesting. Japanese styles were emulated, and it is believed that the renowned designer Christopher Dresser had designs produced at Watcombe. Certainly, many motifs (painted or transfer-printed) had been taken from Owen Jones' "Grammar of Ornament," published from 1856.

The use of an overall glaze on some art wares was an interesting departure from normal practice, and some of these wares were marked "WATCOMBE PORCELAIN." Many bore a darker and harder body than the usual ranges.

From about 1885, the new company commenced the production of wares painted in oil, which began to replace the old form of enamelled decoration. Coloured slips were used to paint tiles and plaques in the biscuit state; and a few rarely signed pieces of the oil-painting work of the artist Holland Birbeck have been found. The quality of oil-painting was high, with detailed brush-work and often elaborate decoration. The surface of the terracotta was particularly suited to oil-painting, and anything with a flat enough surface, such as plaques, tiles and pilgrim-bottles, was decorated to good effect. As at Torquay Terracotta, blanks were produced for amateur artists to paint.

Besides the detailed landscapes, seascapes and other patterns, some interesting designs of geometrical motifs were produced. These and other simple decorations were often painted in black for increased effect.

Some cheaper ranges of terracotta wares were produced during the late 1890s, as well as some white-bodied experimental pieces. Wares painted to high quality, however, are much sought after by collectors, and are somewhat scarcely found currently.

From 1901, output was often identical to that of Aller Vale, with motto and Scandy wares being produced, for example, using a white clay body. Refer to the chapter on Aller Vale for information on these types of product.

After the First World War underglaze painted scenes increased and decoration became brighter. The "Marine Views" series featured sailing-boats and coastal landscapes, and was particularly effective on jardinières. Floral subjects, such as clematis, were popular decorative themes through to the 1920s, and some plain green wares (known as "Art Green Ware") were also produced, green being a colour which featured strongly as a background on earlier wares.

One of the most famous Watcombe patterns of the 1920s was "Kingfisher," which featured a brightly coloured kingfisher diving from a branch into water against a blue background. The scene was completed with water-lilies and bull-rushes.

An attempt at art deco patterns was made during the 1930s, though the classic Devon shapes rather negated the effect.

Watcombe Teapot, 120mm high, glazed terracotta, marked "Watcombe Porcelain", "A5105".

Suggestions for Further Study

The Victoria & Albert Museum, London, has some fine enamelled vases of the classical type.

Thomas, D & E Lloyd. *The Old Torquay Potteries.* Stockwell, 1978.

"The Watcombe Terra-Cotta Works." *The Art Journal* XI, 1872.

Archer, T.C., Prof. "The Watcombe Terra-Cotta Company." *The Art Journal* XVII, 1878.

"Catalogue of an Exhbition of Torquay Marble & Terracotta Ware at Sotheby Bearne, Torquay," Sotheby Parke Bernet & Co., 1979.

"Torquay Pottery 1870-1940;" catalogue of an exhibition at Bearne's & Bonham's Auctioneers in Knightsbridge, London, August, 1986; Torquay Pottery Collector's Society.

Cashmore, Carol. "Ceramics for Gentlemen of Taste: The Torquay Potteries & Their Products." *The Antique Dealer & Collectors' Guide*, August, 1986.

Brisco, Virginia. "Best Forms from the Antique..." (Watcombe); *The Antique Dealer & Collectors' Guide*, August, 1989.

Watcombe Jug, 215mm high, Grecian inspired decoration, transfer printed mark in black "WATCOMBE PORCELAIN".

WATCOMBE POTTERY

Types of Ware	Production	Quality	Availability
Early classical wares	Moderate	Good to Excellent	Uncommon
Art wares (1883-1901)	Moderate	Good to Very Good	Uncommon
Wares post-1901	High	Poor to Good	Common

Marks

Impressed	WATCOMBE TORQUAY	1871 - c.1875
	WATCOMBE POTTERY	1871 - 1901
Printed:	A woodpecker in a landscape, surrounded by a double circle containing the words: Watcombe South Devon. (An earlier version of this mark, c.1875 - 1883, states "Watcombe Torquay")	1884 - 1901
	WATCOMBE	c.1880 - c.1890
Painted:	Watcombe Torquay England	c.1891 - c.1914
Impressed	WATCOMBE TORQUAY MADE IN ENGLAND	c.1920 - c.1927
Stamped:	WATCOMBE TORQUAY ENGLAND	c.1928 - c.1945

+/- pattern or batch numbers.
+/- artist's mark, eg. "H.B." (Holland Birbeck) (few Watcombe artists signed their work).
(NB1: The author has also noted the impressed mark "W" and "T" together on some wares)
+/- turner's symbol, impressed.
+/- price of item, in pencil on terracotta base.

—earthenware
—porcelain
—moulded wares
—tiles
—lustres

Burslem, Stoke-on-Trent, Staffs. (1656-1769)
Etruria, Stoke-on-Trent, Staffs. (1769-1940)
Barlaston, Staffordshire (1940 to present)

Historical Background

In 1656, Thomas Wedgwood established his pottery at Burslem, Stoke-on-Trent, in order to exploit the clay of the Etruria Marls. Josiah Wedgwood I (1730-1795) established Josiah Wedgwood & Sons in 1759, and ten years later moved to a new site at Etruria.

The company made its name in tableware, of which their "Queensware" (cream-coloured earthenware) was particularly popular, selling throughout the world. Still sold today, it is one of the longest running ceramic wares ever produced.

"Jasperware," for which Wedgwood was also famous, was produced from an early date, commencing as plaques and medallions, and extending to vases and other shapes during the latter part of the eighteenth century.

Josiah Wedgwood's sons succeeded him in managing the business, and from 1847, the company produced parian-like figures and busts from a new clay body, which they marketed as "Carrara Ware."

Art pottery was produced from 1878, when Thomas Allen was appointed Art Director, but the most popular art wares were made during the 20th. Century, and in particular during the 1920s and 1930s. Under the artistic direction of John E. Goodwin (Art Director 1902-1934), a wide range of highly individual art wares was produced, including tiles.

Wedgwood was keen to fund the search for new and unusual glazes, and towards the turn of the 20th. Century, the chemist William Burton (at Wedgwood 1877-1892) experimented with lustre-painting, producing some original blue and orange coloured glazes.

In 1893, Burton became director of the Pilkington Pottery, but his lustre-painting experiments were continued by Daisy Mackeig-Jones, such that from 1914, she was able to produce some high quality ornamental wares, which were continued throughout the 1920s until 1931. These she termed "Fairyland Lustre" and "Dragon Lustre."

Wedgwood always had a tradition of using the designs of competent artists, and during the 1920s and 1930s, several artists and designers were employed who have since become renowned for their high quality work. Artists such as Grace Barnsley (later to work at Upchurch with her husband) were decorating wares during this period, and during the 1930s, in particular, original designs were created by Anna Zinkeisen, Harry Threthowan, John Skeaping, Rex Whistler, Eric Ravilious and the architect Keith Murray.

The architect Alfred Powell and his wife Louise also designed pottery for Wedgwood. From about 1905 to 1928, they produced designs from their studio in London.

Wedgwood Vase, 300mm high, yellow, red and blue with gold lustre.

Wedgwood Vase, 185mm high, by Keith Murray, moonstone glaze, marked "Moonstone" and signature of Keith Murray.

223

Wedgwood Examples of 'Fairyand Lustre' by Daisy Mackeig-Jones. l to r:-i) bowl, 70mm high, marked "Z11968". ii) jar and cover, 215mm high, marked "Z4968". (both with gold Portland Vase factory mark).

Wedgwood Lustre bowl, 203mm diam., by Alfred Powell. (courtesy HCMS, ACM 1946.113).

Wedgwood Model of a monkey with young, by John Skeaping, pale green monochrome glaze.

Wedgwood opened a special studio at Etruria in 1926 for the production of hand-decorated wares, and several young women were recruited, having trained at local art schools. The Powells regularly supplied designs for this studio, but the more talented paintresses, such as Millicent Taplin, were often allowed to implement their own designs.

In 1935, Victor Skellern became art director at Wedgwood, succeeding John E. Goodwin. Skellern trained at Burslem School of Art under the renowned artist, Gordon Forsyth. He carried on the fine tradition of experiment and originality that his predecessor had introduced.

In 1940, the factory moved from Etruria to new premises at Barlaston, designed by Keith Murray. The company continues on this site today, trading as Waterford Wedgwood, following a merger with Waterford Glass in 1986.

Products

The prime output from Wedgwood was tablewares, though ornamental wares were regularly produced alongside this production.

The artist, Walter Crane received a commission in 1867 for the design of some vases and trays, and Christopher Dresser is recorded as having designed shapes for tableware and majolica for Wedgwood about this time. Majolica was produced in monochrome colours of brown, green and blue from about 1863, and, with Carrara Ware, continued in general production until the end of the nineteenth century.

Thomas Allen's influence on decorative design at Wedgwood was significant. About 1880, some earthenware vases were produced as art pottery, decorated in coloured slips and incorporating Japanese or Gothic designs. These early art wares were of good quality, but are scarcely found today.

The ceramic designer, Frederick Rhead, joined Wedgwood in 1878, and specialised in pâte-sur-pâte decorated pieces and slipwares, until leaving a few years later. Another well-known ceramic designer, Harry Barnard, joined Wedgwood in 1897 from James Macintyre & Sons, commencing a long association with the company, managing the tile department from 1899, and Wedgwood's London shop from 1902.

Wedgwood produced tiles in a wide range of styles and processes, from glazed encaustic tiles in Gothic styles for church flooring to Jasperware inserts for English furniture. From about 1870 to 1900, transfer-printed tiles were produced, which included sets with titles such as "Robin Hood," "A Midsummer Night's Dream" and "Red Riding Hood."

From about 1905, Alfred and Louise Powell were designing highly decorative wares for Wedgwood, using lustre glazes on earthenware. They comprised mostly simply-shaped vases, jugs and bowls, using pastoral scenes or geometric and floral motifs, with scrolled and floral borders. Silver lustre on blue, green and brown were common colour combinations used.

From 1914, Daisy Mackeig-Jones' "Fairyland Lustres" (fantasy paintings of fairies and stars, etc.) and "Dragon Lustres" (Chinese inspired paintings of birds, butterflies and dragons) were produced.

Mackeig-Jones' lustres were executed on a porcelain body, the colours being applied over a painted surface, which caused them to streak under the glaze. Occasionally gold was used over the glaze to emphasise the underlying design. Bowls of all sizes, saki cups, plates, vases and plaques were the main items decorated with these lustres.

The high quality and originality of these lustres have made them much sought after by collectors. The decoration is particularly impressive against the midnight-blue or black backgrounds, and the simple, Chinese style shapes enhance the spectacle.

Daisy Mackeig-Jones also created some ranges of nursery-ware, which were released from 1914 as "Noah's Ark" and "Brownies."

In 1920, Wedgwood launched a ware called "Rhodian," closely followed by "Persian." Both were influenced by Near-Eastern designs and featured hand-painted decoration designed by Alfred and Louise Powell.

Tablewares were exhibiting more individuality of design during the 1920s and 1930s, and Wedgwood produced several ranges which reflected both the demand for creative hand-painted designs and the need for more mass-produced wares. Both art deco and modernist designs were produced, and artists such as Millicent Taplin contributed high quality designs in both styles. Her modernist "Falling Leaves" pattern in grey and green was particularly successful.

About 1927, the sculptor John Skeaping designed a series of animal sculptures which appeared in monochrome colours with a matt glaze, ranging from the renowned Wedgwood black "Basalt" ware to white, cream and pale green. Of the sculptures produced, the "Polar Bear," "Lion," "Mountain Goat" and "Tiger and Buck" were particularly effective.

Modelling generally became popular at Wedgwood during the late 1920s and early 1930s, with other sculptors designing work, such as the figures produced by the American Alan Best.

During the early 1930s, a series of ornamental wares entitled "Veronese" was launched. These wares consisted of simple shapes with equally simple lustre floral motifs on single coloured grounds, such as plum, green and cream. Some experiments in painting over a tin glaze were carried out around 1935, and a few good quality gilt art deco vases were produced.

During the 1930s, Keith Murray created a range of technically precise engine-turned wares, which are now popular with collectors. Jugs, vases, bowls, trays, beer-mugs and some tablewares were amongst the output of Murray's designs, and most carried a characteristically monochrome matt glaze, as well as a simple shape with concentric grooves or ribbing.

The matt glazes were developed by Norman Wilson (at Wedgwood 1927 to 1962), and appeared in a variety of individual colours: straw, pale blue, white moonstone, pale grey, pale green, basalt black, in particular. Some special glazes, such as copper basalt, were also used.

Murray was engaged to produce a new form of art ware that could be adapted for domestic use; and he modelled his wares on the German "Bauhaus" style, as well as on various Chinese and Korean designs. In 1933, many of these designs were exhibited at the John Lewis store in London as "An Exhibition of New Wedgwood Shapes Designed by Keith Murray." Favourable comments were expressed at this exhibition as well as at other international exhibitions: Milan the same year, London (1935) and Paris (1937).

In 1935, Wedgwood produced a range of tea-sets named "Farnol" in an art deco style similar to Shelley's "Mode" and "Vogue" ranges. In 1937, Eric Ravilious created a range of "Alphabet" nursery-ware, using a lithographic process of decoration, and the following year his pattern "Persephone" was produced for tablewares.

Ravilious often depicted scenes of everyday life in his designs, as exemplified by the "Garden" and "Garden Implements" series. Many of his designs, however, were not released until the early 1950s, his death in 1942 cutting short a promising career.

Suggestions for Further Study

Batkin, Maureen. *Wedgwood Ceramic 1846-1959.* Richard Dennis, 1982.

Batkin, Maureen and Robert Harling. *Ravilious & Wedgwood.* Dalrymple Press, 1986.

Mackeig-Jones, M. *Some Glimpses of Fairyland.* Buten Museum of Wedgwood, 1921 (reprinted 1963).

Reilly, Robin and George Savage. *The Dictionary of Wedgwood.* Woodbridge, Suffolk: Antique Collectors' Club, 1980.

Dawson, Aileen. *Masterpieces of Wedgwood in the British Museum.* London: British Museum, 1984.

Dawes, Nicholas M. *Majolica.* New York: Crown Publishers Inc., 1990.

Des Fontaines, Una. *"Wedgwood Fairyland Lustre, the Work of Daisy Mackeig-Jones;"* catalogue of an exhibition at Sotheby's; Richard Dennis, 1978.

"Eric Ravilious 1903-1942: A Re-assessment of His Life and Work;" catalogue of an exhibition at The Towner Art Gallery, Eastbourne, 1986.

Des Fontaines, Una, Lionel Lambourne and Ann Eatwell. *"Miss Jones & Her Fairyland;"* catalogue of a gift collection from Suzanne & Frederic Weinstein to the Victoria & Albert Museum, London; London: V & A, 1990.

"Wedgwood Catalogue of Bodies, Glazes and Recipes" (presented to the British Museum by Wedgwood in 1941).

Rumsey, Jill. "Keith Murray." *Antique Collector's Club* 16(11), April, 1982.

The Wedgwood factory at Barlaston, Stoke-on-Trent, welcomes visitors, and displays an extensive range of Wedgwood creations in novel settings.

Wedgwood Specimen signature of Keith Murray on bowl.

JOSIAH WEDGWOOD & SONS			
Types of Ware	**Production**	**Quality**	**Availability**
Art wares	Moderate	Good to Very Good	Uncommon
Lustres	Low	Good to Excellent	Scarce
Marks			
Impressed	WEDGWOOD	1929 - 1940	
Painted:	WEDGWOOD *	1780 - 1940	

+/- year letter
+/- artist's mark (eg. 'Keith Murray' in signature, stamped in pastel blue or green; 'John Skeaping' impressed). Daisy Mackeig-Jones rarely signed her work.
+/- 'Made in England' (after 1891)
* (in gold with outline of 'Portland Vase' on many lustrewares and bone china)
(NB. Wares marked "Wedgwood & Co." are not Josiah Wedgwood & Sons.)

Coldrum Farm, Coldrum, Wrotham, Kent (c.1909)
College Street, Chelsea, London (1909-1914)
417, Kings Road, Chelsea, London (1918-1924)
Storrington, Sussex (1924-1940)

Historical Background

Reginald Fairfax Wells trained at the Royal College of Art, South Kensington, London in sculpture during the late 1890s, followed by a period of study in ceramics at Camberwell School of Arts & Crafts.

At first he concentrated on bronze sculpture and achieved some recognition with statuettes, such as "The Sower," "Athlete" and "First Steps." From 1900, he produced several bronze pieces, including a series of small bronze figures, such as "Girl with the Faggot" and "Farm Horse," cast by himself using the lost-wax process. A notable commission was fulfilled for New Place, the home of Lady Methuen at Hindhead in Surrey, where a large statue "Girl with the Scythe" was installed complete with a fountain to his own design.

The bronze figures proved an admirable source for Wells's interest in the cermamic medium, which seems to have born fruit about 1909, whilst at Coldrum, near Wrotham in Kent. Here he produced rough earthenwares decorated very much in the English slipware tradition. Little is currently known about this early work, but it is recorded that some terra-cotta figures were produced, most of which were originally models for bronze subjects.

His affinity with Kent continued when he moved to Chelsea, where until the outbreak of the First World War he produced stoneware which he termed "Coldrum Ware."

During the war he became involved with aircraft design and established his own aviation company in Chelsea. After the war he resumed his pottery work at new premises in Kings Road, Chelsea, where he produced wares often marked "SOON" (though apparently having nothing to do with Chinese Sung wares).

The collector George Eumorfopoulos, who lived in Chelsea, is known to have purchased pieces and Wells exhibited some figures at the Beaux Arts Gallery in Bruton Place, London, amongst which his "Mother and Child" was particularly noted.

In 1924 he moved to Storrington in Sussex, where he built a new and larger kiln. Here he was also involved in tile making and apparently enjoyed fulfilling commissions for old country cottages. At Storrington his stonewares were often Chinese inspired, though he continued to make pieces marked "SOON."

It seems that the Second World War brought an end to Wells' pottery production, as it did for many potteries. He died in 1951.

Reginald Wells "Coldrum" pieces, tallest 265mm. All with impressed mark
COLDRUM except jug which is impressed COLDRUM CHELSEA.

Reginald Wells "Soon pots, tallest 120mm high. All with impressed mark "SOON".

R. Wells Farmhorse, 310mm high, incised mark "R F Wells" on front base.

Products

A variety of figures was produced, many of which were variants or direct copies of his bronze subjects. A series of terracotta figures and figure groups was an early product, with titles such as "The Blacksmith," "Woman Carrying a Basket," "Peasant Girl," "A Father and Child" and "Farm Horses with Riders." Some of these were also later produced in stoneware.

Stoneware figures had titles such as "Motherhood," "Sleep," "Feeding Chickens," etc. Models of animals were also produced in stoneware, such as runner ducks, rams, bulls, Rhone and Shire horses. Colours were either monochrome with mottled glazes or multi-coloured. Wells experimented widely with glaze effects as well as clay bodies. Many of the figures were characterised by thick solid bases, and some were sold with special wooden stands which were particularly artistic in their own right.

Early Wrotham wares were typical earthenware of the English slipware tradition, with light coloured slip trailed designs on dark glazed grounds. Designs tended to reproduce a form of early English crude decoration, often with motto inscriptions.

Wares of the Chelsea Coldrum period were typically heavily potted earthenware of simple shape and minimal surface decoration. Glazes were thick, generally streaked monochrome or bichrome and ran over the base of a piece. Many two- or three-handled vases were produced with small ear-like handles at the vase necks.

Stoneware pieces of the Chelsea Coldrum period exhibit a similar heaviness of potting, massive shape and thick glaze. The ribs of a pot are frequently emphasised on the surface. A variety of coloured glazes was employed, mainly as mottled monochromes, such as sang-de-boeuf, matt mauve, cream, grey, blue, green, and white crackle. Handles were sometimes modelled in the form of ram's heads.

Whilst mainly vases were produced, some plates and bowls were also made in a variety of glazes.

The Soon wares were mainly orientally inspired in shape and glaze. Glazes were more adventurous but quality of potting varied widely, as it did for the earlier wares. Vases, jugs and bowls were still heavily potted and massive in appearance. Many vases bore characteristic scroll-like "ears" which protruded equidistant out from the neck, emulating a Chinese style.

Suggestions for Further Study

The Victoria and Albert Museum, London, has a large collection of Reginald Wells' work, which is well documented (see below).

Marsh, Ernest. "R.F. Wells—Sculptor and Potter." *Apollo* 1, 1925.

Rackham, Bernard. "The Pottery of Mr. Reginald Wells." *The Studio*, December, 1925.

Watson, Oliver. *British Studio Pottery—The Victoria and Albert Museum Collection.* Oxford: Phaidon & Christie's, 1990.

Riddick, Sarah. *Pioneer Studio Pottery—The Milner-White Collection.* London: Lund Humphries Publishers Limited and York City Art Gallery, 1990.

Reginald Wells Stoneware vase, 100mm high, incised "SOON".

REGINALD WELLS

Types of Ware	Production	Quality	Availability
Figures	Low	Good to Very Good	Scarce
Pots	Moderate	Poor to Very Good	Uncommon

Marks

The majority of Wells' wares were marked.

Impressed:	COLDRUM	c.1909 - 1910
Impressed:	COLDRUM WROTHAM	c.1909 - 1910
Impressed:	COLDRUM CHELSEA	1909 - 1914
Incised or painted:	R.F. Wells (signature)	c.1910 onwards
Impressed in relief: +/- production number	SOON (in rectangle)	c.1918 onwards
Incised: +/- "R.F. Wells" incised	SOON	c.1918 onwards
Incised:	RFW (within angles of a "Y")	c.1910 onwards
Incised:	S	1924 onwards

Fife Pottery, Kirkcaldy, Fife, Scotland (1817-1930)

Historical Background

The town of Kirkcaldy in Fife boasted at least four potteries during the nineteenth century, two of which were for many years owned by the same family, the Methven family.

The most significant of the Kirkcaldy potteries were the Links Pottery at Linktown (owned by David Methven, and an important producer of sponge-printed ware), the Rosslyn Pottery (owned by Morrison and Crawford, and known for its spatterware) and the Fife Pottery (owned by John Methven and later Robert Heron, and famous for its Wemyss Ware).

The Fife Pottery originated as the Gallatoun Pottery, which was established in 1790 by Gray & Company at Gallatown, Kirkaldy. In 1817, the pottery moved to larger premises and became known as The Fife Pottery. In 1827, Gray & Company sold the pottery because of financial difficulties to John Methven, who was David Methven's son.

When John Methven died in 1837 his daughter Mary and her husband Robert Heron inherited the pottery. During this time the pottery was producing a decorative cream glazed earthenware with transfer-printed floral patterns, but from 1880 Robert Heron introduced the famous boldy coloured Wemyss Ware, which was named to honour Lady Grosvenor of Wemyss Castle, and which was to dominate the output of the Fife Pottery until its closure in 1930.

Whilst undertaking a grand tour of Europe Robert Heron managed to recruit a few artists from Bohemia (Czechoslovakia), the most renowned of whom in the development of Wemyss Ware was Karel Nekola. He settled in Gallatown, eventually introducing his two sons Carl and Joseph to the pottery, but the remainder of the artists could not acclimatise to Scottish life and returned home.

When Mary Methven Heron died in 1887 her son, Robert Methven Heron, inherited the Pottery. Wemyss Ware became immensely popular, particularly the many commemorative items produced (such as for Queen Victoria's Diamond Jubilee of 1897). Items were retailed in London at Thomas Goode & Company in South Audley Street and many pieces were so marked. Some wares are also believed to have been exported to America.

T.B. Johnston of Pountney's Bristol Pottery (1905-1969)[1] at Fishponds, near Bath, was particularly attracted to the Wemyss hand-painted style and recruited at least two Fife Pottery artists to work at Bristol (George Stewart and David Grinton) as well as securing the rights to reproduce several Wemyss designs.

When Robert Methven Heron died in 1906, the Fife Pottery passed to William Williamson. Karel Nekola died in 1915, and the following year another decorator was employed, Edwin Sandland (1873-1928). He designed an art deco range of Wemyss Ware entitled "Langtoun Ware."

After Sandland's death the Fife Pottery continued for another two years, but was unable to sustain its market, as was the plight of other Kirkcaldy potteries. The Bovey Pottery (T.B. Johnston) at Bovey Tracey in Devon bought the moulds and rights to produce the Wemyss patterns and recruited Joseph Nekola as decorator. Wemyss-like wares were thus carried on at Bovey until its closure in 1952. Royal Doulton is recorded as having bought the designs in 1958.

Products

Prior to the Wemyss Ware phase Robert Heron produced Rockingham style creamwares and also a red-bodied earthenware with a glossy jet black glaze known as "Rosslyn Jet." Mainly functional items were produced, such as teapots and salt buckets.

Wemyss Ware is often popularly associated with hand-painted pink cabbage roses or portaits of cocks and hens similar to the Devon potteries' motto ware. The style of the Bohemian artists at the Fife Pottery was certainly characteristic. Bold, colourful portraits of flowers and fruit (with usually only one type depicted on any one article) produced on functional everyday articles (inkwells, breakfast sets, plates, bowls, jam pots, candlesticks, etc.) epitomised the range of wares known as Wemyss Ware. It was little wonder that the Fife Pottery's Wemyss Ware was so refreshingly different from the transfer-printed creamware produced prior to 1880.

At first, pieces were hand-thrown, then when mass-production was possible in later years, jolleyed and jigged items were produced, followed by slip-cast items. Painting was undertaken in the biscuit state and a clear lead glaze was applied. Pieces were then fired at low temperatures to preserve the brightness of the painting. Unfortunately, this, coupled with the thinness of the glaze has resulted in pieces becoming crazed with time.[2]

Wemyss Ware, however, is just as popular now as it was during its production. The initial patronage of Wemyss Castle, the ware's everyday functionality, the large and varied range of decorative subjects and the distinctive bright patterns have contributed to its current popular collectability.

Another Wemyss-like ware produced by Robert Heron was "Earlshall Ware," produced especially for the "Earlshall Faire" held at St. Andrews castle. The design of rooks in trees silhouetted against a pale background was the inspiration of R.W. Mackenzie who lived at Earlshall House, Leuchars.

Slip-cast models of pigs (in many sizes) and cats with green glass eyes were popular, and seem to command high auction prices today. They were often decorated with masses of painted flowers.

Commemorative items (mugs, cups and goblets) were regularly produced from 1897. Royal marriages, coronations, Boer War and First World War events were all commemorated.

230

Karel Nekola painted some impressive chargers with local scenes, which usually bear his signature. Sandland's work is noticeably different. His painting is more stippled and his "Langtoun Ware" of the late 1920s, which was not commercially succesful, depicted more stylised fruit and flowers in a bold, colourful art deco style.

Many pieces of Wemyss Ware bear distinctive characteristics such as painted rims and bases of mugs, goblets, vases, etc. with scallop or stylised leaf shapes.

Collectors should be careful to differentiate between the Fife Pottery's Wemyss Ware and the later Wemyss style produced at the Bovey Tracey Pottery. The latter ware was fired at higher temperatures so tends not to exhibit the crazing effect, and was usually marked differently. Jan Plichta distributed many of the Bovey Tracey wares, which were often marked "Plichta". Wemyss style pieces produced at Pountney's Bristol Pottery were also very similar to the Fife Pottery's wares. They were marked, however, with marks such as "Pountney's Bristol Cock and Hen Pottery" on cock and hen style wares or more simply "Made at Fishponds."

Collectors should also note that some good modern reproductions of Wemyss Ware have been produced, particularly by Brian Adams and Esther Weeks. Their "Essex Wemyss Wares" are marked "Wemyss Ware Exon".

Suggestions for Further Study

Kirkcaldy Museum and Art Gallery has an extensive collection of Wemyss Ware.

Davis, Peter and Robert Rankine. *Wemyss Ware—a decorative Scottish Pottery.* Edinburgh: Scottish Academic Press, 1986.

Cruickshank, Graeme. *Scottish Pottery.* Shire Publications Ltd., 1987.

Hill, Robin A. "Wemyss Ware—The Pride of the Scottish Potteries." *Antique Collector's Club* 11(8), 12/76.

"To Honour our Queen Elizabeth the Queen Mother and Mark the Wemyss Centenary." *Antique Collector's Club* 15(4), 9/80.

Jones, David. "Notes on Wemyss Ware by a Collector." *Antique Collector's Club* 25(9), 3/91.

[1] Pountney's at the turn of the century was one of the largest potteries in Europe, and were noted suppliers of glaze and clay materials to other potteries.
[2] Collectors should be wary of washing such pieces, since water entering the cracks could cause pieces of glaze to flake away.

Wemyss Vase, 140mm high, cabbage roses; impressed mark WEMYSS with painted mark WEMYSS.

Wemyss Large model of a pig, 44 cm long. (courtesy of Christie's Images)

WEMYSS WARE

Types of Ware	Production	Quality	Availability
Wemyss Ware	High	Fair to Very Good	Common

Marks

Most of the following marks may or may not include a painted decorator's name or initials, plus or minus year of manufacture.

Impressed	WEMYSS WARE R H & S		c.1883 - c.1900
Painted or impressed: (or both)	Wemyss. WEMYSS		c.1900 - 1930
Stamped:	ROBERT HERON & SON KIRKCALDY SCOTLAND EST. 1820	(In circle surmounted by a thistle)	1920 - 1930
	HANDPAINTED WEMYSS WARE	(within the circle)	
Printed:	T. GOODE & CO. SOUTH AUDLEY ST LONDON W	(in oval)	c.1900 - 1918

Appendix I

BARBOTINE—slip-wash ornamentation in low relief. (Ref. Aller Vale).

BISCUIT—pottery which has undergone a first firing at low temperatures, prior to the application of colour or glaze.

CELADON—greenish feldspathic glaze derived from iron, applied before firing. (Ref. Charles Vyse).

CLOISONNE—decoration using enamel on a metal base, and secured to the pottery body.

ENCAUSTIC—a method of tile production first used in medieval times, whereby slabs of clay are inlaid into a square (or other shape) of clay. (Ref. Maw & Co.).

FAIENCE—decorated pottery painted with opaque glazes on a white tin-oxide ground.

FLAMBE—a type of glaze, usally bright red, created by "reduction" (see below). (Ref. Bernard Moore).

FLOWN GLAZE—several coloured glazes streaked together and fused during firing (ref. Linthorpe).

HIGH GLAZE—a highly reflective glaze. (Lead glazes can be particularly reflective).

IMPASTO—the application of colour to the raw, unfired, clay.

JARDINIERE—a plant pot with or without a pedestal.

JOLLEYING—using a shaping tool to form a pot in a rotating mould.

LUSTREWARE—ware decorated with a "metallic" glaze, which, when fired at high temperatures, gives a strong light reflection. (Ref. Pilkington Pottery).

MAJOLICA—see "FAIENCE." (Ref. Della Robbia)

PARIAN WARE—unglazed biscuit porcelain named after Paros in Greece.(Ref. Wedgwood).

PATE-SUR-PATE—decoration by building up layers of white slip into cameo-like motifs, often against a tinted background for effect. (Ref. Mintons).

RAKU—a coarse textured, low-fired earthenware, usually deep-brown in colour, composed of an aggregate of previously fired clay; Japanese in origin. (Ref. Bernard Leach).

REDUCTION—the process of firing in a kiln where the amount of oxygen has been "reduced." Flambé colours are created in a "reducing atmosphere."

SALT-GLAZE—the application of salt in the last stage of firing in the kiln, generally on stone-ware, to produce a glaze with a silky finish. (Ref. Doulton, Martin Brothers).

SANG-DE-BOEUF—a type of flambé glaze, wine-red in colour, resembling ox blood.

SGRAFFITO—the technique of incising decoration into the raw clay, or incising through a coating of coloured slip to reveal the pottery body beneath. (Ref. Hannah Barlow at Doulton; Fremington; Della Robbia).

SLIP—clay dissolved in water to the consistency of thick cream, to which colour may be added, and the whole used for applying a decorative pattern to a piece.

TENMOKU—a glaze of Japanese origin, usually brown-black in colour. (Ref. Charles Vyse).

TERRACOTTA—a fine, unglazed red-bodied ware, light in weight.(Ref. Torquay Terra-Cotta; Watcombe).

THROWING—the process of throwing a lump of clay on to a potter's wheel and shaping it.

TUBE-LINE—decoration with clay slip squeezed from a hand-held rubber bag, to form tubular lines, in the manner of icing a cake. (Ref. Charlotte Rhead).

WARE—pieces which exhibit a particular style or design; thus, "a range of wares" pertains to a collection of individual styles or designs.

Appendix II

DIAMOND REGISTRATION MARKS

The following coded categories were employed in the diamond registration mark, as issued by the British Patent Office (ref. Public Records Office, Kew, source files BT43-48):-

Class of goods (C). For ceramics this was IV. Year Code (Y). See below. Month Code (M). See below. Day Number (D). 1 for Monday, etc. Bundle Number (B).

From 1868 the arrangement of code letters changed.

1842-1867   1868-1883

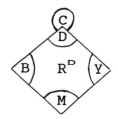

1) Year Codes

A = 1845	I = 1846	Q = 1866	Y = 1853	E = 1881	S = 1875
B = 1858	J = 1854	R = 1861	Z = 1860	F = 1873	U = 1874
C = 1844	K = 1857	S = 1849		H = 1869	V = 1876
D = 1852	L = 1856	T = 1867	A = 1871	I = 1872	W = 1-6
E = 1855	M = 1859	U = 1848	C = 1870	J = 1880	March,
F = 1847	N = 1864	V = 1850	D = 7 Mar	K = 1883	1878
G = 1863	O = 1862	W = 1865	onwards,	L = 1882	X = 1868
H = 1843	P = 1851	X = 1842	1878	P = 1877	Y = 1879

2) Month Codes

A = December	G = February	M = June
B = October	H = April	R = August (and
C = January	I = July	1-19 Sept., 1857)
D = September	K = November (and	W = March
E = May	December, 1860)	

Appendix III

REGISTRATION NUMBERS

The Patents, Designs & Trade Marks Act of 1883 provided for a single registered number to be used on ornamental designs. On ceramics this number, where used, was normally preceeded by an abbreviation for Registered, such as *Rd* or *Reg*.

The following numbers (source, Public Records Office, Kew, BT51 & BT53) give a general idea of the years in which designs were registered. Note that these numbers apply not only to ceramics, but to a range of media, except textiles.

Registered Numbers	Dates Registered	Registered Numbers	Dates Registered
1—18,868	Jan.1 1884—Dec.15 , 1884	592,432—610,963	Nov.17 1911—Nov.23 1912
18,869—39,953	Dec.15 1884—Dec.21 1885	610,964—629,940	Nov.23 1912—Dec.22 1913
39,954—63,874	Dec.21 1885—Dec.21 1886	629,941—644,055	Dec.22 1913—Nov.24 1914
63,875—87,324	Dec.21 1886—Nov.17 1887	644,056—648,254	Nov.29 1914—May 6 1915
87,325—114,048	Nov.17 1887—Nov.17 1888	648,255—656,583	May 6 1915—Jul.5 1916
114,049—139,295	Nov.17 1888—Nov.29 1889	656,584—660,416	Jul.5 1916—May 16 1917
139,296—165,353	Nov.29 1889—Jan.27 1891	660,417—664,322	May 16 1917—May 28 1918
165,354—185,824	Jan.27 1891—Jan.5 1892	664,323—672,512	May 29 1918—Nov.6 1919
185,825—205,137	Jan.5 1892—Dec.30 1892	672,513—680,282	Nov.7 1919—Jan.11 1921
205,138—224,604	Dec.30 1892—Dec.28 1893	680,283—688,220	Jan.11 1921—Feb.16 1922
224,605—247,418	Dec.28 1893—Jan.9 1895	688,221—696,323	Feb.16 1922—Mar.2 1923
247,419—266,237	Jan.9 1895—Nov.21 1895	696,324—709,012	Mar.2 1923—Nov.6 1924
266,238—289,290	Nov.21 1895—Nov.28 1896	709,013—717,778	Nov.6 1924—Dec.15 1925
289,291—311,177	Nov.28 1896—Dec.22 1897	717,779—726,866	Dec.15 1925—Jan.27 1927
311,178—329,512	Dec.22 1897—Nov.28 1898	726,867—740,897	Jan.27 1927—Oct.3 1928
329,513—348,670	Nov.22 1898—Nov.4 1899	740,898—749,695	Oct.3 1928—Oct.30 1929
348,671—367,216	Nov.4 1899—Dec.6 1900	749,696—758,458	Oct.31 1929—Oct.4 1930
367,217—384,526	Dec.6 1900—Dec.12 1901	758,459—771,135	Oct.4 1930—Feb.5 1932
384,527—401,621	Dec.12 1901—Dec.3 1902	771,136—779,893	Feb.6 1932—Jan.24 1933
401,622—424,184	Dec.3 1902—Jan.5 1904	779,894—788,498	Jan.25 1933—Dec.17 1933
424,185—447,602	Jan.5 1904—Jan.3 1905	788,499—797,486	Dec.17 1933—Oct.26 1934
447,603—471,608	Jan.3 1905—Jan.3 1906	797,487—806,973	Oct.27 1934—Oct.5 1935
471,609—491,472	Jan.3 1906—Nov.19 1906	806,974—815,888	Oct.7 1935—Oct.19 1936
491,473—517,231	Nov.19 1906—Dec.7 1907	815,889—825,248	Oct.20 1936—Jan.4 1938
517,232—530,717	Dec.7 1907—Dec.29 1908	825,249—834,429	Jan.5 1938—Mar.3 1939
530,711—552,897	Dec.29 1908—Nov.20 1909	834,430—837,945	Mar.4 1939—Apr.10 1940
552,898—570,588	Nov.20 1909—Sep.26 1910	837,946—843,242	Apr.10 1940—Mar.22 1945
570,589—592,431	Sep.26 1910—Nov.17 1911		

Bibliography

This section lists publications on the subject of pottery as relevant to this book. The bibliography is not exhaustive, but it is hoped that a sufficient cross-section of titles is provided for the reader to seek more detailed information.

Not all references listed have been used in the preparation of this book, and those prior to 1950 have been excluded from this list, unless readily available or of particular importance. References are also given under the appropriate chapter for each pottery.

1. General Period
(A selection of the many references available which relate to the general period covered by this book).

Adburgham, Alison. *Liberty's, A Biography of a Shop*. London: George Allen & Unwin Ltd., 1975.

Arwas, Victor. *The Liberty Style*. London: Academy Editions, 1979.

Battersby, Martin. *The Decorative Twenties*. London: Studio Vista, 1969; reprinted 1976; revised Philippe Garner, 1988.

_____ *The Decorative Thirties*. London: Studio Vista, 1971; reprinted 1976; revised Philippe Garner, 1988.

Bayer, Patricia. *Art Deco Source Book—A Visual Reference to a Decorative Style 1920-40*. London: Phaidon Press Ltd., 1988.

Cameron, I. et al. *The Collectors' Encyclopaedia: Victoriana to Art Deco*. London: William Collins & Co., 1974 (reprinted 1990 by Studio Editions).

Dore, Helen. *William Morris*. London: Pyramid Books, 1990.

Dresser, Dr. Charles. *Studies in Design*. London, 1875 (reprinted Studio Editions, 1988).

Duncan, Alastair, ed. *Encyclopaedia of Art Deco*. London: Headline Book Publishing PLC, 1988.

Garner, Philippe. *The World of Edwardiana*. London: Hamlyn Publishing, 1974.

Halen, Widar. *Christopher Dresser*. London: Phaidon Press Ltd., 1990.

Hannal, Frances. *Ceramics—Twentieth Century Design*. Bell & Hyman, 1986.

Hardy, William. *A Guide to Art Nouveau Style*. London: Quintet Publishing Ltd., 1986.

Haslam, Malcolm. *Marks & Monograms of the Modern Movement 1875-1930*. Cambridge: Lutterworth Press, 1977.

_____ *Art Nouveau—A Buyer's Guide to the Decorative Arts of the 1900s* London: MacDonald Orbis Publishing Ltd., 1988.

Hillier, Bevis. *Art Deco—A Design Handbook*. The Hubert Press Ltd., 1985.

Jones, Owen. *The Grammar of Ornament*. Day & Son, 1856, reprinted Studio Editions 1986/7/8.

_____ *The Grammar of Chinese Ornament*. London: , 1866 (reprinted Studio Editions 1988).

Klein, Dan & Margaret Bishop. *Decorative Art 1880-1980*. London: Phaidon Press Ltd., 1986, 1988.

Klein, Dan, Nancy McClelland and Malcolm Haslam. *In the Deco Style*. London: Thames & Hudson Ltd., 1987.

Lemme, A Van De. *A Guide to Art Deco Style*. London: Quintet Publishing Ltd., 1986.

Levy, Mervyn. *Liberty Style*. London: George Weidenfeld & Nicolson Limited, 1986.

Naylor, Gillian. *The Arts & Crafts Movement*. London: Studio Vista, 1971.

Poulson, Christine. *William Morris*. London: Quintet Publishing Ltd., 1989.

Spencer, Isobel. *Walter Crane*. London: Studio Vista, 1975.

2. Pertaining to British Ceramics in General
Barnard, J. *Victorian Ceramic Tiles*. London: Studio Vista, 1972.

Bartlett, J. *English Decorative Ceramics*. London: Kevin Francis Publishing, 1989.

Battie, David & Michael Turner. *The Price Guide to 19th. & 20th. Century British Porcelain*. Woodbridge, Suffolk, United Kingdom: Antique Collectors' Club, 1975.

Beaulah, Kenneth. *Church Tiles of the Nineteenth Century*. Princes Risborough Buckinghamshire: Shire Publications, 1987.

Bergesen, Victoria. *Encyclopaedia of British Art Pottery*. London: Barrie & Jenkins, 1992.

Blacker, J.F. *ABC of 19th. Century Ceramic Art*. London: Stanley Paul, 1911.

Blunt, Reginald. *The Cheney Book of Chelsea China & Pottery*. EP Publishing, 1973.

Brears, Peter C.D. *The Collector's Book of English Country Pottery*. Devon: David & Charles Ltd., 1974.

Buckley, Cheryl. *Potters & Paintresses—Women Designers in the Pottery Industry 1870-1955*. The Women's Press, 1990.

Cameron. Elisabeth, ed. *Encyclopaedia of Pottery & Porcelain: the 19th. & 20th. Centuries*. London: Faber & Faber Ltd., 1986.

Cruickshank, Graeme. *Scottish Pottery*. Princes Risborough, Buckinghamshire: Shire Publications Ltd., 1987.

Coysh, A.W. *British Art Pottery 1870-1940*. Devon: David & Charles Ltd., 1976.

Dawes, Nicholas M. *Majolica*. New York: Crown Publishers Inc., 1990.

Digby, G. Wingfield. *The Work of the Modern Potter in England*. London: John Murray Ltd., 1952.

Godden, Geoffrey A. *British Pottery, An Illustrated Guide*. London: Barrie & Jenkins, 1974.

_____ *Jewitt's Ceramic Art of Great Britain 1800-1900*. revised by G.A. Godden. London: Barrie & Jenkins, 1974.

_____ *Encyclopaedia of British Pottery & Porcelain Marks*. London: Barrie & Jenkins, 1966 (revised 1979).

_____ *Encyclopaedia of British Pottery & Porcelain*. London: Barrie & Jenkins, 1966 (revised 1980).

Haggar, Reginald. *English Country Pottery*. Phoenix House Ltd., 1950.

Haslam, Malcolm. *English Art Pottery 1865-1915*. Woodbridge, Suffolk, United Kingdom: Antique Collectors' Club, 1975.

Jewitt, Llewellynn. *The Ceramic Art of Great Britain*. 1883; London: New Orchard Editions Ltd., 1985.

Lemmen, Hans Van. *Tiled Furniture*. Princes Risborough, Buckinghamshire: Shire Publications Ltd., 1989.

Lewis, Griselda. *The Collector's History of English Pottery*. Woodbridge, Suffolk, United Kingdom: Antique Collectors' Club, 1987.

Lockett, Terence A. *Collecting Victorian Tiles*. Woodbridge, Suffolk, United Kingdom: Antique Collectors' Club, 1982.

Mainwaring-Baines, J. *Sussex Pottery*. Fisher Publications, 1980.

Rhead, Frederick & George W. Rhead. *Staffordshire Pots & Potters*. London: Hutchinson, 1906 (reprinted by E.P. Publishing, 1977).

Rice, Paul & Christopher Gowing. *British Studio Ceramics in the 20th. Century*. London: Barrie & Jenkins, 1989.

Riddick, Sarah. *Pioneer Studio Pottery—The Milner White Collection*. London: Lund Humphries Publishers Limited, in assoc. with York City Gallery, 1990.

Rose, Muriel. *Artist Potters in England*. London: Faber & Faber Ltd., 1955 (reprinted 1970).

Spours, Judy. *Art Deco Tableware (British Domestic Ceramics 1925-1939)*. London: Ward Lock, 1988.

Thomas, E. Lloyd. *Victorian Art Pottery*. London: Guildart, 1974.

Wakefield, Hugh. *Victorian Pottery*. Herbert Jenkins, 1962.

Watson, Oliver. *British Studio Pottery—The Victoria & Albert Museum Collection*. Oxford: Phaidon & Christie's, 1990.

Watson, Pat. *Collecting Art Deco Ceramics*. London: Kevin Francis Publishing, 1989.

3. Specific to Artists or Potteries

Atterbury, Paul. *Dictionary of Minton*. Woodbridge, Suffolk, United Kingdom: Antique Collectors' Club, 1988.

_____ *Moorcroft Pottery*. London: Richard Dennis & H. Edwards, 1987, 1990, 1993.

Atterbury, Paul & Louise Irvine. *The Royal Doulton Story*. Royal Doulton Tableware Ltd., 1979.

Barker, Ray. *The Crown Devon Story*. published privately, 1991.

Batkin, Maureen & Robert Harling. *Ravilious & Wedgwood*. Dalrymple Press, 1986.

Batkin, Maureen. *Wedgwood Ceramics 1846-1959*. London: Richard Dennis, 1982.

Bell, R.C. *Maling & Other Tyneside Pottery*. Princes Risborough, Buckinghamshire: Shire Publications Ltd., 1986.

Bell, R.C; L. Dixon & S.H. Cottle. *Maling, A Tyneside Pottery*. Tyne & Wear County Council Museums, 1981, 1985.

Birks, Tony and Cornelia Wingfield Digby. *Bernard Leach, Hamada & Their Circle*. London: Phaidon Press Ltd., 1990.

Brannam, Peter. *A Family Business—The Story of a Pottery*. pub. privately, 1982.

Brears, P.C.D. *The Farnham Pottery*. Chichester, Sussex: Phillimore & Co. Ltd., 1971.

Bumpas, Bernard. *Charlotte Rhead, Potter & Designer*. London: Kevin Francis Publishing, 1988.

Cardew. Michael. *Pioneer Pottery*. London: Longman Group UK Ltd., 1969.

_____ *Michael Cardew—A Pioneer Potter. An Autobiography*. London: William Collins & Co., 1988.

Casey, Andrew. *Susie Cooper—A Collectors'Guide*. Stratford-on-Avon: Jazz Publications, 1992.

Cashmore, Carol & Chris. *Collard, the Honiton and Dorset Potter*. pub. privately, 1983. (includes details of Aller Vale pattern codes). Obtainable from 5, Sussex Road, Brentwood, Essex, United Kingdom.

Catleugh, J. *William De Morgan Tiles*. Trefoil, 1983.

Clark, G. *Michael Cardew*. London: Faber & Faber Ltd., 1978.

Collins, M. & D. *An Introduction to Sylvac*. Sylvac Collectors' Circle, 1988.

Cox, George, ARCA. *Pottery for Artists, Craftsmen & Teachers*. New York: Macmillan Inc., 1914.

Cross, A.J. *Pilkington Royal Lancastrian Pottery & Tiles*. London: Richard Dennis, 1980.

Davis, Peter and Robert Rankine. *Wemyss Ware—a Decorative Scottish Pottery*. Edinburgh: Scottish Academic Press, 1986.

Dawson, Aileen. *Bernard Moore Master Potter (1815-1935)*. London: Richard Dennis, 1982.

_____ *Masterpieces of Wedgwood in the British Museum*. London: British Museum, 1984.

Edgeler, Audrey. *Art Potters of Barnstaple*. Alton, Hampshire: Nimrod Press Ltd., 1990.

Eyles, Desmond. *The Doulton Burslem Wares*. London: Barrie & Jenkins, 1980.

_____ *The Doulton Lambeth Wares*. London: Hutchinson, 1975.

_____ *Royal Doulton 1815-1965*. London: Hutchinson, 1965.

Eyles, Desmond and Richard Dennis. *Royal Doulton Figures Produced at Burslem 1890-1978*. Royal Doulton Tableware, 1978 (see below for new edition 1987).

Eyles, Desmond, Richard Dennis, and Louise Irvine. *Royal Doulton Figures Produced at Staffordshire*. Royal Doulton & Richard Dennis, 1987.

Gaunt, W. & M.D.E. Clayton-Smith. *William De Morgan*. London: Studio Vista, 1971.

Gosse, Edmund. *Sir Henry Doulton*. Edited by Desmond Eyles. London: Hutchinson, 1970.

Hallam, Edward. *Ashtead Potters Ltd. in Surrey. 1923-35*. pub. privately, 1990; obtainable from PO Box 159, Epsom, Surrey, KT17 1NR, England.

Hart, Clive W. *Linthorpe Art Pottery*. Guisborough: Aisling Publications, 1988.

Haslam, Malcolm. *The Martin Brothers, Potters*. London: Richard Dennis, 1978.

_____ *The Story of Sir Edmund Elton*. London: Richard Dennis, 1989.

_____ *William Staite Murray*. Crafts Council, 1984.

Hawkins, Jennifer. *The Poole Potteries*. Barrie & Jenkins, 1980.

Hill, Susan. *The Shelley Style—A Collectors' Guide*. Stratford-on-Avon: Jazz Publications Ltd., 1990.

Holland, William Fishley. *Fifty Years a Potter*. Pottery Quarterly, 1958.

Hopwood, Irene & Gordon. *The Shorter Connection—A J Wilkinson, Clarice Cliff, Crown Devon*. London: Richard Dennis, 1992.

Irvine, Louise. *Royal Doulton Figures*. London: Richard Dennis, 1981.

Irvine, Louise. *Royal Doulton Series Ware*. London: Richard Dennis, Vol.1 1980, Vol.2 1984, Vol.3 1986, Vol.4 1988.

Leach, Bernard. *A Potter's Book*. London: Faber & Faber Ltd., 1940, revised 1976.

Leach, Bernard. *A Potter's Portfolio*. London: Lund Humphries Publishers Limited, 1951 (reissued as *"The Potter's Challenge."* New York: E.P. Dutton, 1975 & London: Souvenir Press, 1976).

Lewis, J.M. *The Ewenny Potteries*. Cardiff: National Museum of Wales, 1982.

Lomax, Abraham. *Royal Lancastrian Pottery 1900-1938*. pub. privately, 1957.

Lukins, Jocelyn. *Doulton Flambé Animals*. pub. privately, 1981.

Mackeig-Jones, M. *Some Glimpses of Fairyland*. Buten Museum of Wedgwood, 1921 (reprinted 1963).

McKeown, Jo. *Poole Pottery—The First 100 Years*. Dorset: Poole Pottery, 1973.

Meisel, Louis K. *Clarice Cliff—The Bizarre Affair*. London: Thames & Hudson Ltd., 1988.

Messenger, Michael. *Pottery & Tiles of the Severn Valley (catalogue of the Clive House Museum collection)*. Remploy Ltd., 1979.

Niblett, Paul. *Hand Painted Gray's Pottery*. Stoke-on-Trent: City Museum & Art Gallery, 1982, 1983; new edition 1987.

Pearson, Kevin. *The Doulton Figure Collectors' Handbook*. London: Kevin Francis Publishing, 1986, 1988.

Reilly, Robert & George Savage. *The Dictionary of Wedgwood*. Woodbridge, Suffolk, United Kingdom: Antique Collectors' Club, 1980.

Roscoe, Barley. *Katharine Pleydell-Bouverie: A Potter's Life 1895-1985*. Bath: Bath University Press, 1980.

Rose, Peter. *George Tinworth*. London: Richard Dennis, 1990.

Ross, Dr. Catherine & Stephen Moore. *Maling, Trademark of Excellence*. Tyne & Wear County Council Museums, 1989.

Ruston, James H. *Ruskin Pottery*. Sandwell: Metropolitan Borough of Sandwell, 1975 and 1990 with corrections.

Thomas, D & E Lloyd. *The Old Torquay Potteries.* Ilfracombe, Devon: Arthur H. Stockwell, Ltd., 1978. (in association with Guildart, London)

Torquay Pottery Collectors' Society. *Torquay Motto Wares.* TPCS, 1990.

Verbeek, Susan Jean. *The Sylvac Story—The History & Products of Shaw & Copestake Ltd.* Pottery Productions, 1989.

Watkins, Chris, William Harvey, and Robert Senft. *Shelley Potteries, The History & Production of a Staffordshire Family of Potters;* London: Barrie & Jenkins, 1980, 1986.

Watson, Howard. *Collecting Clarice Cliff.* London: Kevin Francis Publishing, 1988.

Wentworth-Shields, Peter and Kay Johnson. *Clarice Cliff.* L'Odeon, 1976 & 1981.

Williamson, Art Gallery & Museum. *Della Robbia Pottery, Birkenhead 1894-1906, An Interim Report.* Birkenhead: Metropolitan Borough of Wirral, c.1974.

Yeman, Mick. *The Lyle Price Guide to Doulton.* Lyle Publications, 1987.

4. Exhibition Catalogues

Catalogues relating to major exhibitions since 1970, arranged in date order.

1970—Linthorpe Ware; catalogue by J Le Vine of an exhibition at Billingham Art Gallery, Jan. 1970; pub. Teesside Museums & Art Galleries.

1971—Catalogue of an Exhibition of Doulton Stoneware & Terracotta 1870-1925, Part 1; pub. Richard Dennis, 1971.

1972—Christopher Dresser 1834-1904; illustrated catalogue by Richard Dennis & J. Jeffe of an exhibition at the Fine Arts Society, 1972; pub. Richard Dennis, 1972.

1972—Clarice Cliff; catalogue of an Exhibition at The Museum & Art Gallery, Brighton, 1972.

1972—William De Morgan (1839-1917); catalogue of an exhibition at Leighton House, 1972 ; pub. De Morgan Foundation.

1973—William Moorcroft & Walter Moorcroft (1897-1973); catalogue of an exhibition at The Fine Arts Society, 1973; pub. Richard Dennis, 1973.

1973—"Doulton Ware & Products of Other British Potteries, the Woolley Collection, including 'Lambeth Stoneware'," by Rhoda Edwards; catalogue pub. by London Borough of Lambeth, Directorate of Amenity Services, 1973.

1973—Catalogue of Pottery by William De Morgan, by Roger Pinkham; pub. Victoria & Albert Museum, 1973.

1974—Charles Vyse 1882-1971; catalogue of an exhibition by Richard Dennis at The Fine Art Society, London, 1974; pub. Richard Dennis.

1975—Doulton Pottery from the Lambeth & Burslem Studios 1873-1939, Part 2; pub. Richard Dennis, 1975. (see also 1971)

1976—Minton 1798-1910; catalogue of an exhibition by E.Aslin & Paul Atterbury at the Victoria & Albert Museum, London, 1976; pub. V & A. Museum, 1976.

1977—The Art of Bernard Leach; retrospective exhibition catalogue; pub. Victoria & Albert Museum, London, 1977.

1978—Elegance & Utility 1924-1978: The Work of Susie Cooper, A Tribute from Wedgwood; catalogue by Adrian Woodhouse of an Exhibition at Sanderson's Showrooms, London, 1978.

1978—Wedgwood Fairyland Lustre, the Work of Daisy Mackeig-Jones; catalogue by Una Des Fontaines of an exhibition at Sotheby's; pub. Richard Dennis, 1978.

1978—The Poole Potteries; catalogue of an exhibition at the Victoria & Albert Museum, London, 1978; pub. V & A.

1979—Catalogue of an Exhibition of Torquay Marble and Terracotta Ware at Sotheby Bearne, Torquay, 1979; pub. Sotheby Parke Bernet & Co.

1979—Mabel Lucie Attwell; catalogue by A. Packer of a centenary exhibition at Brighton Museum, 1979.

1979—Christopher Dresser 1834-1904; catalogue by Michael Collins of an exhibition held at Camden Arts Centre (1979) and the Dorman Museum, Middlesbrough (1980); pub. Arkwright Trust.

1980—Katharine Pleydell-Bouverie, catalogue of an exhibition at the Crafts Study Centre, Holburne Museum, Bath, 1980.

1980—Shelley Potteries; catalogue of an exhibition at the Geffrye Museum, 1980.

1980—The Birkenhead Della Robbia Pottery, 1893 (sic)—1906; catalogue of an exhibition in 1980; pub. Jeremy Cooper Ltd.

1981—Ruskin Pottery and the European Ceramic Revival; catalogue by I. Bennett of an exhibition at Ferneyhough, 1981.

1981—Christopher Dresser Phd; catalogue by Andy Tilbrook of an exhibition by Andy Tilbrook and Dan Klein at The Halkin Arcade, London, Autumn, 1981.

1983—Burmantofts Pottery; catalogue of an exhibition at Cartwright Hall, Bradford; pub. Bradford Art Galleries & Museums, Nov. 1983.

1983—Michael Cardew and Pupils; catalogue of an exhibition at York City Art Gallery 1983; pub. York City Art Gallery.

1984—The Oxshott Pottery; catalogue by Denise & Henry Wren of a retrospective exhibition; pub. Crafts Study Centre, 1984.

1984—Minton Tiles 1835-1935; catalogue of an exhibition, edited by D. Skinner & Hans Van Lemmen; pub. Stoke-on-Trent City Museum & Art Gallery, 1984.

1984—By Potters Art and Skill: Pottery by the Fishleys of Fremington; catalogue by Emmeline Leary and Jeremy Pearson of an exhibition at the Royal Albert Memorial Museum, Exeter, 1984.

1985—Hannah Barlow; catalogue of an exhibition at Christie's, South Kensington, by Peter Rose; pub. Richard Dennis, 1985.

1986—Rhead Artists & Potters 1870-1950; catalogue by Bernard Bumpas of an exhibition at the Geffrye Museum, London, 1986 (touring exhibition).

1986—Torquay Pottery 1870-1940; catalogue of an Exhibition at Bearne's & Bonham's in Knightsbridge, London, August, 1986; pub. Torquay Pottery Collectors' Society.

1986—Eric Ravilious 1903-1942: A Re-assessment of His Life and Work; catalogue of an exhibition at The Towner Art Gallery, Eastbourne, 1986.

1987—Susie Cooper Productions; catalogue by Ann Eatwell of an Exhibition at the Victoria & Albert Museum, London and the City Museum & Art Gallery, Stoke-on-Trent, 1987.

1988—Bretby Art Pottery; museum catalogue by Judith Anderson; Derby Art Gallery, March, 1988.

1989—The Designs of William De Morgan; catalogue by Martin Greenwood; pub. Richard Dennis & William Wiltshire III, 1989, to coincide with an exhibition at the Victoria & Albert Museum, London.

1990—Miss Jones & Her Fairyland; catalogue by Una Des Fontaines, Lionel Lambourne and Ann Eatwell of a gift collection from Suzanne & Frederic Weinstein to the Victoria & Albert Museum, London; pub. V & A, 1990.

1990—Christopher Dresser 1834-1904; catalogue of an exhibition at The Fine Art Society, London, Autumn, 1990; pub. The Fine Art Society & Haslam & Whiteway Ltd.

1991—C.H. Brannam Barum Ware; catalogue by Harry Lyons of a display of Barum Ware at the Liberty Arts & Crafts Exhibition, London, 1991.

5. Magazines

a) Contemporary to the period covered by this book.

Some specific contemporary magazine articles have been referenced under the relevant chapter. The following is a selection of magazine and journal types:-
The Art Journal (1849-1912)

The Magazine of Art (1878-1902)
The Magazine of Fine Arts
The Potter (1893-1894)
The Pottery Gazette (1875 onwards) (becoming The Pottery & Glass Trades' Review & Gazette after 1877)
Pottery & Glass
The Studio (1893 onwards)

b) Magazine articles from 1970 onwards.

The following is a selection, mainly from "The Antique Collector" (AC), "The Antique Dealer & Collectors Guide" (ADC) and "Antique Collecting" (the journal of the Antique Collectors' Club, Woodbridge (ACC).

Bartlett, John: Elton Ware Rediscovered; *AC,* July, 1985.

_____, *Elton Ware; Bristol Illustrated,* Nov. 1986.

_____, *Elton Ware—The Genius of Sir Edmund Elton, Potter-Baronet; ACC* 21(9), Feb. 1987.

Bennett, Ian: Ruskin Pottery & The Ferneyhough Collection; *ACC* 27(1), May 1992.

Botting, Meg: A Wielding Force in the Shadows (Compton); *Country Life,* 20/9/79.

Bracegirdle, Cyril: Linthorpe the Forgotten Pottery; *Country Life,* 1971.

Bradley, R.J.: Castle Hedingham Pottery 1837-1905; article in three parts; *The Connoisseur,* Feb., Mar, Apr., 1968.

Brisco, Virginia: Best Forms from the Antique... (The Watcombe Pottery); *ADC,* August, 1989.

Bumpas, Bernard: Pottery Designed by Charlotte Rhead. *AC,* January, 1983.

_____: *Tube-Line Variations. AC,* December, 1985.

_____: *Cheerful Charlotte Rhead. ADC,* August, 1988.

Cashmore, Carol: Ceramics for Gentlemen of Taste: The Torquay Potteries and Their Products. *ADC,* August, 1986.

Cashmore, Carol: Honiton—A Neglected Pottery. *ADC,* May, 1987.

Cecil, Victoria: For House & Garden (Compton). *AC,* January, 1981.

Cross, A.J.: Pilkington's Royal Lancastrian Pottery 1904-1957. *ADC,* September, 1973.

_____: *Pilkington's Tile & Pottery Co. Ltd. ACC* 15(2), June, 1980.

Crossingham-Gower: The Potters of Poole. *Art & Antiques,* March 22nd, 1975.

_____: *Susie Cooper—Pride of the Potteries. Art & Antiques,* April 12, 1975.

Eatwell, Ann: A Bold Experiment in Tableware Design (1934 Harrod's Exhibition). *ACC,* 19(6) November, 1984.

Elton, Julia: Eltonware at Clevedon Court. *National Trust magazine,* 1980.

Fletcher, Neil: Sixty Glorious Years—The Work of Susie Cooper, OBE. *ACC,* 19(5) October, 1984.

Haslam, Malcolm: Some Vorticist Pottery. *The Connoisseur,* Oct.1975.

Hill, Robin A.: Wemyss Ware—The Pride of the Scottish Potteries; ACC, 11(8), Dec. 1976.

James, Susan: Barum Ware—The Work of C.H. Brannam (1855-1937). *AC,* August 1973.

Jones, David: Notes on Wemyss Ware by a Collector. *ACC* 25(9), March, 1991.

King, C. Eileen: Curious Pottery of Castle Hedingham. *Art & Antiques,* 26/7/1975.

Kinghorn, Jonathan: The Allander Pottery 1904-1908. *ACC* 21(1), May, 1986.

Knowles, Eric: Photographic Portrait Tiles (George Cartlidge, Sherwin & Cotton). *AC,* August, 1977.

McDonald, C. Haig: Excellent in its Simplicity (Susie Cooper). *AC,* July, 1987.

Mortimer, Tony L.: The Royal Lancastrian Pottery. *ACC* 20(4), September, 1985.

Mutler, Grant: Minton Secessionist Ware. *The Connoisseur,* August, 1980.

Peake, Graham: In the Advance Spirit (Susie Cooper). *ADC,* July 1987.

Pinkham, Roger: A Tale of Three Potteries. *Antique Collectors' Fayre,* Sept. 1977.

Ruck, Pamela: A Victorian Squire & His Eccentric Pottery. *Art & Antiques,* March 27, 1976.

Rumsey, Jill: Keith Murray. *ACC* 16(11), April, 1982.

Snodin, Su: Susie Cooper, Diverse Designer. *AC,* August, 1982.

Stirling, Robert: Carlton Ware: Naturalistic Patterns of the 1930s and 1940s. *ACC,* May 1984.

Summerfield, Angela: The Martin Brothers. *AC,* November, 1987.

Tharp, Lars: William Moorcroft: Master Potter of the 20th.Century. *ACC* 24(6), Nov. 1989.

Thornton, Lynne: Pilkington's Royal Lancastrian Lustre Pottery. *The Connoisseur,* May 1970.

Tattersall, B.: The Birkenhead Della Robbia Pottery. *Apollo,* Feb. 1973.

Wade, Hilary: Christopher Dresser & The Linthorpe Potteries. *AC,* February, 1984.

Watson, Pat: Commercial Courage (Clarice Cliff). *ADC,* August 1988.

Watson, Pat: The Gentle Art of E. Radford. *Antique Collectors' Fayre,* 2(10) April, 1988.

Weaver, Cynthia, The Astra Ware of Minton, Hollins & Co. *ACC* 26(6), Nov. 1991.

Winstone, Victor: As Fresh as 50 Years Ago (Susie Cooper). *Art & Antiques,* June 10, 1978.

Anon, Antique Collectors' Club: De Morgan Wares. *ACC* 19(5), Sept. 1974.

Anon, Antique Collectors' Club: To Honour our Queen Elizabeth the Queen Mother and Mark the Wemyss Centenary. *ACC* 15(4), Sept. 1980.

PRICE GUIDE FOR BRITISH CERAMIC ART

Values vary immensely according to an article's condition, location of the market, parts of the country, materials, craftsmanship, demand and overall quality of design. While estimates from our survey of different markets may serve as a general guide for evaluation, collectors must use their own judgement and make their own decisions. Values given are in British pound sterling. The left hand number is the page number. The letters following the page number indicate the position of the photograph on the page: T=top, L=left, TL=top left, TR=top right, C=center, CL=center left, CR= center right, R=right, B=bottom, BL=bottom left, BR=bottom right. The name following the position is the Pottery. The prices are listed in British pounds sterling.

6	BL	Cranston	30-60
9	B	Minton Hollins	40-70 each
10	B	Fielding's	70-120
16	T	Aller Vale	30-70 each
	B	Aller Vale	30-60 each
18	T	Aller Vale	40-90 each
19	L	Ashby Guild	25-40
	R	Ashby Guild	25-40
20	B	Ashtead, face tankards	90-170 each
21	TL	Ashtead	25-40
	TR	Ashtead	70-140
	B	Ashtead	15-25 each
22	B	Ashtead;condiments	50-90 each
23	T	Ashtead	40-100 each
	BR	Ashtead	450-750
24	L	Ashworth	70-150
	R	Ashworth	40-80
25	B	Ault	25-60 each
26	T	Ault	15-30 each
	B	Ault	40-70
	R	Ault	200-450
27	T	Ault	30 60 each
28	B	C.J.C. Bailey	80-150
29	B	Baron	10-50 each
30	L	Baron	30-70
	R	Baron	30-70
31	R	Braden	400-800 each
32	B	Brannam	60-180 each
33	TL	Brannam	60-120
	TR	Brannam	30-50
	BL	Brannam	150-250
	BR	Brannam	250-400
34	TL	Brannam	250-400 each
	TR	Brannam	150-200
	BL	Brannam	250-400
	BR	Brannam, lg.vase	200-300
	BR	Brannam, sm.vase	40-60
36	TL	Brannam	60-150 each
	B	Brannam	200-300
37	TR	Brannam	140-190
38	B	Bretby	40-90 each
39	TC	Bretby	160-300
	TR	Bretby	30-60
40	T	Bretby, candlesticks	30-60 each
		Bretby, vases	50-90 each
		Bretby, jardiniere	60-120
	BL	Bretby	40-70
	BR	Bretby	30-70
42	BL	Burmantofts	200-300
	BR	Burmantofts	200-300
43	TL	Burmantofts	200-350
	TR	Burmantofts	250-400
	B	Burmantofts, monkey	200-400
44	B	Burmantofts	40-120
45	TL	Burmantofts	100-250
	TR	Burmantofts	350-450
46	B	Bushey Heath	350-500
47	T	Bushey Heath	90-175
48	B	Cardew	120-250 each
49	B	Cardew	190-270
50	B	Carlton	20-50 each
51	TL	Carlton	100-200 each
	TR	Carlton	50-140
52	TL	Carlton	50-120
	TR	Carlton	180-400 each
53	B	Castle Hedingham	40-90 each
54	B	Castle Hedingham	70-150
55	B	Clarice Cliff sugar sifters	250-600 each
	B	Clarice Cliff Isis & Lotus jugs	700-1600 each
56	T	Clarice Cliff	700-900 set
	BL	Clarice Cliff	
		"Caravan" pattern plate	1600-2300
		small "Bizarre" plate	250-350
		"Fantasque" wall mask	1500-2000
		"Bizarre" Lotus jugs	2000-2500 ea.
		"Bizarre" Sunray vase	2000-2500
		"Bizarre" Yo yo vase	2000-2500
	BR	Clarice Cliff	600-900 set
58	TL	Clarice Cliff	80-170
	TR	Clarice Cliff	70-150
	B	Clarice Cliff	400-900 each
59	T	Clarice Cliff	170-350
	CL	Clarice Cliff	700-1200
	CR	Clarice Cliff	700-1300
	BL	Wilkinson	60-170
	BR	Clarice Cliff	80-190
60	T	Clarice Cliff, T row	400-1300
		Clarice Cliff, others	400-900
61	B	S & E Collier	20-40
63	B	Compton	50-120 each
64	TL	Compton	60-120 each
	TR	Compton	100-200
66	T	Compton	80-200
	B	Compton	50-90
68	T	Craven Dunnill	70-150 each
	B	Craven Dunnill	30-60 each
69	B	De Morgan, tile	100-200
		De Morgan, other	600-1600
71	TL	De Morgan	400-700
	TR	De Morgan	250-350
	BL	De Morgan	200-300
	BR	De Morgan	400-800
73	B	Della Robbia	400-700
74	B	Della Robbia, vase & cover	60-150
		Della Robbia, lg.vase	200-300
75	TL	Della Robbia	250-450
	TR	Della Robbia	300-550
76	B	Denby	20-90 each
78	T	Denby	30-70 each
79	T	Denby	20-80 each
	C	Denby	15 50 each
	B	Denby	50-90
80	B	Dicker	20-60 each
81	T	Dicker	20-60 each
82	T	Dicker	10-70 each
	B	Dicker	20-60 each
83	B	Doulton	250-550 each
84	TL	Doulton	50-90 each
	TR	Doulton	170-290 each
	B	Doulton	250-650 each
86	BL	Doulton	180-300
	BR	Doulton	70-130 each
87	T	Doulton	90-300 each
88	T	Doulton	50 90 each
	BL	Doulton	200-300
	BR	Doulton	100-150
89	T	Doulton	40-90
	BL	Doulton	180-250
	BR	Doulton	130-200
90	TL	Doulton	120-250
	TR	Doulton	120-250
	B	Doulton	90-175
91	B	Doulton	150-250 each
92	TL	Doulton	40-60
	TR	Doulton	60-120
	B	Doulton	350-700
93	TL	Doulton	70-140
	TR	Doulton	70-120
	B	Doulton	200-300
97	B	Dunmore	20-40 each
99	B	Elton, small vase	60-90
		Elton, lge vase	150-300
100	TL	Elton, candlestick	80-120
		Elton, bulb vase	50-80
	TR	Elton	150-300 each
	BL	Elton	100-350 each
	BR	Elton	100-300 each
101	TL	Elton	500-800
	TR	Elton	500-800
	B	Elton	450-900 each
103	TL	Elton	150-250
104	L	Elton	600-900
	TR	Elton	100190
	B	Elton	250-400
105	TL	Elton	120-200
	C	Elton	150-250
	TR	Elton	170-250
	B	Elton	500-800
107	B	Ewenny	15-40 each
108	B	Farnham	40-90 each
109	T	Farnham	30-70
110	TL	Farnham	90-190
	TR	Farnham	120-200
	B	Farnham	30-70
111	B	Foley	
		Shelley "Mabel Lucie Attwell", animal teaset	400-750
		Shelley "Mabel Lucie Attwell", pixie jugs	150-180 each
		Shelley "Hilda Cowham", tent teapots	150-180 each
112	BL	Foley	700-1300
	BR	Foley	600-1100
113	T	Foley	150-800 each
114	TL	Foley	400-700
	TR	Foley	70-120
	BL	Foley	60-150
	BR	Foley	40-70
115	T	Foley	70-250 each
	B	Foley	700-1400
117	T	Foley	350-600
	B	Foley	70-150
118	B	Fremington, jug	60-150
		Fremington, beaker	50-120
119	T	Fremington	350-450
121	L	Granville	70-90
	R	Granville	70-120 each
122	L/R	Susie Cooper	90-190
123		Susie Cooper	150-300
124	B	A.E. Gray Ltd.	20-40 each
125	T	Susie Cooper	250-350
	B	Gray	40-80
127	C	Holyrood	40-100
128	B	Honiton	40-130 each
129	T	Honiton	40-130 each
130	T	Honiton	50-140 each
	B	Honiton	40-90 each
131	T	Honiton	60-180 each
	B	Honiton	60-120 each
132	BL	Isle of Wight	30-60 each
133	T	Isle of Wight	40-100 each
134	B	Lauder	90-190
135	TL	Lauder	90-170 each
	TR	Lauder	90-200 each
	BR	Lauder	20-40
136	B	Leach	250-700 each
138	TL	Leach	70-180
	C	Leach	120-200
139	B	Linthorpe	270-700 each
140	TL	Linthorpe	120-200
	TR	Linthorpe	350-700
141	T	Linthorpe	180-600 each
142	B	Maling	70-120
144	B	Martin Bros.	400-850 each
146	T	Martin Bros.	500-800
147	T	Martin Bros.	230-350 each
	B	Martin Bros., bird	1700-2700
		vase	500-800
149	T	Martin Bros.	100-250
150	B	Maw	1100-2500 ea.
151	T	Maw	90-180 each
	B	Maw	150-230 each
152	B	Maw	50-90
153	B	Maw	250-300
155	T	Mintons	140-280 each
156	TL	Mintons	40-120 each
	TR	Mintons	200-300 set
	B	Mintons	40-90 each
158	TL	Mintons	60-140 each
	BL	Mintons	120-190
	R	Mintons	400-600
159	TR	Mintons	30-60
	B	Mintons	800-1600
161	T	Moorcroft	180-2300 each
	B	Moorcroft	700-1200
162	T	Moorcroft	500-900
	B	Moorcroft	400-2900 each
163	T	Moorcroft	700-2200 each
165	TL	Moorcroft, Flamminian	350-500 each
	TR	Moorcroft	300-500
	B	Moorcroft, Aurelian	250-750 each
167	B	Moore	180-550 each
168	B	Moore	270-350
169	T	Moore	120-230 each
	B	Moore	120-250
170	B	Mortlake	50-180 each
171	T	Mortlake	120-200
	B	Mortlake	160-250
172	T	Mortlake	120-190
	B	Mortlake	170-250
173	B	Murray	500-900
174	B	Murray	600-1200
175	B	Myott	50-100
176	T	Myott	90-170 set
	C	Myott	50-90
	B	Myott	40-70
177	B	Oxshott	40-90 each
178	BL	Oxshott	90-150
	BR	Oxshott	90-150
179	T	Oxshott	50-90 each
	B	Oxshott	40-90
182	TL	Pilkington	90170
	TR	Pilkington	60-150
	BL	Pilkington	70-120
	BR	Pilkington	150-250 each
183	L	Pilkington	850-1200
	TR	Pilkington	250-400
	BR	Pilkington	350 500
184	T	Pilkington	750-1100
	B	Pilkington, baluster vase	250-350
		oviform vase	250-350
		charger	400-500
		bowl	250-350
		oviform vase	200-300
		elongated vase	250-350
185	T	Pilkington	250-350
	B	Pilkington	250-350
186	B	Pleydell Bouverie	200-400 each
187	B	Pleydell Bouverie	250-400
188	B	Poole	80-350 each
190	TL	Poole	50-80 each
	TR	Poole	400-600
	B	Poole	120-180
191	BR	Poole	250-350
192	T	Radford	40-130 each
	BL	Radford	80-150
	BR	Radford	40-70
193	TL	Radford	30-60
	TR	Radford	90-180
	B	Radford	30-160 each
194	B	Radford	30-50
195	BL/R	C.Rhead	110-170
196	B	C.Rhead	70-140 each
197	T	C.Rhead	120-200
198	B	Ruskin	700-1800 each
199	TL	Ruskin	150-190
	BL	Ruskin	150-230
	R	Ruskin	80-160
200	B	Ruskin	170-250
201	BL	Rye	120-200
	BR	Rye	100-170
203	B	Salopian	50-200 each
204	B	Salopian	90-180 each
205	T	Salopian	50-200 each
	B	Salopian	150-200
206	B	Cartlidge tiles	120-190 each
207	R	Sherwin	250-350 each panel
209	TL	Torquay	80-140
	TR	Torquay	300-500 each
	B	Longpark	90-150
210	B	Upchurch	70-190 each
211	L	Upchurch	70-120
	R	Upchurch	60-100
212	B	Charles Vyse	250-350
213	T	Charles Vyse	200-250
214	T	Charles Vyse	400-700
	B	Charles Vyse	400-500
		Harry Parr	600-900
215	B	Wardle	130-190 each
216	T	Wardle	20-70 each
	BL	Wardle	60-150 each
	BR	Wardle	60-180 each
217	T	Wardle	50-170 each
	B	Wardle	70-250 each
218	T	Wardle	120-250 each
219	B	Wardle	150-200
221	B	Watcombe	350-600
222	B	Watcombe	250-350
223	BL	Wedgwood	150-250
	BR	Wedgwood	100-200
224	T	Wedgwood	700-4000 each
	BL	Wedgwood	250-350
	BR	Wedgwood	200-300
227	B	Wells	40-190 each
228	T	Wells	90-180 each
	B	Wells	400-700
229	B	Wells	170-250
231	T	Wemyss	250-350
	B	Wemyss	2500-3300

Index

239

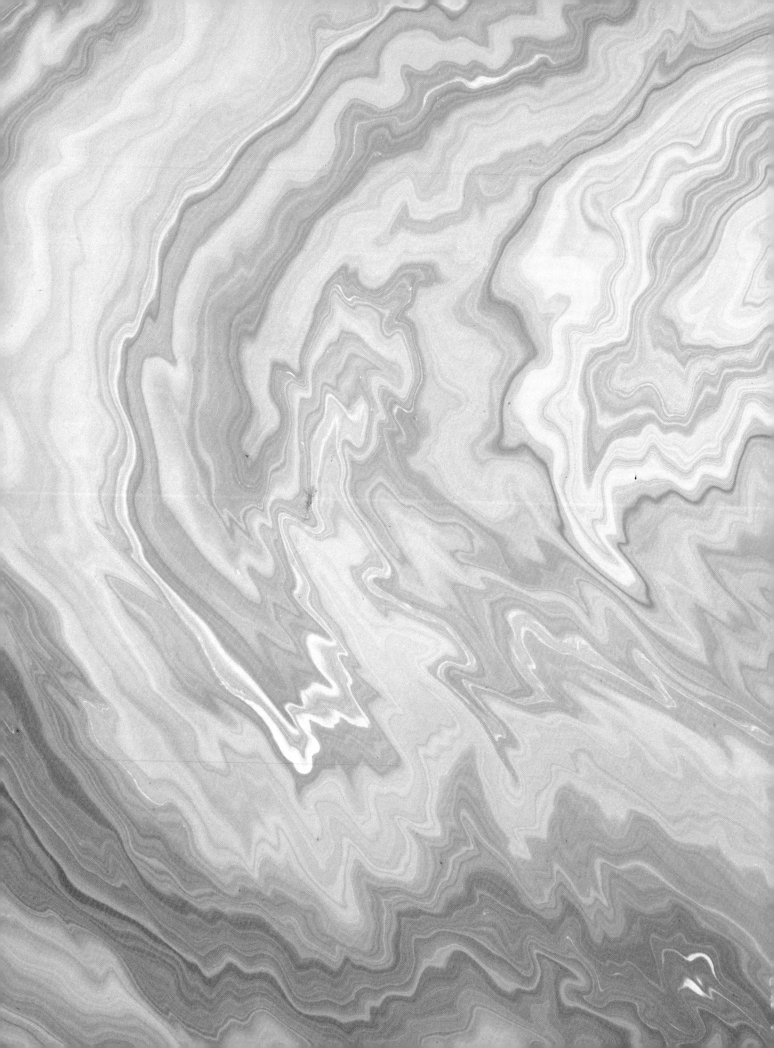